Treatment Integrity

SCHOOL PSYCHOLOGY BOOK SERIES

Treatment Integrity

A Foundation for Evidence-Based Practice in Applied Psychology

Edited by

Lisa M. Hagermoser Sanetti

Thomas R. Kratochwill

American Psychological Association

Washington, DC

Published by
American Psychological Association
750 First Street, NE
Washington, DC 20002
www.apa.org

To order
APA Order Department
P.O. Box 92984
Washington, DC 20090-2984
Tel: (800) 374-2721; Direct: (202) 336-5510
Fax: (202) 336-5502; TDD/TTY: (202) 336-6123
Online: www.apa.org/pubs/books
E-mail: order@apa.org

In the U.K., Europe, Africa, and the Middle East, copies may be ordered from
American Psychological Association
3 Henrietta Street
Covent Garden, London
WC2E 8LU England

Typeset in Goudy by Circle Graphics, Inc., Columbia, MD

Printer: United Book Press, Baltimore, MD
Cover Designer: Minker Design, Sarasota, FL

The opinions and statements published are the responsibility of the authors, and such opinions and statements do not necessarily represent the policies of the American Psychological Association.

Library of Congress Cataloging-in-Publication Data

Treatment integrity : a foundation for evidence-based practice in applied psychology /
  Lisa M. Hagermoser Sanetti and Thomas R. Kratochwill, Editors-in-Chief. — First edition.
    pages cm. — (School psychology book series)
  Includes bibliographical references and index.
  ISBN-13: 978-1-4338-1581-2
  ISBN-10: 1-4338-1581-8
  1. Mental health services. 2. Behavior modification. 3. Evidence-based psychotherapy.
4. Psychology, Applied. I. Sanetti, Lisa M. Hagermoser. II. Kratochwill, Thomas R.
  RA790.5.T74 2014
  616.89'14—dc23
                                22013018273

British Library Cataloguing-in-Publication Data

A CIP record is available from the British Library.

Printed in the United States of America
First Edition

http://dx.doi.org/10.1037/14275-000

To my husband, Christopher, a model of great integrity.
—*Lisa M. Hagermoser Sanetti*

To my son, Tyler, moving forward with integrity.
—*Thomas R. Kratochwill*

CONTENTS

SERIES FOREWORD

Outside of their homes, children spend more time in schools than any other setting. From tragedies such as Sandy Hook and Columbine to more hopeful developments such as the movement towards improved mental health, health, and academic achievement, there is an ongoing need for high-quality writing that speaks to ways in which children, families, and communities associated with schools worldwide can be supported through the application of sound psychological research, theory, and practice.

As such, for the past several years the American Psychological Association (APA Books) and its Division 16 (School Psychology) have partnered to produce the School Psychology Book Series. The mission of this series is to increase the visibility of the science, practice, and policy for children and adolescents in schools and communities. The result has been a strong collection of scholarly work that appeals not only to psychologists but to individuals from all fields who have reason to seek and use what psychology has to offer in schools.

Many individuals have made significant contributions to the School Psychology Book Series. First, we would like to acknowledge the dedication of past series editors: Sandra L. Christensen, Jan Hughes, R. Steve McCallum,

David McIntosh, LeAdelle Phelps, Susan Sheridan, and Christopher H. Skinner. Second, we would like to acknowledge the outstanding editorial visions of the scholars who have edited or authored books for the series. The work of these scholars has significantly advanced the science and practice for children and adolescents worldwide.

We welcome your comments about this volume and other topics you would like to see explored in this series. To share your thoughts, please visit the Division 16 website at www.apadivisions.org/division-16.

Linda A. Reddy, PhD
Series Editor

CONTRIBUTORS

Courtney N. Baker, PhD, Department of Psychology, Tulane University, New Orleans, LA

Katherine Bevans, PhD, The Children's Hospital of Philadelphia and the Perelman School of Medicine at the University of Pennsylvania, Philadelphia

Karen A. Blase, PhD, National Implementation Research Network, Frank Porter Graham Child Development Institute, University of North Carolina at Chapel Hill

Hayden Bosworth, PhD, Departments of Medicine, Psychiatry, and Nursing, Duke University Medical Center, Durham, NC

Brian K. Bumbarger, MEd, Evidence-Based Prevention and Intervention Support Center, Prevention Research Center, Pennsylvania State University, State College

Amy Cassata, PhD, Center for Elementary Mathematics and Science Education, The University of Chicago, Chicago, IL

Jeanne Century, EdD, Center for Elementary Mathematics and Science Education, The University of Chicago, Chicago, IL

Florence D. DiGennaro Reed, PhD, BCBA-D, Department of Applied Behavioral Science, University of Kansas, Lawrence

Dean L. Fixsen, PhD, National Implementation Research Network, Frank Porter Graham Child Development Institute, University of North Carolina at Chapel Hill

Kristin A. Gansle, PhD, School of Education, College of Human Sciences and Education, Louisiana State University, Baton Rouge

Frank M. Gresham, PhD, Department of Psychology, Louisiana State University, Baton Rouge

Jason M. Hirst, BS, Department of Applied Behavioral Science, University of Kansas, Lawrence

Shannon R. Holmes, MA, Nebraska Center for Research on Children, Youth, Families and Schools, University of Nebraska–Lincoln

Veronica J. Howard, MA, Department of Psychology, University of Alaska, Anchorage

Heather A. King, PhD, Center for Health Services Research in Primary Care, Health Services Research and Development, Department of Veterans Affairs Medical Center, Durham, NC

Thomas R. Kratochwill, PhD, School Psychology Program, University of Wisconsin–Madison

Stephen S. Leff, PhD, The Children's Hospital of Philadelphia and the Perelman School of Medicine at the University of Pennsylvania, Philadelphia

Anna C. J. Long, PhD, Department of Psychology, Louisiana State University, Baton Rouge

Brandy R. Maynard, PhD, School of Social Work, Saint Louis University, Saint Louis, MO

Julia E. McGivern, PhD, Educational Psychology, School of Education, University of Wisconsin–Madison

Allison J. Metz, PhD, National Implementation Research Network, Frank Porter Graham Child Development Institute, University of North Carolina at Chapel Hill

Sandra F. Naoom, MSPH, National Implementation Research Network, Frank Porter Graham Child Development Institute, University of North Carolina at Chapel Hill

George H. Noell, PhD, Department of Psychology, Louisiana State University, Baton Rouge

Francheska Perepletchikova, PhD, Department of Psychiatry, Child and Adolescent Psychiatry Division, Weill Cornell Medical College, White Plains, NY

Thomas J. Power, PhD, The Children's Hospital of Philadelphia and the Perelman School of Medicine at the University of Pennsylvania, Philadelphia

Kristin M. Rispoli, PhD, Nebraska Center for Research on Children, Youth, Families and Schools, University of Nebraska–Lincoln

Lisa M. Hagermoser Sanetti, PhD, Department of Psychology and the Center for Behavioral Education and Research, University of Connecticut, Storrs

Susan M. Sheridan, PhD, Nebraska Center for Research on Children, Youth, Families and Schools, University of Nebraska–Lincoln

Martha J. Walter, PhD, Educational Psychology, School of Education, University of Wisconsin–Madison

Treatment Integrity

INTRODUCTION: TREATMENT INTEGRITY IN PSYCHOLOGICAL RESEARCH AND PRACTICE

LISA M. HAGERMOSER SANETTI AND THOMAS R. KRATOCHWILL

Act as if what you do makes a difference. It does.

—William James

Evolution in psychological theory and science has resulted in significant progress for the treatment of those who experience social, emotional, and behavioral problems. Treatments are no longer informed primarily by fear and ignorance, as they were in centuries past (when lobotomies, marginalization, and institutionalization were common practice), but rather by humane understanding, theoretical models, and empirical support (Mash & Wolfe, 2010). Over the past two decades, the focus on accountability and evidence-based practice has significantly increased in managed care agencies, policies (e.g., Individuals With Disabilities Education Improvement Act, 2004; No Child

Preparation of this book was supported in part through Grant R324A10005 from the Institute for Education Sciences, U.S. Department of Education, to the University of Connecticut. The opinions expressed are those of the authors and do not represent views of the Institute for Education Sciences or the U.S. Department of Education. Opinions expressed herein do not necessarily reflect the position of the U.S. Department of Education, and such endorsements should not be inferred. We thank Melissa Collier-Meek for her editorial assistance.

http://dx.doi.org/10.1037/14275-001
Treatment Integrity: A Foundation for Evidence-Based Practice in Applied Psychology, L. M. H. Sanetti and T. R. Kratochwill (Editors)

Left Behind Act, 2001; Patient Protection and Affordable Care Act, 2010), professional organizations (American Psychological Association, 2005), and granting agencies (Institute of Education Sciences, 2012; National Institute of Mental Health, 2012) that represent, finance, and regulate psychological services. A significant increase in the evaluation and dissemination of evidence-based treatments (Kazak et al., 2010; Kazdin, 2008; Kratochwill, 2007; Roberts & Yeager, 2004; Weisz, Sandler, Durlak, & Anton, 2005) has occurred contemporaneously. For example, registries of evidence-based programs and practices (e.g., http://www.nrepp.samhsa.gov/), a clearinghouse of clinical practice guidelines (http://www.guideline.gov/), and treatment consensus statements (http://consensus.nih.gov/) have been developed to help psychologists identify evidence-based practices.

Identifying an appropriate evidence-based practice is necessary but insufficient for producing behavior change in clients, however (Durlak & DuPre, 2008; Peterson, Homer, & Wonderlich, 1982; Wickstrom, Jones, LaFleur, & Witt, 1998). An intervention must be implemented as planned to produce behavior change. In the broadest sense, *treatment integrity* (also referred to as treatment fidelity, fidelity of implementation, procedural fidelity, or implementation integrity) refers to the extent to which an intervention is implemented as intended (Century, Rudnick, & Freeman, 2010; Perepletchikova & Kazdin, 2005; Sanetti & Kratochwill, 2009). If critical components of an evidence-based treatment are not implemented, the intended recipients are unlikely to benefit. Among the many variables identified as influencing the efficacy of interventions, treatment integrity is the most proximal and definitive (Noell, 2008). If practitioners are truly to engage in evidence-based practice and researchers are to further test intervention efficacy, they must have a foundational knowledge of treatment integrity as well as its assessment and promotion.

TREATMENT INTEGRITY AND IMPLEMENTATION SCIENCE

Treatment integrity is related to the discrete delivery of evidence-based treatments or programs to recipients. Such treatment delivery is essential to achieving positive outcomes for recipients. Yet, it is only one part of the broader field of *implementation science,* which Eccles and Mittman (2006) defined as "the scientific study of methods to promote the systemic uptake of research findings and other evidence-based practices into routine practice" (p. 1). Implementation science includes activities at both the intervention level (i.e., treatment integrity) and the implementation level (Fixsen, Naoom, Blase, Friedman, & Wallace, 2005). Implementation-level activities refer to systems- or organizational-level actions that facilitate intervention delivery to clients. Conceptual models of implementation science (e.g., Fixsen et al., 2005) and initial empirical evidence suggest that implementation-level activities (e.g., organizational policies, leadership, resources) can influence intervention-level activities (i.e., treatment integrity; see Sanetti & Kratochwill, 2009). The primary focus of the content in this book, however, is on treatment integrity and intervention-level activities. These factors are where "the rubber meets the road"; practitioners and researchers often are not able to significantly or expediently influence implementation-level activities, but they are able to influence the treatment integrity of evidence-based practices to improve recipients' outcomes.

EVOLUTION OF TREATMENT INTEGRITY

Current researchers and practitioners have acknowledged the importance of measuring and promoting treatment integrity in their work (Cochrane & Laux, 2008; Perepletchikova, Treat, & Kazdin, 2007; Sanetti & DiGennaro Reed, 2012). Recognition of the clinical and methodological importance of treatment integrity has increased only relatively recently, however. For decades, intervention outcome researchers assumed that the interventions they were studying were implemented competently, consistently, and accurately. This assumption rendered unnecessary attention to treatment integrity as an important variable in either effective practice or intervention evaluation research. Challenges to the stringency of treatment outcome research and concerns for accountability related to intervention delivery resulted in an increased concern for accountability related to intervention delivery in the 1980s, and systematic research on treatment integrity in psychology and education began a decade later (Peterson et al., 1982; Sanetti & Kratochwill, 2009; VandenBos & Pino, 1980; Yeaton & Sechrest, 1981).

Today, there is a growing literature base on treatment integrity in psychology and education, and there are extensive literature bases on treatment integrity in related fields (e.g., medicine, prevention science). The important information contained in these literature bases is highly inaccessible to most researchers and practitioners who are attending to treatment integrity as a component, not the sole focus, of their work. To obtain a foundational knowledge of treatment integrity conceptual models, assessment practices, and promotion strategies, one currently must find, read, and synthesize myriad journal articles and texts from multiple fields and then determine how these results can be applied to one's work. The fact that practitioners and researchers simply do not have the time or resources to devote to such activities is a commonly presented hypothesis as to why treatment integrity continues to be ignored in most practice and research settings (Cochrane

& Laux, 2008; Dane & Schneider, 1998; McIntyre, Gresham, DiGennaro, & Reed, 2007; Moncher & Prinz, 1991; Perepletchikova, Hilt, Chereji, & Kazdin, 2009; Perepletchikova et al., 2007; Peterson et al., 1982; Sanetti & DiGennaro Reed, 2012; Sanetti, Dobey, & Gritter, 2012; Sanetti, Gritter, & Dobey, 2011; Schoenwald, 2011).

PURPOSE OF THE BOOK

This book is meant to provide the first comprehensive source on the current state of knowledge related to the conceptualization, assessment, and promotion of treatment integrity across psychology, education, and related fields. Given this context, we hope to accomplish the following goals:

- Provide an accessible resource that summarizes the current state of the research on the conceptual models, assessment, and promotion related to treatment integrity.
- Take a broad view of treatment integrity by including summaries of conceptual and empirical work on treatment integrity within multiple areas of psychology, education, and related fields (i.e., medicine, prevention science).
- Situate treatment integrity within the ethical and legal context in which psychologists practice and conduct research.
- Offer balanced content that will benefit both practitioners implementing evidence-based treatments and researchers building the evidence base.
- Promote evidence-based practices by providing an overview of assessment and promotion strategies that are based on research findings.
- Illustrate how treatment integrity practices may be implemented across intervention types and service-delivery models.
- Include content relevant to psychologists as well as professionals who provide or supervise the provision of intervention services, such as social workers, counselors, speech-language pathologists, educators, and administrators.

In short, the chapters in this book present a broad, multielement view of treatment integrity to specify what is known and what is not yet known about the implementation of evidence-based interventions. For example, the reader will note that some findings have been consistent across studies and fields (e.g., higher levels of treatment integrity result in improved outcomes), whereas other findings have not (e.g., self-report of treatment integrity has been found to be acceptable by some researchers and unreliable by others).

Similarly, the chapters in this book present diverse definitions of treatment integrity. This variation in definitions reflects the emerging, evolving, and complex nature of this area of inquiry and further underscores the need for a comprehensive resource on the topic.

OVERVIEW OF THE BOOK

This book consists of four primary sections: (a) conceptualizing treatment integrity, (b) assessing treatment integrity, (c) promoting treatment integrity, and (d) applying treatment integrity assessment and promotion methods.

The first section, "Conceptualizing Treatment Integrity," provides a broad overview of conceptual models related to treatment integrity from fields in which significant work has been conducted over several decades. In Chapter 1, Heather A. King and Hayden Bosworth, researchers who have made important contributions to the medical literature on treatment adherence, provide an overview of current conceptualizations of treatment fidelity in human services research. The medical literature arguably has the best developed literature base on treatment fidelity across a wide spectrum of disorders and interventions (e.g., medication adherence). Without question, practitioners and researchers in psychology, education, and social science have knowledge to gain regarding intervention implementation from the depth of work conducted in medicine. In Chapter 2, Brian K. Bumbarger, a prevention science researcher who has been involved in the development of conceptual models of treatment integrity for school- and community-based prevention programs, provides an overview of the predominant conceptualizations of treatment integrity in prevention science. In Chapter 3, Anna C. J. Long and Brandy R. Maynard explicate theoretical models of adult behavior change. Because implementation of many interventions requires adult behavior change, promoting high levels of treatment integrity can be conceptualized as an adult behavior change process. Thus, empirically supported theoretical models of adult behavior change can inform development of intervention strategies to promote adoption and sustained implementation of interventions.

The second section, "Assessing Treatment Integrity," provides an overview of the conceptual and empirical development in two areas: measure development and data analysis. In Chapter 4, Jeanne Century and Amy Cassata provide an overview of the conceptual underpinnings of school-based treatment integrity assessment and the development of a battery of treatment integrity assessments for application in applied and research settings. In Chapter 5, Frank M. Gresham provides an overview of measuring and interpreting treatment integrity, including discussions of the relationship between treatment integrity and validity, variables hypothesized to influence treatment integrity, psychometric issues to consider, and methods of treatment integrity assessment. In Chapter 6, Francheska Perepletchikova provides an overview of treatment integrity assessment within the domain of psychotherapy research.

The third section, "Promoting Treatment Integrity," includes an overview of three common methods for improving educators' level of treatment integrity. In Chapter 7, George H. Noell and Kristen A. Gansle provide an overview of the systematic line of research supporting and the procedures for implementing performance feedback. Performance feedback is the treatment integrity promotion strategy with the most empirical support; however, to date no resource has synthesized the research findings and explicated the supported feedback procedures. In Chapter 8, Dean L. Fixsen, Karen A. Blase, Allison J. Metz, and Sandra F. Naoom provide an overview of the empirical bases for and factors related to preparing practitioners to implement interventions, including interventionist selection, training, and coaching. In Chapter 9, Florence D. DiGennaro Reed, Jason M. Hirst, and Veronica J. Howard provide a review of behavior analytic principles that are relevant to promoting and maintaining treatment integrity.

The final section, "Applying Treatment Integrity Assessment and Promotion Methods," provides an overview of the legal and ethical issues associated with treatment integrity and examples of how various strategies for treatment integrity assessment and promotion can be applied to different service delivery models and settings. In Chapter 10, Julia E. McGivern and Martha J. Walter discuss the legal and ethical issues associated with treatment integrity assessment, documentation, and promotion in research and practice as well as the role of treatment integrity in special education eligibility determination and due process in multitiered intervention models of service delivery. In Chapter 11, Susan M. Sheridan, Kristin M. Rispoli, and Shannon R. Holmes provide an overview of how treatment integrity can be assessed and promoted in conjoint behavioral consultation, an indirect service delivery model; both the consultation level (i.e., implementation of the conjoint consultation model) and the intervention level (i.e., implementation of the intervention by the consultee) are discussed. In Chapter 12, Courtney N. Baker, Stephen S. Leff, Katherine Bevans, and Thomas J. Power provide an overview of the challenges and successes of assessing treatment integrity and adapting practices to promote higher levels of treatment integrity in community-based programs.

The available conceptual and empirical knowledge regarding treatment integrity has been compiled in this volume. We hope this book will (a) provide researchers and practitioners with the information they need to develop a foundational knowledge related to treatment integrity and identify treatment integrity assessment methods and promotion strategies appropriate for their practice, (b) improve the methodological quality of intervention evaluation in research and practice, and (c) help advance the science of treatment integrity.

REFERENCES

American Psychological Association. (2005). *Policy statement on evidence-based practice in psychology*. Retrieved from http://www.apa.org/practice/ebp.html

Century, J., Rudnick, M., & Freeman, C. (2010). A framework for measuring fidelity of implementation: A foundation for shared language and accumulation of knowledge. *American Journal of Evaluation, 31*, 199–218. doi:10.1177/1098214010366173

Cochrane, W. S., & Laux, J. M. (2008). A survey investigating school psychologists' measurement of treatment integrity in school-based interventions and their beliefs about its importance. *Psychology in the Schools, 45*, 499–507. doi:10.1002/pits.20319

Dane, A. V., & Schneider, B. H. (1998). Program integrity in primary and early secondary prevention: Are implementation effects out of control? *Clinical Psychology Review, 18*, 23–45. doi:10.1016/S0272-7358(97)00043-3

Durlak, J. A., & DuPre, E. P. (2008). Implementation matters: A review of research on the influence of implementation on program outcomes and the factors affecting implementation. *American Journal of Community Psychology, 41*, 327–350. doi:10.1007/s10464-008-9165-0

Eccles, M. P., & Mittman, B. S. (2006). Welcome to implementation science. *Implementation Science, 1*, 1–3. doi:10.1186/1748-5908-1-1

Fixsen, D. L., Naoom, S. F., Blase, K. A., Friedman, R. M., & Wallace, F. (2005). *Implementation research: A synthesis of the literature*. Tampa: University of South Florida, Louis de la Parte Florida Mental Health Institute, National Implementation Research Network.

Individuals With Disabilities Education Improvement Act, 20 U.S.C. § 1400 (2004).

Institute of Education Sciences. (2012). *Request for applications: Special education research grants*. Retrieved from http://ies.ed.gov/funding/pdf/2013_84324a.pdf

Kazak, A. E., Hoagwood, K., Weisz, J. R., Hood, K., Kratochwill, T. R., Vargas, L. A., & Banez, G. A. (2010). A meta-systems approach to evidence-based practice for children and adolescents. *American Psychologist, 65*, 85–97. doi:10.1037/a0017784

Kazdin, A. E. (2008). Evidence-based treatment and practice: New opportunities to bridge clinical research and practice, enhance the knowledge base, and improve patient care. *American Psychologist, 63*, 146–159. doi:10.1037/0003-066X.63.3.146

Kratochwill, T. R. (2007). Preparing psychologists for evidence-based practice: Lessons learned and challenges ahead. *American Psychologist, 62*, 829–843. doi:10.1037/0003-066X.62.8.829

Mash, E. J., & Wolfe, D. A. (2010). *Abnormal child psychology* (4th ed.). Belmont, CA: Wadsworth Cengage Learning.

McIntyre, L. L., Gresham, F. M., DiGennaro, F. D., & Reed, D. D. (2007). Treatment integrity of school-based interventions with children in the *Journal of Applied Behavior Analysis* 1991–2005. *Journal of Applied Behavior Analysis, 40*, 659–672. doi:10.1901/jaba.2007.659-672

Moncher, F. J., & Prinz, R. J. (1991). Treatment fidelity in outcome studies. *Clinical Psychology Review, 11*, 247–266. doi:10.1016/0272-7358(91)90103-2

National Institute of Mental Health. (2012). Dissemination and implementation research in health (R01). Retrieved from http://www.nimh.nih.gov/research-funding/grants/foas.jsp?type=ALL

No Child Left Behind Act, 20 U.S.C. § 16301 (2001).

Noell, G. H. (2008). Research examining the relationships among consultation process, treatment integrity, and outcomes. In W. P. Erchul & S. M. Sheridan (Eds.), *Handbook of research in school consultation: Empirical foundations for the field* (pp. 315–334). Mahwah, NJ: Erlbaum.

Patient Protection and Affordable Care Act, Pub. L. No. 111-148, § 2702, 124 Stat. 119 (2010).

Perepletchikova, F., Hilt, L. M., Chereji, E., & Kazdin, A. E. (2009). Barriers to implementing treatment integrity procedures: Survey of treatment outcome researchers. *Journal of Consulting and Clinical Psychology, 77*, 212–218. doi:10.1037/a0015232

Perepletchikova, F., & Kazdin, A. E. (2005). Treatment integrity and therapeutic change: Issues and research recommendations. *Clinical Psychology: Science and Practice, 12*, 365–383. doi:10.1093/clipsy.bpi045

Perepletchikova, F., Treat, T., & Kazdin, A. E. (2007). Treatment integrity in psychotherapy research: Analysis of the studies and examination of the associated factors. *Journal of Consulting and Clinical Psychology, 75*, 829–841. doi:10.1037/0022-006X.75.6.829

Peterson, L., Homer, A. L., & Wonderlich, S. A. (1982). The integrity of independent variables in behavior analysis. *Journal of Applied Behavior Analysis, 15*, 477–492. doi:10.1901/jaba.1982.15-477

Roberts, A. R., & Yeager, K. (2004). *Evidence-based practice manual: Research and outcome measures in health and human services*. New York, NY: Oxford University Press.

Sanetti, L. M. H., & DiGennaro Reed, F. D. (2012). Barriers to implementing treatment integrity procedures in school psychology research: Survey of treatment outcome researchers. *Assessment for Effective Intervention, 37*, 195–202. doi:10.1177/1534508411432466

Sanetti, L. M. H., Dobey, L., & Gritter, K. L. (2012). Treatment integrity of interventions with children in the *Journal of Positive Behavior Interventions* from 1995 to 2009. *Journal of Positive Behavior Interventions, 14,* 29–46. doi:10.1177/1098300711405853

Sanetti, L. M. H., Gritter, K. L., & Dobey, L. (2011). Treatment integrity of interventions with children in the school psychology literature from 1995 to 2008. *School Psychology Review, 40,* 72–84.

Sanetti, L. M. H., & Kratochwill, T. R. (2009). Toward developing a science of treatment integrity: Introduction to the special series. *School Psychology Review, 38,* 445–459.

Schoenwald, S. K. (2011). It's a bird, it's a plane, it's . . . fidelity measurement in the real world. *Clinical Psychology: Science and Practice, 18,* 142–147. doi:10.1111/j.1468-2850.2011.01245.x

VandenBos, G. R., & Pino, C. D. (1980). Research on the outcome of psychotherapy. In G. R. VandenBos (Ed.), *Psychotherapy: Practice, research, policy* (pp. 23–69). Beverly Hills, CA: Sage.

Weisz, J. R., Sandler, I. N., Durlak, J. A., & Anton, B. S. (2005). Promoting and protecting youth mental health through evidence-based prevention and treatment. *American Psychologist, 60,* 628–648. doi:10.1037/0003-066X.60.6.628

Wickstrom, K. F., Jones, K. M., LaFleur, L. H., & Witt, J. C. (1998). An analysis of treatment integrity in school-based behavioral consultation. *School Psychology Quarterly, 13,* 141–154. doi:10.1037/h0088978

Yeaton, W. H., & Sechrest, L. (1981). Critical dimensions in the choice and maintenance of successful treatments: Strength, integrity, and effectiveness. *Journal of Consulting and Clinical Psychology, 49,* 156–167. doi:10.1037/0022-006X.49.2.156

I
CONCEPTUALIZING TREATMENT INTEGRITY

1

TREATMENT FIDELITY IN HEALTH SERVICES RESEARCH

HEATHER A. KING AND HAYDEN BOSWORTH

The extent to which individuals engage in healthy lifestyles and have access to supportive resources dramatically reduces the risk of chronic diseases such as cardiovascular disease (CVD), asthma, heart failure, arthritis, and diabetes (Chiuve, McCullough, Sacks, & Rimm, 2006; Lanas et al., 2007; Lichtenstein et al., 2006; Richardson, Kriska, Lantz, & Hayward, 2004). Unhealthy behaviors account for an estimated 50% of mortality in the United States (McGinnis & Foege, 1993) and lead to significant health care utilization; the direct cost of treating CVD, for example, will triple from $272.5 billion in 2010 to $818.1 billion in 2030 (Heidenreich et al., 2011). Unhealthy behaviors such as smoking, poor diet, and sedentary lifestyles account for as

This chapter was supported by a postdoctoral fellowship from the Department of Veterans Affairs, Office of Academic Affiliations, Health Services Research and Development (TPP 21-020), to the first author and by a Career Scientist Award from the Department of Veterans Affairs, Veterans Health Administration, Office of Research and Development, Health Services Research and Development (IIR 08-027), to the second author. The views expressed in this chapter are those of the authors and do not necessarily represent the position or policy of the Department of Veterans Affairs or the United States government.

http://dx.doi.org/10.1037/14275-003
Treatment Integrity: A Foundation for Evidence-Based Practice in Applied Psychology, L. M. H. Sanetti and T. R. Kratochwill (Editors)

much as 40% of premature deaths in the United States, whereas deficiencies in health care delivery account for only 10% (Schroeder, 2007). Further, one of the largest contributing factors to disease complications is poor medication adherence; 20% to 50% of patients are nonadherent and experience worse health outcomes as a result (DiMatteo, Giordani, Lepper, & Croghan, 2002). Cardiovascular medications alone are estimated to be responsible for half of the 50% reduction in mortality from coronary heart disease over the past 20 years (Ford et al., 2007). Individuals' health and medication-regime adherence behaviors clearly have a great influence on the actual achievement of intervention benefits. Thus, the potential benefit of interventions to improve patients' health behaviors exceeds that of interventions aimed at improving service delivery by health care providers.

Our goal in this chapter is to frame the importance of treatment fidelity in research examining patient treatment adherence to lifestyle interventions in the medical setting. Our discussion of treatment fidelity applied to health services research includes definitions of treatment fidelity; the importance of treatment fidelity to research and clinical practice; the prevalence of examining treatment fidelity; treatment fidelity methods and techniques; and additional treatment fidelity considerations in health services contexts. We discuss intervention tailoring and technology within the section on growing trends in health services research and implications for treatment fidelity. Finally, we discuss the role of treatment fidelity in the context of dissemination. Although many authors in this book use the term *treatment integrity*, *treatment fidelity* is more common in medicine and, as such, is used in this chapter.

TREATMENT FIDELITY APPLIED TO HEALTH SERVICES RESEARCH

In this section, we discuss how the concept of treatment fidelity applies to health services research. We define treatment fidelity and review its importance to research and clinical practice as well as its prevalence. Next, we discuss methods and techniques used to monitor and improve treatment fidelity followed by additional treatment-fidelity-related considerations in health services contexts.

Treatment Fidelity Defined

Treatment fidelity involves the "methodological strategies used to monitor and enhance the reliability and validity of behavioral interventions" (Bellg et al., 2004, p. 443). The definition of treatment fidelity, particularly the proposed components, has evolved over time (Bellg et al., 2004).

According to Moncher and Prinz (1991), treatment fidelity includes two connected but separate components. The first component, *treatment integrity*, refers to whether intervention delivery occurred as planned (Vermilyea, Barlow, & O'Brien, 1984; Yeaton & Sechrest, 1981). The second component, *treatment differentiation*, refers to the degree to which treatment conditions are distinct in critical dimensions (Kazdin, 1986a, 1986b).

Other investigators have further expanded the concept of treatment fidelity. According to Perepletchikova and Kazdin (2005), for example, three components are involved, one of which is *treatment differentiation* as described above. The other two components are (a) *treatment adherence* (i.e., the degree to which certain predetermined procedures are used by the interventionist during treatment delivery) and (b) *therapist competence* (i.e., the skillfulness of the interventionist delivering the treatment; e.g., Perepletchikova & Kazdin, 2005; Waltz, Addis, Koerner, & Jacobson, 1993). Alternatively, Lichstein, Riedel, and Grieve (1994) focused on patient experiences, rather than solely treatment delivery by the interventionist, and added *treatment receipt* (i.e., whether the patient understands and is able to use the treatment skills) and *treatment enactment* (i.e., whether the patient is able to actually implement the learned behavior in everyday life).

The Treatment Fidelity Workgroup of the National Institutes of Health (NIH) Behavior Change Consortium (BCC) developed yet another treatment fidelity framework expanding on the Lichstein et al. (1994) model. This framework addresses five areas: (a) design of study, (b) training of providers, (c) delivery of treatment, (d) receipt of treatment, and (e) enactment of treatment skills (Bellg et al., 2004). This conceptualization integrates and expands prior components (i.e., treatment delivery, receipt, and enactment as defined in previous frameworks) and adds components (i.e., design of study and training providers). It is tailored to increase relevancy to health behavior change trials and research as well as clinical practice (Borrelli et al., 2005). *Design of study* involves factors to be considered prior to trial initiation, such as content, dose, and congruence, with applicable theory and clinical experience guiding the intervention. *Training of providers* (e.g., provider training standardization, interventionist skill acquisition and maintenance) should be considered at the beginning of studies and throughout (Bellg et al., 2004; Borrelli et al., 2005). Of all these various components of treatment fidelity, enactment is perhaps the most conceptually and practically challenging (Bellg et al., 2004).

Importance of Treatment Fidelity

The concept of treatment fidelity and its components are significant to health services research. In particular, treatment fidelity is important for both research and clinical practice.

Research

Accurate conclusions with regard to the interpretation of results and confidence in study findings cannot be formed or stated in the absence of assessment of treatment fidelity (Bellg et al., 2004; Borrelli, 2011). For example, if significant results were found without monitoring and optimizing treatment fidelity, whether the outcome was due to a successful intervention or to other, unknown, and perhaps unintentional elements added to or omitted from the treatment would be unclear. In this scenario, a Type I error may occur (i.e., the treatment effect is believed to be significant when this is not the case); the resulting potential danger is implementation and dissemination of ineffective treatments. Alternatively, if there were nonsignificant findings and level of treatment fidelity was not measured, whether an ineffective treatment or a lack of treatment fidelity produced these results could not be determined. The mistaken belief that a treatment effect is nonsignificant is a Type II error, which may lead to rejection of potentially effective interventions. These errors (i.e., discarding effective programs or accepting ineffective ones as a result of limited attention to treatment fidelity) are costly, both financially and scientifically; there is a substantial cost to multiple individuals in clinical practice, including patients, providers, and organizations (Bellg et al., 2004; Borrelli, 2011).

Clinical Practice

Addressing and monitoring treatment fidelity comprehensively in pilot studies facilitates conducting large-scale clinical trials (Bruckenthal & Broderick, 2007). Strengths and weaknesses of components of treatment fidelity (e.g., study design, training providers, provider delivery of treatment, patient receipt of treatment, patient enactment of treatment skills) identified during pilot work can inform trial improvements and future research (Bruckenthal & Broderick, 2007). In addition, treatment fidelity may be critical to successful dissemination of research findings from trials (e.g., effective new procedures, behavioral change interventions) to clinical practice (Bellg et al., 2004; Bruckenthal & Broderick, 2007). Health professionals in medical settings have clinical expertise, but they often lack knowledge of and experience with behavior change research. Treatment fidelity promotion and verification strategies utilized and described by researchers could serve as guidelines and recommendations for translating interventions to clinical practice as well as implementing them accordingly (Bellg et al., 2004).

Prevalence of Treatment Fidelity

Components of treatment fidelity have been examined and evaluated within medicine and particular subfields, such as complementary and alternative medicine in cancer treatment (i.e., reflexology trial among female patients with advanced breast cancer; Wyatt, Sikorskii, Rahbar, Victorson, & Adams, 2010). In addition, components of treatment fidelity and corresponding promotion, monitoring, and assessment strategies have been incorporated in health behavior change research, such as in a program designed to increase exercise among older women who had experienced a hip fracture (Resnick et al., 2005). Despite its importance, however, treatment fidelity often is not fully addressed in health behavior intervention articles, public health clinical trial reports, and the clinical psychology, psychiatry, and psychotherapy literatures (Borrelli et al., 2005; Mayo-Wilson, 2007; Moncher & Prinz, 1991).

Moncher and Prinz (1991) reviewed 359 treatment outcome studies (i.e., psychosocial interventions designed to treat a particular problem) from 1980 to 1988 to determine the degree to which researchers sufficiently considered treatment fidelity. The evaluation focused on major journals in four domains: clinical psychology, behavior therapy, psychiatry, and marital and family therapy. Moncher and Prinz reported that the majority of the studies (~55%) basically ignored treatment fidelity promotion and verification with regard to three specific strategies: using a treatment manual, supervising treatment agents/implementers, and examining implementer adherence to protocol. Of those studies that assessed the latter and had multiple-session treatments, only approximately 32% sampled from more than one session. In addition, just about 13% of the studies reviewed relied on multiple sources of verification for treatment fidelity, both independent coders/observers and participants. Furthermore, only approximately 26% of the studies reported that the interventionists were trained in the intervention protocol.

Moncher and Prinz (1991) concluded that, despite some progress (i.e., significant increases over the time frame selected in treatment agent supervision and inspection of implementer adherence), improvement is needed with regard to the attention paid to treatment fidelity and reporting as well. Researchers should also acknowledge that treatment fidelity is not dichotomous (i.e., present/absent) and that it exists on a continuum (Moncher & Prinz, 1991). This evaluation was restricted to the fields of psychology and psychiatry and focused on therapy and mental health; these findings, therefore, may or may not apply to other settings and contexts in medicine and health behavior change research. Other aspects of treatment fidelity more recently proposed, such as treatment receipt and enactment of treatment skills by the patient, were not considered.

Borrelli et al. (2005) conducted a more recent review of treatment fidelity. As in Moncher and Prinz (1991), articles involving psychosocial interventions designed to address a specific problem were included; however, this evaluation focused on health behavior change literature. Examples of specific health behaviors targeted include smoking, physical activity, diet, and alcohol/drug use. Articles published in five journals over 10 years (1990–2000) were identified, and 342 studies met the inclusion criteria. Of the health behavior change studies reviewed, 54% did not report using any of the three treatment fidelity strategies originally explored by Moncher and Prinz (i.e., use of a treatment manual, supervision of treatment providers, checking adherence to treatment protocol). Despite the difference in time period and literature, the results of Borrelli et al. were very similar to those of Moncher and Prinz (about 55%). Borrelli et al. did not find significant changes (i.e., increases) in the use of these strategies from the early to late 1990s; rather, there were actually nonsignificant trends for decreases in reporting over time.

Borrelli et al. (2005) considered 22 strategies in addition to the three examined by Moncher and Prinz (1991) and employed a total of 25 to evaluate reporting of and adherence to treatment fidelity. These 25 strategies were distributed across the five parts of the framework developed by the Treatment Fidelity Workgroup of the NIH BCC; examples of strategies by component include providing information about treatment dose in the various conditions (*design*); describing and measuring training of providers (*training*); assessing provider adherence to protocol (*delivery*); examining patient understanding of and ability to perform treatment skills during the study period (*receipt*); and evaluating patient application of treatment skills in other, real-world settings (*enactment;* Borrelli et al., 2005).

The mean proportion of adherence to treatment fidelity strategies for the design, training, delivery, receipt, and enactment components was .80, .22, .35, .49, and .57, respectively (Borrelli et al., 2005). These results demonstrate considerable variation across the components, with the highest mean proportion of adherence to strategies found in the component of design and the lowest found in the training component. On average, the mean proportion of overall adherence was .55 when all individual strategies were considered. Finally, few studies achieved high levels of treatment fidelity, defined as .80 or greater proportion adherence, across all strategies (15.5%) as well as all strategies and all components (6.5%; Borrelli et al., 2005). Both evaluations (Borrelli et al., 2005; Moncher & Prinz, 1991) are limited in that it is unclear whether the studies included did not use the strategies or whether the strategies were employed but just not described and completely reported in the published articles. As Borrelli et al. pointed out, however, these are critical details that are required for readers and interested parties to form conclusions, perform replications, or translate the interventions to more applied clinical settings.

Perepletchikova, Treat, and Kazdin (2007) examined the adequacy of procedures for implementation of treatment integrity (i.e., the degree to which an intervention is delivered as intended) in randomized controlled trials (RCTs) in psychotherapy research from six influential journals in the field (years 2000–2004). Results focusing on 147 selected articles, including 202 treatments (i.e., psychosocial interventions), revealed that very few studies (3.5%) were rated as adequately addressing total treatment integrity. Perepletchikova et al. highlighted that less attention is paid to treatment integrity than to operational definitions and measurement (e.g., reliability) of outcomes. They also extended prior reviews, including those discussed above, by examining correlates of treatment integrity. Both journal of publication and treatment approach (skill-building interventions as compared with non-skill-building treatments) were related to implementation of integrity procedures (Perepletchikova et al., 2007).

Perepletchikova, Hilt, Chereji, and Kazdin (2009) contacted the corresponding authors of the articles identified above and asked them to complete an online survey examining perceived barriers to implementing treatment integrity procedures. Of the authors, 74 responded and met the criteria for inclusion (i.e., completed at least one demographic item as well as one item measuring barriers). The authors generally appreciated treatment integrity, which was not reported to be a barrier to implementation. Both an absence of editorial/publication requirements related to treatment integrity and a dearth of general knowledge regarding this concept were identified as barriers to addressing treatment fidelity, however. Strong barriers to implementation of treatment integrity procedures included (a) limited theory and a deficiency in specific, related guidelines and (b) demands associated with time, cost, and labor. Finally, there was an inverse relationship between the number of perceived barriers and actual adequacy of treatment integrity procedures in practice (Perepletchikova et al., 2009).

The realization is growing that taking treatment fidelity into consideration is important when performing research, particularly in the public health and health behavior arenas (Bellg et al., 2004; Borrelli, 2011). Increasing the focus on evidence-based practices in medicine is also important (Institute of Medicine, 2001). Given the importance of treatment fidelity to the internal and external validity of studies such as health behavior change clinical trials (Borrelli, 2011), some have suggested that funding requests, reviewer guidelines, and requirements for publication explicitly address the techniques employed by investigators to enhance and monitor treatment fidelity (Bellg et al., 2004; Perepletchikova et al., 2009). Such policies could motivate and encourage researchers to include treatment fidelity in their designs and work; with increased attention paid to the concept, it could become more prevalent in the literature and eventually become part of standard research practice (Bellg et al., 2004; Perepletchikova et al., 2009).

Treatment Fidelity Methods and Techniques

A number of practices and strategies for monitoring and improving treatment fidelity that correspond to the five-component model previously introduced and described by the Treatment Fidelity Workgroup of the NIH BCC (Bellg et al., 2004; Resnick et al., 2005) have been proposed. With regard to *study design*, researchers should (a) clarify the intervention protocol fits with a theory, (b) consider dose within and across conditions, and (c) prepare in advance for potential implementation difficulties. *Training of interventionists* can be supported by (a) standardizing training, (b) using manuals and role playing, and (c) incorporating differences among providers. Assessment and observation of provider knowledge and performance as well as training throughout the study are important and may prevent skill decay (i.e., drift) over time. In terms of *treatment delivery*, session observation and checklists are useful for ensuring protocol adherence; they are also critical for preventing contamination across treatment and control conditions. *Participant receipt of treatment* (i.e., comprehension and ability to use and perform skills addressed in the intervention) as well as *enactment*, or use of skills in everyday life, can be assessed with self-report, behavioral, or observational measures (Bellg et al., 2004; Resnick et al., 2005).

In the case of clinical trials focusing on treatment adherence to lifestyle interventions in the medical environment, multiple interventionists might provide an intervention, particularly if the intervention was a multisite trial. In the case of the Hypertension Intervention Nurse Telemedicine Study (HINTS), a Veterans Affairs (VA)–funded trial, we evaluated a novel hypertension treatment delivery method based on home telemonitoring of blood pressure (BP) and tested which of three interventions delivered via telephone was most effective in improving BP control (Bosworth et al., 2011). In the trial, two nurses administered three telephonic interventions to 593 veterans with poor BP control. Eligible patients were randomized to either usual care or one of three telephone-based intervention groups: (a) nurse-administered behavioral management, (b) nurse- and physician-administered medication management, or (c) a combination of the two.

The five-component model described by the Treatment Fidelity Workgroup of the NIH BCC (Bellg et al., 2004; Resnick et al., 2005) was used for the HINTS trial. With regard to *study design*, we ensured that the intervention protocol was based on a theory (e.g., transtheoretical theory), and we scripted out the intervention in anticipation of potential implementation difficulties. *Training of interventionists* consisted of ensuring that the nurses administered the intervention consistently to patients. We tracked this by periodically listening to phone conversations, recording the length of time of each contact, and examining process and outcome measures by each nurse interventionist. We compared values across these various domains as periodic checks for intervention fidelity of delivery of the intervention. Internal validity may be threatened as interventionists become less adherent to the study protocol over time (Heimberg & Becker, 1984). Thus, we checked fidelity throughout the 3 years that the 18-month intervention was administered. We randomly listened to nurses' calls to ensure protocol adherence (*treatment delivery*). *Participant receipt of treatment* (i.e., comprehension and ability to use and perform skills addressed in the intervention) as well as *enactment* or use of skills such as home BP monitoring were assessed with self-report, behavioral, and observational measures. This attention to fidelity has allowed us to further disseminate and implement the program into other health care systems (Bosworth et al., 2011). The program is being implemented by case managers in North Carolina Medicaid and the United Kingdom National Health System.

Additional Treatment Fidelity Considerations in Health Services Contexts

The concept of treatment fidelity has received attention within a variety of fields, particularly the social and behavioral disciplines (Moncher & Prinz, 1991). Kirchhoff and Dille (1994) argued that there are a number of complications to treatment fidelity among interventions conducted in clinical contexts; however, such complications have received limited consideration until recently. Examples of these challenges include selection of providers and sites, fit of the intervention with usual care, and difficulties in altering current standards and practices. Medical and health services environments involve various complexities of care that may influence assessment, monitoring, and enhancement of treatment fidelity (Kirchhoff & Dille, 1994). Evaluating treatment fidelity is particularly important when it cannot be guaranteed, such as in community treatment settings and other real-world applications (Neff, 2011).

Community treatment settings are often quite diverse in regard both to providers and to participants (Campbell, 2011). Characteristics of these individuals as well as aspects of the provider–patient relationship may be important moderators that impact treatment effects. Leventhal and Friedman (2004) suggested that a lack of knowledge regarding "processes between the steps," where both the steps and the transitions are influenced by clinician and patient traits and interactions, significantly contributes to the well-documented gap between efficacy and effectiveness that is present in health services research (p. 453). Campbell (2011) posited that consideration of these individual characteristics of patients and providers and their relational factors in the context of monitoring treatment fidelity can inform not only research but also practice, allowing for the matching of patients, providers, and treatments in medicine. In fact, such tailoring and approaches are becoming increasingly common, and, as such, they are highlighted below.

GROWING TRENDS IN HEALTH SERVICES RESEARCH AND IMPLICATIONS FOR TREATMENT FIDELITY

Intervention research and delivery are constantly evolving. Tailored interventions and increased use of technology are two current trends that influence treatment fidelity.

Tailoring

Tailored, individualized, and individual-centered interventions focus on and/or respond to patients' characteristics, such as personality traits, goals, motivations, and preferences (Beck et al., 2010). These types of interventions are appreciated by participants and by providers or health professionals and are therefore becoming more common in the treatment and intervention literature, particularly in medical and health services contexts. Despite challenges associated with tailored interventions related to, for example, development, implementation, evaluation, and standardization, the potential benefits of tailoring may outweigh the challenges if improved cost efficiency and outcomes as well as adherence are achieved (Beck et al., 2010). Because greater attention to treatment fidelity has been requested and goals and strategies for fidelity monitoring and enhancement have been recommended for future health behavior research, public health investigations, and clinical trials (Bellg et al., 2004; Borrelli, 2011; Mayo-Wilson, 2007), treatment fidelity must be maintained when interventions are tailored. With proper planning, training, and attention to previous research and relevant theoretical backgrounds and frameworks achieved (Beck et al., 2010), reaching this goal is feasible.

In considering intervention tailoring, one should also consider that standardized interventions do not always demonstrate effects and that they may not be successful or be adopted by clinicians in actual practice (Beck et al., 2010). Leventhal and Friedman (2004) argued that rigidity in implementation and strict efforts to achieve high standards of fidelity, which are generally not even well defined, might negatively influence behavioral health intervention research and preclude translation and dissemination into clinical practice. Furthermore, in treatment fidelity models such as that proposed by Bellg et al. (2004), patients and participants are viewed as reactive rather than as "active, self-regulating, problem solvers capable of inventing solutions to their own behavioral problems" (Leventhal & Friedman, 2004, p. 455). However, patients and participants may play an active role in their own health promotion and disease management; this possibility warrants acknowledgment and consideration in intervention development as well as strategies to promote treatment fidelity.

Use of Technology

Health technologies and technology-based behavioral interventions (i.e., "use of information and communication technology applications to promote behavioral outcomes"; DeVito Dabbs et al., 2011, p. 340) are becoming increasingly common. Given this rise in utilization and application, considering the unique issues these interventions present to treatment fidelity—which are currently lacking in the literature—is particularly important. DeVito Dabbs et al. (2011), therefore, proposed a fidelity framework that is potentially more suitable for and applicable to technology-based behavioral interventions. In this case, where interactions between the participant and the technology are involved, technology is a distinct component of the intervention rather than solely a delivery method; note that system quality (e.g., reliability) of the technology is not an element of fidelity (DeVito Dabbs et al., 2011).

DeVito Dabbs et al. (2011) accounted for various technology-specific elements (i.e., features and interfaces) in the fidelity framework, as well as additional factors important to fidelity of these programs in particular. These factors include (a) receipt, (b) the reciprocal delivery–receipt relationship, and (c) patient technology acceptance (i.e., perceptions, attitudes, and intentions related to use), which are all critical to adoption (i.e., actual use of technology). Technology acceptance is hypothesized to moderate the relationship between delivery/receipt and adoption, which then mediates enactment (i.e., performing targeted health behaviors). To illustrate use of the framework in practice, DeVito Dabbs et al. applied it to Pocket PATH (Personal Assistant for Tracking Health); a mobile health application intended to promote self-care behaviors following lung transplantation. An intervention fidelity evaluation plan was developed accordingly (DeVito Dabbs et al., 2011).

Others have focused on web-based behavioral interventions, such as an RCT of a web-based cognitive behavioral stress management intervention for improving coping skills among survivors of breast cancer (Eaton, Doorenbos, Schmitz, Carpenter, & McGregor, 2011). Another example of the use of a web-based intervention is the secondary prevention risk interventions via telemedicine and tailored patient education (SPRITE; Shah et al., 2011). The latter study is a secondary prevention intervention for individuals who have had a myocardial infarction in the past 36 months. In this three-arm RCT, the first arm receives home BP monitors plus a nurse-delivered, telephone-based tailored patient education intervention and is enrolled into HealthVault, a Microsoft electronic health record platform. The second arm also receives BP monitors plus a tailored patient education intervention and is enrolled in HealthVault. However, the patient education intervention is delivered via a web-based program and covers topics identical to those in the nurse-delivered intervention. Both arms are compared with a control group receiving standard care. To ensure treatment fidelity, Shah et al. track that individuals are accessing the website or are being contacted by the nurse interventionist. In the latter case, they randomly review inter-actions, and, in the case of the website arm, they track closely the frequency of individuals using the website and send reminders when individuals have not visited the site in a prescribed time. Shah et al. have scripted material for both the website and the nurse-administered intervention and can ensure that everyone has access to the same material. Computer prompts are used for contacts to ensure fixed length, number, and frequency of contact sessions (Shah et al., 2011).

The Internet and smartphones are becoming more pervasive in inter-vention delivery, particularly in health care, where the programs are easily scalable (i.e., implemented) and can potentially include many patients with lower staff and organizational costs (Eaton et al., 2011). Delivery of behav-ioral interventions via the web (or smartphones) can be a strength as well as a threat to treatment fidelity. Adequate treatment fidelity can be ensured, however, if challenges such as self-administration (e.g., there is an increased risk that participants will receive an inadequate dose of the intervention) are addressed; different considerations regarding treatment fidelity are required when an intervention is not necessarily delivered by an interventionist or provided in person (Eaton et al., 2011). These considerations involve being able to track usage, such as frequency in contacting or receiving material, as well to examine doses of contacts (e.g., time on a website). Individuals typi-cally engage in these technology-based interventions, but long-term use is rarely examined and continues to be a problem (Shaw & Bosworth, 2012).

The discussions and examples provided by DeVito Dabbs et al. (2011) and Eaton et al. (2011) demonstrate that suggested treatment fidelity strate-gies, such as those described by the Treatment Fidelity Workgroup of the NIH BCC, can be applied successfully to behavioral interventions involv-ing technology. Treatment fidelity strategies that are particularly relevant for behavioral interventions using technology and that are automated include (a) design of study (e.g., ensure the same treatment dose within and across conditions); (b) delivery of treatment (e.g., reduce differences within treat-ment, ensure adherence to treatment protocol, and minimize contamination between conditions); and (c) receipt of treatment (e.g., ensure participant comprehension and ability to perform behavioral skills; Bellg et al., 2004). However, treatment fidelity strategies of behavioral interventions involving technology may require some modifications; these are important to consider, given the growing role of technology in health care and related interventions. Technology can also play an important role in supporting treatment fidelity and quality control, regardless of the type of intervention and delivery method (Farran et al., 2011).

DISSEMINATION AND TREATMENT FIDELITY

As discussed, treatment fidelity may contribute to the successful dissemination of research in clinical practice and applied settings. In fact, the lack of attention to and limited reporting of treatment fidelity may be among the main reasons for the delays and challenges of implementing programs in the health care system. A substantial gap exists between clinical research and clinical practice; research findings are being "lost in translation" (Lenfant, 2003). Research discoveries often take years or decades to reach clinical practice (Westfall, Mold, & Fagnan, 2007). One source suggests that 17 years are required, on average, for just 14% of new outcomes or results to penetrate daily clinical practice (Balas & Boren, 2000, as cited in Westfall et al., 2007).

Others argue, however, that a two-way process and exchange between researchers and practitioners, rather than attention to treatment fidelity, is the most critical aspect of successful dissemination (King, Hawe, & Wise, 1998). A disconnect exists between efficacy and effectiveness research; linear progression from the former to the latter is generally unsuccessful (Glasgow, Lichtenstein, & Marcus, 2003). This debate regarding fidelity and adaptation (i.e., tensions, fit, balance, and negotiation) will likely continue as behavioral interventions increase in complexity (e.g., Hawe, Shiell, & Riley, 2004; Spillane et al., 2007).

TREATMENT FIDELITY RECOMMENDATIONS

Within the context of study design, treatment fidelity ensures the same treatment dose within conditions. Treatment fidelity ensures equivalent dosage across conditions, and planning for implementation setbacks is important. Those designing studies should standardize provider training, ensure provider skills acquisition, minimize "drift" in provider skills, and accommodate provider differences. In terms of delivery, a description of the training in the administration of the treatment protocol and of the implementers' competence should be reported (Moncher & Prinz, 1991). Training should be versatile. Training manuals, didactics sessions, modeling, and supervision of cases with feedback regarding adherence to protocol can be used. Training should include periodic booster sessions to ensure maintenance of protocol adherence (McMahon, 1987). Competence should be assessed through observation of pilot cases or assessment of the interventionist's knowledge of the treatment regimen. We typically use a canary group in our research. Such a group contains approximately twenty individuals who meet all the same inclusion/exclusion criteria of the larger sample; these individuals allow the interventionists to practice and familiarize themselves with the program. This canary group usually receives material approximately two months ahead of the intervention group, which provides an opportunity to identify and fix any new intervention material as it is deployed. This model is also used for technology-based interventions that allow us to identify potential "bugs" before the actual intervention group encounters them.

The assessment should document the intensity and length of treatment, occurrence of sessions, adherence to the specific and global aspects of the protocol, and absence of inappropriate techniques or fidelity violations (Luborsky & DeReubeis, 1984). Special attention may be given to selecting observation periods and evaluation criteria that are sensitive, so that similarities and differences in treatment are evaluated, yet are not too costly to implement or too complex. Whenever possible, multiple observers should be used and observers should be calibrated with criteria.

Researchers may need to conceptualize and measure treatment fidelity differently at various stages in the research-to-practice sequence. Particularly in the dissemination stage, in which an intervention is implemented broadly under a wide range of circumstances, understanding the active ingredients of the intervention, as well as specifying the allowable and prohibited changes, may be key to successful use in practice (Dusenbury, Brannigan, Hansen, Walsh, & Falco, 2005).

Policymakers, administrators, and researchers need treatment fidelity data to (a) assess generalizability of findings, (b) design future trials, (c) determine the feasibility of interventions, (Dusenbury, Brannigan, Falco, & Hansen, 2003), and (d) develop treatment guidelines (Jackson & Waters, 2005). The importance of treatment fidelity data is emphasized in the Transparent Reporting of Evaluations with Nonrandomized Designs (TREND) statement (Altman et al., 2001). A guide for reporting nonrandomized controlled trials, TREND complements the Consolidated Standards of Reporting Trials (CONSORT) statement (Des Jarlais, Lyles, & Crepaz, 2004), a guide for reporting RCTs.

Researchers should provide some quantitative measure of fidelity, and articles should be interpreted in light of achieved fidelity. Researchers should consider discussing prescribed techniques and the absence of prohibited techniques used for acceptable implementation. Careful consideration of treatment fidelity helps researchers explain study findings, revise interventions for future testing, and increase statistical power and effect size by reducing random and unintended variability (Moncher & Prinz, 1991).

CONCLUSION

Treatment fidelity criteria deserve more attention in research and evaluation studies. Treatment fidelity in the context of intervention implementation is not an all-or-none phenomenon; rather, it falls on a measurable continuum that should be incorporated in the design of research projects and dissemination/implementation programs. A wide range of procedures, from simple to elaborate, can be used to promote fidelity. Such procedures include clear treatment definitions, intensive training, careful supervision, and corrective remediation to prevent repeated violations of treatment protocol. One of the greatest obstacles to progress in health services and outcome research has been incomplete reporting of information pertinent to treatment fidelity so that research consumers can critically evaluate the evidence (Moncher & Prinz, 1991). An issue is balancing enough treatment fidelity assessment in which easily administered and general measures are used to ensure successful reproducibility of programs and measuring the extent to which more subtle critical components are present and operating as expected.

REFERENCES

Altman, D. G., Schulz, K. F., Moher, D., Egger, M., Davidoff, F., Elbourne, D., . . . Lang, T. (2001). The revised CONSORT statement for reporting randomized trials: Explanation and elaboration. *Annals of Internal Medicine, 134*, 663–694. doi:10.7326/0003-4819-134-8-200104170-00012

Beck, C., McSweeney, J. C., Richards, K. C., Roberson, P. K., Tsai, P. F., & Souder, E. (2010). Challenges in tailored intervention research. *Nursing Outlook, 58*, 104–110. doi:10.1016/j.outlook.2009.10.004

Bellg, A. J., Borrelli, B., Resnick, B., Hecht, J., Minicucci, D. S., Ory, M., . . . Czajkowski, S. (2004). Enhancing treatment fidelity in health behavior change studies: Best practices and recommendations from the NIH Behavior Change Consortium. *Health Psychology, 23*, 443–451. doi:10.1037/0278-6133.23.5.443

Borrelli, B. (2011). The assessment, monitoring, and enhancement of treatment fidelity in public health clinical trials. *Journal of Public Health Dentistry, 71*, S52–S63. doi:10.1111/j.1752-7325.2011.00233.x

Borrelli, B., Sepinwall, D., Ernst, D., Bellg, A. J., Czajkowski, S., Breger, R., . . . Orwig, D. (2005). A new tool to assess treatment fidelity and evaluation of treatment fidelity across 10 years of health behavior research. *Journal of Consulting and Clinical Psychology, 73,* 852–860. doi:10.1037/0022-006X.73.5.852

Bosworth, H. B., Powers, B. J., Olsen, M. K., McCant, F., Grubber, J., Smith, V., . . . Oddone, E. Z. (2011). Home blood pressure management and improved blood pressure control: Results from a randomized controlled trial. *Archives of Internal Medicine, 171,* 1173–1180. doi:10.1001/archinternmed.2011.276

Bruckenthal, P., & Broderick, J. E. (2007). Assessing treatment fidelity in pilot studies assist in designing clinical trials: An illustration from a nurse practitioner community-based intervention for pain. *Advances in Nursing Science, 30*(1), E72–E84.

Campbell, B. K. (2011). Fidelity in public health clinical trials: Considering provider–participant relationship factors in community treatment settings. *Journal of Public Health Dentistry, 71,* S64–S65. doi:10.1111/j.1752-7325.2011.00227.x

Chiuve, S. E., McCullough, M. L., Sacks, F. M., & Rimm, E. B. (2006). Healthy lifestyle factors in the primary prevention of coronary heart disease among men: Benefits among users and nonusers of lipid-lowering and antihypertensive medications. *Circulation, 114,* 160–167. doi:10.1161/CIRCULATIONAHA.106.621417

Des Jarlais, D. C., Lyles, C., & Crepaz, N. (2004). Improving the reporting quality of nonrandomized evaluations of behavioral and public health interventions: The TREND statement. *American Journal of Public Health, 94,* 361–366. doi:10.2105/AJPH.94.3.361

DeVito Dabbs, A., Song, M.-K., Hawkins, R., Aubrecht, J., Kovach, K., Terhorst, L., . . . Callan, J. (2011). An intervention fidelity framework for technology-based behavioral interventions. *Nursing Research, 60,* 340–347. doi:10.1097/NNR.0b013e31822cc87d

DiMatteo, M. R., Giordani, P. J., Lepper, H. S., & Croghan, T. W. (2002). Patient adherence and medical treatment outcomes: A meta-analysis. *Medical Care, 40,* 794–811. doi:10.1097/00005650-200209000-00009

Dusenbury, L., Brannigan, R., Falco, M., & Hansen, W. B. (2003). A review of research on fidelity of implementation: Implications for drug abuse prevention in school settings. *Health Education Research, 18,* 237–256. doi:10.1093/her/18.2.237

Dusenbury, L., Brannigan, R., Hansen, W. B., Walsh, J., & Falco, M. (2005). Quality of implementation: Developing measures crucial to understanding the diffusion of preventive interventions. *Health Education Research, 20,* 308–313. doi:10.1093/her/cyg134

Eaton, L. H., Doorenbos, A. Z., Schmitz, K. L., Carpenter, K. M., & McGregor, B. A. (2011). Establishing treatment fidelity in a web-based behavioral intervention study. *Nursing Research, 60,* 430–435. doi:10.1097/NNR.0b013e31823386aa

Farran, C. J., Etkin, C. D., McCann, J. J., Paun, O., Eisenstein, A. R., & Wilbur, J. (2011). Role of technology in supporting quality control and treatment fidelity in a family caregiver clinical trial. *Western Journal of Nursing Research*, *33*, 953–978. doi:10.1177/0193945910394453

Ford, E. S., Ajani, U. A., Croft, J. B., Critchley, J. A., Labarthe, D. R., Kottke, T. E., . . . Capewell, S. (2007). Explaining the decrease in U.S. deaths from coronary disease, 1980–2000. *New England Journal of Medicine, 356*, 2388–2398. doi:10.1056/NEJMsa053935

Glasgow, R. E., Lichtenstein, E., & Marcus, A. C. (2003). Why don't we see more translation of health promotion research to practice? Rethinking the efficacy-to-effectiveness transition. *American Journal of Public Health, 93*, 1261–1267. doi:10.2105/AJPH.93.8.1261

Hawe, P., Shiell, A., & Riley, T. (2004). Complex interventions: How "out of control" can a randomised controlled trial be? *BMJ: British Medical Journal, 328*, 1561–1563. doi:10.1136/bmj.328.7455.1561

Heidenreich, P. A., Trogdon, J. G., Khavjou, O. A., Butler, J., Dracup, K., Ezekowitz, M. D., . . . Woo, Y. J. (2011). Forecasting the future of cardiovascular disease in the United States: A policy statement from the American Heart Association. *Circulation, 123*, 933–944. doi:10.1161/CIR.0b013e31820a55f5

Heimberg, R. G., & Becker, R. E. (1984). Comparative outcome research. In M. Hersen, L. Michelson, & A. S. Bellack (Eds.), *Issues in psychotherapy research* (pp. 251–283). New York, NY: Plenum Press.

Institute of Medicine. (2001). *Crossing the quality chasm: A new health system for the 21st century*. Washington, DC: National Academy Press.

Jackson, N., & Waters, E. (2005). Criteria for the systematic review of health promotion and public health interventions. *Health Promotion International, 20*, 367–374. doi:10.1093/heapro/dai022

Kazdin, A. E. (1986a). Comparative outcome studies of psychotherapy: Methodological issues and strategies. *Journal of Consulting and Clinical Psychology, 54*, 95–105. doi:10.1037/0022-006X.54.1.95

Kazdin, A. E. (1986b). The evaluation of psychotherapy: Research, design and methodology. In S. L. Garfield & A. E. Bergin (Eds.), *Handbook of psychotherapy and behavior change* (3rd ed., pp. 23–68). New York, NY: Wiley.

King, L., Hawe, P., & Wise, M. (1998). Making dissemination a two-way process. *Health Promotion International, 13*, 237–244. doi:10.1093/heapro/13.3.237

Kirchhoff, K. T., & Dille, C. A. (1994). Issues in intervention research: Maintaining integrity. *Applied Nursing Research, 7*, 32–38. doi:10.1016/0897-1897(94)90018-3

Lanas, F., Avezum, A., Bautista, L. E., Diaz, R., Luna, M., Islam, S., & Yusuf, S. (2007). Risk factors for acute myocardial infarction in Latin America: The INTERHEART Latin American study. *Circulation, 115*, 1067–1074. doi:10.1161/CIRCULATIONAHA.106.633552

Lenfant, C. (2003). Clinical research to clinical practice—Lost in translation? *New England Journal of Medicine, 349*, 868–874. doi:10.1056/NEJMsa035507

Leventhal, H., & Friedman, M. A. (2004). Does establishing fidelity of treatment help in understanding treatment efficacy? Comment on Bellg et al. (2004). *Health Psychology, 23,* 452–456. doi:10.1037/0278-6133.23.5.452

Lichstein, K. L., Riedel, B. W., & Grieve, R. (1994). Fair tests of clinical trials: A treatment implementation model. *Advances in Behaviour Research and Therapy, 16,* 1–29. doi:10.1016/0146-6402(94)90001-9

Lichtenstein, A. H., Appel, L. J., Brands, M., Carnethon, M., Daniels, S., Franch, H. A., . . . Wylie-Rosett, J. (2006). Diet and lifestyle recommendations revision 2006: A scientific statement from the American Heart Association Nutrition Committee. *Circulation, 114,* 82–96. doi:10.1161/CIRCULATIONAHA.106.176158

Luborsky, L., & DeReubeis, R. J. (1984). The use of psychotherapy treatment manuals: A small revolution in psychotherapy research style. *Clinical Psychology Review, 4,* 5–14. doi:10.1016/0272-7358(84)90034-5

Mayo-Wilson, E. (2007). Reporting implementation in randomized trials: Proposed additions to the Consolidated Standards of Reporting Trials statement. *American Journal of Public Health, 97,* 630–633. doi:10.2105/AJPH.2006.094169

McGinnis, J. M., & Foege, W. H. (1993). Actual causes of death in the United States. JAMA: *Journal of the American Medical Association, 270,* 2207–2212. doi:10.1001/jama.1993.03510180077038

McMahon, P. M. (1987). Shifts in intervention procedures: A problem in evaluating human service interventions. *Social Work Research and Abstracts, 23,* 13–16. doi:10.1093/swra/23.4.13

Moncher, F. J., & Prinz, R. J. (1991). Treatment fidelity in outcome studies. *Clinical Psychology Review, 11,* 247–266. doi:10.1016/0272-7358(91)90103-2

Neff, J. A. (2011). Maximizing treatment fidelity in public health clinical trials. *Journal of Public Health Dentistry, 71*(Suppl. 1), S66. doi:10.1111/j.1752-7325.2011.00226.x

Perepletchikova, F., Hilt, L. M., Chereji, E., & Kazdin, A. E. (2009). Barriers to implementing treatment integrity procedures: Survey of treatment outcome researchers. *Journal of Consulting and Clinical Psychology, 77,* 212–218. doi:10.1037/a0015232

Perepletchikova, F., & Kazdin, A. E. (2005). Treatment integrity and therapeutic change: Issues and research recommendations. *Clinical Psychology: Science and Practice, 12,* 365–383. doi:10.1093/clipsy.bpi045

Perepletchikova, F., Treat, T. A., & Kazdin, A. E. (2007). Treatment integrity in psychotherapy research: Analysis of the studies and examination of the associated factors. *Journal of Consulting and Clinical Psychology, 75,* 829–841. doi:10.1037/0022-006X.75.6.829

Resnick, B., Inguito, P., Orwig, D., Yahiro, J. Y., Hawkes, W., Werner, M., . . . Magaziner, J. (2005). Treatment fidelity in behavior change research: A case example. *Nursing Research, 54,* 139–143. doi:10.1097/00006199-200503000-00010

Richardson, C. R., Kriska, A. M., Lantz, P. M., & Hayward, R. A. (2004). Physical activity and mortality across cardiovascular disease risk groups. *Medicine and Science in Sports and Exercise, 36,* 1923–1929. doi:10.1249/01.MSS.0000145443.02568.7A

Schroeder, S. A. (2007). We can do better—Improving the health of the American people. *New England Journal of Medicine, 357,* 1221–1228. doi:10.1056/NEJMsa073350

Shah, B. R., Adams, M., Peterson, E. D., Powers, B., Oddone, E. Z., Royal, K., . . . Bosworth, H. B. (2011). Secondary prevention risk interventions via telemedicine and tailored patient education (SPRITE): A randomized trial to improve post myocardial infarction management. *Circulation: Cardiovascular Quality and Outcomes, 4,* 235–242. doi:10.1161/CIRCOUTCOMES.110.951160

Shaw, R., & Bosworth, H. (2012). Short message service (SMS) text messaging as an intervention medium for weight loss: A literature review. *Health Informatics Journal, 18,* 235–250.

Spillane, V., Byrne, M. C., Byrne, M., Leathem, C. S., O'Malley, M., & Cupples, M. E. (2007). Monitoring treatment fidelity in a randomized controlled trial of a complex intervention. *Journal of Advanced Nursing, 60,* 343–352. doi:10.1111/j.1365-2648.2007.04386.x

Vermilyea, B. B., Barlow, D. H., & O'Brien, G. T. (1984). The importance of assessing treatment integrity: An example in the anxiety disorders. *Journal of Behavioral Assessment, 6,* 1–11. doi:10.1007/BF01321456

Waltz, J., Addis, M. E., Koerner, K., & Jacobson, N. S. (1993). Testing the integrity of a psychotherapy protocol: Assessment of adherence and competence. *Journal of Consulting and Clinical Psychology, 61,* 620–630. doi:10.1037/0022-006X.61.4.620

Westfall, J. M., Mold, J., & Fagnan, L. (2007). Practice-based research—"Blue highways" on the NIH roadmap. *JAMA: Journal of the American Medical Association, 297,* 403–406. doi:10.1001/jama.297.4.403

Wyatt, G., Sikorskii, A., Rahbar, M. H., Victorson, D., & Adams, L. (2010). Intervention fidelity: Aspects of complementary and alternative medicine research. *Cancer Nursing, 33,* 331–342. doi:10.1097/NCC.0b013e3181d0b4b7

Yeaton, W. H., & Sechrest, L. (1981). Critical dimensions in the choice and maintenance of successful treatments: Strength, integrity, and effectiveness. *Journal of Consulting and Clinical Psychology, 49,* 156–167. doi:10.1037/0022-006X.49.2.156

2

UNDERSTANDING AND PROMOTING TREATMENT INTEGRITY IN PREVENTION

BRIAN K. BUMBARGER

Researchers in psychology have made significant progress in understanding how to prevent and treat mental illness and youth behavioral problems such as violence and substance abuse (National Research Council & Institute of Medicine, 2009), particularly over the past 40 years. However, these increases in knowledge have not yet resulted in significant population-level public health improvement at the levels seen in clinical trials (Bumbarger & Perkins, 2008). In both treatment and prevention, increasing the adoption and implementation of effective interventions and ensuring that these interventions are delivered with integrity are of equal importance. In this chapter, I (a) discuss the issue of treatment integrity from the perspective of

Brian K. Bumbarger is founding director of the Evidence-Based Prevention and Intervention Support Center of the Prevention Research Center at Penn State University. He has been engaged in a large-scale effort to disseminate effective preventive interventions for over a decade. The initiative seeks to promote high-quality implementation and fidelity and involves nearly 200 replications of a diverse menu of interventions.

http://dx.doi.org/10.1037/14275-004
Treatment Integrity: A Foundation for Evidence-Based Practice in Applied Psychology, L. M. H. Sanetti and T. R. Kratochwill (Editors)

prevention; (b) highlight key considerations in encouraging treatment integrity within a prevention framework; and (c) provide a number of recommendations for addressing the challenges to promoting, monitoring, measuring, and achieving high-quality prevention service delivery.

THE EMERGENCE OF EVIDENCE-BASED PREVENTION

Tremendous growth in the development and evaluation of intervention models has occurred in the past half-century. Arguably, more has been learned about what causes and what works to prevent poor outcomes for youths in the past 40 years than in the 1,000 years prior (Lerner, 2001). Today, many prevention programs have been proven effective in well-designed studies, with many independently replicated and showing sizable effects sustained for years beyond the intervention (Greenberg, Domitrovich, & Bumbarger, 2001). Randomized trials have yielded convincing evidence in preventing substance use, violence, and aggression and in promoting children's mental health and academic achievement (National Research Council & Institute of Medicine, 2009). Subsequent reviews and meta-analyses have resulted in a number of lists of what are now commonly referred to as *evidence-based programs* (EBPs). As a result, policy makers and practitioners can now readily choose from a variety of effective preventive interventions targeting a broad range of populations, settings, and outcomes.

BARRIERS TO ACHIEVING PUBLIC HEALTH IMPROVEMENT

Despite these advances in the identification of EBPs, a number of specific barriers to moving from lists of effective programs to broad public health impact have been identified. In particular, issues of dissemination/adoption, implementation quality, and sustainability represent the most prevalent and salient challenges (Bruns et al., 2008; Elias, Zins, Graczyk, & Weissburg, 2003; Elliott & Mihalic, 2004). More than 20 years after the first lists of EBPs were published, these programs still represent the minority of prevention strategies used by schools and communities (U.S. Department of Education, 2011). Even the most successfully disseminated EBPs are estimated to be reaching only 1% of the children and youths who could benefit from them (Ginexi & Hilton, 2006). Further, considerable evidence suggests that when EBPs are broadly disseminated they are rarely implemented with treatment integrity or sufficient quality; in fact, it is rare for prevention programs to specifically measure or monitor implementation integrity and quality except under research conditions (Durlak & DuPre, 2008; Fixsen, Naoom, Blase,

Friedman, & Wallace, 2005). This lack of monitoring can lead to poor implementation quality, adaptation, and variability across implementers and contexts (Moore, Bumbarger, & Rhoades Cooper, 2013).

Sustainability represents yet another considerable challenge to prevention services because, unlike in other fields such as health care, corrections, or education, no stable "system" exists for prevention. In most communities, the field of prevention is represented by a loosely based coalition of nonprofits, schools, religious organizations, and service providers operating on a patchwork of short-term grants and local fund-raising, often with little coordination or strategic direction (Altman, 2009). This characteristic instability of prevention may be unique among human and social services. With practitioners struggling to sustain programs long enough to develop substantial competence or mastery, such instability has a significant detrimental impact on treatment integrity.

WHAT IS TREATMENT INTEGRITY IN PREVENTION

Promotion of treatment integrity in prevention requires the establishment of a common definition that encompasses the critical elements of intervention delivery. Although throughout this chapter I refer generally to *implementation quality and fidelity* as the term encompassing all of the broad concepts of program delivery, the currently accepted models of treatment integrity in prevention science acknowledge four broad constructs: adherence, dosage, quality, and engagement (Backer, 2001; Dane & Schneider, 1998; Durlak, Weissberg, & Pachan, 2010; Dusenbury, Brannigan, Falco, & Hansen, 2003; Fixsen et al., 2005). These constructs collectively describe how a program is delivered and received. The concept of *adherence*, which refers to the extent to which required program content is delivered and core concepts are conveyed, is at the center of treatment integrity. EBP developers or distributors usually define required content to be taught and activities to be carried out. Structured interventions with discrete lessons often have session-specific checklists. Thus, an adherence or fidelity score can be calculated as the percentage of required content (objectives or activities) delivered. This is the most commonly assessed construct of program delivery, although it may not be the most important. One can imagine (and indeed may have seen in classroom observations) scenarios in which a teacher covers all of the required lesson content but delivers it in a way that is not engaging, or is in the wrong sequence, or with other adaptations (e.g., adding ad hoc content) that may reduce the likelihood of program effectiveness. In this circumstance, implementation integrity can be high while implementation quality is low.

Dosage is a second aspect of treatment integrity that is important to consider. Saying that a drug is effective implies that the drug is effective when taken at the prescribed dose at the recommended intervals. Similarly, EBPs often prescribe a specific number of lessons or sessions as well as a specific sequence and frequency of delivery. These recommendations are generally grounded in theory and are based on the structure of the intervention used in the trials that demonstrated its effectiveness. Thus, deviations from the recommended dosage, sequence, or frequency may reduce the program's efficacy or render it ineffective or even harmful (Grossman & Rhodes, 2002; Grossman & Tierney, 1998).

A third aspect of treatment integrity, *quality of delivery*, may relate to the practitioner's skill and preparation, the practitioner's ability to manage program delivery, and the types of teaching techniques used. In some EBPs, the manner of instruction, rather than the content, is thought to be most important to program effectiveness (Bumbarger & Miller, 2007). The LifeSkills Training curriculum (Botvin, 2001), for example, involves specific interactive teaching techniques, small group student problem solving and rehearsal, and a Socratic style of conveying important concepts. The program's underlying theory postulates that this highly engaging form of delivery promotes greater knowledge uptake and skill development than does traditional didactic instruction. Some teachers may find this style of education unfamiliar or uncomfortable or may have difficulty managing the classroom during this type of instruction; thus, they may be more apt to deliver the required content but in a more traditional teaching style (Bumbarger, 2009). In this scenario, ironically, content adherence and implementation quality may be in direct conflict.

Engagement (sometimes referred to as reach or participation) is a fourth aspect of treatment integrity. Because prevention focuses primarily on universal rather than targeted intervention, it relies on reaching enough participants to impact mean levels of outcome improvement measured across groups. For this reason, treatment integrity in the case of prevention requires sufficient reach and engagement; that is, reaching enough of the population and having the participants be sufficiently engaged for the intervention to have the intended effect (Offord, 1996).

THE IMPORTANCE OF IMPLEMENTATION QUALITY AND INTEGRITY

Why does treatment integrity matter in prevention? First and foremost, it matters because quality implementation is clearly related to positive outcomes (Fixsen et al., 2005). That achieving positive outcomes would require high-quality implementation is both logical and empirically supported. A growing number of individual interventions have included treatment integrity measures in trials and found this relationship between better implementation quality and better outcomes (Botvin, Baker, Dusenbury, Botvin, & Diaz, 1995; Kam, Greenberg, & Walls, 2003; Rohrbach, Sun, &, Sussman, 2010). Dusenbury et al. (2003) reported that across a diverse menu of school-based substance abuse prevention programs, adherence was associated both with student outcomes and with mediating factors related to those outcomes. Likewise, several recent meta-analyses have established the correlation clearly (Durlak & DuPre, 2008; Durlak et al., 2010; Fixsen et al., 2005) and have shown that implementation factors accounted for significant variability in outcome effect sizes (Tobler et al., 2000; Wilson, Lipsey, & Derzon, 2003).

There are additional reasons to assess treatment integrity. First, measuring and monitoring treatment integrity provides important information about the feasibility of programs that may not be established in efficacy trials. Proving that a program works is not the same as proving that a program is usable. Assessing implementation quality, especially under natural (i.e., non-research) conditions, allows one to determine (a) whether the program can actually be delivered in common contexts, (b) what adaptations are likely to occur, and (c) what additional supports may be necessary or advantageous to improve program delivery.

Assessing program implementation is also important in prevention when the distal behavioral outcome of interest cannot reasonably be assessed, either because the outcome would not likely emerge for many years or because the differential preventive benefits of the intervention cannot be assessed without a comparison group. In these quite common circumstances, detailed information on implementation quality and integrity coupled with evidence from previous experimental trials can be combined with measures of proximal mediators, such as skills, knowledge, attitudes, or intentions, to establish a credible argument that the program is having (or will have) the intended impact.

ADAPTATION AND PROGRAM DRIFT

Understanding adaptation and program drift is critical to promoting treatment integrity in prevention practice. *Adaptation* refers to conscious changes to the content or method of delivering an intervention (regardless of intent or rationale); program *drift* refers to unwitting deviation from the original intervention design. Consideration of adaptation and program drift includes understanding the type of change or deviation, the timing of the change, and the catalyst or cause (Moore et al., 2013). Adaptation can include adding, changing, or omitting key program content; changing the method, style, or context of delivery; changing the sequence or frequency of the intervention; or even changing the target population. These adaptations can occur intentionally prior to implementation or reactively as unanticipated barriers are encountered. Further, they may be initiated in reaction to logistical barriers or in response to cultural or philosophical differences.

One of the significant challenges to taking effective prevention to scale has been the conflict between advocates of strict adherence and proponents of local adaptation (Backer, 2001). When the field of prevention practice began moving toward an agenda of promoting EBPs, there was a strong emphasis on complete fidelity. These interventions typically have been evaluated in efficacy trials meant to test hypothesized theories of behavior change. In such trials, the researcher attempts to offer the greatest level of intervention possible with the least amount of drift and interference from extraneous variables that might reduce effectiveness or offer alternative hypotheses for effects. This design is appropriate for evaluating efficacy, but it is not as helpful in designing a scalable intervention. Such a design sometimes results in an efficacious intervention that is not well suited to replication in real-world contexts. Successful efficacy trials would optimally be followed by effectiveness trials that would carefully unpack the intervention and optimize it for scale-up. However, practitioners and policymakers are so hungry for effective interventions that this step has effectively been skipped, leaving a hole in our knowledge (Durlak & DuPre, 2008). Without knowing for sure what specific elements of these interventions are critical for program success, program developers and funders have mostly advocated for adherence and against adaptation (Backer, 2001).

This dogmatic approach has been met with some criticism from researchers and practitioners (Blakely et al., 1987). Proponents of adaptation argue that practitioners should be allowed and even encouraged to adapt programs to their local context and populations. In addition to honoring the knowledge and experiences of local practitioners, some have theorized that this type of proactive adaptation (especially cultural tailoring) might increase engagement and community buy-in. Such increases might in turn increase reach and sustainability, thus potentially increasing program impact (Bernal & Sa'ez-Santiago, 2006; Castro, Barrerra, & Martinez, 2004). Empirical examination of the issue has recently begun to emerge in two forms: comparative tests of adapted versions of interventions and meta-analyses on the differential effects of interventions for population subgroups. Both can inform the debate and contribute to our understanding of cultural adaptation and its relationship to treatment integrity.

In a relatively small number of studies, EBPs were intentionally tailored to meet the specific needs of cultural, racial, or ethnic groups, or local groups were encouraged to proactively adapt a program to meet local needs (Carpentier et al., 2007; Coatsworth, Duncan, Pantin, & Szapocznik, 2006; Domenech Rodríguez, Baumann, & Schwartz, 2011; Komro et al., 2006; Kumpfer, Alvarado, Smith, & Bellamy, 2002; Marek, Brock, & Sullivan, 2006; Martinez, McClure, Eddy, Ruth, & Hyers, 2012; Okamoto et al., 2006). Both types of designs offer a comparison with the original EBP and thus speak to the question of the potential added value of cultural adaptation. Taken as a whole, although there is some evidence that such adaptation may encourage greater participation and engagement (e.g., Kumpfer et al., 2002), these studies do not provide convincing evidence that culturally adapted interventions produce the same or greater positive outcomes than those seen in the original efficacy studies or studies of similar nontailored interventions. Further, most of the widely disseminated EBPs have shown similar effects across diverse populations, and meta-analyses examining differential outcomes of effective programs have failed to find significant differences across population subgroups (Wilson, Lipsey, & Soydan, 2003). This is not to say that there is no value to cultural adaptation, only that the call for such adaptation may be overstated and that it cannot rest on purely empirical grounds. Indeed, researchers have been advocating for a more centrist model that strives for the greatest possible implementation integrity to core elements (to the degree that they can be identified or reasonably hypothesized) but allows for adaptation of the "surface structure" of interventions—the pictures, language, and vignettes, for example (Castro et al., 2004; Domitrovich & Greenberg, 2000).

REASONS FOR POOR TREATMENT INTEGRITY

A growing empirical literature informs our understanding of why treatment integrity in prevention is generally poor. This knowledge can help researchers identify and prioritize efforts to improve implementation quality and integrity. As EBPs have begun to be widely replicated over the past decade, a number of studies have assessed implementation quality and integrity and sought to identify correlates of high versus low adherence (Dariotis, Bumbarger, Duncan, & Greenberg, 2008; Dusenbury et al., 2003; Elliott & Mihalic, 2004; Hallfors & Godette, 2002; Rohrbach, Grana, Sussman, & Valente, 2006; Spoth & Molgaard, 1999; U.S. Department of Education, 2011). These correlates can be organized into five domains: characteristics of the implementer, characteristics of the implementing organization, characteristics of the intervention, characteristics of the program recipients, and characteristics of the school or community in which the program is delivered. In their study of a statewide scale-up of EBPs, Dariotis et al. (2008) found correlates of high versus low adherence in each of these domains and found important differences by program type (i.e., school-based, community-based, family-focused) in the barriers and assets with the most robust correlation to adherence. These findings underscore the complexity and fluidity of the implementation environment and the interaction among a variety of factors that can lead to good or poor quality and integrity. However, these findings also suggest that within certain prevention environments (schools, communities), a common set of implementation assets and barriers can reasonably be predicted and proactively planned for by practitioners, program developers and trainers, and funders and policymakers.

ADDITIONAL CHALLENGES TO TREATMENT INTEGRITY IN PREVENTION

When considering treatment integrity in the framework of prevention, one should recognize that, in contrast to treatment or therapy, prevention practice often occurs in contexts that are not conducive to high-quality implementation and that may in fact present additional barriers to adherence and quality (Ringeisen, Henderson, & Hoagwood, 2003). Especially in school-based prevention practice, programs are often considered "add-ons" that compete with the core academic mission (Greenberg, 2004). Inadequate time, space, and resources all work against quality program implementation and treatment integrity. In addition, prevention services are often delivered by practitioners who are less formally trained and who are not acculturated to structures of "clinical supervision." In community-based prevention, practitioners may be volunteers, students, or entry-level human services staff without a specific background or preparation other than what has been provided as part of the intervention's training. Classroom teachers, who often are the primary deliverers of prevention programs, generally have little or no specific training in child development or prevention science, and they may have little knowledge of etiological models of the youth substance use, mental health, or behavioral problems they are tasked with preventing (Bumbarger, 2009; Bumbarger & Miller, 2007). Aside from engaging in preservice periods of student teaching, teachers receive far less observation and clinical supervision than one would find in therapeutic practice, and social structures and union rules often create significant barriers to establishing such coaching and supervision (Greenberg, 2004; Kam et al., 2003).

Other challenges to treatment integrity stem from more conceptual and academic gaps in our knowledge of implementation. The relationship between implementation quality and positive outcomes has been clearly documented in the literature, but whether this relationship is perfectly linear is not clear. A plateau effect—a tipping point at which treatment integrity and quality are

sufficient to generate positive outcomes and beyond which the additional benefit may be negligible—is likely. For instance, results of research on the LifeSkills
Training Program suggest that positive outcomes are seen when implementers achieve over 60% treatment integrity (Botvin et al., 1995). Below that
point, program impact is greatly reduced; however, whether much difference
in targeted outcomes would be seen if, for example, treatment integrity were
increased from 65% to 80% or more when implementers achieve over 60%
treatment integrity is unclear. The implication is that perfect implementation
is not necessary for achieving outcomes. Program implementation merely has
to be good enough. However, because increasing (and for that matter measuring) treatment integrity or quality is not such a precise practice, achieving the
optimal ratio of effort to impact is elusive. This is again a shortcoming of the traditional model of research-to-practice, in which the important conceptual and
experimental steps between efficacy testing and wide-scale replication are often
given short shrift (Emshoff, 2008; Glasgow, Lichtenstein, & Marcus, 2003).
An exciting development in this area is recent work by Collins, Chakraborty,
Murphy, and Strecher (2009) to develop trials designed specifically to optimize interventions. In addition, some program developers have purposefully
embedded feedback loops into efforts to disseminate their intervention models,
wherein experience from replications is quickly used to reengineer the intervention and/or the training and dissemination infrastructure (Fagan, Hanson,
Hawkins, & Arthur, 2008; Hansen, Bishop, & Bryant, 2009).

RECOMMENDATIONS FOR IMPROVING IMPLEMENTATION QUALITY AND INTEGRITY

In light of the challenges and considerations discussed previously, steps
clearly can be taken to proactively promote treatment integrity as EBPs are
taken to scale. The following six broad recommendations are offered for
improving implementation quality and integrity in prevention:

1. Make Careful Program Selection Decisions

When prevention programs represent a poor fit with community
needs, organizational resources, or the skills or beliefs of practitioners, treatment integrity becomes much more challenging (Gorman-Smith, 2006).
High-quality implementation and integrity begin with the basic decision
about which prevention program or strategy to adopt. This point may seem
elementary, but the reality is that very often program adoption decisions are
made hastily and arbitrarily, without careful consideration of important questions about fit and feasibility.

Those making careful program selection and adoption decisions should consider three issues: evidence, fit, and feasibility. Communities should opt for preventive interventions that have been rigorously evaluated and found to be effective. In addition to providing the greatest confidence about producing client impacts, EBPs mitigate the inherent inability of prevention programs to demonstrate distal behavioral outcomes in the absence of a comparison group (by relying on impacts demonstrated in previous research). However, some programs are simply less prepared for dissemination and more difficult to implement, and they require greater planning and readiness. Program adoption decisions should follow a careful consideration of fit and feasibility. When programs are carefully matched to the specific needs of a community and to the resources, mission, and beliefs of practitioners and organizations, fewer barriers, more natural supports for fidelity and high-quality implementation, and, thus, better treatment integrity are likely.

2. Develop a Deep Understanding of the Intervention

Another key to promoting treatment integrity is developing a deep understanding of the intervention being delivered. Doing so is particularly challenging for prevention practitioners, who seldom have much (if any) formal training in child development or the specific etiology of the outcome they are trying to prevent (e.g., drug use, bullying, violence). High-quality implementation requires a clear understanding of how the problem develops and how the specific intervention interacts with that pathway to change its developmental trajectory. Often, prevention practitioners have only a superficial understanding of how the program they are delivering is hypothesized to effect distal behavioral outcomes. The causal model between program delivery and program impact is essentially a "black box" that they find difficult to articulate or do not understand. When barriers to implementation arise, practitioners are forced to make uninformed decisions that may negatively impact program effectiveness.

The problem is exacerbated by the conventional model of preimplementation training used in nearly all prevention programs. This model typically involves a 1- or 2-day training, often months before program implementation, that focuses almost solely on the "mechanics" of delivering the intervention. In my experience attending trainings for the most widely disseminated EBPs over the past decade, there is often very little instruction on the underlying theory of the intervention or discussion of how specific lessons or objectives connect to a causal model of behavior change. Practitioners learn the *how* of delivering the program but not the *why*.

Adopters should identify the core elements for each aspect of implementation (i.e., adherence, dosage, quality, and engagement) and communicate these elements to implementers as the minimum expectations for treatment integrity in program delivery as part of developing a deeper understanding of the intervention. A clear understanding of the underlying logic model and core elements of the intervention allows practitioners to make important decisions about implementation and adaptation. Most adaptations are made on the fly, in response to unanticipated barriers (e.g., leaving out lesson content because an off-topic conversation meant there was not enough time in the class period), or nonconsciously, due to a lack of understanding of the program's theory (e.g., not correcting misperceptions of peer norms in a classroom discussion). Ensuring that implementers understand and can clearly articulate the program's conceptual model greatly reduces the likelihood of unintended negative adaptations (or poor treatment integrity) and enables implementers to make informed decisions when adaptation cannot be avoided. Asking them to complete a simple worksheet in which they create a visual logic model of the program or having them narratively describe the program's theory after training provides good checks for understanding. Facilitating "learning communities" of practitioners during implementation provides an opportunity to discuss implementation challenges with peers and to continue developing program understanding and expertise during implementation (Bumbarger, 2009). This model, which is very different from the traditional training paradigm, can help to address some of the most common causes of poor treatment integrity.

3. Assess Readiness for Implementation

Researchers should not assume that any prevention program, even an EBP, can be effectively implemented in any community or context. However, schools, providers, or agencies often begin adopting an intervention without having conducted any formal or informal assessment of their readiness to do so (Hawkins, Catalano, & Arthur, 2002; Lehman, Greener, & Simpson, 2002). This aspect of scaling-up EBPs is perhaps the least developed. In fact, few established prevention programs have clearly specified minimum implementation requirements or developed a standardized readiness assessment tool for communities looking to adopt an intervention.

Readiness assessment involves consideration of the minimum conditions necessary for effective implementation of the intervention, including resources, staff skills and qualifications, environmental and administrative supports, and access to populations. When a specific readiness assessment tool is not available, adopting organizations can often look to the program developer or to others who have successfully adopted the program to identify critical preimplementation conditions and resources. Identifying and addressing gaps in resources, staff skills or qualifications, or necessary supports before beginning program implementation may significantly improve treatment integrity. Because this area of dissemination is so poorly developed, states or federal agencies may find it advantageous to address this need at the initiative level, rather than the community level. Such initiatives commonly promote the diffusion of specific EBPs or menus of endorsed interventions. The inclusion of program-specific readiness assessment tools, training, and resources when such initiatives promote dissemination of programs would potentially increase treatment integrity and result in a more efficient and productive use of the funds being invested in such initiatives.

4. Engage in Formal Preimplementation Planning

Once it has decided to adopt an intervention, the community or organization should engage in a formal and thoughtful preimplementation planning process. An implementation plan should outline the specifics of identifying or recruiting implementers (to include ensuring they meet minimum qualifications and are supportive of the program) and outline the process for training, including plans for booster and replacement training, ongoing coaching, or other types of clinical supervision. The plan should describe the implementation context and how it will be managed (including specific program delivery logistics) and specify the target population and a plan for recruiting participants if necessary. This aspect of planning (participant recruitment) is often overlooked or underestimated, especially in family- or parent-focused interventions. Finally, the plan should articulate how the program will be monitored and specify the tools and processes for assessing both program implementation (i.e., adherence, dosage, quality, and engagement) and program impact (i.e., changes in proximal indicators and distal outcomes). Preimplementation planning should be completed collaboratively with both administrators and line staff. Such collaboration facilitates practitioner buy-in and demonstrates administrative support, both of which promote better program implementation quality and integrity.

5. Develop an Infrastructure to Support Continuous Quality Improvement

Although planning for implementation of a specific intervention is useful and necessary, the development of a sustained infrastructure to support prevention implementation within organizations and systems (including schools, which are continuously engaged in prevention practice) is essential to move the field forward. This kind of development implies an organizational commitment to high-quality implementation, across multiple interventions, sustained over time. Such an infrastructure should encompass and systematize all of the recommendations described above: the processes and resources necessary for careful selection and adoption of interventions (including consideration of known facilitators and barriers). Development of a sustained infrastructure would ensure that practitioners fully understand and assess readiness to adopt interventions prior to implementation and carefully and thoroughly plan to achieve high-quality implementation and adherence.

The goal in developing such an infrastructure is not only to prevent poor treatment integrity but also to change the organizational dynamics and build internal capacity and desire for continuous quality improvement. An organization committed to continuous quality improvement has the processes and resources to enable practitioners (a) to assess how well they are doing and what impact they are having (monitoring) and (b) to identify and pursue steps to strengthen practice based on that information (improvement). This infrastructure should emphasize and support self-monitoring and individual goal setting to increase self-efficacy and promote intrinsic motivation and desire for mastery. Most practitioners in education and human services entered those professions to help and serve others, so the intrinsic motivation to excel is likely already there but is being thwarted by a lack of readily available tools and resources to support that desire (Midgley, 2009).

Supportive infrastructure includes coaching and mentoring, opportunities for peer support and reflective practice, and safe avenues for giving and receiving feedback. Implementers should be involved in both the development of process and performance measures and the establishment of benchmarks. Assessment of implementation and outcomes should be meaningful (e.g., should include measures and benchmarks that have face validity and merit to practitioners) and should promote an understanding and belief in the logical connections among prevention service delivery, implementation quality, and outcomes. Feedback in the form of practical and actionable data can empower practitioners to self-monitor and strive for improved practice (Hamilton & Bickman, 2008). This is in stark contrast to the current status quo, where practitioners often feel judged, administrators primarily rely on extrinsic motivation (e.g., high-stakes tests or accountability-focused benchmarks that are not well grounded in the realities of practice), and data are seen as a bureaucratic burden rather than a useful tool for self-assessment and improvement.

Many programs now have standard implementation monitoring tools, although at times these have been created for research contexts and may be unnecessarily burdensome in the "real world." Developers' implementation monitoring instruments or checklists can be adapted for local needs, or new instruments can be created with a good understanding of the intervention. Program developers and trainers are often happy to help adapt instruments and may welcome the feedback from practitioners.

6. Frame Programs in a Larger Public Health Context

EBPs are most often adopted by single schools or agencies working in isolation from the larger community. However, a growing body of evidence indicates that prevention programs connected to a broader community coalition effort are more likely to monitor and promote implementation quality and integrity and to achieve higher levels of adherence (Brown, Feinberg, & Greenberg, 2010; Bumbarger, 2006; Spoth, Guyll, Lillehoj, Redmond, & Greenberg, 2007). A public health approach to prevention recognizes that multiple programs and strategies addressing different stages of youth development and coordinated across different domains (community, school, individual, family, peer group) are necessary for improving population-level health and well-being. This type of multistakeholder coordination is often challenging and has, in fact, developed into its own distinct science, but such coordination can be critical for achieving the tipping point necessary for individual interventions to impact community-level outcomes (Butterfoss, 2008). Having multiple prevention efforts connected across a community can provide a synergy that results in a whole greater than the sum of its parts. This type of collaboration allows prevention practitioners to see themselves as part of a larger community health promotion effort and provides opportunities to network and create ad hoc learning communities with other practitioners. Such communities of practice increase intrinsic motivation for continuous quality improvement and promote a desire for mastery and increased accountability, which encourage greater implementation quality and adherence.

CONCLUSION

The second half of the 20th century saw enormous growth in the development of interventions capable of significantly preventing or reducing poor mental and behavioral health outcomes for youths. The challenge for the 21st century will be taking such effective interventions to scale, to reach a tipping point at which they can influence population-level public health. Doing so will require careful attention to balancing the sometimes competing goals of dissemination and high-quality implementation.

Early attempts at broad dissemination have generally resulted in poor treatment integrity, but they have taught us important lessons about the characteristics of programs, practitioners, and contexts that support or impede implementation. Pioneering efforts to scale up effective prevention have led to the emergence of a distinct science of translational research that will inform future dissemination efforts as well as the development of the next generation of interventions (Rohrbach et al., 2006). Improvements are being made in the conceptualization and measurement of treatment integrity, moving from narrowly defined assessments of content adherence to a more holistic definition that recognizes the equal importance of quality of delivery and engagement. And important questions about adapting core elements are beginning to be empirically tested.

Recognition of the unique set of challenges to treatment integrity within prevention is growing. Such challenges may stem from a lack of stable infrastructure and funding; practitioners and environment, often "co-opted" from other fields, that bring competing demands for attention and resources; and interventions that have been taken to scale before they were fully developed or understood. Researchers, policymakers, and practitioners have responded to these challenges with innovation and creativity because they recognize the promise and the ethical responsibility that come with the demonstration of prevention's effectiveness and cost-effectiveness. Through careful planning and creation of infrastructure to support program adoption and implementation, effective preventive interventions can be taken to scale and the high-quality implementation and integrity necessary to achieve the strength of effects seen in trials and to significantly impact children, families, and communities can be maintained.

REFERENCES

Altman, D. G. (2009). Challenges in sustaining public health interventions. *Health Education & Behavior, 36*, 24–28. doi:10.1177/1090198107299788

Backer, T. E. (2001). *Finding the balance: Program fidelity in substance use prevention: A state-of-the-art review*. Rockville, MD: Substance Abuse Mental Health Services Administration, Center for Substance Abuse Prevention.

Bernal, G., & Sa'ez-Santiago, E. (2006). Culturally centered psychosocial interventions. *Journal of Community Psychology, 34*, 121–132. doi:10.1002/jcop.20096

Blakely, C. H., Mayer, J. P., Gottschalk, R. G., Schmitt, N., Davidson, W. S., Roitman, D. B., & Emshoff, J. G. (1987). The fidelity–adaptation debate: Implications for the implementation of public sector social programs. *American Journal of Community Psychology, 15*, 253–268. doi:10.1007/BF00922697

Botvin, G. (2001). *Life skills training*. Princeton, NJ: Princeton Health Press.

Botvin, G. J., Baker, E., Dusenbury, L., Botvin, E. M., & Diaz, T. (1995). Long-term follow-up results of a randomized drug abuse prevention trial in a White middle-class population. *JAMA: Journal of the American Medical Association, 273*, 1106–1112. doi:10.1001/jama.1995.03520380042033

Brown, L. D., Feinberg, M. E., & Greenberg, M. T. (2010). Determinants of community coalition ability to support evidence-based programs. *Prevention Science, 11*, 287–297. doi:10.1007/s11121-010-0173-6

Bruns, E. J., Hoagwood, K. E., Rivard, J. C., Wotring, J., Marsenich, L., & Carter, B. (2008). State implementation of evidence-based practice for youths, part II: Recommendations for research and policy. *Journal of the American Academy of Child & Adolescent Psychiatry, 47,* 499–504. doi:10.1097/CHI.0b013e3181684557

Bumbarger, B. (2006, May). *The effectiveness of community prevention coalitions: Results from a large-scale study in Pennsylvania.* Paper presented at the conference of the Society for Prevention Research, San Antonio, TX.

Bumbarger, B. (2009, March). *Dissemination of evidence-based programs: A low-cost model for improving implementation quality.* Paper presented at the National Institutes of Health Conference on the Science of Implementation and Dissemination, Bethesda, MD.

Bumbarger, B. K., & Miller, A. (2007). *Is there a role for police in school-based drug prevention? The Law Enforcement–Education Partnership to Promote LifeSkills Training (LEEP-LST) Project.* Retrieved from www.portal.state.pa.us/portal/server.pt/document/350504/leep-lst_project_highlights_-_revised_pdf

Bumbarger, B. K., & Perkins, D. F. (2008). After randomised trials: Issues related to dissemination of evidence-based interventions. *Journal of Children's Services, 3*(2), 53–61.

Butterfoss, F. D. (2008). *Coalitions and partnerships in community health.* San Francisco, CA: Jossey-Bass.

Carpentier, F. R. D., Mauricio, A. M., Gonzales, N. A., Millsap, R. E., Meza, C. M., Dumka, L. E., . . . Genalo, M. T. (2007). Engaging Mexican origin families in a school-based preventive intervention. *Journal of Primary Prevention, 28,* 521–546. doi:10.1007/s10935-007-0110-z

Castro, F. G., Barrerra, M. J., & Martinez, C. R., Jr. (2004). The cultural adaptation of prevention interventions: Resolving tensions between fidelity and fit. *Prevention Science, 5,* 41–45. doi:10.1023/B:PREV.0000013980.12412.cd

Coatsworth, J. D., Duncan, L. G., Pantin, H., & Szapocznik, J. (2006). Patterns of retention in a preventive intervention with ethnic minority families. *Journal of Primary Prevention, 27,* 171–193. doi:10.1007/s10935-005-0028-2

Collins, L. M., Chakraborty, B., Murphy, S. A., & Strecher, V. (2009). Comparison of a phased experimental approach and a single randomized clinical trial for developing multicomponent behavioral interventions. *Clinical Trials, 6,* 5–15. doi:10.1177/1740774508100973

Dane, A. V., & Schneider, B. H. (1998). Program integrity in primary and early secondary prevention: Are implementation effects out of control? *Clinical Psychology Review, 18,* 23–45. doi:10.1016/S0272-7358(97)00043-3

Dariotis, J. K., Bumbarger, B. K., Duncan, L. G., & Greenberg, M. T. (2008). How do implementation efforts relate to program adherence? Examining the role of organizational, implementer, and program factors. *Journal of Community Psychology, 36,* 744–760. doi:10.1002/jcop.20255

Domenech Rodríguez, M. M., Baumann, A. A., & Schwartz, A. L. (2011). Cultural adaptation of an evidence based intervention: From theory to practice in a Latino/a community context. *American Journal of Community Psychology, 47,* 170–186. doi:10.1007/s10464-010-9371-4

Domitrovich, C. E., & Greenberg, M. T. (2000). The study of implementation: Current findings from effective programs that prevent mental disorders in school-age children. *Journal of Educational and Psychological Consultation, 11,* 193–221. doi:10.1207/S1532768XJEPC1102_04

Durlak, J. A., & DuPre, E. P. (2008). Implementation matters: A review of research on the influence of implementation on program outcomes and the factors affecting implementation. *American Journal of Community Psychology, 41,* 327–350. doi:10.1007/s10464-008-9165-0

Durlak, J. A., Weissberg, R. P., & Pachan, M. (2010). A meta-analysis of after-school programs that seek to promote personal and social skills in children and adolescents. *American Journal of Community Psychology, 45,* 294–309. doi:10.1007/s10464-010-9300-6

Dusenbury, L., Brannigan, R., Falco, M., & Hansen, W. B. (2003). A review of fidelity of implementation: Implications for drug abuse prevention in school settings. *Health Education Research, 18,* 237–256.

Elias, M. J., Zins, J. E., Graczyk, P. A., & Weissburg, R. P. (2003). Implementation, sustainability, and scaling up of social-emotional and academic innovations in public schools. *School Psychology Review, 32,* 303–319.

Elliott, D. S., & Mihalic, S. (2004). Issues in disseminating and replicating effective prevention programs. *Prevention Science, 5,* 47–53. doi:10.1023/B:PREV.0000013981.28071.52

Emshoff, J. G. (2008). Researchers, practitioners, and funders: Using the framework to get us on the same page. *American Journal of Community Psychology, 41,* 393–403. doi:10.1007/s10464-008-9168-x

Fagan, A. A., Hanson, K., Hawkins, J. D., & Arthur, M. W. (2008). Bridging science to practice: Achieving prevention program implementation fidelity in the Community Youth Development Study. *American Journal of Community Psychology, 41,* 235–249. doi:10.1007/s10464-008-9176-x

Fixsen, D. L., Naoom, S. F., Blase, K. A., Friedman, R. M., & Wallace, F. (2005). *Implementation research: A synthesis of the literature.* Tampa: University of South Florida, Louis de la Parte Florida Mental Health Institute, National Implementation Research Network.

Ginexi, E. M., & Hilton, T. F. (2006). What's next for translation research? *Evaluation & the Health Professions, 29,* 334–347. doi:10.1177/0163278706290409

Glasgow, R. E., Lichtenstein, E., & Marcus, A. C. (2003). Why don't we see more translation of health promotion research to practice? Rethinking the efficacy-to-effectiveness transition. *American Journal of Public Health, 93,* 1261–1267. doi:10.2105/AJPH.93.8.1261

Gorman-Smith, D. (2006). *How to successfully implement evidence-based social programs: A brief overview for policymakers and program providers.* Retrieved from http://coalition4evidence.org/wp-content/uploads/2012/12/Publication HowToSuccessfullyImplement06.pdf

Greenberg, M. T. (2004). Current and future challenges in school-based prevention: The researcher perspective. *Prevention Science, 5,* 5–13. doi:10.1023/B:PREV.0000013976.84939.55

Greenberg, M. T., Domitrovich, C., & Bumbarger, B. (2001). The prevention of mental disorders in school-aged children: Current state of the field. *Prevention & Treatment, 4,* Article 1. Retrieved from http://psycnet.apa.journals/pre/4/1/1a.pdf

Grossman, J. B., & Rhodes, J. E. (2002). The test of time: Predictors and effects of duration in youth mentoring relationships. *American Journal of Community Psychology, 30,* 199–219. doi:10.1023/A:1014680827552

Grossman, J. B., & Tierney, J. P. (1998). Does mentoring work? An impact study of the Big Brothers Big Sisters program. *Evaluation Review, 22,* 403–426. doi:10.1177/0193841X9802200304

Hallfors, D., & Godette, D. (2002). Will the "Principles of Effectiveness" improve prevention practice? Early findings from a diffusion study. *Health Education Research, 17,* 461–470. doi:10.1093/her/17.4.461

Hamilton, J. D., & Bickman, L. (2008). A measurement feedback system (MFS) is necessary to improve mental health outcomes. *Journal of the American Academy of Child & Adolescent Psychiatry, 47,* 1114–1119. doi:10.1097/CHI.0b013e3181825af8

Hansen, W. B., Bishop, D. C., & Bryant, K. S. (2009). Using online components to facilitate program implementation: Impact of technological enhancements to All Stars on ease and quality of program delivery. *Prevention Science, 10,* 66–75. doi:10.1007/s11121-008-0118-5

Hawkins, J. D., Catalano, R. F., & Arthur, M. W. (2002). Promoting science-based prevention in communities. *Addictive Behaviors, 27,* 951–976.

Kam, C.-M., Greenberg, M. T., & Walls, C. T. (2003). Examining the role of implementation quality in school-based prevention using a PATHS curriculum. *Prevention Science, 4,* 55–63. doi:10.1023/A:1021786811186

Komro, K. A., Perry, C. L., Veblen-Mortenson, S., Farbakhsh, K., Kugler, K. C., Alfano, K. A., . . . Jones-Webb, R. (2006). Cross-cultural adaptation and evaluation of a home-based program for alcohol use prevention among urban youth: The "Slick Tracy Home Team Program." *Journal of Primary Prevention, 27,* 135–154. doi:10.1007/s10935-005-0029-1

Kumpfer, K. L., Alvarado, R., Smith, P., & Bellamy, N. (2002). Cultural sensitivity and adaptation in family-based prevention interventions. *Prevention Science, 3,* 241–246. doi:10.1023/A:1019902902119

Lehman, W. E. K., Greener, J. M., & Simpson, D. D. (2002). Assessing organizational readiness for change. *Journal of Substance Abuse Treatment, 22,* 197–209. doi:10.1016/S0740-5472(02)00233-7

Lerner, R. (2001). Promoting promotion in the development of prevention science. *Applied Developmental Science, 5*, 254–257. doi:10.1207/S1532480XADS0504_06

Marek, L. I., Brock, D. P., & Sullivan, R. (2006). Cultural adaptations to a family life skills program: Implementation in rural Appalachia. *Journal of Primary Prevention, 27*, 113–133.

Martinez, C. R., Jr., McClure, H. H., Eddy, J. M., Ruth, B., & Hyers, M. J. (2012). Recruitment and retention of Latino immigrant families in prevention research. *Prevention Science, 13*, 15–26. doi:10.1007/s11121-011-0239-0

Midgley, N. (2009). Editorial: Improvers, adapters and rejecters—The link between "evidence-based practice" and "evidence-based practitioners." *Clinical Journal of Child Psychology and Psychiatry, 14*, 323–327. doi:10.1177/1359104509104045

Moore, J. E., Bumbarger, B. K., & Rhoades Cooper, B. (2013). Examining adaptations of evidence-based programs in natural contexts. *Journal of Primary Prevention.* Advance online publication. doi:1007/s10935-013-0303-6

National Research Council & Institute of Medicine. (2009). *Preventing mental, emotional, and behavioral disorders among young people: Progress and possibilities.* Washington, DC: National Academies Press.

Offord, D. R. (1996). The state of prevention and early intervention. In R. D. Peters & R. J. McMahon (Eds.), *Preventing childhood disorders, substance abuse, and delinquency* (pp. 329–344). Thousand Oaks, CA: Sage.

Okamoto, S. K., LeCroy, C. W., Tann, S. S., Rayle, A. D., Kulis, S., Dustman, P., & Berceli, D. (2006). The implications of ecologically based assessment for prevention science with indigenous youth populations. *Journal of Primary Prevention, 27*, 155–170. doi:10.1007/s10935-005-0016-6

Ringeisen, H., Henderson, K., & Hoagwood, K. (2003). Context matters: Schools and the "research to practice gap" in children's mental health. *School Psychology Review, 32*, 153–168.

Rohrbach, L. A., Grana, R., Sussman, S., & Valente, T. W. (2006). Type II translation: Transporting prevention interventions from research to real-world settings. *Evaluation & the Health Professions, 29*, 302–333. doi:10.1177/0163278706290408

Rohrbach, L. A., Sun, P., & Sussman, S. (2010). One-year follow-up evaluation of the Project Towards No Drug Abuse (TND) dissemination trial. *Preventive Medicine, 51*, 313–319. doi:10.1016/j.ypmed.2010.07.016

Spoth, R., Guyll, M., Lillehoj, C. J., Redmond, C., & Greenberg, M. (2007). PROSPER study of evidence-based intervention implementation quality by community–university partnerships. *Journal of Community Psychology, 35*, 981–999. doi:10.1002/jcop.20207

Spoth, R., & Molgaard, V. (1999). Project Family: A partnership integrating research with the practice of promoting family and youth competencies. In T. R. Chibucos & R. Lerner (Eds.), *Serving children and families through community–university partnerships: Success stories* (pp. 127–137). Boston, MA: Kluwer Academic. doi:10.1007/978-1-4615-5053-2_18

Tobler, N. S., Roona, M. R., Ochshorn, P., Marshall, D. G., Streke, A. V., & Stackpole, K. M. (2000). School-based adolescent drug prevention programs: 1998 meta-analysis. *Journal of Primary Prevention, 20,* 275–336. doi:10.1023/A:1021314704811

U.S. Department of Education. (2011). *Prevalence and implementation fidelity of research-based prevention programs in public schools: Final report.* Washington, DC: Office of Planning, Evaluation and Policy Development, Policy and Program Studies Service.

Wilson, S. J., Lipsey, M. W., & Derzon, J. H. (2003). The effects of school-based intervention programs on aggressive behavior: A meta-analysis. *Journal of Consulting and Clinical Psychology, 71,* 136–149. doi:10.1037/0022-006X.71.1.136

Wilson, S. J., Lipsey, M. W., & Soydan, H. (2003). Are mainstream programs for juvenile delinquency less effective with minority youth than majority youth? A meta-analysis of outcomes research. *Research on Social Work Practice, 13,* 3–26. doi:10.1177/1049731502238754

3

TREATMENT INTEGRITY AS ADULT BEHAVIOR CHANGE: A REVIEW OF THEORETICAL MODELS

ANNA C. J. LONG AND BRANDY R. MAYNARD

Despite the impetus to improve practice and client outcomes through the dissemination of evidence-based practices (EBPs), the promise of achieving desired outcomes in practice settings has yet to be fully realized (Walrath, Sheehan, Holden, Hernandez, & Blau, 2006). Evidence suggests that the effectiveness and impact of an EBP are reduced when the EBP is not implemented in the way it was designed and tested (Walrath et al., 2006). If practitioners are to achieve outcomes similar to those obtained in efficacy studies, EBPs must be implemented with treatment integrity (Greenwood, 2009). Put simply, if clients are to benefit from broad dissemination of EBPs, practitioners must be certain the EBPs are implemented in the way intended.

Research on the extent to which EBPs are implemented with treatment integrity consistently finds that a large number of mental health and education practitioners demonstrate insufficient implementation levels even when they receive intervention training (Durlak & DuPre, 2008; Fixsen, Naoom, Blase, Friedman, & Wallace, 2005; Noell, Witt, Gilbertson, Ranier, & Freeland,

http://dx.doi.org/10.1037/14275-005
Treatment Integrity: A Foundation for Evidence-Based Practice in Applied Psychology, L. M. H. Sanetti and T. R. Kratochwill (Editors)

1997; Noell et al., 2005). Factors hypothesized to be associated with facilitating or impeding intervention implementation have been categorized as being related to (a) the intervention agent (individual practitioner), (b) the intervention, (c) the organization, or (d) the external environment (for a review, see Durlak & DuPre, 2008; Sanetti & Kratochwill, 2009). Although these factors have been acknowledged frequently in research, they have received limited attention in the intervention context (Sanetti & Kratochwill, 2009). The dearth of research in this area may, in part, be due to the large number of factors thought to be associated with treatment integrity. Therefore, determining how to influence client outcomes most swiftly is difficult. EBPs are typically enacted by individual practitioners; thus, it may be prudent to begin addressing this gap in the research by focusing on factors related to the practitioner. This focus on the practitioner is particularly appropriate given the challenges of implementing EBPs, which often require practitioners to integrate new intervention-related behavior into their routines and methods of practice. These changes may run counter to practitioners' philosophical or theoretical beliefs, prior training, and/or experience (Kratochwill & Shernoff, 2003). Promoting the treatment integrity of EBPs can be considered an adult behavior change process (Noell, 2008) that can draw on established theories of behavior change to inform and guide effective EBP implementation.

Our primary purpose in this chapter is to illustrate how adult behavior change theory may inform the conceptualization and promotion of treatment integrity. The chapter focuses on supporting practitioners' treatment integrity as informed by preliminary work to occasion behavior change. Four major theories demonstrating broad application are presented: (a) *social cognitive theory*, (b) *theory of planned behavior*, (c) *transtheoretical model*, and (d) *health action process approach*. Because an exhaustive literature review of each theory goes far beyond the scope of this chapter, our discussion includes a brief overview of each theory, its empirical support, and its potential application to treatment integrity.

THEORIES OF BEHAVIOR CHANGE

There are many theories of behavior change. We selected four prominent models for inclusion in this chapter, due to the varied explanations of behavior change they provide and the distinct set of potential targets for promoting treatment integrity indicated. We discuss the four models and the possible applications they have to treatment integrity below.

Social Cognitive Theory

Social cognitive theory (SCT; Bandura, 1986, 1997) is a learning theory that explains behavior as a function of the interaction among three factors: the person, the environment, and behavioral experiences (see Figure 3.1; Bandura, 1986). The dynamic relationship among these factors emphasizes, on the one hand, the critical role of cognitive processes in one's ability to exercise control over one's actions and, on the other hand, the influence of the environment or social system on one's behavior (Bandura, 1986, 2001). Although SCT presents a myriad of factors that explain changes in behavior, the model posits a set of core determinants. In particular, one's behavior is largely determined by one's perceived self-efficacy and expectations regarding outcomes of one's action (outcome expectations), along with behavioral goals and perceived sociostructural factors (i.e., social and structural influences; Bandura, 2004).

SCT underscores the importance of one's perceived self-efficacy (Bandura, 1997). Bandura (1986) defined *self-efficacy* as "people's judgments of their capabilities to organize and execute courses of action required to attain designated types of performances" (p. 391). Self-efficacy is the basis for personal agency (i.e., the ability to intentionally produce desired changes)

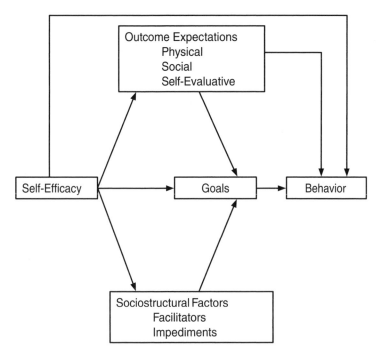

Figure 3.1. Social cognitive theory. Schematic of the structural paths of influence wherein perceived self-efficacy affects behavior both directly and through its impact on goals, outcome expectations, and perception of sociostructural facilitators and impediments. From "Health Promotion by Social Cognitive Means," by A. Bandura, 2004, *Health Education & Behavior, 31,* p. 146. Copyright 2004 by SAGE Publications. Adapted with permission.

and is the dominant predictor of behavior, having both a direct and an indirect effect on behavior via other core sociocognitive determinants (Bandura, 1997, 2004). Although self-efficacy varies across different behaviors and circumstances (Bandura, 1986), in general, the stronger one's self-efficacy, the higher the behavioral goals one sets, the more favorable the outcomes anticipated, and the greater one's self-regulation and persistence (Bandura, 2004).

SCT also posits that behavior is affected by the outcomes people expect their actions to produce. *Outcome expectations* are people's judgments of the probability that a particular behavior will produce particular consequences (Bandura, 1997). In most cases, those who perceive themselves as highly efficacious will expect outcomes that are beneficial, whereas those who perceive themselves as inefficacious will expect their actions to result in poor outcomes (Bandura, 2004). The type of outcome—physical (beliefs about positive and aversive physical experiences), social (anticipated social reactions), and self-evaluation (beliefs related to self-satisfaction and worth)—varies, with the positive or negative expectation of such an outcome being a function of the subjective values individuals assign to it (Bandura, 1997). Each positive expectation motivates behavior, whereas each negative expectation discourages behavior.

Two other key determinants of behavior in SCT are one's goals and one's perceptions of sociostructural factors, including facilitators and impediments (Bandura, 2004). First, goals provide self-incentives and help one guide and regulate one's actions. Indeed, individuals can evaluate their current behavior through the generation of personal standards (Bandura, 1997, 2005). When individuals set challenging personal goals, a discrepancy is created between current behavior and a desired action. This discrepancy leads to an exertion of effort and use of personal resources to achieve the desired behavior change (Bandura, 2005). In general, long-term goals set a general course for change, whereas short-term subgoals incrementally direct what an individual does in the present (Bandura, 2001, 2004). Second, sociostructural factors influence behavior through individuals' perceptions of the impediments and facilitators to behavior change (Bandura, 2005). Human behavior takes place in a social system. Thus, individuals' regulation of their behavior toward the attainment of goals can vary as a function of this system (Bandura, 2005). That is, individuals' behavior is influenced by available resources and opportunities, as well as by social rules, practices, guides, or sanctions that might deter or facilitate behavior change (Bandura, 2001, 2004).

Empirical Support

Researchers have used SCT to explain behavior across many disciplines, including education, health, psychopathology, athletics, and business (Bandura, 1997). Research results support intercorrelations among SCT determinants and their significant combined contribution to the prediction of behavior (Anderson, Winett, & Wojcik, 2007; Petosa, Suminski, & Hortz, 2003). For example, goal setting and self-efficacy are positively correlated and explain unique variance in behavior (Lozano & Stephens, 2010). Outcome expectations have also been found to be positively associated with self-efficacy; however, their prediction of behavior independent of self-efficacy has not been consistently demonstrated (Taber, Meischke, & Maciejewski, 2010). Similarly, sociostructural factors, such as social supports, increase the explained variance in behavior but do so indirectly, primarily via other core determinants (self-efficacy, outcome expectations, goals; e.g., Anderson et al., 2007).

As the vast body of literature on self-efficacy reveals, an individual's efficacy beliefs play a central role in the causal structure of SCT (Bandura, 1997; Bandura & Locke, 2003). Studies have shown that self-efficacy influences goal setting and commitment, outcome expectations, and perceptions of impediments (sociostructural factors) to behavior change (Anderson et al., 2007; Bandura, 1997). Several meta-analyses conducted across a diverse range of behaviors and contexts have demonstrated the predictive power of self-efficacy and, in some instances, have shown self-efficacy to be a better predictor of future behavior than is past performance (see Bandura & Locke, 2003). Together, these results support both the emphasis Bandura (1997) placed on self-efficacy and the central role that self-efficacy plays within the broader system of sociocognitive determinants. Overall, research has revealed that interventions targeting more SCT determinants demonstrate significantly larger effect sizes than do interventions targeting fewer or none of the model's determinants (Graves, 2003). Additionally, research results support that interventions targeting SCT components effectively increase and maintain behavior change (Graves, 2003; Webb, Sniehotta, & Michie, 2010).

Application to Promoting Treatment Integrity

SCT helps to explain how practitioners may change their behavior, and it provides direction on the selection of implementation supports to promote such change prior to and during intervention implementation. Bandura (2004) put forth a stepwise model for promoting behavior change, with the intensity of support increasing on the basis of each individual practitioner's need. At the first level are individuals with a high sense of self-efficacy and positive outcome expectations who require minimal support to successfully change their behavior. The second level consists of individuals who doubt their personal efficacy and the likely positive outcomes of their behavior. These individuals need additional support and guidance to help them get through difficult periods. Individuals at the third level hold the belief that behavior change is completely outside their control. These individuals require a substantial amount of support. Use of this stepwise model and consideration of other key sociocognitive determinants, such as goals and sociostructural factors, may promote a practitioner's treatment integrity.

For instance, if a clinical supervisor wants to proactively address the quality of client care, he or she could promote trainees' treatment integrity to an offered EBP (e.g., trauma-focused group therapy [TFGT]). To start, the supervisor could determine the level of support a trainee needs according to Bandura's stepwise model. Then, on the basis of that need, the supervisor could enhance the trainee's self-efficacy and outcome expectations regarding the TFGT through supports targeting the trainee's sources of personal efficacy. Such supports might include (a) using verbal persuasion (i.e., expressions of belief in the trainee's capabilities to perform the behavior), (b) helping the trainee to develop coping strategies to manage physiological states that might debilitate performance, or (c) building up the trainee's positive enactive experiences (i.e., successes with the behavior) and vicarious experiences, such as observation of models' successes with the behavior (Bandura, 1986). Thus, if the trainee expresses a high sense of self-efficacy and positive outcome expectations, verbal persuasion might be all that is needed to support TFGT implementation. In contrast, if the trainee expresses substantial reservations about TFGT execution, the supervisor could use an intensive support such as a mastery program that includes participant modeling to build on the trainee's successes.

With adequate self-efficacy and positive outcome expectations achieved, the supervisor might further promote effective TFGT delivery through goal setting and attention to salient sociostructural factors. First, the trainee could be assisted in creating materials to support self-monitoring and regulation toward meeting short-term subgoals. For example, the trainee could be supplied with adherence checklists and plans of action for implementing the TFGT lessons each week. Second, the trainee could be assisted in developing a general goal that would guide implementation toward a long-term aim (e.g., the TFGT will be completed with an average of 80% adherence or greater; generalization of skills will be actively promoted with clients, as designed). Finally, to target the trainee's perceptions of sociostructural factors, the supervisor could (a) circumvent perceived impediments, (b) provide social supports that foster self-efficacy, and (c) ensure that necessary resources and opportunities for implementation are present.

Theory of Planned Behavior

The theory of planned behavior (TPB; Ajzen, 1985, 1991) is a largely motivation-based theory designed to predict and explain behavior in specific contexts. The theory posits that behavior change is directly determined by

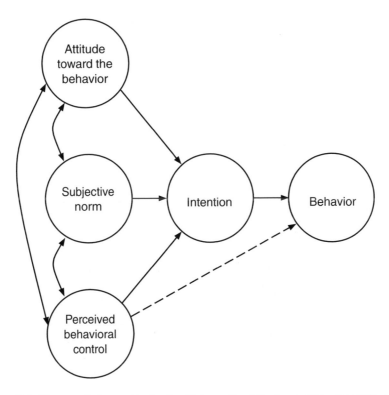

Figure 3.2. Theory of planned behavior. Schematic of the immediate determinants of intention and behavior. From "The Theory of Planned Behavior," by I. Ajzen, 1991, *Organizational Behavior and Human Decision Processes, 50,* p. 182. Copyright 1991 by Elsevier. Adapted with permission.

two factors: behavioral intentions (hereafter referred to as intentions) and perceived behavioral control (see Figure 3.2; Ajzen, 1985, 1991). Intentions develop from one's attitudes toward a behavior (ATT; i.e., positive or negative evaluation about performing the behavior), subjective norms (SN; i.e., perceived social pressure to perform or not perform a behavior), and perceived behavioral control (PBC; i.e., perception of the ease or difficulty of performing a behavior; Ajzen, 1985). Intentions are the driving force of one's motivation to engage in a behavior, and they provide information about the amount of effort an individual is likely to put forth. Not all behavior is completely within individual control. Therefore, PBC plays an important direct role in the prediction of behavior by helping account for the extent to which an individual has the opportunities and resources needed to enact a behavior (Ajzen, 1991).

Three types of beliefs underlie and predict one's ATT, SN, and PBC. These beliefs indirectly determine behavior. First, an individual's ATT is the product of behavioral beliefs that link a specific behavior with outcomes or attributes that are positively or negatively valued (Ajzen, 1985; Ajzen & Fishbein, 1980). An individual who believes mostly positive outcomes will result from engaging in a behavior will have a favorable ATT. Second, an individual's SN is based on normative beliefs that are weighted by the individual's motivation to comply with important others. These beliefs include two types of social pressure: injunctive, or the perceptions of important others approving of a behavior, and descriptive, or the perceptions of important others also performing the behavior (Fishbein & Ajzen, 2010). An individual who believes that others want him or her to perform a behavior will perceive social pressure to do so. Finally, an individual's PBC develops from control beliefs. Control beliefs integrate information from past experiences with the behavior and factors impeding or facilitating the behavior (Ajzen, 1991). An individual who perceives control is one who believes that he or she can sufficiently manage factors that might influence the behavior.

According to the TPB, the stronger an individual's intention, the more likely it is that he or she will attempt to perform the behavior in question. Intention is, therefore, assumed to be the immediate antecedent of behavior. However, the success of the behavioral attempt will be based on an individual's actual control over factors that may influence behavior attainment (Ajzen, 1985). For the best prediction of behavior, Ajzen (1991) proposed, two conditions should be met. First, intention and PBC must be measured for a specific behavior and within the same context in which the behavior will take place. Second, these determinants must remain stable between initial assessment and behavior measurement. Thus, an extended period of time between assessment and observation of a behavior is not recommended, because an increasing number of events may affect underlying beliefs and thereby generate new or revised intentions (Ajzen, 2011).

Empirical Support

The TPB is one of the most widely known and researched models from social psychology (Ajzen, 2011). The parsimoniousness of the model and its ease of application in applied settings partly explain its popularity (McEachan, Conner, Taylor, & Lawton, 2011). Researchers have used the TPB to explain a wide range of behaviors across multiple disciplines (Armitage & Conner, 2001; Fishbein & Ajzen, 2010). In addition, Ajzen and Madden (1986) demonstrated the ability of the TPB to predict individuals' intentions and behavior more accurately than did its predecessor, the theory of reasoned action (Ajzen & Fishbein, 1980). This improvement in the model's predictive ability is due to the addition of PBC, which affords the capacity to explain nonvolitional behaviors (e.g., behaviors not within the full control of a person, such as quitting smoking and weight loss) in addition to volitional behaviors (e.g., behaviors that can typically be performed at will, such as teeth brushing or other mundane tasks; Ajzen, 1991; Armitage & Conner, 2001). A vast body of research has shown that, together, the TPB determinants account for a substantial proportion (approximately 40–45%) of the variance in intention formation and a significant percentage (approximately 20–25%) of the variance in behavior (Armitage & Conner, 2001; McEachan et al., 2011). As well, research has shown that determinants are related to the corresponding sets of underlying beliefs (Ajzen, 1991). However, the explanatory power of the TPB may be reduced if measures of the determinants are not compatible with the behavior that is to be predicted (specific to target action, context, and time; Fishbein & Ajzen, 1975) or if the PBC of an individual is too discrepant from his or her actual control over the behavior (Ajzen, 1991).

Ajzen (1991) stated that "the relative importance of ATT, SN, and PBC in the prediction of intention is expected to vary across behaviors and situations" (p. 188). Consequently, the weight of influence given to each determinant varies on the basis of the specific intention to be formed. However, to date, across the range of behaviors studied, ATT and PBC are stronger predictors of intention than is SN (Armitage & Conner, 2001).

Application to Promoting Treatment Integrity

Because the TPB focuses solely on determinants preceding behavior change, the model identifies potential variables to target prior to intervention implementation. Thus, as indicated by the model, if implementation is to occur, a practitioner must have a favorable attitude about the intervention, a belief that other relevant practitioners encourage its use, and a perception that carrying out the intervention is feasible. Using Ajzen's (2006) guidelines for preparing a standard questionnaire, practitioners can develop a measure of these determinants for a specific intervention and context.

Consider the case of a teacher who needs to implement an evidence-based reading intervention with a student (e.g., Repeated Reading). The teacher must implement the intervention with high treatment integrity if placement and instructional decisions are to be made on the basis of the student's response to the intervention. To proactively promote the teacher's treatment integrity, a school psychologist could assess the teacher's behavioral, normative, and control beliefs related to intervention implementation. Then, the school psychologist could target any counterproductive beliefs by using persuasive communication to change those beliefs and thus, ultimately, the teacher's behavior. For example, persuasive messaging can target negative beliefs (e.g., dislike for the intervention), contrasting beliefs (e.g., perception that others disapprove of the intervention), or insufficiently strong beliefs (e.g., uncertainty about intervention feasibility) about Repeated Reading to enhance the teacher's intentions and PBC, which are the immediate antecedents to implementation. Conversely, the school psychologist could take a more direct approach by assessing the teacher's ATT, SN, and PBC independently of the underlying beliefs. This approach might lead the school psychologist to (a) encourage the development of a positive attitude toward Repeated Reading by explicitly linking important student outcomes to its implementation (e.g., Repeated Reading leads to increased reading fluency), (b) actively promote the teacher's motivation (social pressure) to comply with implementation by highlighting colleagues who use Repeated Reading and speak highly of it, and/or (c) increase the teacher's PBC by reducing the immediate obstacles to implementation and providing adequate training and resources.

Transtheoretical Model

The transtheoretical model (TTM; Prochaska & DiClemente, 1984; Prochaska, Johnson, & Lee, 2009) is an integrative theory for understanding intentional behavior change. The TTM was developed from two parallel bodies of work: (a) Prochaska's (1979) work to systematically distill major theories of psychotherapy into a single integrative model, and (b) the work of Prochaska and DiClemente (1984) to understand how individuals effectively change their own behavior. From these bodies of work and additional research over the past 30 years, four primary determinants are prevalently discussed: processes of change, stages of change, decisional balance, and self-efficacy. For a discussion of a fifth core determinant, temptation, and critical assumptions about the nature of behavior change, see Prochaska et al. (2009).

The processes of change (POC) determinant comprises a set of covert and overt activities that individuals engage in as they attempt to modify their behavior (see Figure 3.3; Prochaska et al., 2009). These POC are important because they delineate the mechanisms by which individuals initiate, adopt, and maintain a desired behavior. Put simply, the POC outline how to change one's behavior at each point of the behavior change process (Prochaska & Norcross, 2007). Ten POC have been revealed through continued validation of the TTM (Prochaska et al., 2009): (a) consciousness raising (i.e., increasing awareness of a problem behavior and the circumstances surrounding it); (b) dramatic relief (i.e., catharsis, or the production of a heightened emotional experience followed by appropriate action to reduce or discharge the emotion); (c) self-reevaluation (i.e., self-assessments of one's image with and without a problem behavior); (d) environmental reevaluation (i.e., assessments of how the presence or absence of a problem behavior affect's one's social environment); (e) self-liberation (i.e., one's commitment to and belief

Stages by Processes of Change

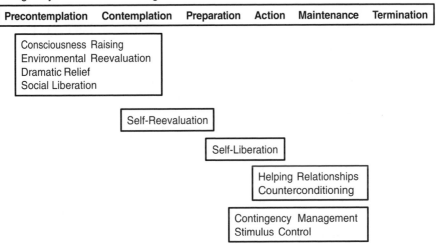

Figure 3.3. The transtheoretical model. Schematic of stages by processes of change. From "Stages and Processes of Self-Change of Smoking: Toward an Integrative Model of Change," by J. O. Prochaska and C. C. DiClemente, 1983, *Journal of Consulting and Clinical Psychology, 51,* p. 394. Copyright 1983 by the American Psychological Association.

in one's ability to change); (f) social liberation (i.e., increasing acceptance of and opportunities for change within the broader social system); (g) counterconditioning (i.e., learning alternate behaviors that can replace the problem behavior); (h) stimulus control (i.e., removal of cues for problem behavior and addition of prompts for desired behavior); (i) contingency management (i.e., provision of consequences to increase the likelihood of a particular action); and (j) helping relationships (i.e., the openness, trust, care, acceptance and support of another).

While investigating the POC individuals use to change their own problematic smoking behavior, DiClemente and Prochaska (1982) discovered that individuals were using different POC at different times. From this study, they identified the second core determinant of the TTM: the stages of change (SOC). Although the SOC determinant has undergone modifications, it remains an organizing framework of the TTM. The SOC emphasize the temporal dimension of behavior change (i.e., behavior change occurs over time; Prochaska et al., 2009) and represent how individuals' attitudes, intentions, and behaviors differ at different points in the behavior change process (Prochaska & Norcross, 2007). In its most current form, the SOC comprises six stages through which individuals progress by use of POC: (a) *precontemplation* (i.e., unaware of problem and have no intention to change behavior in the foreseeable future); (b) *contemplation* (i.e., aware of problem and intending to change behavior in the near future but may be ambivalent); (c) *preparation* (i.e., intending to change behavior in the immediate future and has a plan for doing so); (d) *action* (i.e., making observable changes in behavior); (e) *maintenance* (i.e., working to prevent relapse to former behavior); and (f) *termination* (i.e., no longer at risk of relapse and new behavior is fully part of current habits; Prochaska, Wright, & Velicer, 2008). Although the SOC are visually represented in a linear progression, the stages are more accurately described as spiraling in nature. That is, relapse to earlier stages is common before permanent behavior change is attained (Prochaska & DiClemente, 1983).

The TTM comprises two primary determinants in addition to the SOC and POC: decisional balance, or one's weighing of the pros and cons of behavior change; and self-efficacy, or one's confidence in one's ability to change and not relapse (Prochaska et al., 2009). Although these two determinants do not receive as much attention in the literature as do the SOC and POC, they remain essential to the integrative perspective of the TTM. Along with POC, these two determinants help explain individuals' progression through the SOC. In particular, as one progresses through the stages, one's self-efficacy and awareness of the pros of changing increase, and one's perception of the cons of changing decreases (Prochaska & DiClemente, 1984; Prochaska et al., 2009).

Empirical Support

The TTM has been applied to a broad range of problem and health behaviors and to the promotion of individuals' physical and mental health (Prochaska et al., 2009) over the past 25 years. The individual core determinants of the TTM (i.e., the POC, SOC, decisional balance, and self-efficacy) and its use as an integrative framework have garnered empirical support. For example, the POC have been identified, verified, and refined through empirical testing across a variety of behaviors (Prochaska & DiClemente, 1986; Prochaska et al., 2009). Researchers have also studied the SOC across a range of behaviors and have shown them to be predictive of subsequent behavior (e.g., a smoker in contemplation is twice as likely to be abstinent 1 month following treatment as is a smoker in precontemplation; DiClemente et al., 1991). Further, decisional balance has demonstrated remarkable stability across 48 different behaviors; the number of pros increases and the number of cons decreases in a consistent pattern as people move from precontemplation to maintenance (Hall & Rossi, 2008). Last, research indicates that self-efficacy is an important determinant across behaviors (for a review, see Bandura, 1997; Schwarzer, 1992) as well as when examined within a stage model. For instance, researchers have found a positive association between levels of self-efficacy and movement through the SOC (i.e., self-efficacy increases as participants move through the stages; DiClemente, Prochaska, & Gilbertini, 1985; Velicer, DiClemente, Rossi, & Prochaska, 1990).

Empirical support for the integration of SOC and POC has been demonstrated with some behaviors, although not as consistently or strongly as has the relationship between decisional balance and an individual's SOC (Prochaska, DiClemente, & Norcross, 1992). Results from randomized controlled trials evaluating the TTM as an integrative framework have demonstrated promising outcomes for its application (Marcus et al., 1998; Velicer, Redding, Sun, & Prochaska, 2007). For example, a review of 23 interventions using part or all of the TTM found greater effects in behavior change when all key model determinants were used together than when just one or two were used (Spencer, Pagell, Hallion, & Adams, 2002).

Application to Promoting Treatment Integrity

The TTM provides a framework for determining practitioners' readiness for change and guidance for the selection of strategies to facilitate change both prior to and during intervention implementation. In application to treatment integrity, the model may be used to identify the specific POC (i.e., types of implementation support) most effective during a given SOC (Prochaska & Norcross, 2007) to move a practitioner to adoption and ultimately sustainment of an EBP. According to Prochaska et al. (2009), implementation supports that address practitioners' resistance and ambivalence to change (e.g., motivational interviewing) might be most beneficial at early stages of behavior change. In contrast, a behavioral approach to implementation support (e.g., counterconditioning) might be most successful at later stages of change.

For example, if a mental health agency planned to add an EBP to its outpatient services (e.g., cognitive behavior therapy [CBT]), it could conduct an assessment of each practitioner's readiness (i.e., SOC, decisional balance, and/or self-efficacy) to implement CBT to ensure best practice. This assessment could help the agency provide the appropriate supports at the appropriate times to its practitioners. To this end, a review of current measures of key TTM determinants (for a list of measures, see http://www.uri.edu/research/cprc/measures.htm) might inform the development of a practitioner readiness questionnaire. This questionnaire could delineate practitioners' current SOC, as well as highlight markers of readiness to move to the next stage. These markers might include practitioners' current balance of the pros and cons of changing their practice as well as their level of self-efficacy regarding CBT. With specific information about practitioner readiness, tailored supports could be selected and supplied to practitioners to best facilitate their progression toward effective, sustained CBT implementation. For practitioners in precontemplation who do not believe there is a need to change their practice, the agency might focus on consciousness raising. The agency could provide feedback regarding outcomes that need improvement for a specific client population and education on the benefits of CBT. On the other hand, for practitioners in preparation who are ready for immediate adoption of CBT, the agency might focus its efforts on CBT training and support to develop specific goals and a plan of action for implementation. Once CBT implementation has commenced, the agency can reinforce practitioners' efforts by (a) providing ongoing support through supervisory or peer relationships (helping relationships) and (b) providing incentives for CBT use and effective implementation (contingency management).

Health Action Process Approach

The health action process approach (HAPA; Schwarzer, 1992, 2008a) is an empirically supported behavior change theory from health psychology. The HAPA describes the mechanisms that underlie both the development of an intention to act (i.e., the act of goal setting) and the enactment of the action (i.e., the act of goal pursuit). Thus, the HAPA may help illuminate cognitive processes that translate individuals' intentions into actions, bridging the intention–behavior gap (Schwarzer, 2008a). The HAPA explains behavior change as comprising two phases (see Figure 3.4). First, a motivational phase leads to the development of an explicit behavioral intention (e.g., "I intend to do moderate exercise for 30 minutes twice weekly").

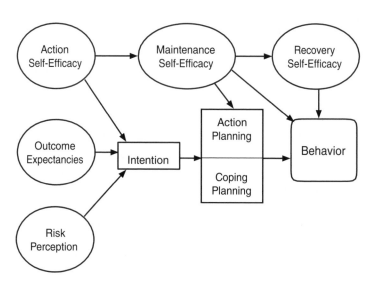

Motivational Phase   Volitional Phase

Figure 3.4. Health action process approach. Schematic of immediate determinants of intention and behavior across the two phases of behavior change. From *The Health Action Process Approach*, by R. Schwarzer. Retrieved from http://www.hapa-model.de/. Copyright by R. Schwarzer. Adapted with permission.

Second, a volitional phase leads to the adoption and maintenance of the new behavior (e.g., "I am completing 30-minute jogs twice weekly prior to work"). On the basis of the two phases, an individual must form an intention to change his or her behavior before doing so.

The motivational phase comprises three key determinants that together contribute to the development of an explicit behavioral intention: outcome expectancies, action self-efficacy, and risk perception (Schwarzer, 2008b). *Outcome expectancies* involve the contemplation of different behaviors and their potential outcomes. Through consideration of the pros and cons of different actions, an individual gathers important information for making decisions about developing an intention to act (Schwarzer, 2008a). In addition to outcome expectancies, *action self-efficacy*, or confidence in one's ability to perform a new behavior, is critical to the formation of an intention (Schwarzer & Luszczynska, 2008). Action self-efficacy is a central determinant of intention and is regarded as its best individual predictor (Luszczynska & Schwarzer, 2003). Finally, to begin contemplation to develop an intention, one must first perceive a need for doing so. *Risk perception* is the recognition of a problem that has to be addressed (Schwarzer, 2008a). Although a less proximal contributor to intention, risk perception plays a vital role in intention formation by providing the foundation for an individual to further consider behavior change (Schwarzer & Luszczynska, 2008).

Once an explicit intention has been formed, an individual moves from the motivational phase to the volitional phase. During the volitional phase, the HAPA suggests, adoption and maintenance of a behavior is predicted by two determinants, planning and volitional self-efficacy (Luszczynska & Schwarzer, 2003; Schwarzer & Luszczynska, 2008). *Planning* processes include action and coping planning. Action plans support the adoption of behaviors by providing precise instructions on the when, where, and how of implementing an intended behavior (Scholz, Schüz, Ziegelmann, Lippke, & Schwarzer, 2008). Coping plans help to facilitate the maintenance of behaviors by predetermining strategies for overcoming barriers to performance, including managing distractions and competing influences (Gollwitzer, 1999). To further ensure persistence in implementation of a behavior, high *volitional self-efficacy* (comprising maintenance and recovery self-efficacies, such as confidence in one's ability to maintain a behavior over time and recover it after a lapse) is important because it signifies an individual's confidence to sustain a behavior and persist when faced with challenges (Luszczynska & Schwarzer, 2003).

Empirical Support

The HAPA is one of the most frequently researched models from health psychology and has proven utility across a diverse range of health behaviors, from physical exercise to breast self-examination to seat belt use (Schwarzer, 2008a). In addition, empirical support for the relationships among HAPA determinants and their influence on behavioral outcomes has been replicated (Garcia & Mann, 2003; Lippke, Ziegelmann, & Schwarzer, 2005; Schüz, Sniehotta, Mallach, Wiedemann, & Schwarzer 2009). Although self-efficacy is the strongest predictor of intention, research has shown that, together, outcome expectancies, action self-efficacy, and risk perception provide the best prediction of intention formation (Schwarzer & Luszczynska, 2008; Schwarzer, Luszczynska, Ziegelmann, Scholz, & Lippke, 2008) and explain a significant proportion of the variance in the development of intentions (Scholz et al., 2008). Additionally, these three determinants are significantly associated with the planning processes that are important during the volitional phase (Renner, Spivak, Kwon, & Schwarzer, 2007).

Because performing a desired behavior is not a single event, inclusion of postintentional processes is critical to the HAPA for ensuring that individuals who have an intention successfully translate it into action. Several studies have demonstrated that a strong intention plus action and coping planning increase the likelihood of a new behavior being implemented and maintained more than does intention alone (Gollwitzer & Sheeran, 2006; Sniehotta, Schwarzer, Scholz, & Schüz, 2005). Volitional self-efficacy also plays a central role in the enactment of intentions across time (Parschau et al., 2012). For instance, it helps to predict which individuals will progress from having a specific behavioral intention to actually performing the behavior (Schüz et al., 2009). Thus, volitional self-efficacy supports the individual's commitment to sustaining a behavior, even after a lapse.

Application to Promoting Treatment Integrity

The HAPA shows promise for promoting the treatment integrity of EBPs by focusing on determinants both prior to and during intervention implementation. First, each phase of the model is explicit about what determinants to target to facilitate an individual's progression from development of a strong intention to implement an intervention to actual intervention implementation and maintenance. Second, by operating as a hybrid model (neither a stage nor continuum theory; Schwarzer, 2008b), the HAPA allows for the linear prediction of behavior without losing the benefits of having the ability to select the most appropriate implementation supports, given an individual's present phase of behavior change (i.e., motivational or volitional).

Consider, for example, a practitioner who must work indirectly through a parent to improve a client's behavior. The practitioner completes a functional assessment and develops a behavior support plan (BSP). The practitioner realizes that although the parent is invested in seeing her child's behavior change, changing her own behavior to effectively implement the BSP may be challenging. By applying the HAPA, the practitioner has a comprehensive and resource-efficient framework for supporting the parent's BSP implementation.

First, the practitioner must ensure that the parent develops a strong intention to implement the BSP. During the evaluation process the parent demonstrates an accurate perception of the risk related to her child's behavior and a sense of urgency about intervening. However, her action self-efficacy and outcome expectancies (key determinants for intention) related to her child's BSP remain unclear. To assess the parent's intention to implement, the practitioner can either assess her intention directly (e.g., "What intention do you have for the next weeks and months to carry out this BSP?") or assess it indirectly by inquiring about (a) the parent's confidence in her ability to integrate and execute all components of the BSP (e.g., "How confident are you that you can provide the scheduled attention as outlined in your child's BSP?" "Do you believe you have the necessary skills to carry out this BSP?") and (b) the outcomes the parent anticipates as a result of BSP implementation (e.g., "What do you believe will occur as a result of providing scheduled attention?" "What changes do you expect to see in your child's behavior related to implementation of this BSP?"). The latter assessment approach seems preferable. First, it may reduce the likelihood of receiving a socially desirable (inaccurate) parent response. Second, it helps to define specific targets for efficient provision of implementation support.

When the assessment process is complete, the practitioner has important information with which to promote BSP implementation. If the assessment reveals that the parent has many positive expectations regarding the BSP but does not feel confident in her ability to implement its components, the practitioner can provide direct training (i.e., modeling, behavioral rehearsal, feedback) to increase the parent's efficacy beliefs. Next, the practitioner can support the translation of the parent's intent to implement the BSP into action. According to Schwarzer (2008a), this translation of intentions to actions is achieved through two types of strategic planning: action and coping planning. The practitioner could initially assist the parent in mapping each implementation step into her regular routines and activities in the home (action planning). Then, the practitioner could help the parent problem solve around potential threats to sustaining the BSP (coping planning). Last, to increase the likelihood of consistent implementation for the duration required, the practitioner might periodically reevaluate the parent's self-efficacy beliefs, especially regarding her confidence in her ability to maintain or recover BSP implementation (volitional self-efficacy), and intervene as needed.

CONCLUSION

In this chapter, we have described treatment integrity as an adult behavior change process that may be facilitated through the application of adult behavior change theory. We provided an overview of four empirically supported behavior change theories and discussed their application to facilitate intervention-related behavior. Although the four theories include some similar determinants, most notably the prominence of self-efficacy (or a similar construct, such as PBC), each of them provides a unique framework for understanding and promoting practitioners' intervention implementation.

The adoption of a behavior change theory in the development of implementation supports has direct implications for the identification of targets for support, the timing of those supports, the selection of specific techniques, and the evaluation of those techniques (Improved Clinical Effectiveness Through Behavioral Research Group [ICEBeRG], 2006; Webb et al., 2010). The models presented in this chapter are widely accepted and broadly applied, but their use in the promotion of treatment integrity is in its infancy; few investigations have been tested in efforts to change professional practices (ICEBeRG, 2006). Given the emergent state of research-based implementation supports (French et al., 2012), a few considerations warrant attention during early investigations of applying adult behavior change theory to the improvement of treatment integrity.

First, no single, widely agreed-upon process currently exists for taking theoretically based constructs and translating them into the components of a specific technique (Bhattacharyya, Reeves, Garfinkel, & Zwarenstein, 2006). Determining which procedures seem beneficial for replication will require a review of approaches outlined and supported in the literature. Having a clearly defined, reproducible method for translating theory into practice is necessary because poor operationalization of theories can lead to the development of ineffective implementation supports (ICEBeRG, 2006). Second, due to the multitude of variables proposed to influence treatment integrity, it may become apparent that a focus on the individual practitioner alone, although prudent, is insufficient (Bhattacharyya, Reeves, & Zwarenstein, 2009). Rather, the redesign of service delivery systems might be necessary to effectively attend to implementation barriers and needed incentives (or facilitators).

The theories presented in this chapter may hold great promise for facilitating the effective implementation of EBPs; however, both feasibility and efficacy testing are needed for examining the translation of these theories for the purpose of promoting treatment integrity. Researchers in psychology and related fields are well suited to advance the EBP movement beyond passive dissemination of EBPs to active, theoretically based approaches that will increase the likelihood of successful implementation. If such advances can be achieved, mental health practice settings and schools will finally be able to experience the full realization of the promises asserted by EBPs.

REFERENCES

Ajzen, I. (1985). From intentions to action: A theory of planned behavior. In J. Kuhl & J. Beckman (Eds.), *Action control: From cognitions to behaviors* (pp. 11–39). New York, NY: Springer. doi:10.1007/978-3-642-69746-3_2

Ajzen, I. (1991). The theory of planned behavior. *Organizational Behavior and Human Decision Processes, 50,* 179–211. doi:10.1016/0749-5978(91)90020-T

Ajzen, I. (2006). Constructing a theory of planned behavior questionnaire. Retrieved from http://people.umass.edu/aizen/pdf/tpb.measurement.pdf

Ajzen, I. (2011). The theory of planned behavior: Reactions and reflections. *Psychology & Health, 26,* 1113–1127. doi:10.1080/08870446.2011.613995

Ajzen, I., & Fishbein, M. (1980). *Understanding attitudes and predicting social behavior.* Englewood-Cliffs, NJ: Prentice-Hall.

Ajzen, I., & Madden, T. J. (1986). Prediction of goal-directed behavior: Attitudes, intentions, and perceived behavioral control. *Journal of Experimental Social Psychology, 22,* 453–474. doi:10.1016/0022-1031(86)90045-4

Anderson, E. S., Winett, R. A., & Wojcik, J. R. (2007). Self-regulation, self-efficacy, outcome expectations, and social support: Social cognitive theory and nutrition behavior. *Annals of Behavioral Medicine, 34,* 304–312. doi:10.1007/BF02874555

Armitage, C. J., & Conner, M. (2001). Efficacy of the theory of planned behavior: A meta-analytic review. *British Journal of Social Psychology, 40,* 471–499. doi:10.1348/014466601164939

Bandura, A. (1986). *Social foundations of thought and action: A social cognitive theory.* Englewood Cliffs, NJ: Prentice-Hall.

Bandura, A. (1997). *Self-efficacy: The exercise of control.* New York, NY: Freeman.

Bandura, A. (2001). Social cognitive theory: An agentic perspective. *Annual Review of Psychology, 52,* 1–26. doi:0066-4308/01/0201-0001

Bandura, A. (2004). Health promotion by social cognitive means. *Health Education & Behavior, 31,* 143–164. doi:10.1177/1090198104263660

Bandura, A. (2005). The evolution of social cognitive theory. In K. G. Smith & M. A. Hitt (Eds.), *Great minds in management* (pp. 9–35). Oxford, England: Oxford University Press.

Bandura, A., & Locke, E. A. (2003). Negative self-efficacy and goal effects revisited. *Journal of Applied Psychology, 88,* 87–99. doi:10.1037/0021-9010.88.1.87

Bhattacharyya, O., Reeves, S., Garfinkel, S., & Zwarenstein, M. (2006). Designing theoretically-informed implementation interventions: Fine in theory, but evidence of effectiveness in practice is needed. *Implementation Science, 1,* Article 5. doi:10.1186/1748-5908-1-5

Bhattacharyya, O., Reeves, S., & Zwarenstein, M. (2009). What is implementation research? Rationale, concepts, and practices. *Research on Social Work Practice, 19,* 491–502. doi:10.1177/1049731509335528

DiClemente, C. C., & Prochaska, J. O. (1982). Self-change and therapy change of smoking behavior: A comparison of processes of change in cessation and maintenance. *Addictive Behaviors, 7,* 133–142. doi:10.1016/0306-4603(82)90038-7

DiClemente, C. C., Prochaska, J. O., Fairhurst, S. K., Velicer, W. F., Velasquez, M. M., & Rossi, J. S. (1991). The processes of smoking cessation: An analysis of precontemplation, contemplation, and preparation stages of change. *Journal of Consulting and Clinical Psychology, 59,* 295–304. doi:10.1037/0022-006X.59.2.295

DiClemente, C. C., Prochaska, J. O., & Gilbertini, M. (1985). Self-efficacy and the stages of change of smoking. *Cognitive Therapy and Research, 9,* 181–200. doi:10.1007/BF01204849

Durlak, J. A., & DuPre, E. P. (2008). Implementation matters: A review of research on the influence of implementation on program outcomes and the factors affecting implementation. *American Journal of Community Psychology, 41,* 327–350. doi:10.1007/s10464-008-9165-0

Fishbein, M., & Ajzen, I. (1975). *Belief, attitude, intention, and behavior: An introduction to theory and research.* Retrieved from http://people.umass.edu/aizen/f&a1975.html

Fishbein, M., & Ajzen, I. (2010). *Predicting and changing behavior: The reasoned action approach.* New York, NY: Psychology Press.

Fixsen, D. L., Naoom, S. F., Blase, K. A., Friedman, R. M., & Wallace, F. (2005). *Implementation research: A synthesis of the literature.* Tampa: University of South Florida, Louis de la Parte Florida Mental Health Institute, National Implementation Research Network.

French, S. D., Green, S. E., O'Connor, D. A., McKenzie, J. E., Francis, J. J., Michie, S., . . . Grismshaw, J. M. (2012). Developing theory-informed behavior change interventions to implement evidence into practice: A systematic approach using the theoretical domains framework. *Implementation Science, 7,* Article 38. doi:10.1186/1748-5908-7-38

Garcia, K., & Mann, T. (2003). From "I wish" to "I will": Social-cognitive predictors of behavioral intentions. *Journal of Health Psychology, 8,* 347–360. doi:10.1177/13591053030083005

Gollwitzer, P. M. (1999). Implementation intentions: Strong effects of simple plans. *American Psychologist, 54,* 493–503. doi:10.1037/0003-066X.54.7.493

Gollwitzer, P. M., & Sheeran, P. (2006). Implementation intentions and goal achievement: A meta-analysis of effects and processes. *Advances in Experimental Social Psychology, 38,* 69–119. doi:10.1016/S0065-2601(06)38002-1

Graves, K. D. (2003). Social cognitive theory and cancer patients' quality of life: A meta-analysis of psychosocial intervention components. *Health Psychology, 22,* 210–219. doi:10.1037/0278-6133.22.2.210

Greenwood, C. R. (2009). Treatment integrity: Revisiting some big ideas. *School Psychology Review, 38,* 547–553.

Hall, K. L., & Rossi, J. S. (2008). Meta-analytic examination of the strong and weak principles across 48 health behaviors. *Preventive Medicine, 46,* 266–274. doi:10.1016/j.ypmed.2007.11.006

Improved Clinical Effectiveness Through Behavioral Research Group. (2006). Designing theoretically-informed implementation interventions. *Implementation Science, 1,* Article 4. doi:10.1186/1748-5908-1-4

Kratochwill, T. R., & Shernoff, E. S. (2003). Evidence-based practice: Promoting evidence-based interventions in school psychology. *School Psychology Quarterly, 18,* 389–408. doi:10.1521/scpq.18.4.389.27000

Lippke, S., Ziegelmann, J. P., & Schwarzer, R. (2005). Stage-specific adoption and maintenance of physical activity: Testing a three-stage model. *Psychology of Sport and Exercise, 6,* 585–603. doi:10.1016/j.psychsport.2004.11.002

Lozano, B. E., & Stephens, R. S. (2010). Comparison of participatively set and assigned goals in the reduction of alcohol use. *Psychology of Addictive Behaviors, 24,* 581–591. doi:10.1037/a0021444

Luszczynska, A., & Schwarzer, R. (2003). Planning and self-efficacy in the adoption and maintenance of breast self-examination: A longitudinal study on self-regulatory cognitions. *Psychology & Health, 18,* 93–108. doi:10.1080/0887044021000019358

Marcus, B. H., Bock, B. C., Pinto, B. M., Forsyth, L. H., Roberts, M. B., & Traficante, R. M. (1998). Efficacy of an individualized, motivationally-tailored physical activity intervention. *Annals of Behavioral Medicine, 20,* 174–180. doi:10.1007/BF02884958

McEachan, R. R. C., Conner, M., Taylor, N. J., & Lawton, R. J. (2011). Prospective prediction of health-related behaviours with the theory of planned behaviour: A meta-analysis. *Health Psychology Review, 5,* 97–144. doi:10.1080/17437199.2010.521684

Noell, G. H. (2008). Research examining the relationships among consultation process, treatment integrity, and outcomes. In W. P. Erchul & S. M. Sheridan (Eds.), *Handbook of research in school consultation: Empirical foundations for the field* (pp. 315–334). Mahwah, NJ: Erlbaum.

Noell, G. H., Witt, J. C., Gilbertson, D. N., Ranier, D. D., & Freeland, J. T. (1997). Increasing teacher intervention implementation in general education settings through consultation and performance feedback. *School Psychology Quarterly, 12,* 77–88. doi:10.1037/h0088949

Noell, G. H., Witt, J. C., Slider, N. J., Connell, J. E., Gatti, S. L., Williams, K. L., . . . Duhon, G. J. (2005). Treatment implementation following behavioral consultation in schools: A comparison of three follow-up strategies. *School Psychology Review, 34,* 87–106.

Parschau, L., Richert, J., Koring, M., Ernsting, A., Lippke, S., & Schwarzer, R. (2012). Changes in social-cognitive variables are associated with stage transitions in physical activity. *Health Education Research, 27,* 129–140. doi:10.1093/her/cyr085

Petosa, R. L., Suminski, R., & Hortz, B. (2003). Predicting vigorous physical activity using social cognitive theory. *American Journal of Health Behavior, 27,* 301–310. doi:10.5993/AJHB.27.4.2

Prochaska, J. O. (1979). *Systems of psychotherapy: A transtheoretical analysis.* Homewood, IL: Dorsey Press.

Prochaska, J. O., & DiClemente, C. C. (1983). Stages and processes of self-change of smoking: Toward an integrative model of change. *Journal of Consulting and Clinical Psychology, 51,* 390–395. doi:10.1037/0022-006X.51.3.390

Prochaska, J. O., & DiClemente, C. C. (1984). *The transtheoretical approach: Crossing traditional boundaries of therapy.* Homewood, IL: Dorsey Press.

Prochaska, J. O., & DiClemente, C. C. (1986). Toward a comprehensive model of behavior change. In W. R. Miller & N. Heather (Eds.), *Treating addictive behavior: Processes of change* (pp. 3–27). New York, NY: Plenum Press. doi:10.1007/978-1-4613-2191-0_1

Prochaska, J. O., DiClemente, C. C., & Norcross, J. C. (1992). In search of how people change: Applications to addictive behaviors. *American Psychologist, 47,* 1102–1114. doi:10.1037/0003-066X.47.9.1102

Prochaska, J. O., Johnson, S., & Lee, P. (2009). The transtheoretical model of behavior change. In S. A. Shumaker, J. K. Ockene, & K. A. Riekert (Eds.), *The handbook of health behavior change* (pp. 59–83). New York, NY: Springer.

Prochaska, J. O., & Norcross, J. C. (2007). Comparative conclusions: Toward a transtheoretical therapy. In J. O. Prochaska & J. C. Norcross (Eds.), *Systems of psychotherapy: A transtheoretical analysis* (6th ed., pp. 507–539). Belmont, CA: Brooks/Cole.

Prochaska, J. O., Wright, J. A., & Velicer, W. F. (2008). Evaluating theories of health behavior change: A hierarchy of criteria applied to the transtheoretical model. *Applied Psychology, 57,* 561–588. doi:10.1111/j.1464-0597.2008.00345.x

Renner, B., Spivak, Y., Kwon, S., & Schwarzer, R. (2007). Does age make a difference? Predicting physical activity of South Koreans. *Psychology and Aging, 22,* 482–493. doi:10.1037/0882-7974.22.3.482

Sanetti, L. M. H., & Kratochwill, T. R. (2009). Toward developing a science of treatment integrity: Introduction to the special series. *School Psychology Review, 38,* 445–459.

Scholz, U., Schüz, B., Ziegelmann, J. P., Lippke, S., & Schwarzer, R. (2008). Beyond behavioural intentions: Planning mediates between intentions and physical activity. *British Journal of Health Psychology, 13,* 479–494. doi:10.1348/135910707X216062

Schüz, B., Sniehotta, F. F., Mallach, N., Wiedemann, A., & Schwarzer, R. (2009). Predicting transitions from preintentional, intentional and actional stages of change: Adherence to oral self-care recommendations. *Health Education Research, 24,* 64–75. doi:10.1093/her/cym092

Schwarzer, R. (1992). Self-efficacy in the adoption and maintenance of health behaviors: Theoretical approaches and a new model. In R. Schwarzer (Ed.), *Self-efficacy: Thought control of action* (pp. 217–243). Washington, DC: Hemisphere.

Schwarzer, R. (2008a). Modeling health behavior change: How to predict and modify the adoption and maintenance of health behaviors. *Applied Psychology, 57*, 1–29. doi:10.1111/j.1464-0597.2007.00325.x

Schwarzer, R. (2008b). Response: Some burning issues in research on health behavior change. *Applied Psychology, 57*, 84–93. doi:10.1111/j.1464-0597.2007.00324.x

Schwarzer, R., & Luszczynska, A. (2008). How to overcome health-compromising behaviors: The health action process approach. *European Psychologist, 13*, 141–151. doi:10.1027/1016-9040.13.2.141

Schwarzer, R., Luszczynska, A., Ziegelmann, J. P., Scholz, U., & Lippke, S. (2008). Social-cognitive predictors of physical exercise adherence: Three longitudinal studies in rehabilitation. *Health Psychology, 27*(Suppl. 1), S54–S63. doi:10.1037/0278-6133.27.1(Suppl.).S54

Sniehotta, F. F., Schwarzer, R., Scholz, U., & Schüz, B. (2005). Action plans and coping plans for long-term lifestyle change: Theory and assessment. *European Journal of Social Psychology, 35*, 565–576. doi:10.1002/ejsp.258

Spencer, L., Pagell, F., Hallion, M. E., & Adams, T. B. (2002). Applying the transtheoretical model to tobacco cessation and prevention: A review of the literature. *American Journal of Health Promotion, 17*, 7–71. doi:10.4278/0890-1171-17.1.7

Taber, D. R., Meischke, H., & Maciejewski, M. L. (2010). Testing social cognitive mechanisms of exercise in college students. *American Journal of Health Behavior, 34*, 156–165. doi:10.5993/AJHB.34.2.3

Velicer, W. F., DiClemente, C., Rossi, J. S., & Prochaska, J. O. (1990). Relapse situations and self-efficacy: An integrative model. *Addictive Behaviors, 15*, 271–283. doi:10.1016/0306-4603(90)90070-E

Velicer, W. F., Redding, C. A., Sun, X., & Prochaska, J. O. (2007). Demographic variables, smoking variables, and outcomes across five studies. *Health Psychology, 26*, 278–287. doi:10.1037/0278-6133.26.3.278

Walrath, C. M., Sheehan, A. K., Holden, E. W., Hernandez, M., & Blau, G. M. (2006). Evidence-based treatments in the field: A brief report on provider knowledge, implementation, and practice. *Journal of Behavioral Health Services & Research, 33*, 244–253. doi:10.1007/s11414-005-9008-9

Webb, T. L., Sniehotta, F. F., & Michie, S. (2010). Using theories of behaviour change to inform interventions for addictive behaviours. *Addiction, 105*, 1879–1892. doi:10.1111/j.1360-0443.2010.03028.x

II

ASSESSING TREATMENT INTEGRITY

4

CONCEPTUAL FOUNDATIONS FOR MEASURING THE IMPLEMENTATION OF EDUCATIONAL INNOVATIONS

JEANNE CENTURY AND AMY CASSATA

Measuring the extent and nature of innovation implementation and measuring the factors affecting the implementation process are critical steps for understanding how, why, and under what circumstances educational innovations work (Durlak, 2010; Hulleman & Cordray, 2009; O'Donnell, 2008; Ruiz-Primo, 2005; Sanetti & Kratochwill, 2009). Before this can happen, however, the implementation research field needs to take some fundamental and essential steps. In this chapter, we address the critical need for shared conceptual frameworks for measuring innovation implementation and factors that affect implementation. We describe how our work has led to the

This material is based on work supported by the National Science Foundation under Grants 0628052, 0635598, 1008569, and 1109595. Any opinions, findings, conclusions, or recommendations expressed in this material are those of the authors and do not necessarily reflect the views of the National Science Foundation. The authors are part of the Research and Evaluation Group at the Center for Elementary Mathematics and Science Education (CEMSE) at the University of Chicago. CEMSE is committed to the sharing of knowledge and the creation of useful products and programs to make a positive difference for instruction throughout the nation.

http://dx.doi.org/10.1037/14275-006
Treatment Integrity: A Foundation for Evidence-Based Practice in Applied Psychology, L. M. H. Sanetti and T. R. Kratochwill (Editors)

development of such frameworks as well as the application of those frameworks in studies using related data collection tools and analysis approaches. We also highlight some of the persistent questions that emerge in innovation implementation studies and how we have addressed them.

Researchers now acknowledge that educational innovations are complex and include the enactment of interrelated components that must each be measured if the status of innovation implementation is to be fully understood. Domitrovich et al. (2008), for example, defined *intervention* as "a set of features or practices that are directly related to the underlying theory of the intervention and describe the mechanisms of change" (p. 8). As such, the notion that innovations can be operationally defined according to their essential parts—parts that are believed to lead to intended outcomes—is now increasingly accepted in the field of implementation research.

These innovation parts, which have been referred to as *components or building blocks*, *critical program dimensions*, *model dimensions*, *fidelity criteria*, *essential characteristics*, and *critical parts*, are hereafter referred to as *components* (Bond et al., 2000; Hall & Hord, 1987; Huntley, 2005; Mowbray, Holter, Teague, & Bybee, 2003; Sabelli & Dede, 2001; Wang, Nojan, Strom, & Walberg, 1984). Notwithstanding the different labels used, researchers appear to increasingly agree that innovations consist of essential components that must be specifically described and measured to determine which of them bolster or hinder student performance and to understand the differential effects of incomplete or incorrect implementation (Fullan, 1983; Lynch & O'Donnell, 2005; Ruiz-Primo, 2005; Wang et al., 1984). However, few tools are available to measure the enactment of educational innovations at this level of specificity (Levy, Pasquale, & Marco, 2008; Mowbray et al., 2003).

Clarifying some terms at this point will be useful. We use the term *innovation* in this chapter to refer to any practice that is new to the user. The innovation does not have to be new to the field at large; rather, the practice should require that the users in a particular setting change what they are doing. Across the literature, one might see the terms *program*, *intervention*, *practice*, or *reform* used, sometimes interchangeably and sometimes with nuanced differences. In the context of our work, the focus is on the notion that the practice of interest—whether considered to be an intervention, reform, or program—is different from the current practice.

Over the past several years, our research team at the Center for Elementary Mathematics and Science Education (CEMSE) at the University of Chicago has engaged in a learning process focused on creating tools to measure enactment of innovations through developing approaches for conceptualizing, operationally defining, organizing, and measuring their essential elements. CEMSE's work in this area has focused on a range of innovations but originally grew out of two projects supported by the National Science Foundation

(NSF): Applied Research on Science Materials Implementation: Bringing Measurement of Fidelity of Implementation (FOI) to Scale (2007–2010; referred to as the *implementation study*) and Accumulating Knowledge on Scaling and Sustaining Reform: A Foundation for Future Research (2007–2011; referred to as the *factor study*).

We began the implementation study as a result of a conversation with a school district administrator who expressed a need to understand, as she put it, "what is happening in my classrooms" or, more broadly put, how her district was implementing its reform-based elementary science program. She was unable to gather these implementation data efficiently, in part because her district was so large and in part because the district science "program" (i.e., innovation) consisted of over 25 separate units from at least four different published curricula. It became clear early in this work that we needed to look beyond the curricula as "wholes" and instead take a component-based approach to answering her question. By identifying and measuring enactment of innovation components that were common across and unique to the instructional materials being used in the district, we would be able to accurately describe innovation implementation. This work, described in detail in Century, Rudnick, and Freeman (2010), led to the development of a conceptual framework for organizing innovation components and a suite of instruments for measuring the implementation of the curricula. The development of these instruments included a 15-school pilot test and a 39-school field test to establish item reliability and validity and resulted in (a) a teacher instructional questionnaire, (b) a teacher instructional log, (c) a teacher interview protocol, (d) a classroom observation protocol, (e) a school leader questionnaire, and (f) a school leader interview protocol. We have found over time that this framework can be applied to other kinds of innovations, and we currently refer to it as the *innovation implementation conceptual framework*.

We have come to agree from a conceptual standpoint with Sanetti and Kratochwill (2009), who suggested that understandings about implementation as a whole will be enhanced if researchers begin to conceptualize implementation more broadly, so that implementation models can be applied across disciplines. Using the notion of components, our framework provides a clear and broadly applicable foundation for identifying, defining, and organizing the essential elements of an innovation. This framework can then support one's ability to measure and describe innovation implementation, or the extent to which each component is enacted. A result of this approach is the ability to collect data on implementation of particular components in multiple innovations, so that knowledge is accumulated about enactment of those components and their impacts on outcomes.

Although specific and clear descriptions of enacted components are essential to understanding innovation impact, this activity is only part of understanding, conceptualizing, and measuring implementation. Understanding why implementation happens as it does is equally important. This imperative motivated the factor study mentioned above, which was a comprehensive cross-disciplinary literature review that identified and defined variables that contribute to and/or inhibit innovation implementation. The findings of this study confirmed that, contrary to the assumptions of some, implementers' decisions to adopt new practices and the subsequent ways the implementers enact these practices are influenced by more than an innovation's actual or perceived effectiveness. Rather, a wide range of individual, organizational, and contextual influences (Century, Cassata, Freeman, & Rudnick, 2012; Cranney, Warren, Barton, Gardner, & Walley, 2001; Fixsen, Naoom, Blase, Friedman, & Wallace, 2005), which we refer to as *factors*, have an impact on users' decisions to adopt, use, and continue using innovations. Further, these factors interact with one another and have varying degrees of impact over time, influencing the extent to which enactments of particular innovation components are sustained.

These factors are not part of the innovation itself, and, therefore, their measurement is not part of measuring innovation implementation as we define it. Rather, together with measures of innovation implementation (i.e., measuring enactment of innovation components), the related factors shed light on the larger implementation process. By systematically measuring the enactment of the innovation itself and the factors that affect its implementation, we can develop knowledge about what can improve education and the contexts and conditions in which that improvement can happen.

For the remainder of the chapter, we describe how we brought the implementation study and the factor study together to create a foundation for rigorously measuring the implementation process and accumulating knowledge about successful innovations in education. In doing so, we discuss (a) the development of the innovation implementation conceptual framework and the factor framework and (b) applications of these frameworks in current innovation implementation studies. We also highlight some of the challenges we face in innovation implementation measurement that come from use of different terminology, definitions, and conceptual approaches.

THE CHALLENGING INNOVATION
IMPLEMENTATION LANDSCAPE

The absence of consistent measures for assessing enacted innovation components is due, in part, to the lack of consensus in education about a clear conceptual framework that can guide and organize the constructs to be measured. In a comprehensive review of the implementation literature, Sanetti and Kratochwill (2009) highlighted the need for "consensus regarding the critical dimensions within a conceptual model of treatment integrity and the operational definitions of those dimensions" (p. 453). This call has been echoed by others for over a decade (e.g., Dane & Schneider, 1998); however, despite the development of multiple conceptual frameworks of treatment integrity, the needed comprehensiveness, consistency, and definitional clarity have not yet been achieved.

A comparison of the conceptual frameworks proposed a decade apart by Dane and Schneider (1998) and Domitrovich et al. (2008) illustrates this ongoing issue. Dane and Schneider identified five dimensions of program integrity (i.e., adherence, exposure, differentiation, quality, and participant responsiveness). Upon identifying these dimensions in their review of prevention programs, they stated, "The definitions and labels assigned to these aspects vary considerably and are often not consistent with the terms used in the present review" (p. 39). They offered provisional definitions (see Table 4.1) but suggested that the adoption of uniform definitions would be necessary to move forward. Unfortunately, many education researchers have used Dane and Schneider's dimensions as originally defined or have used the dimensions with different definitions, without regard to the authors' clear call for definitional consensus and clarity.

The conceptual framework offered by Domitrovich et al. (2008) provides an example of how conceptual frameworks are evolving, but consensus and clarity remain lacking. The focus of this detailed conceptual framework is understanding implementation within the domain of school-based preventive health interventions. Their framework incorporates key program elements ("core components") as well as clearly articulated contextual factors that may support or inhibit implementation (e.g., training, infrastructure, mentoring) that are independent of the intervention itself. Although there is some overlap between the Domitrovich et al. framework and the one proposed by Dane and Schneider (1998), examination of the frameworks side by side illustrates that similar terms (e.g., *quality*) have divergent operational definitions at the same time that similar constructs are represented by different terms (e.g., *adherence, fidelity;* see Table 4.1). This is not an uncommon phenomenon among available conceptual frameworks of implementation.

This phenomenon has important practical implications for improving education. Implementation researchers who evaluate the implementation and subsequent student outcomes of educational interventions, often describe implementation process in the absence of detailed operational definitions. As a result, reliably measuring and, just as importantly, communicating about implementation is impossible. For example,

TABLE 4.1
Alignment of Frameworks for Implementation of Innovations
in Educational Settings

Dane & Schneider (1998)	Domitrovich et al. (2008)
Adherence: The extent to which specified program components were delivered as prescribed in program manuals (p. 45).	*Fidelity*: The degree to which the intervention and its support system are conducted as planned (p. 11). • The *intervention* (program, policy, process, or principal) includes strategies or innovations linked by a causal mechanism to specified, intended outcomes (p. 7). • The *support system* includes pre-intervention training, professional development, opportunities for active learning, and other forms of technical assistance (p. 7).
Exposure: An index that may include any of the following: (a) the number of sessions implemented, (b) the length of each session, or (c) the frequency with which program techniques were implemented (p. 45).	*Dosage*: Specific units of an intervention, amount of time of exposure (p. 11). *Delivery strategy*: The frequency, duration, timing, and mode of delivering the core components, as well as the individuals actually responsible for implementing the intervention (p. 9).
Participant responsiveness: A measure of participant response to program sessions, which may include indicators such as levels of participation and enthusiasm (p. 45).	
Quality: A measure of *qualitative aspects* of program delivery that are not directly related to the implementation of prescribed content, such as implementer enthusiasm, leader preparedness, global estimates of session effectiveness, and leader attitudes toward program (p. 45).	*Quality*: Affective engagement, sensitivity, responsiveness, engaging participants, interpersonal skills (p. 11). *Contextual factors*: Individual-level and school-level factors (pp. 13–17) • *Individual-level factors* include professional characteristics, psychological characteristics, perceptions of and attitudes to the intervention. • *School-level factors* include mission-policy alignment, decision structure, resources, personnel expertise, administrative leadership, school culture, school climate and organizational health, characteristics of the school, classroom climate. *Contextual factors*: Macro-level factors (pp. 12–13).

TABLE 4.1
Alignment of Frameworks for Implementation of Innovations
in Educational Settings   *(Continued)*

Dane & Schneider (1998)	Domitrovich et al. (2008)
	• *Macro-level factors* include federal, state, and district policies; leadership and human capital; and community-university partnerships.
Differentiation: A manipulation check that is performed to safeguard against the diffusion (unintentional spread) of treatments; that is, to ensure that the subjects in each experimental condition receive only planned intervention (p. 45).	

guidelines for evaluating the effectiveness of mathematics instructional materials ask researchers to present evidence that provides "reliable and valid indicators of the extent, quality, and type of the implementation of the materials" (National Research Council Committee for a Review of the Evaluation Data on the Effectiveness of NSF-Supported and Commercially Generated Mathematics Curriculum Materials, 2004, p. 6). The guidelines mention the importance of documenting content coverage and the extent of professional development provided but go no further in describing what "extent, quality, and type" actually mean. This lack of detail presents a challenge for researchers, who rely on these frameworks to guide the development of measurement constructs. Consequently, the lack of clarity stands in the way of developing a cumulative body of knowledge.

THE INNOVATION IMPLEMENTATION FRAMEWORK: A COMPONENT APPROACH

Recognizing the limitations of existing conceptual frameworks (see Century et al., 2010, for a discussion of our consideration of Dane & Schneider's 1998 work), we developed the innovation implementation framework. Our framework development process was guided by the premise that educational interventions have both implicit and explicit models that comprise a set of components thought to be essential to implementation of the interventions (Bauman, Stein, & Ireys, 1991; Ruiz-Primo, 2005; Wang et al., 1984). Thus, we define *innovation implementation* as the extent to which innovation components are in use at a particular moment in time. Our framework (see Table 4.2) then categorizes those program components into conceptually coherent groups.

As we developed our framework, we were careful to attend to already existing approaches. For example, we considered frameworks that reflect a "structure/process" dichotomy for organizing program elements. Mowbray et al. (2003) organized fidelity criteria into two groups: "framework for service delivery" (structure) and "the ways in which services are delivered" (process). Similarly, Wang et al. (1984) categorized program elements "related to resources" (structural) and those related to "roles and behaviors" (process). We created the innovation implementation conceptual framework through an iterative process that took these frameworks and other previous work (e.g., Dane & Schneider, 1998; Dusenbury, Brannigan, Falco, & Hansen, 2003; Lastica & O'Donnell, 2007; Mowbray et al., 2003) into account. The innovation implementation conceptual framework can be applied across multiple innovations and, through its applicability and component approach, can improve ability to accumulate knowledge in the field.

The innovation implementation conceptual framework (see Table 4.2) appears simple, but the spare foundation provides an adaptable structure for describing and measuring very complex innovations. We organize program components into two broad categories: structural and interactional. *Structural* components include the organizational, design, and support elements that are the building blocks of the innovation. These components are further divided into two subcategories: *Structural–procedural* components are the organizing steps and design elements of the innovation, and *structural–educative* components are the support elements that communicate what the user needs to know to implement the innovation. The *interactional* components include the behaviors, interactions, and practices of innovation "users" during enactment and are organized to reflect user groups. User groups can include teachers, school leaders, students, partners, and others, depending on the innovation,

TABLE 4.2
The Innovation Implementation Conceptual Framework

Innovation implementation framework				
Structural components		Interactional components		
Structural–procedural	Structural–educative	User Group 1	User Group 2	User Group 3

its design, and components in the model. See Century et al. (2010) for more details on the framework development and component identification. For an instructional materials innovation, for example, the *structural–procedural* components include organizational and design elements such as time spent on instruction, lesson order, materials presence, use of reading and writing structures, and various instructional delivery formats (e.g., discussion, games, student interaction with materials). The *structural–educative* components, on the other hand, include the information and skills users need to enact an instructional materials innovation as intended (e.g., background information on content, pedagogy, national standards). The *interactional* components also fall into categories, organized by groups of users (i.e., teachers and learners). *Interactional–pedagogical* components include the actions, behaviors, and interactions that teachers are expected to engage in when enacting the intervention, and *interactional–learner engagement* components represent the actions, behaviors, and interactions that learners are expected to engage in when participating in the enactment of the intervention (see Table 4.3). A second type of innovation—the STEM (science, technology, engineering, and mathematics) school model—illustrates how the same framework adapts to a slightly more complex innovation. In this case, the structural components categories remain, but the interactional components expand to include the interactions that take place at the whole-school level and at the learning experience level (note that we did not say classroom level, because learning experiences happen within and outside of classroom walls in these schools). This framework yielded six user groups: all staff (school level), students (school level), school leaders (school level), partners (at the school level), teachers (learning experience level), and students (learning experience level). In some cases, the structural components would increase to reflect different levels of the innovation as well. One can extrapolate from these two examples that this approach can apply to even more complex innovations that operate at three or more levels. Consider that there is potentially a set of structural (procedural structures, educative supports) and interactional (user/participant/stakeholder) components at each level of an innovation.

Not all innovations will have similar numbers of components across all categories. For example, some innovations are more focused on interactions, and others are more structural; some focus on particular user groups more than others. Due to the clarity of component definitions and placement of components in the framework, the innovation implementation conceptual framework allows for a conceptually sound component approach. This approach will (a) bring more specificity to implementation descriptions, (b) facilitate cross program learning, and (c) allow for the accumulation of implementation knowledge across innovations.

TABLE 4.3
The Innovation Implementation Conceptual Framework Applied to Two Innovations

	Innovation implementation framework							
	Structural components		Interactional components					
			School level				Learning experience level	
	Structural procedural	Structural educative	All staff	Students	School leaders	Partners	Interactional pedagogical	Interactional learner engagement
Innovation 1: Instructional materials	Structural procedural	Structural educative	N/A				Teachers	Students
Innovation 2: STEM school model	Structural procedural	Structural educative	All staff	Students	School leaders	Partners	Teachers	Students

Note. STEM = Science, technology, engineering, and mathematics.

THE FACTOR FRAMEWORK: ORGANIZING CONTEXTS AND CONDITIONS THAT AFFECT THE IMPLEMENTATION PROCESS

The development of the innovation implementation conceptual framework led to approaches for describing and measuring innovation implementation. We consider innovation implementation to be the extent to which innovation components are in use at a particular moment in time. As noted above, however, it is important to understand not only what was implemented but also why implementation occurs as it does; that is, the *implementation process*. We consider implementation process to be innovation implementation in the context of all of the factors that contribute to and inhibit implementation and their ongoing interactions over time. As noted by Sanetti and Kratochwill (2009), measuring the relationships between dimensions of innovation implementation and variables known to mediate or moderate the effects of an innovation has received limited attention in the literature. Our recognition of this problem and the importance of addressing the "why" of implementation process was at the heart of the factor study.

In that study, we identified individual, organizational, and contextual factors that appeared to influence the extent to which users enacted key innovation components. This work moved beyond the boundaries of conventional implementation studies because it sought to identify not only the factors affecting implementation but also those that have an impact on innovation *spread*, the movement of innovation implementation from one user (individual or organizational) to another, and *sustainability*, innovation implementation over time.

The factor study began with an extensive literature search and review (Century, Cassata, et al., 2012). Using a range of search terms related to sustainability and innovation, our team retrieved 69,801 abstracts from the fields of education, public health, marketing, business, and economics. We reviewed the abstracts to yield 657 sources to be reviewed, with 572 of these sources retrievable. Each source was coded, and the themes we identified evolved into a preliminary list of over 25 factors and processes that the sources suggested affect innovation implementation and sustainability. We grouped these factors and processes into categories and began mapping out relationships. (For more information on this work, refer to http://cemse.uchicago.edu/research-and-evaluation).

As we operationalized the factors into measures (Century, Cassata, Rudnick, & Freeman, 2012), we discussed and refined specific definitions of each factor. This process sometimes resulted in a shift in the framework categories and at other times in a reorganization of factors. We continued with this iterative process until we arrived at the first draft of our factor framework. As we continued to revise this framework, we began to systematically review other implementation frameworks (e.g., Domitrovich et al., 2008; Fixsen et al., 2005; Wandersman et al., 2008). This process further informed our framework development and revisions until we arrived at the current factor framework described in Appendix 4.1.

Our factor framework has four broad categories that, like other frameworks (e.g., Domitrovich et al., 2008; Fixsen et al., 2005; Sanetti & Kratochwill, 2009), suggest that innovations reside in the embedded systems by which they are enacted by individual users who function within organizations that exist within a larger environmental context. Our categories include (a) characteristics of the innovation, (b) characteristics of individual users (e.g., teachers, students, leadership), (c) characteristics of the organization (e.g., classroom, school, health center), and (d) elements of the environment external to the organization (e.g., district, state, community). We have also identified a fifth category, (e) enacted networks, which describes the nature and extent to which interactions occur among individuals in different organizations. This factor is unique in that it exists across two of our broad categories, in the space between elements of the environment and characteristics of the user. We created subcategories and more specific definitions for each of the factors within these broad categories.

In the special case of leaders as users, rather than list all leadership characteristics, we identified leadership characteristics that were specific to the innovations we were examining. We recognize that leaders have many characteristics that could influence innovation implementation and that these might shift, depending on the innovation. With regard to organizational factors, the "characteristics related to people in the organization" are characteristics that reside in individuals but come together as a collective characteristic of the organization as a whole. For example, an individual may have a strong sense of self-efficacy (e.g., "I can do this practice") about an innovation but not have a strong sense of organizational efficacy (e.g., "I can do this practice, but as an organization my school cannot"). Another necessary clarification in the organizational factor category is that our factors *information sharing, information sufficiency* and *collaboration* are sometimes grouped by others into larger categories that they refer to as *organizational climate* or *operational network*. Along similar lines, our factor *shared beliefs and values* is what others might refer to as *organizational culture*. We choose to use the more specific terms with the intention of bringing more clarity to communication and measurement.

Finally, note that we account for factors falling into more than one category in our factor framework. For example, innovativeness is present in three places: (a) as a characteristic of an individual, (b) as a special characteristic of leadership, and (c) as an organizational characteristic. Similarly, learning opportunities may originate both from within the organization and from outside of the organization, so we place opportunities for learning and utility of opportunities for learning in more than one category and define and measure them separately.

The implementation literature demonstrates, with regard to spread and sustainability, that whereas some have measured innovation implementation, many fewer have monitored spread or persistence (Hargreaves & Goodson, 2006). Simply put, "there is a paucity of field-based, empirical research that focuses intensively on the issues revolving around the question of whether or not . . . changes can and will be institutionalized in schools" (Prestine, 2000, p. 126). Taking this into consideration, we have shaped our work with the view that if we are to understand innovation implementation and the implementation process, we need to do so while taking into account of both short- and long-term time frames.

Some implementation frameworks address the issue of time by including *stages of implementation*. Fixsen et al. (2005), for example, described an implementation process with discernible stages, including initial exploration and the decision to adopt something new, program installation or start-up, initial implementation, and full operation. We agree with their suggestion that different factors and combinations of factors influence implementation depending on the length of time that an innovation has been in place. We differ, however, in that we do not focus on identifying stages of implementation overall; rather, we focus on innovation implementation as a continuous evolutionary process within which innovation components change over time as a result of surrounding factors.

Given this evolutionary point of view, sustaining an innovation is a far more complex process than embedding a program, as designed, into an existing system so that all of its elements become standard practice. Sustainability is, by its nature, a continuous process of adaptation (Century & Levy, 2002). This is where the intersection of the innovation implementation conceptual framework and the factor framework come together to create a comprehensive landscape for measuring implementation process. Together, these frameworks support clear measurement of implementation of innovation components and the factors that affect innovation implementation over time.

APPLICATION OF THE INNOVATION IMPLEMENTATION AND FACTOR FRAMEWORKS

We hope that measuring the enactment of educational innovations and the factors that affect them will contribute to a growing theoretical base for understanding how and why innovations are implemented and sustained. Thus, after completing our first cycle of theory and framework development, we set out to operationalize these ideas in collaborative research with school-based practitioners. We developed two additional NSF-supported studies. The first study, "The Ohio STEM Learning Network: A Study of Factors Affecting Implementation, Spread and Sustainability" (2010–2013; referred to hereafter as the *STEM school study*), as referenced earlier in the description of our innovation implementation conceptual framework, focuses on the STEM school model, a school-wide innovation. Therefore, this innovation has program elements that exist at the school level and the "learning experience" level as well as expectations for interactions of partners and community members.

The second study, "Factors That Affect Implementation, Spread, and Sustainability: An Implementation Study of Everyday Mathematics" (2011–2014; referred to hereafter as the *EM study*), focuses on the implementation of *Everyday Mathematics* (EM), an instructional materials program for elementary mathematics, within four school districts that have been implementing the program for a range of years. The differences in years of implementation afford us the opportunity not only to measure and describe the status of EM implementation but also to identify and measure the factors that contribute to and inhibit implementation and sustainability of EM at different points in the implementation process.

We consider these studies "sister studies" in that they are rooted in the same early work and theory. They differ, however, by what the innovation is, which provides the opportunity to consider the factors in the "characteristics of the innovation" category (see Appendix 4.1). Although two studies is only a small first step in understanding the role that characteristics of the innovation play in the implementation process, together they enable us to consider the differences in innovations and contribute to a more robust and further developed theory than either study could provide on its own.

Measuring the Enactment of STEM School Models: The STEM School Study

The STEM school study focuses on describing the implementation of the STEM school model across five STEM platform schools in Ohio. *Platform schools* are specifically designed to be sources of communication and spread of new practices to other schools. Thus, in this study we focused on (a) understanding implementation of the STEM school model at each school and (b) measuring and understanding the presence of factors that affect innovation implementation and spread. This study provided us with the opportunity to build from our earlier frameworks in two ways. First, this was our first opportunity to operationalize our innovation implementation conceptual framework for a school-level innovation and to use it in a focused implementation study. Second, this project provided us with the opportunity to operationalize the factor framework into measurable constructs and data collection instruments.

Innovation Implementation Measurement

To measure enactment of the STEM school model innovation, we used a component identification process that we had developed in the implementation study described at the beginning of this chapter. This process entailed reviewing innovation materials, speaking with developers, and talking with users (for more on this process, see Century et al., 2010). Throughout, we used the innovation implementation conceptual framework to organize the structural and interactional critical components that STEM school leaders identified as essential. Because this innovation was at both a school-wide and a learning experience (classroom) level, we included interactions for all user/ participant groups at each of these levels (see Table 4.2).

The current list of STEM school model components can be found online (http://researcherswithoutborders.org/projects/understanding-stem-schools/components). Using this set of components and the instruments developed in the implementation study (see http://cemse.uchicago.edu/research-and-evaluation), we developed a suite of instruments to measure the presence of the STEM school model innovation implementation. The suite of instruments includes (a) a teacher instructional questionnaire, (b) a teacher interview protocol, (c) a school observation protocol, (d) a school leader interview protocol, (e) a student questionnaire, and (f) a student focus group protocol.

Factor Measurement

We developed instruments to measure the factors in the factor frame-work concurrently with our identification of the STEM school model components and associated instruments. The factor instrument development process was an essential step in gaining clarity about (a) the definition of each factor, (b) confirmation of the place of each factor in the framework, and (c) measurement of each factor. Prior to this work, there was no set of tools that measured the range of factors within the factor framework. Rather, there were many tools, most of which focused on only one or two factors but measured them very much in depth. To consider the relative impact of factors on innovation implementation, however, we had to develop tools that could measure the range of factors that might influence implementation and spread in a way that was practical and unobtrusive for our practitioner collaborators.

We measured factors with a suite of instruments, including (a) factor questionnaires for teachers, (b) interview protocols (for school partners, teachers, and school leaders) and focus group protocols (for teachers and students), and (c) a school visit observation protocol. Students did not have a separate factor questionnaire; rather, they had one questionnaire with both component and factor items. Not all factors are measured in all instruments; instead, we made decisions about the best ways to measure each of the factors to best account for them in our analysis.

Measuring the Enactment of Mathematics Instructional Materials: The EM Study

The EM study was a direct outgrowth of the implementation study described in the introduction, and it built on the innovation implementation instruments developed as part of the implementation study. We began with the initial set of EM components identified in the implementation study and refined them and their definitions so that they could be more clearly and appropriately measured. Then, with the updated set of EM components, we revised the implementation study instruments and combined them with the factor instruments developed in the STEM school study so that we could collect data on the entire implementation process. (See http://cemse.uchicago.edu/research-and-evaluation/research/ to review our current framework for measuring the implementation of EM, including the complete list of components and their definitions.)

Analysis of Implementation

We are currently in the process of examining a range of ways to analyze our innovation implementation and implementation process data for both the STEM school study and the EM study. We have conducted preliminary analyses for the STEM school study that have included exploratory factor analyses to identify component indices using teacher questionnaire data. The analysis resulted in one to four indices for each component category. We are considering using these indices to create an implementation "profile" for teachers that would include index scores for each component category. We anticipate that users of educational innovations will vary in the extent to which they enact components within each of the categories. Thus, different users will have different profiles represented as a set of index scores. We will conduct similar analyses in the EM study. In this case, we expect to have enough teachers so that we can further cluster them into implementation "types." We are also exploring ways to represent implementation profiles and types using data visualization. Creating ways to represent implementation types is at the heart of our analysis work using this approach and among the potential important contributions this work can make.

With the identification of implementation types, we can take our analyses in two further directions. In the case of our EM study, we will examine relationships between implementation types and student outcomes. These analyses will shed light on which combinations of innovation components are related to desired student outcomes and, of these components, which are in fact most critical. Further, in both the EM and the STEM school studies, we will examine the impact of the presence of factors on innovation implementation. We will have data on the presence of factors that affect individual and organizational use of an innovation and will examine the relationships between factors and the implementation types.

ISSUES TO CONSIDER DURING IMPLEMENTATION STUDIES

Even with strong conceptual frameworks and systematic data collection approaches, implementation studies still face some persistent challenges. There are no single answers to these challenges, but making principled decisions about how to handle them is essential. We discuss two such challenges in this section.

Measuring Innovation Fidelity Versus Measuring Innovation Use

The implementation study began with the intention to create instruments for measuring "fidelity of implementation" of instructional materials. As we proceeded with the work, however, we came to recognize that there is a difference between measuring "fidelity" and measuring "use," or what we refer to more specifically as *innovation implementation*. The instruments derived from our innovation implementation conceptual framework measure the status of component enactment at a given time. From those data we can determine the status of implementation, or what we refer to above as an *implementation profile* (or, with a different analytic approach, an *implementation type*). Our approach is well suited for the kinds of research questions we ask that focus on understanding how users actually enact innovations in real settings and the relationships between those enactments, the factors that affect them, and outcomes. Put more simply, our primary interest is in questions of "use."

Notwithstanding our primary interests, the instruments and resulting data can also be used to examine questions of fidelity. In those cases, the primary questions focus on examining relationships between the current status of implementation and an ideal. To be clear, fidelity studies analyze the relationships between actual enactment (e.g., implementation profiles or types) and a theoretically ideal enactment. Implementation process studies, on the other hand, examine the ways innovations are used in practice, the impact of contextual factors on enactment, and the extent to which particular enactments have strong relationships to desired outcomes.

This difference, though sometimes nuanced, is important to explicitly discuss. The fidelity perspective prevails within the literature, described with a range of terms, including *treatment integrity* (Sanetti & Kratochwill, 2009), *program integrity* (Dane & Schneider, 1998), *program adherence* (Dusenbury et al., 2003; Ruiz-Primo, 2005), *fidelity of implementation* (O'Donnell, 2008), *treatment fidelity* (Hulleman & Cordray, 2009), and *implementation quality* (Domitrovich et al., 2008). All have an underlying theme that focuses on the space between the program "in theory" and the program "as applied" in a given context. Implied in these labels is the notion that a user should be enacting a program "ideally," or as intended by the developer (Durlak, 2010; O'Donnell, 2008).

We agree that in the context of intervention development or efficacy or effectiveness testing, the standard should be one of fidelity. However, our work has focused on implementation in real settings that have widely varied conditions and contexts. In these settings, the enactment of innovation components will necessarily vary by individual, organizational, and environmental factors. In these cases, the question of what is "ideal" becomes an empirical one, borne out only by examining relationships between the enacted intervention and outcomes in those settings.

Further, from a practical perspective, researchers widely acknowledge that teachers rarely implement a program exactly as written, and some suggest that principled adaptations made by high-quality teachers can yield improved outcomes. We agree with Sanetti and Kratochwill (2009) and Durlak and DuPre (2008), who suggested that "high" fidelity or "more" fidelity does not necessarily lead to improved outcomes. In certain circumstances, adaptations or deviations from the original model may in fact have a positive effect if they make the intervention more contextually relevant.

This point of view further affirms the merits of a component approach to measuring innovation implementation. Treating an innovation as a whole and expecting a group of educators to implement all components with high fidelity is sensible only if there are sufficient data to support that the components that constitute that innovation are effective with that particular population in that particular context. A component approach supports efforts to understand which parts of the program work and why. There may even be a critical threshold of innovation implementation above which increased implementation does not meaningfully influence outcomes. Only with more clear and specific data about components and a framework for organizing and accumulating findings about those components will researchers be able to determine with more confidence which innovation components are "critical" and should be implemented with "high fidelity" and which can or should be adapted.

Establishing Boundaries of the Innovation: What Is the "It"

As we applied the framework to a range of innovations that differ in complexity, scope, and specificity, we found it necessary to be conceptually clear about the boundaries between the innovation itself (the "it") and the factors that influence innovation implementation. On first glance, this task may not seem difficult, but a careful look at a range of innovations reveals that innovation elements can shift from being innovation components to being factors that affect the implementation process, depending on where the developers (and in some cases the users) of the innovation draw the boundary. For example, when considering the use of instructional materials, many recognize the importance of professional development support (Arbaugh, Lannin, Jones, & Park-Rogers, 2006; Kent, Pligge, & Spence, 2003; Krebs & Burgis, 2003; SRI International, Center for Technology in Learning, 2009). In some cases, a professional development strategy and plan is part of the innovation, along with the instructional materials themselves. In the case of our EM study, however, professional development is not part of the innovation. Rather, professional development (referred to as *opportunities for learning* in the factor framework) is a factor that affects the implementation process.

The issue of where to draw the boundary around the intervention is not only one of measurement; it is also a concern as we build our conceptual frameworks for innovation implementation and the innovation process. Some theories of implementation have frameworks that include both the innovation and the surrounding factors (e.g., Domitrovich et al., 2008; Fixsen et al., 2005; Wandersman et al., 2008). We agree that measuring contexts and conditions is key to understanding the implementation process. However, we believe that the lack of coherency in the field regarding descriptions of implementation is exacerbated by the blurring of innovation and factor boundaries. Our approach clearly separates the innovation implementation components and the factors affecting the implementation process.

CONCLUSION

We seek to move the field forward toward specific measures of innovation implementation and the implementation process. Our innovation implementation and factor frameworks (and the instruments that are grounded in them) provide sound tools for specifically and rigorously answering the questions of "what works, why, and under what circumstances." By explicitly measuring the enactment of innovation components and the factors that influence their enactment, our tools provide an improved way to understand why programs are enacted as they are and why certain aspects of programs do or do not endure. Our approach provides sound conceptual organization while also supporting collection of a wide range of data that informs initial development of statistical models to explain program implementation in ways that reflect the complex reality of the contexts in which educational innovations are enacted.

We hope that, through these efforts, we can ultimately bring coherency to research on innovation implementation and the implementation process. We wish to establish a strong starting point for developing common language and shared conceptual understanding and even perhaps some shared measures. With these tools, researchers and practitioners can, together, make progress toward bringing strategic, impactful, and lasting improvements to schools.

APPENDIX 4.1
Factors, Processes, and Mechanisms That Influence the Implementation, Spread, and Sustainability of Educational Innovations

Characteristics of the innovation	Attributes of an innovation that are uninfluenced by other factors at a given point in time
Complexity	Number of an innovation's parts and extent of their interdependence
Specificity	Level of detail in which the operationalization of an innovation is described
Adaptability	A combination of complexity and specificity
Scope	Innovation's target area(s) within the field of education
Empirical effectiveness	Evidence that an innovation accomplishes desired outcomes
Results demonstrability	Extent to which the impacts of an innovation can be communicated/shown to others
Age	Total time an innovation has been in existence in the context of the setting
Duration	Number of years that an innovation has been enacted in a particular setting and/or the stage of enactment (e.g., "start-up," "maintenance")
In the context of the innovation	
Self-efficacy	Competency and confidence in the user's (or potential user's) own abilities to enact the innovation
Understanding of the innovation	Extent to which a user (or potential user) understands the strategies, components, and goals of an innovation

Factors, Processes, and Mechanisms That Influence the Implementation,
Spread, and Sustainability of Educational Innovations *(Continued)*

Characteristics of individual users	Attributes of users (or potential users) of the innovation. Users include teachers, administrators, school leaders, policymakers, students, and others.
Attitude toward the innovation	Extent to which the user (or potential user) is in favor of (or not) use of the innovation
Attitudes toward things related to the innovation	Enjoyment of topics/areas related to the innovation (also related to intrinsic motivation)
Intrinsic motivation	Influence on an individual's decision making that comes from the level of enjoyment of or sense of ownership toward an innovation as well as the sense of commitment to or trust in the innovation and/or those leading it
Extrinsic motivation	Influence on an individual's decision making that comes from external incentives (e.g., to gain recognition, money, and power) or from negative consequences from an external source (e.g., to avoid being penalized)

Not in the context of the innovation

Innovativeness	Extent to which a user (or potential user) seeks out, creates, and/or enacts new ways of doing things
Resourcefulness and coping	Ability of a user (or potential user) to combat stress and persist with difficult goals/tasks
Networkedness	Tendency for an individual to participate in a social network (inside or outside the organization). Example for inside the organization: level of social participation (e.g., attendance at meetings, density of network). Example for outside the organization: number of links a person has outside the organization (Greenhalgh, Robert, Macfarlane, Bate, & Kyriakidou, 2004).
Time management and organizational skills	The act or process of planning and exercising conscious control over the amount of time spent on specific activities, especially to increase efficiency or productivity The skills enable people to plan and carry on activities effectively (i.e., to put order to a situation, objects, or people).

(continues)

Factors, Processes, and Mechanisms That Influence the Implementation,
Spread, and Sustainability of Educational Innovations *(Continued)*

Characteristics of individual users	Attributes of users (or potential users) of the innovation. Users include teachers, administrators, school leaders, policymakers, students, and others.

User perceptions of the innovation

Perceived adaptability	User's (or potential user's) perceptions of an innovation's permissible flexibility
Perceived visibility	Extent to which a user or potential user has seen or heard about the innovation
Ease of use	User's (or potential user's) perceptions of an innovation's ease of implementation
Perceived effectiveness	User's (or potential user's) impression that an innovation accomplishes desired outcomes

Descriptive characteristics of the individual user

Demographic	Includes gender, age, SES
Education	Includes formal education and training
Experience	Includes number of years in position and/or experience with the innovation

Characteristics of the organization	Attributes of the organization in which the innovation resides. The "organization" can be any size (e.g., state network, district, school, classroom).

Characteristics related to people in the organization

Organizational innovativeness	Extent to which users perceive that their organization is a place that seeks out, creates, and/or enacts new ways of doing things
Organizational efficacy	Extent to which people in the organization perceive it as being competent at and capable of implementing the innovation
Clarity of organizational goals	Extent to which people in the organization perceive the intended direction of the organization as it pertains to the innovation is clear
Collaboration[a]	Extent to which people in the organization perceive that interactions between individuals in an organization are rooted in trust, are mutually beneficial, and make progress toward a goal
Information sufficiency	Extent to which people in the organization perceive that the organization shares information about the innovation that is sufficient for individuals to enact their roles

Factors, Processes, and Mechanisms That Influence the Implementation,
Spread, and Sustainability of Educational Innovations   *(Continued)*

Characteristics of the organization	Attributes of the organization in which the innovation resides. The "organization" can be any size (e.g., state network, district, school, classroom).
Information sharing	Extent to which people in the organization feel that information sharing about the innovation takes place within the organization
Shared beliefs and values[b]	Extent to which people in the organization perceive that the norms, values and beliefs about education are shared by individuals in an organization and the extent to which this perception engenders trust (Domitrovich et al., 2008)
Locus of decision making	Extent to which individuals perceive they are involved in decision-making processes
Resources	Extent to which users feel they have enough resources (financial, material, human) to implement the innovation
Time	Extent to which users feel they have enough time to implement the innovation
Utility of opportunities for learning inside the organization	Extent to which users feel the opportunities for learning inside the organization are useful
Utility of opportunities for learning in the environment	Extent to which users feel the opportunities for learning outside the organization are useful
Personal support	Extent to which users feel they have sufficient personal and emotional support. In the cases of particular innovations, users can include students
Instructional leadership	Extent to which the leadership and others communicate knowledge, expertise, and understanding about the innovation content and pedagogy
Innovation advocacy	Extent to which the leadership visibly and vocally communicates about the merits and benefits of the innovation
Leadership innovativeness	Extent to which the leadership seeks out and enacts new ways of doing things throughout the organization

Descriptive characteristics of the organization	
Organizational structures	Formal rules, policies, and guidelines for operations of an organization in which an innovation resides. Includes decision-making structures, reporting structures, and supervisory structures.

(continues)

Factors, Processes, and Mechanisms That Influence the Implementation,
Spread, and Sustainability of Educational Innovations *(Continued)*

Characteristics of the organization	Attributes of the organization in which the innovation resides. The "organization" can be any size (e.g., state network, district, school, classroom).
Financial resource allocation	Distribution of financial resources to the innovation relative to the financial resources available
Physical environment	Characteristics of the physical space in which the innovation is enacted
Population characteristics	Demographic, education, and experience of the whole organizational population. These characteristics also include organization size, student mobility, and staff turnover.
Extraneous events, initiatives, and/or incidents	Events or initiatives that occur within the organization that can cause distraction from or support for the innovation
Stakeholder community support	The human, material, and other resources provided by the community of individuals and organizations invested in the success of the organization (e.g., volunteers, partners, families)
Presence of opportunities for learning inside the organization	Extent to which sources of growth and development for users (including leaders) of an innovation are present inside the organization
Organizational strategies	
Ongoing improvement structures	Includes planning (ongoing strategizing about the continuation of an innovation) and formative evaluation (ongoing evaluation that provides users with data intended to inform decision making about an innovation)
Leveraging	One organization capitalizing on another organization's resources, contacts, or practices across participants in the network
Dissemination	Steps taken to actively share the innovation with others
Implementation strategy	Population in number and category of participants in the innovation at any given point in time
Family/community/stakeholder communication	Extent to which individuals in the organization share information about the innovation with family members, community members, and/or other stakeholders

Factors, Processes, and Mechanisms That Influence the Implementation,
Spread, and Sustainability of Educational Innovations *(Continued)*

Elements of the environment	Attributes of the environment surrounding the organization in which the innovation resides
Political environment	The policies, guidelines, and rules outside the organization that can affect implementation and spread of the innovation (district mandates are included here)
Community beliefs and values	Extent to which the population (e.g., community, parents) surrounding the organization in which the innovation resides has beliefs and values that pertain to education and/or the innovation
Descriptive characteristics of the community	Includes community size, SES, and geographic region
Presence of opportunities for learning in the environment	Extent to which sources of growth and development for users (including leaders) of an innovation are present outside the organization
Network structures	Intentionally designed opportunities for interactions between individuals in different organizations
Descriptive visibility	Evidence of the innovation in places where it can be seen or heard
Extraneous events or initiatives	Events that occur around the organization that can cause distraction from the innovation
Networks	Networks exist in the space between elements of the environment and characteristics of the user.
Enacted networks	Nature and extent to which interactions occur between individuals in different organizations

Note. Fit: One approach to processing the interactions of factors is to consider the concept of "fit." There are three kinds of "fit": fit with needs, fit with current practice, and fit with values and beliefs. If an innovation meets all areas of fit, a user is much more likely to use it. However, that is seldom the case. More often, the range of factors influencing a user's decision to enact an innovation create a conflict between the three kinds of fit that then can stand in the way of change. SES = socioeconomic status.
[a]Collaboration, information sufficiency, and information sharing constitute what some refer to as *organizational climate.*
[b]Some people refer to this as *organizational culture.*

REFERENCES

Arbaugh, F., Lannin, J., Jones, D. L., & Park-Rogers, M. (2006). Examining instructional practices in Core-Plus lessons: Implications for professional development. *Journal of Mathematics Teacher Education, 9,* 517–550. doi:1007/s10857-006-9019-3

Bauman, L. J., Stein, R. E. K., & Ireys, H. T. (1991). Reinventing fidelity: The transfer of social technology among settings. *American Journal of Community Psychology, 19,* 619–639. doi:10.1007/BF00937995

Bond, G., Williams, J., Evans, L., Salyers, M., Kim, H.-W., Sharpe, H., & Leff, H. S. (2000). *Psychiatric rehabilitation fidelity toolkit.* Cambridge, MA: Human Services Research Institute.

Century, J., Cassata, A., Freeman, C., & Rudnick, M. (2012, April). *Measuring implementation, spread and sustainability of educational innovations: Innovating for coordinated collaborative research.* Paper presented at the meeting of the American Educational Research Association, Vancouver, British Columbia, Canada.

Century, J., Cassata, A., Rudnick, M., & Freeman, C. (2012). Measuring enactment of innovations and the factors that affect implementation and sustainability: Moving toward common language and shared conceptual understanding. *Journal of Behavioral Health Services & Research, 39,* 343–361. doi:10.1007/s11414-012-9287-x

Century, J., & Levy, A. J. (2002). Sustaining your reform: Five lessons from research. *Benchmarks, 3*(3), 1–7. Retrieved from http://sustainability2003.terc.edu/media/data/media_000000000208.pdf

Century, J., Rudnick, M., & Freeman, C. (2010). A framework for measuring fidelity of implementation: A foundation for shared language and accumulation of knowledge. *American Journal of Evaluation, 31,* 199–218. doi:10.1177/1098214010366173

Cranney, M., Warren, E., Barton, S., Gardner, K., & Walley, T. (2001). Why do GPs not implement evidence-based guidelines? A descriptive study. *Family Practice, 18,* 359–363. doi:10.1093/fampra/18.4.359

Dane, A. V., & Schneider, B. H. (1998). Program integrity in primary and early secondary prevention: Are implementation effects out of control? *Clinical Psychology Review, 18,* 23–45. doi:10.1016/S0272-7358(97)00043-3

Domitrovich, C. E., Bradshaw, C. P., Poduska, J. M., Hoagwood, K., Buckley, J. A., Olin, S., . . . Ialongo, N. S. (2008). Maximizing the implementation quality of evidence-based preventive interventions in schools: A conceptual framework. *Advances in School Mental Health Promotion, 1*(3), 6–28. doi:10.1080/1754730X.2008.9715730

Durlak, J. A. (2010). The importance of doing well in whatever you do: A commentary on the special section, "Implementation research in early childhood education." *Early Childhood Research Quarterly, 25,* 348–357. doi:10.1016/j.ecresq.2010.03.003

Durlak, J. A., & DuPre, E. P. (2008). Implementation matters: A review of research on the influence of implementation on program outcomes and the factors affecting implementation. *American Journal of Community Psychology, 41*, 327–350. doi:10.1007/s10464-008-9165-0

Dusenbury, L., Brannigan, R., Falco, M., & Hansen, W. B. (2003). A review of research on fidelity of implementation: Implications for drug abuse prevention in school settings. *Health Education Research, 18*, 237–256. doi:10.1093/her/18.2.237

Fixsen, D. L., Naoom, S. F., Blase, K., Friedman, R. M., & Wallace, F. (2005). *Implementation research: A synthesis of the literature*. Tampa: University of South Florida, Louis de la Parte Florida Mental Health Institute, National Implementation Research Network.

Fullan, M. (1983). Evaluating program implementation: What can be learned from follow through. *Curriculum Inquiry, 13*, 215–227. doi:10.2307/1179640

Greenhalgh, T., Robert, G., Macfarlane, F., Bate, P., & Kyriakidou, O. (2004). Diffusion of innovations in service organizations: Systematic review and recommendations. *Milbank Quarterly, 82*, 581–629. doi:10.1111/j.0887-378X.2004.00325.x

Hall, G. E., & Hord, S. M. (1987). *Change in schools: Facilitating the process*. New York: State University of New York Press.

Hargreaves, A., & Goodson, I. (2006). Educational change over time? The sustainability and non-sustainability of three decades of secondary school change and continuity. *Educational Administration Quarterly, 42*, 3–41. doi:10.1177/0013161X05277975

Hulleman, C. S., & Cordray, D. S. (2009). Moving from the lab to the field: The role of fidelity and achieved relative intervention strength. *Journal of Research on Educational Effectiveness, 2*, 88–110. doi:10.1080/19345740802539325

Huntley, M. A. (2005). *Operationalizing the concept of "fidelity of implementation" for NSF-funded mathematics curricula*. Unpublished manuscript.

Kent, L. B., Pligge, M., & Spence, M. (2003). Enhancing teacher knowledge through curriculum reform. *Middle School Journal, 34*(4), 42–46.

Krebs, A. S., & Burgis, K. (2003). Using standards-based curriculum materials: A professional development model. *Journal of Mathematics Education Leadership, 6*(2), 8–12.

Lastica, J., & O'Donnell, C. (2007, April). *Considering the role of fidelity of implementation in science education research: Fidelity as teacher and student adherence to structure*. Paper presented at the meeting of the American Educational Research Association, Chicago, IL.

Levy, A. J., Pasquale, M. M., & Marco, L. (2008). Models of providing science instruction in the elementary grades: A research agenda to inform decision makers. *Science Educator, 17*(2), 1–18.

Lynch, S., & O'Donnell, C. (2005). *The evolving definition, measurement, and conceptualization of fidelity of implementation in scale-up of highly rated science curriculum units in diverse middle schools*. Unpublished manuscript.

Mowbray, C. T., Holter, M. C., Teague, G. B., & Bybee, D. (2003). Fidelity criteria: Development, measurement, and validation. *American Journal of Evaluation, 24*, 315–340. doi:10.1177/109821400302400303

National Research Council Committee for a Review of the Evaluation Data on the Effectiveness of NSF-Supported and Commercially Generated Mathematics Curriculum Materials. (2004). *On evaluating curricular effectiveness: Judging the quality of K–12 mathematics evaluations.* Washington, DC: National Academies Press.

O'Donnell, C. L. (2008). Defining, conceptualizing, and measuring fidelity of implementation and its relationship to outcomes in K–12 curriculum intervention research. *Review of Educational Research, 78*, 33–84. doi:10.3102/0034654307313793

Prestine, N. A. (2000). Disposable reform? Assessing the durability of secondary school reform. *Planning and Changing, 31*, 124–147.

Ruiz-Primo, M. A. (2005). *A multi-method and multi-source approach for studying fidelity of implementation* (Tech. Rep. No. 677). Los Angeles, CA: National Center for Research on Evaluation, Standards, and Student Testing, University of California, Los Angeles.

Sabelli, N., & Dede, C. (2001). Integrating educational research and practice: Reconceptualizing goals and policies: How to make what works work for us? Retrieved from http://www.forschungsnetzwerk.at/downloadpub/2001_sabelli_policy.pdf

Sanetti, L. M. H., & Kratochwill, T. R. (2009). Toward developing a science of treatment integrity: Introduction to the special series. *School Psychology Review, 38*, 445–459.

SRI International, Center for Technology in Learning. (2009). *Systemic vs. one-time teacher professional development: What does research say?* (Research Note 15). Retrieved from http://education.ti.com/sites/UK/downloads/pdf/Research%20Notes%20-%20Ongoing%20vs%20one-time%20PD.pdf

Wandersman, A., Duffy, J., Flaspohler, P., Noonan, R., Lubell, K., Stillman, L., . . . Saul, J. (2008). Bridging the gap between prevention research and practice: The interactive systems framework for dissemination and implementation. *American Journal of Community Psychology, 41*, 171–181. doi:10.1007/s10464-008-9174-z

Wang, M. C., Nojan, M., Strom, C. D., & Walberg, H. J. (1984). The utility of degree of implementation measures in program implementation and evaluation research. *Curriculum Inquiry, 14*, 249–286. doi:10.2307/3202214

5

MEASURING AND ANALYZING TREATMENT INTEGRITY DATA IN RESEARCH

FRANK M. GRESHAM

The accuracy with which interventions are implemented as planned, intended, or programmed is known as *treatment integrity* (Peterson, Homer, & Wonderlich, 1982). The notion of treatment integrity exists across a variety of fields involved with providing treatments or interventions to individuals. In medicine, the concept of treatment compliance, or *treatment adherence*, is an important and problematic issue. In clinical psychology, a common term for this concept is *treatment fidelity*. In applied behavior analysis the term *procedural reliability* has been used, and in the field of rehabilitation and substance abuse the term *program implementation* is common. Although these variations in terminology exist across fields, the concern that treatments or interventions are implemented as planned, intended, or programmed is crucial in documenting that changes in an individual's functioning (medical,

This writing of this chapter was supported by Grants R324A090098 and R324A087113 from the Institute of Educational Science, United States Department of Education.

http://dx.doi.org/10.1037/14275-007
Treatment Integrity: A Foundation for Evidence-Based Practice in Applied Psychology, L. M. H. Sanetti and T. R. Kratochwill (Editors)

psychological, or behavioral) are due to treatments and not to extraneous or confounding variables.

The implementation of evidence-based intervention practices in schools is predicated on the assumption that demonstrable changes in academic or social behavior (i.e., the dependent variable) are related to systematic, manipulated changes in the environment (i.e., the independent variable) and are not due to extraneous variables. The absence of objective and measured specification of an operationally defined independent variable (the "treatment") and its subsequent measured application in a natural environment (e.g., a classroom) compromises any incontrovertible conclusions that might be drawn concerning the relation between a treatment and behavior change (Gresham, 1989; McIntyre, Gresham, DiGennaro, & Reed, 2007). Establishing the accuracy of treatment implementation is a critical aspect of scientific investigation and of the practical application of behavior change strategies or instructional procedures. The ineffectiveness of many instructional or behavioral interventions is likely due to the low accuracy of implementation of these procedures rather than the inert or weak nature of interventions in changing behavior (Gresham, 2009).

My purpose in the current chapter is to describe the evolution of the concept of treatment integrity over the past 30 years and to discuss key issues in the measurement of the treatment integrity construct. A discussion of how lapses in maintaining adequate treatment integrity produce threats to valid inference making in terms of internal, external, and statistical conclusion validity and of construct validity is provided. The chapter concludes with a discussion of technical issues involved in the measurement of the treatment integrity construct.

HISTORICAL CONTEXT OF TREATMENT INTEGRITY

Much of the foundation for treatment integrity can be traced back to the development of naturalistic observation technology in the field of applied behavior analysis. Early laboratory work in operant learning in the animal laboratory used electromechanical recording of response rates in rats and pigeons (Skinner, 1938). In applied settings, however, accurate and reliable measurement of the dependent variable (behavior) had to be based on an adequate observational technology using frequency, rate, or interval-based recording systems. Some years later, a new literature evolved that dealt with threats to the accuracy of dependent variable observation, such as observer reactivity (Romanczyk, Kent, Diament, & O'Leary, 1973), observer biases (O'Leary, Kent, & Kanowitz, 1975), observer drift (Reid, 1970), observational code complexity (Kazdin, 1977), and fluctuations in various reliability estimates (Hartmann, 1977).

Tight experimental control of the independent variable (treatment) is much more difficult in naturalistic settings than in a controlled laboratory setting. The same sources of error and threats to the accuracy of the dependent variable also apply to observation of the independent variable (Peterson et al., 1982). Delivery of the independent variable in naturalistic settings often involves human judgments, and, as such, the accuracy and reliability of these judgments are necessary for drawing valid scientific conclusions regarding the effect of the independent variable on the dependent variable. Johnston and Pennypacker (1993) stated,

> Unfortunately, experimenters cannot assume once implemented, the independent variable will magically remain constant in its characteristics throughout the treatment condition. Any of its features may vary in unplanned and undesirable ways for one reason or another, which might lead to variability in the data. This means that *experimenters must take steps to insure that the independent variable (as well as the condition in which it is embedded) is maintained exactly as intended* [emphasis added]. This can be a considerable challenge, especially in applied research, in which the independent variable is often a complex condition involving the behavior of others. (p. 194)

Inadequate assessment and implementation of the independent variable may result in faulty conclusions about the relationship between the independent variable and the dependent variable. In fact, Peterson et al. (1982) suggested that a "curious double standard" has evolved in applied behavior analysis, in which certain variables always have operational definitions and some measure of interobserver agreement when the behavior is a dependent variable but not when the observer behavior serves as an independent variable. Research consumers would be unlikely to accept a researcher's claim that the target behavior changed when the treatment was applied if no data on behavior rate were presented to verify this claim. In contrast, a large majority of published research studies in applied behavior analysis, psychotherapy outcome research, interventions for children with specific learning disabilities, and treatment programs for children with autism spectrum disorders fail to report data on the degree to which these various treatments were implemented as planned, intended, or programmed (Gresham, Gansle, Noell, Cohen, & Rosenblum, 1993; Gresham, MacMillan, Beebe-Frankenberger, & Bocian, 2000; McIntyre et al., 2007; Perepletchikova, Treat, & Kazdin, 2007; Wheeler, Baggett, Fox, & Blevins, 2006).

Several studies in the intervention literature highlight the problems associated with not ensuring the accuracy of independent variable delivery. Bernal, Klinnert, and Schultz (1980) showed that parents receiving behavioral parent training reported more child improvement than did parents receiving humanistic counseling, although there were no differences in the observations of child behavior in the two groups. Observation of parents in the two interventions showed that individuals in the behavioral parent training group were not implementing behavioral techniques any more than were parents in the humanistic treatment condition. Wodarski, Feldman, and Pedi (1974) found no effects of a behavioral treatment program and determined that the treatment agents delivering the treatment failed to apply the specific components.

DIMENSIONS OF TREATMENT INTEGRITY

The treatment integrity construct is currently thought of as multidimensional, in contrast with its initial conceptualization as being unidimensional and consisting of adherence to an established treatment protocol (Gresham, 1989; Peterson et al., 1982). Treatment adherence represents a quantitative dimension of treatment integrity because it can be measured in terms of the number or percentage of critical treatment components that are implemented over the course of a treatment. Treatment adherence can be conceptualized as the *accuracy* and *consistency* with which a treatment is implemented. In this view, there are two aspects of treatment adherence: (a) treatment component adherence and (b) session/daily adherence. Table 5.1 depicts an example of how one might present data on these two dimensions of treatment adherence for a social skills intervention implemented twice per week. As shown in Table 5.1, the overall component adherence was 64.3%, with three components being implemented half the time and one component never being implemented. Table 5.1 also shows that daily adherence to the treatment protocol was inconsistent (71.4% vs. 57.1%). Measuring these two aspects of treatment adherence allows one to assess which components are being inconsistently implemented on which days or sessions.

More recently, other dimensions of treatment integrity have evolved in the literature: interventionist competence and treatment differentiation (Nezu & Nezu, 2008; Perepletchikova et al., 2007). *Interventionist competence* refers to the skill and experience of the interventionist in delivering the treatment. Competence in this sense might be best conceptualized as a qualitative dimension of treatment integrity because it reflects judgments of how well a treatment is delivered. *Treatment differentiation* represents theoretical distinctions between different aspects of two or more treatments and how those theoretical differences are represented in treatment delivery. For example, cognitive behavior theory posits that the mechanism accounting for the reduction of anxiety is how an individual perceives or thinks about anxiety-provoking situations and responses. A common technique in cognitive behavior therapy is to challenge thoughts that magnify negative outcomes related to these situations and to replace them with more effective, realistic

TABLE 5.1
Treatment Adherence Data for Social Skills Intervention Implemented Twice per Week

Date: 12/17/11   School: Jones Elementary School   Observer: Sam School Psychologist

Component	Session					Sum	Component adherence
	Monday	Tuesday	Wednesday	Thursday	Friday		
Introduce skill and ask questions about it		X		X		2/2	100%
Define skill and discuss key words		X		0		1/2	50%
Discuss why skill is important		X		0		1/2	50%
Identify skill steps and have student repeat them		X		X		2/2	100%
Model and role-play skill		X		X		2/2	100%
Reinforce occurrences of skill throughout session		0		0		0/0	0%
Correct inappropriate demon-strations of skill		0		X		1/2	50%
Sum		5/7		4/7		9/14	64.3%
Session adherence		71.4%		57.1%			

thoughts. Alternatively, social learning theory posits that observational learning, or viewing an adaptive response in the presence of an anxiety-producing stimulus, might reduce an individual's anxiety response. A common technique based on social learning theory is coping modeling, in which the model initially demonstrates an anxiety response and then gradually becomes more comfortable in the presence of the anxiety-producing stimulus.

The relationship between treatment adherence and interventionist competence sometimes is confusing, because competence presupposes adherence but adherence does not presuppose competence (McGlinchey & Dobson, 2003). One may adhere to a particular treatment with perfect adherence yet do so in an incompetent manner. For example, a teacher might be instructed to deliver contingent praise for appropriate classroom behavior and may do this with perfect integrity. However, the quality of that praise may be stilted and insincere and thereby not be very reinforcing to the student. A breakdown in treatment integrity in this case would suggest training, practice, and feedback to ensure a more competent delivery of treatment. A breakdown in adherence would require performance feedback and training in implementing key components of a treatment plan.

Bellg et al. (2004) described an additional dimension of treatment integrity that they termed *treatment receipt*. Treatment receipt is conceptualized by exposure/dose of the treatment, participant comprehension of the treatment, and participant responsiveness to the treatment. Exposure or dose of a treatment refers to the amount of treatment received by the participant. For example, "dose" of a treatment might be the number of times per day or week the participant is exposed to the treatment. Exposure to a treatment can also be conceptualized as the *duration* of a treatment regimen for a particular problem. Some problems might require only 3 weeks of exposure to a treatment, whereas other problems might require a considerably longer time to reconcile a particular problem (10–15 weeks). Participant comprehension refers to the degree to which a participant understood or comprehended the content of the treatment. For example, a teacher's understanding of the difference between attention-maintained and escape-maintained behaviors would constitute participant comprehension. Participant responsiveness refers to the extent to which a participant is engaged in the treatment and finds it relevant.

TREATMENT INTEGRITY AND THREATS TO VALID INFERENCE MAKING

Failure to ensure the integrity with which treatments are delivered poses several threats to drawing valid inferences in behavioral research (Gresham, 1997; Kazdin, 1992; Moncher & Prinz, 1991; Shadish, Cook, & Campbell,

2002). Experimental research seeks to isolate and measure the effects of independent (treatment) variables on dependent variables. Without control of extraneous factors operating in the experimental situation, no definitive conclusions can be drawn regarding the effects of independent variables on dependent variables.

Shadish et al. (2002) identified four types of experimental validity that allow researchers to draw reasonable conclusions from experiments: (a) internal validity, (b) external validity, (c) construct validity, and (d) statistical conclusion validity. Each of these types of validity is discussed in the following paragraphs.

Internal validity refers to the extent to which changes in a dependent variable can be unequivocally attributed to systematic, manipulated changes in an independent variable. Internally valid experiments allow the researcher to rule out alternative explanations for results. If significant behavior changes occur as reflected in the dependent variable and if no data concerning the accuracy or degree to which the independent variable was implemented are presented, the internal validity of the experiment is compromised. Similarly, if significant changes in the dependent variable do not occur and if the treatment integrity is not monitored, distinguishing between an ineffective treatment and a potentially effective treatment implemented with poor integrity is difficult (Gresham, 1989). Alterations, changes, or deviations from an established treatment protocol have been called "therapist drift" (Peterson et al., 1982). Therapist drift may produce positive effects, negative effects, or no effects at all; however, unless treatment integrity is monitored and measured, such drift precludes definitive conclusions regarding what may have been responsible for treatment outcomes.

External validity refers to the inferences about the extent to which a causal relationship can be generalized over variations in persons, settings, treatments, treatment agents, and outcomes (Shadish et al., 2002). In terms of external validity, poorly defined, inadequately described, and idiosyncratically implemented treatments make replication and evaluation of treatment difficult (Moncher & Prinz, 1991). The absence of information concerning treatment definition and integrity limits the generalizability of treatments across participants, settings, situations, and treatment implementers (Kazdin, 1992).

Construct validity refers to explanations of the causal relation between independent and dependent variables (Kazdin, 1992). Whereas internal validity involves the demonstration that an independent variable was responsible for changes in a dependent variable, construct validity deals with the interpretation or explanation of the causal relation. Construct validity is very close to the statistical concept of *mediation*, which describes the manner or the mechanism by which an independent variable produces a given effect (Baron & Kenny, 1986).

For example, a study in which cognitive strategy training was used to increase reading comprehension might be interpreted as having enhanced the students' working memory (the presumed causal relation). Treatment integrity data might reveal that the treatment involved teaching students an explicit problem-solving strategy, mastery teaching of each step in the strategy, and specific correction procedures for student errors (i.e., direct instruction). Thus, the way in which cognitive strategy training was carried out in this hypothetical study may have been more consistent with a direct instruction explanation than with a cognitive strategy procedure aimed at enhancing working memory. Having no treatment integrity data would prevent a researcher from reaching this conclusion.

Statistical conclusion validity refers to those aspects of the quantitative evaluation of a study that influence the conclusions drawn about the effect of an independent variable (Kazdin, 1992; Shadish et al., 2002). One threat to statistical conclusion validity is the variability with which treatments are implemented. For example, in a study comparing Treatment A with Treatment B, researchers would like to conclude that differences between these two treatments were due to true differences between the groups and not to extraneous factors. However, in calculations of an effect size, the denominator includes a measure of variability—namely, the standard deviation. As such, whatever differences exist between the effects of Treatment A and those of Treatment B is, in part, a function of the variability in the experiment (Kazdin, 1992). This variability may be due to within-group differences of participants in the two treatments, random variability of dependent measures, and/or differences in how experimenters implemented the treatment (i.e., treatment integrity). Inconsistent application of or deviations in how treatments are implemented can increase the variability in an experiment. Increased variability can result in lower effect sizes and thus create a threat to the statistical conclusion validity of a study.

Some researchers may argue that the imprecise application of treatments poses no threats to the validity of conclusions that might be drawn about the relationship between independent and dependent variables. These researchers may maintain that changes in the dependent variable (e.g., reading fluency, phonological awareness) imply the stable and accurate application of the independent variable (the treatment). This assumption, however, may not be justified in all cases because dependent variable changes could also be due to some unrecognized and unmeasured collection of "third variables" or to modifications in treatment protocols that occurred but went undetected.

Some might also argue that explicit assessment and demonstration of treatment integrity is not a necessary condition for intervention research because errors in experimental control are protected by replications within and across participants in experimental research, particularly single-case design research. However, as Johnston and Pennypacker (1993) noted,

> Merely replicating control and experimental conditions (and reproducing their effects), regardless of their similarity to the original version, provides only very indirect and tenuous support for the influence of the independent variable. Direct and convincing evidence can only be obtained by conducting manipulations that clearly rule out all possible extraneous factors, while identifying the necessity of the variables constituting the independent variable. (pp. 266–267)

Further, unless a researcher knows precisely what was done, how it was done, and for how long it was done, replication is impossible. If *replicate* means to duplicate, copy, or repeat what was done, then this replication depends entirely on a complete and unambiguous specification of treatment procedures and an assessment of whether these procedures were implemented as intended or planned (Gresham et al., 2000).

PUTATIVE VARIABLES INFLUENCING TREATMENT INTEGRITY

The foundation of treatment integrity can be traced to Yeaton and Sechrest's (1981) seminal paper; the paper provided a clear conceptualization of treatment integrity, in which several key issues involved in its definition, measurement, and evaluation were outlined. Yeaton and Sechrest hypothesized reciprocal relationships among the *strength, integrity,* and *effectiveness* of treatments. In this view, the strength of treatments implemented with poor integrity is decreased (i.e., active treatment ingredients are diluted), and the effectiveness of those treatments is therefore reduced. As such, treatment integrity is important for evaluating the strength and effectiveness of treatments for different behaviors, in different settings, for different individuals, and across different treatment implementers.

Gresham (1989, 1997), on the basis of a logical or intuitive analysis of the literature, identified several factors or variables that appear to be related to treatment integrity. These variables can be broadly classified into two categories: (a) variables related to the intervention (e.g., complexity, materials/resources, ease of implementation) and (b) variables related to the interventionist (e.g., motivation to implement, skill proficiency, self-efficacy).

It should be noted that there are currently no empirical data to suggest the degree to which each of these putative variables affects treatment outcomes. Empirical moderator (a correlational variable that affects the strength or direction of a relationship between a predictor variable and a criterion variable) and mediator (a causal variable that specifies how a variable leads to changes in an outcome) analyses (Baron & Kenny, 1986) of these variables have received scant attention in the research literature (Sanetti & Kratochwill, 2009). Similarly, the literature contains little evidence that longer treatment or more frequent treatments (dose effects) are more effective than briefer treatments for a particular problem. An exception to this is the Lovaas (1987) study that claimed to produce "autistic recovery" in about half of the children receiving an intense behavioral intervention. In this study, some children received 40 or more hours of treatment per week and other children received 10 hours of treatment per week. Lovaas concluded that strong treatment effects were observed in the 40-hour-per-week group and weak effects were produced in the 10-hour-per-week group. On the basis of these data, Lovaas recommended that children with autism require at least 40 hours of intense behavioral intervention per week and that anything less would be ineffective. This study, although highly cited, suffered from numerous threats to internal, external, and statistical conclusion validity; collected no treatment integrity data; and has enjoyed only partial replication since its publication (Gresham & MacMillan, 1997).

There is also currently little empirical research addressing the relationship among treatment effectiveness (actual and perceived), treatment acceptability, and treatment integrity. Witt and Elliott (1985) suggested that treatments that are perceived to be more effective are likely to be more acceptable and therefore will be implemented with higher treatment integrity. Witt and Elliott's (1985) theoretical model of treatment acceptability stressed the interrelations among four elements of treatments: treatment acceptability, treatment use, treatment integrity, and treatment effectiveness. The hypothesized relationships among these four elements are viewed as sequential and reciprocal. Acceptability is the initial issue in the sequence of treatment selection and use. Once a treatment is viewed as acceptable, the probability of using the treatment rather than less acceptable treatments is high. The key element linking use and effectiveness is treatment integrity. If treatment integrity is high, the probability of that treatment leading to behavior change is enhanced, whereas if treatment integrity is low, the treatment is less likely to result in meaningful behavior change. Practitioners currently lack knowledge concerning how effectiveness data (actual or perceived) and acceptability influence subsequent implementation of these treatments.

PSYCHOMETRIC ISSUES IN MEASURING
TREATMENT INTEGRITY

Unfortunately, there have been few developments in the construction of feasible and efficient measures of treatment integrity that have adequate psychometric properties (Sanetti & Kratochwill, 2009). Assessment of the treatment adherence dimension of treatment integrity requires that treatment components be objectively specified and measured. Measurement issues in treatment integrity can be conceptualized in terms of classical test theory, in which components that make up a treatment can be viewed much like items on a test or scale. The degree to which each component of the treatment is implemented can be thought of as the reliability or consistency with which that component is implemented over the course of a treatment. This would be viewed as stability of each component's implementation over time, much like test–retest reliability.

Some authors have suggested that the reliability of treatment integrity measures could be evaluated with internal consistency indices such as coefficient alpha or factor analysis (Schulte, Easton, & Parker, 2009; Sheridan, Swanger-Gagne, Welch, Kwon, & Garbacz, 2009). This is a questionable recommendation for establishing the reliability of treatment adherence measures. Little evidence indicates that the various components of an intervention should correlate with each other (internal consistency of the treatment). Take the seven components of the social skills intervention presented in Table 5.1. There is little reason to believe that Step 1 (introduce the skill and ask questions about it) should correlate with Step 6 (reinforce occurrences of the skill throughout the session), and it is unclear whether each step should correlate with the intervention's total score, such as would be done in calculating item–total correlations. A factor analysis of these seven components would probably yield a single factor labeled *total treatment integrity*, which would be relatively meaningless in a psychometric sense. Baer (1977) made a similar argument in commenting on the reliability of direct observations in which interval-based recording procedures are used for target behaviors.

The concept of measurement *accuracy* is perhaps a more relevant psychometric principle in evaluating treatment integrity (Cone, 1988). Specifying intervention components in standard and absolute terms and computing the percent accuracy of treatment implementation over time can establish the accuracy of an assessment method. The value of the independent variable (the treatment) is known prior to a treatment's implementation, whereas the value of the dependent variable (target behavior to be changed) is known only after a treatment has been implemented (Peterson et al., 1982). Given that one knows the value of the independent variable a priori, one should be able to assess its accuracy of implementation. The accuracy of implementation of each component can be assessed by simply recording the occurrence and nonoccurrence of each component.

TECHNICAL ISSUES IN MEASURING AND EVALUATING TREATMENT INTEGRITY

Several technical issues are involved in the conceptualization and measurement of the adherence dimension of treatment integrity. These include specification and definition of treatment components, selection of assessment methods, and interpretation of treatment integrity data. Each of these issues is discussed in the following sections.

Specification of Treatment Components

The measurement of the adherence dimension of treatment integrity requires the operational definition of the treatment and its components. Each treatment component must be defined in specific, behavioral terms so that it can accurately be measured. Johnston and Pennypacker (1980) argued,

> There may be a distinction between what the experimenter thinks or says is the independent variable and the actual controlling variables in the experiment. Ideally, the discrepancy is minimal because the independent variable has been defined in terms that refer to real events in the environment. . . . Such a clear description of the independent variable is essential if any factually accurate statement is to issue from the experimental effort. (p. 40)

Based on previous reviews of treatment integrity data in the treatment outcome literature, an average of about 75% of the studies included an operational definition of the treatment (Gresham et al., 1993; McIntyre et al., 2007; Peterson et al., 1982; Wheeler et al., 2006). Although this percentage constitutes the majority of studies, this number should be contrasted with the percentage of reviewed studies that included an operational definition of the dependent variable: 100%. Why, then, is there a discrepancy between the percentage of studies operationally defining the independent and dependent variables? Again, Peterson et al.'s (1982) notion of the "curious double standard" perhaps best explains this finding.

Independent variables can be defined along at least four dimensions: verbal, physical, spatial, and temporal. For example, Mace, Page, Ivancic, and O'Brien (1986) compared time-out with and without contingent delay to decrease disruptive behavior. Mace et al. defined the time-out procedure as follows: (a) Immediately following the occurrence of the target behavior (temporal dimension), (b) the therapist said "No, go to time-out" (verbal dimension), (c) led the child by the arm to a prepositioned time-out chair (physical dimension), and (d) seated the child facing the corner (spatial dimension). (e) If the child's buttocks were raised from the time-out chair, or if the child's head was turned more than 45 degrees (spatial dimension), the therapist used the least amount of force necessary to guide compliance with the time-out procedure (physical dimension). (f) At the end of 2 minutes (temporal dimension), the therapist turned the time-out chair 45 degrees from the corner (physical and spatial dimensions) and (g) walked away (physical dimension).

The operational definition of treatment procedures used by Mace et al. (1986) would make replications and external validation of this procedure relatively easy. Contrast the Mace et al. treatment definition with the definition of a portion of a treatment published in the *Journal of Applied Behavior Analysis* by Stark et al. (1993): "Specifically, parents were initially taught to use differential reinforcement (praising and ignoring) and were gradually introduced to the use of contingent privileges (loss of a privilege contingent on not meeting a meal goal)" (p. 439). The parent training component of the Stark et al. study would clearly be more difficult to replicate than would the time-out study by Mace et al. based on the operational definition of treatment components.

An unresolved question in component specification is the level of specificity required. Does one use global, intermediate, or molecular levels of specification? On the one hand, it makes intuitive sense to define components in very specific terms to ensure clarity of treatment components. On the other hand, a detailed task analysis may be overwhelming to treatment agents and thereby risk consumer rejection of treatments. Additionally, the complexity of the treatment increases as a function of the number of components specified. Paradoxically, treatments with a larger number of well-defined components may be implemented with a lower level of treatment integrity than treatments with fewer and more nebulously defined components because of the perceived complexity of the former.

Global levels of treatment specification would involve stating simple principles of behavior change, such as catch them being good, reward appropriate behavior, and use planned ignoring. Intermediate levels of specification involve writing the major steps of a treatment program, such as construct a reinforcement menu for all students, write classroom rules on poster board in 4-inch letters with colored markers, review classroom rules daily with the class, and remove points contingent on rule violation. A molecular level of specification involves a detailed task analysis of every event in a treatment plan. For example, there may be five to 10 substeps in one step of an intermediate level of specification (e.g., remove points immediately upon rule violations, restate the rule to the offending student, stand in close physical proximity to the student, establish eye contact with the student).

An important, yet unresolved, issue in the specification of treatment components is the weighting of each treatment component. Some components of a treatment are more crucial than other components to treatment success. Providing contingent delivery of a positive reinforcer for a target behavior is likely much more important than telling a student the rationale for an intervention program. Given that some treatment components are more important than others, the weighting of components must be taken into consideration when treatment integrity is evaluated. Little empirical support currently exists for selecting and weighting various components within treatments. The decision of how to weight treatment components should be based on the extent to which each component shows a relationship to the target behavior. This is a fruitful area of investigation in future research on treatment integrity.

Methods of Treatment Integrity Assessment

Treatment integrity can be assessed with either direct or indirect behavioral assessment methods. Direct assessment of treatment integrity is based on the observation of treatment implementation as it is being implemented. A treatment agent bases indirect assessment methods on the assessment of treatment integrity of an intervention subsequent to its implementation. There are advantages and disadvantages to using either direct or indirect methods of treatment integrity assessment.

Direct Assessment

Direct assessment of treatment integrity is identical to the systematic observation of behavior in applied settings. Several factors should be considered in the selection and design of direct observation systems, such as the purpose of making the observations, the content of the observations, the amount of behavior to be observed, and the quality of the data produced (Foster & Cone, 1986). The same factors should guide the design of direct observation systems for treatment integrity.

The ultimate goal of any direct observation assessment is to produce data that accurately represent the behaviors of interest. Content validity is the most important type of validity for direct observation assessment. Representativeness of observational data depends on both the number of observation sessions (i.e., content sampling) and the length of each observation session. In general, the greater the amount of data collected on representative behaviors, the more representative the data are of the content domain.

Little research attention has been devoted to the question of the amount of direct observation data that is required to produce a representative sample of treatment integrity. Researchers simply do not know how many times per day, how long, or over how many days one must observe to produce a representative picture of the level of treatment integrity with which a treatment is being implemented. One methodological approach to determining representativeness would be to conduct studies using the logic of generalizability theory (G theory; Cronbach, Gleser, Nanda, & Rajaratnam, 1972). G theory is concerned with the *dependability* of behavioral measures and the accuracy of generalizing from an observed score to the average score that could be obtained under all possible conditions of measurement. In contrast to classical test theory, G theory can simultaneously evaluate multiple sources of error, called *facets*, in any given measurement. A *generalizability study* on treatment integrity could evaluate multiple facets that influence treatment integrity, such as number of times per day it is assessed, duration of a treatment, number of days of treatment, and the setting in which treatment takes place. After a generalizability study had been conducted, a *decision study* could be conducted to design a measurement that minimizes error for a particular purpose. This methodology has been applied to various behavioral assessment methods including systematic direct observations (Hintze & Matthews, 2004), direct behavior ratings (Chafouleas, Christ, Riley-Tillman, Briesch, & Chanese, 2007), and behavior rating scales (Bergeron, Floyd, McCormack, & Farmer, 2008).

An important consideration in direct assessment of treatment integrity is the potential for reactive effects of the observer's presence in the treatment setting, particularly if the treatment agent knows the observer is assessing the integrity of the intervention. Reactivity during direct observations of treatment integrity is not easily resolved, but some practical solutions may ameliorate reactive effects. One, observers could observe on a random schedule and spot-check the implementation of a treatment plan. Two, observers could attempt to be as unobtrusive as possible in the treatment setting. Three, observers could simply not communicate the purpose of the observation to treatment agents during the treatment integrity assessment phase.

Some may question the need to minimize observer reactivity if the reactive effects tend to be in the desired direction (i.e., treatment agents implement the treatment with greater integrity when observers are present). However, if treatment agents implement treatment plans only while observations are being conducted, the treatment will be less effective or ineffective most of the time (i.e., when observations are not being conducted). Again, little empirical research using systematic direct observations has been conducted on the reactivity of direct assessment of treatment integrity (see Codding, Livanis, Pace, & Vaca, 2008).

Indirect Assessment

Indirect assessment methods include self-reports, behavioral interviews regarding treatment implementation, and various permanent product assessments. Self-report measures involve treatment agents rating the degree to which they implemented the treatment that day. Items on these measures could either be rated dichotomously (Implemented/Not Implemented) or be rated on a Likert scale (e.g., 1 = *Low Treatment Integrity* to 5 = *High Treatment Integrity*). Completion of a self-report may produce reactive implementation effects in the desired direction by cuing treatment agents to implement the treatment with higher integrity. Self-reports also could have no implementation effects but have reactive rating effects. That is, treatment agents continue to implement a treatment with a low level of treatment integrity, but they report high treatment integrity.

Behavioral interviews similar to problem identification interviews (Bergan & Kratochwill, 1990) could also be used to assess treatment integrity (see Wilkinson, 2006). One would expect, based on this method, that the majority of verbalizations would be in the plan and observation content domains and in the process categories of specification, validation, and summarization. Little research, however, has systematically investigated the use of behavioral interviews in the assessment of treatment integrity.

Finally, some treatments leave a permanent product in the environment that can be used to assess treatment integrity. Homework and classwork completion and accuracy, self-monitoring forms, and direct behavior reports all have been used to assess treatment integrity (Chafouleas, McDougal, Riley-Tillman, Panahon, & Hilt, 2005; Gresham, 1989; Sheridan et al., 2009). For some interventions, permanent products will provide a general estimate (often, not every treatment component has a corresponding product) of treatment integrity; however, for others (e.g., implementation of a psychotherapy session), permanent products will not be a feasible method of assessing treatment integrity.

We know that multiple methods can be effectively used to assess treatment integrity. What is not currently known are the relationships among direct and various indirect treatment integrity assessment methods. Investigating such relationships is a fruitful area for future treatment integrity research.

Interpretation of Treatment Integrity Data

A frequent assumption is that interventions must have perfect treatment integrity to be maximally effective. This assumption presumes a perfect linear relationship between level of treatment integrity and level of treatment outcome. This assumption, however, is not based on empirical data, and little published research shows a one-to-one correspondence between level of treatment integrity and level of treatment outcome. In fact, Gresham et al. (1993) found only a .58 correlation between treatment integrity level and treatment outcome level in their review of 158 school-based behavioral interventions studies. Other authors have noted that rigid adherence to a treatment protocol may not necessarily be required or desirable (Sanetti & Kratochwill, 2009; Schulte et al., 2009). There may be a ceiling effect above which treatment integrity improvement may not be helpful or cost beneficial. The problem the field faces is that practitioners do not know what level of treatment integrity is necessary with what treatments to produce beneficial treatment outcomes. Also not known at this time is how far one might "drift" away from a treatment protocol and still have positive treatment outcomes.

One might invoke different standards for adherence to treatment protocols depending on whether a study is an *efficacy* study or an *effectiveness* study. Requiring that efficacy studies would include rather strict adherence to a treatment protocol is reasonable, because these studies focus on establishing intervention effects under tightly controlled conditions with designs that are high in internal validity. Less rigid adherence to treatment protocols would be allowed for effectiveness studies, because these studies seek to establish intervention effects under less controlled conditions and with designs that are high in external validity.

Currently, practitioners have no comprehensive database to guide them in deciding what the optimal levels of treatment integrity are for different treatments across different populations or individuals. Some problems might be effectively resolved with 75% treatment integrity, whereas other problems might require close to 100% treatment integrity to be effective. A potentially useful avenue for future research and research syntheses could be based on the notion of *treatment effect norms* (Yeaton, 1988). A treatment effect norm refers to the average outcomes of given treatments or family of treatments whose goal is to alleviate a problem. Meta-analyses have been used extensively as a means of quantifying what effects, on average, might be produced with what treatments, with what clients or populations, and under what conditions.

Practitioners could establish and catalog *treatment integrity effect norms* by quantifying what levels of treatment integrity, measured by what methods, with what interventions, produce what level of outcomes. In using the Good Behavior Game, for example, they might find that, on average, 75% treatment integrity as measured by direct observations is required to produce socially valid reductions in disruptive behavior for elementary-age students. It might be that lower levels of treatment integrity using this intervention do not produce socially valid effects. Treatment integrity effect norms could be constructed across multiple tiers of interventions using different populations

TABLE 5.2
Relationship Between Treatment Integrity and Treatment Outcomes

| | Level of treatment integrity | | |
Effect size	High (> 80%)	Moderate (60–80%)	Low (< 60%)
Effective (≥ .80)			
Somewhat effective (.40–.79)			
Ineffective (< .39)			

of students. Table 5.2 provides an example of how these norms could be constructed by showing the relationship between integrity level and treatment outcome.

CONCLUSION

The failure to define and measure the degree to which treatments are implemented as planned or intended compromises the development of a true science of evidence-based interventions. The importance of treatment integrity spans multiple fields of endeavor involving the provision of treatment services to individuals, including medicine, education, psychotherapy, and applied behavior analysis. Experimentation in the laboratory can easily control sources of extraneous variance that may confound the interpretation of the phenomenon being studied. In applied settings, however, controlling all possible sources of extraneous influence that affect the phenomenon of interest is extremely difficult. One thing that can and should be controlled is the integrity with which any given treatment is implemented.

Treatment integrity has evolved into a multidimensional construct consisting of treatment adherence, interventionist competence, treatment differentiation, and treatment receipt. This chapter emphasized treatment adherence because it was seen as the keystone dimension of a treatment's success or failure. Unless adherence to a treatment protocol is ensured, the other three dimensions become moot.

From a research methodology standpoint, ignoring treatment integrity poses substantial threats to valid inference making including internal validity, external validity, construct validity, and statistical conclusion validity. Failure to systematically and accurately determine the degree to which treatments are implemented as planned clearly compromises the entire enterprise of establishing evidence-based intervention practices. Although a number of variables have been hypothesized as moderators or mediators of treatment integrity, few of these variables have been empirically and systematically evaluated in controlled research (Sanetti & Kratochwill, 2009).

Professional organizations as well as granting agencies are insisting that researchers attend to treatment integrity. An excellent example of this can be found in the report by the Task Force on Evidence-Based Practice in Special Education by the Council for Exceptional Children. This document states that the treatment integrity of intervention implementation is critical in single-case designs because the independent variable is implemented continuously over time (Horner et al., 2005). Additionally, researchers who submit efficacy grants to the Institute of Education Sciences are now required to describe how treatment integrity will be measured, the frequency of these assessments, and what degree of variation in treatment integrity will be accepted over the course of the study (Institute of Education Sciences, 2012). The National Institute of Mental Health is funding research aimed at optimizing treatment integrity of evidence-based treatments (National Institute of Mental Health, 2011). It is essential that treatment integrity data, in both research and practice, be regularly assessed and reported. Doing so will allow the field to develop a better understanding of the concepts and strategies in evidence-based intervention research and practice.

REFERENCES

Baer, D. M. (1977). Perhaps it would be better not to know everything. *Journal of Applied Behavior Analysis, 10*, 167–172. doi:10.1901/jaba.1977.10-167

Baron, R. M., & Kenny, D. A. (1986). The moderator–mediator variable distinction in social psychological research: Conceptual, strategic, and statistical considerations. *Journal of Personality and Social Psychology, 51*, 1173–1182. doi:10.1037/0022-3514.51.6.1173

Bellg, A. J., Borrelli, B., Resnick, B., Hecht, J., Minicucci, D. S., Ory, M., . . . Czajkowski, S. (2004). Enhancing treatment fidelity in health behavior change studies: Best practices and recommendations from the NIH Behavior Change Consortium. *Health Psychology, 23*, 443–451. doi:10.1037/0278-6133.23.5.443

Bergan, J. R., & Kratochwill, T. R. (1990). *Behavioral consultation and therapy.* New York, NY: Plenum Press.

Bergeron, R., Floyd, R. G., McCormack, A. C., & Farmer, W. L. (2008). The generalizability of externalizing behavior composites and subscale scores across time, rater, and instrument. *School Psychology Review, 37*, 91–108.

Bernal, M. E., Klinnert, M. D., & Schultz, L. A. (1980). Outcome evaluation of behavioral parent training and client-centered parent counseling for children with conduct problems. *Journal of Applied Behavior Analysis, 13*, 677–691. doi:10.1901/jaba.1980.13-677

Chafouleas, S. M., Christ, T. J., Riley-Tillman, C. R., Briesch, A. M., & Chanese, J. A. M. (2007). Generalizability and dependability of direct behavior ratings to assess social behavior of preschoolers. *School Psychology Review, 36*, 63–79.

Chafouleas, S. M., McDougal, J. L., Riley-Tillman, C. R., Panahon, C. J., & Hilt, A. M. (2005). What do daily behavior report cards (DBRCs) measure? An initial comparison of DRBCs with direct observation for off-task behavior. *Psychology in the Schools, 42*, 669–676. doi:10.1002/pits.20102

Codding, R. S., Livanis, A., Pace, G. M., & Vaca, L. (2008). Using performance feedback to improve treatment integrity of classwide behavior plans: An investigation of observer reactivity. *Journal of Applied Behavior Analysis, 41*, 417–422. doi:10.1901/jaba.2008.41-417

Cone, J. (1988). Psychometric considerations and the multiple models of behavioral assessment. In A. Bellack & M. Hersen (Eds.), *Behavioral assessment: A practical handbook* (pp. 42–66). Boston, MA: Pergamon Press.

Cronbach, L. J., Gleser, G. C., Nanda, H., & Rajaratnam, N. (1972). *The dependability of behavioral measures*. New York, NY: Wiley.

Foster, S., & Cone, J. (1986). Design and use of direct observation. In A. Ciminero, K. Calhoun, & H. Adams (Eds.), *Handbook of behavioral assessment* (2nd ed., pp. 253–324). New York, NY: Wiley Interscience.

Gresham, F. M. (1989). Assessment of treatment integrity in school consultation and prereferral intervention. *School Psychology Review, 18*, 37–50.

Gresham, F. M. (1997). Treatment integrity in single-subject research. In R. D. Franklin, D. B. Allison, & B. S. Gorman (Eds.), *Design and analysis of single-case research* (pp. 93–117). Mahwah, NJ: Erlbaum.

Gresham, F. M. (2009). Evolution of the treatment integrity concept: Current status and future directions. *School Psychology Review, 38*, 533–540.

Gresham, F. M., Gansle, K. A., Noell, G. H., Cohen, S., & Rosenblum, S. (1993). Treatment integrity in school-based behavioral intervention studies: 1980–1990. *School Psychology Review, 22*, 254–272.

Gresham, F. M., & MacMillan, D. L. (1997). Autistic recovery? An analysis and critique of the empirical evidence on the Early Intervention Project. *Behavioral Disorders, 22*, 185–201.

Gresham, F. M., MacMillan, D. L., Beebe-Frankenberger, M. E., & Bocian, K. M. (2000). Treatment integrity in learning disabilities intervention research: Do we really know how treatments are implemented? *Learning Disabilities Research & Practice, 15*, 198–205. doi:10.1207/SLDRP1504_4

Hartmann, D. P. (1977). Considerations in the choice of interobserver reliability estimates. *Journal of Applied Behavior Analysis, 10*, 103–116. doi:10.1901/jaba.1977.10-103

Hintze, J. M., & Matthews, W. J. (2004). The generalizability of systematic direct observations across time and setting: A preliminary investigation of the psychometrics of behavioral assessment. *School Psychology Review, 33*, 258–270.

Horner, R. H., Carr, E. G., Halle, J., McGee, G., Odom, S., & Wolery, M. (2005). The use of single-subject research to identify evidence-based practice in special education. *Exceptional Children, 71*, 165–179.

Institute of Education Sciences. (2012). *Requests for applications: Special education grants* (CFDA No. 84-324A). Washington, DC: U.S. Department of Education.

Johnston, J. M., & Pennypacker, H. S. (1980). *Strategies and tactics of human behavioral research*. Hillsdale, NJ: Erlbaum.

Johnston, J. M., & Pennypacker, H. S. (1993). *Strategies and tactics of behavioral research* (2nd ed.). Hillsdale, NJ: Erlbaum.

Kazdin, A. E. (1977). Artifact, bias, and complexity of assessments: The ABCs of reliability. *Journal of Applied Behavior Analysis, 10*, 141–150. doi:10.1901/jaba.1977.10-141

Kazdin, A. E. (1992). *Research design in clinical psychology* (2nd ed.). New York, NY: Macmillan.

Lovaas, O. I. (1987). Behavioral treatment and normal educational and intellectual functioning in young autistic children. *Journal of Consulting and Clinical Psychology, 55*, 3–9. doi:10.1037/0022-006X.55.1.3

Mace, F. C., Page, T., Ivancic, M., & O'Brien, S. (1986). Effectiveness of brief time-out with and without contingent delay: A comparative analysis. *Journal of Applied Behavior Analysis, 19*, 79–86. doi:10.1901/jaba.1986.19-79

McGlinchey, J. B., & Dobson, K. S. (2003). Treatment integrity concerns in cognitive therapy for depression. *Journal of Cognitive Psychotherapy, 17*, 299–318. doi:10.1891/jcop.17.4.299.52543

McIntyre, L. L., Gresham, F. M., DiGennaro, F. D., & Reed, D. D. (2007). Treatment integrity of school-based interventions with children in the *Journal of Applied Behavior Analysis*: 1991–2005. *Journal of Applied Behavior Analysis, 40*, 659–672. doi:10.1901/jaba.2007.659-672

Moncher, F., & Prinz, R. (1991). Treatment fidelity in outcome studies. *Clinical Psychology Review, 11*, 247–266. doi:10.1016/0272-7358(91)90103-2

National Institute of Mental Health. (2011). Funding opportunity announcement: Optimizing fidelity of empirically-supported behavioral treatments for mental disorders (R21/R33). Retrieved from http://grants.nih.gov/grants/guide/rfa-files/RFA-MH-12-050.html

Nezu, A. M., & Nezu, C. M. (2008). Treatment integrity. In D. McKay (Ed.), *Handbook of research methods in abnormal and clinical psychology* (pp. 351–366). Thousand Oaks, CA: Sage.

O'Leary, K. D., Kent, R. N., & Kanowitz, J. (1975). Shaping data collection congruent experimental hypotheses. *Journal of Applied Behavior Analysis, 8*, 43–51. doi:10.1901/jaba.1975.8-43

Perepletchikova, F., Treat, T. A., & Kazdin, A. E. (2007). Treatment integrity in psychotherapy research: Analysis of the studies and examination of the associated factors. *Journal of Consulting and Clinical Psychology, 75*, 829–841. doi:10.1037/0022-006X.75.6.829

Peterson, L., Homer, A. L., & Wonderlich, S. A. (1982). The integrity of independent variables in behavior analysis. *Journal of Applied Behavior Analysis, 15*, 477–492. doi:10.1901/jaba.1982.15-477

Reid, J. (1970). Reliability assessment of observational data: A possible methodological problem. *Child Development, 41*, 1143–1150. doi:10.2307/1127341

Romanczyk, R. G., Kent, R. N., Diament, C., & O'Leary, K. D. (1973). Measuring the reliability of observational data: A reactive process. *Journal of Applied Behavior Analysis, 6*, 175–184. doi:10.1901/jaba.1973.6-175

Sanetti, L. M. H., & Kratochwill, T. R. (2009). Toward developing a science of treatment integrity: Introduction to the special series. *School Psychology Review, 38*, 445–459.

Schulte, A. C., Easton, J. E., & Parker, J. (2009). Advances in treatment integrity research: Multidisciplinary perspectives on the conceptualization, measurement, and enhancement of treatment integrity. *School Psychology Review, 38*, 460–475.

Shadish, W. R., Cook, T. D., & Campbell, D. T. (2002). *Experimental and quasi-experimental designs for generalized causal inference.* New York, NY: Houghton Mifflin.

Sheridan, S. M., Swanger-Gagne, M., Welch, G. W., Kwon, K., & Garbacz, S. A. (2009). Fidelity measurement in consultation: Psychometric issues and preliminary examination. *School Psychology Review, 38*, 476–495.

Skinner, B. F. (1938). *The behavior of organisms.* New York, NY: Appleton-Century-Croft.

Stark, L. J., Knapp, L. G., Bowen, A. M., Powers, S. W., Jelalian, E., Evans, S., . . . Hovell, M. (1993). Increasing caloric consumption in children with cystic fibrosis: Replication with 2-year follow-up. *Journal of Applied Behavior Analysis, 26*, 435–450. doi:10.1901/jaba.1993.26-435

Wheeler, J. J., Baggett, B. A., Fox, J., & Blevins, L. (2006). Treatment integrity: A review of intervention studies conducted with children with autism. *Focus on Autism and Other Developmental Disabilities, 21*, 45–54. doi:10.1177/10883576060210010601

Wilkinson, L. A. (2006). Monitoring treatment integrity: An alternative to the "consult and hope" strategy in school-based behavioural consultation. *School Psychology International, 27*, 426–438. doi:10.1177/0143034306070428

Witt, J. C., & Elliott, S. N. (1985). Acceptability of classroom management strategies. In T. R. Kratochwill (Ed.), *Advances in school psychology* (Vol. 4, pp. 251–288). Hillsdale, NJ: Erlbaum.

Wodarski, J. S., Feldman, R. A., & Pedi, S. J. (1974). Objective measurement of the independent variable: A neglected methodological aspect in community-based behavioral research. *Journal of Abnormal Child Psychology, 2*, 239–244. doi:10.1007/BF00918891

Yeaton, W. H. (1988). Treatment effect norms. In J. C. Witt, S. N. Elliott, & F. M. Gresham (Eds.), *Handbook of behavior therapy in education* (pp. 171–187). New York, NY: Plenum Press. doi:10.1007/978-1-4613-0905-5_7

Yeaton, W. H., & Sechrest, L. (1981). Critical dimensions in the choice and maintenance of successful treatments: Strength, integrity, and effectiveness. *Journal of Consulting and Clinical Psychology, 49*, 156–167. doi:10.1037/0022-006X.49.2.156

6

ASSESSMENT OF TREATMENT INTEGRITY IN PSYCHOTHERAPY RESEARCH

FRANCHESKA PEREPLETCHIKOVA

Precision and control are vital to the methodology of empirical testing of treatment efficacy, and treatment integrity plays an integral role. *Treatment integrity* refers to the extent to which treatment was implemented as intended (Vermilyea, Barlow, & O'Brien, 1984). Treatment outcome research is full of examples of how failure to ensure that the treatment was carried out appropriately resulted in unjustified conclusions, inadequate clinical care, inappropriate

Some of the material used in this chapter is from the following sources:

Treatment Integrity in Treatment Outcome Research: Adequacy of Procedures, Associated Factors, Implications for Research and Practice, Guidelines and Recommendations, by F. Perepletchikova, 2009, Saarbrücken, Germany: Lambert Academic Publishing. Copyright 2009 by F. Perepletchikova. Adapted with permission.

"Treatment Integrity and Therapeutic Change: Issues and Research Recommendations" by F. Perepletchikova & A. E. Kazdin, 2005, *Clinical Psychology: Science and Practice*, 12, 365–383. Copyright 2005 by Wiley. Adapted with permission.

"Treatment Integrity in Psychotherapy Research: Analysis of the Studies and Examination of the Associated Factors" by F. Perepletchikova, T. A. Treat, & A. E. Kazdin, 2007, *Journal of Consulting and Clinical Psychology*, 75, 829–841. Copyright 2007 by the American Psychological Association.

http://dx.doi.org/10.1037/14275-008
Treatment Integrity: A Foundation for Evidence-Based Practice in Applied Psychology, L. M. H. Sanetti and T. R. Kratochwill (Editors)
Copyright © 2014 by the American Psychological Association. All rights reserved.

recommendations, and premature dissemination of treatments into clinical practice (e.g., Krumholz et al., 1998; Lauritsen, 1992; Sechrest, White, & Brown, 1979). Failure to ensure treatment integrity poses threats to the experimental validity of a study and has serious implications for inferences drawn about the relationship between treatment and outcome (e.g., Gresham, MacMillan, Beebe-Frankenberger, & Bocian, 2000; Moncher & Prinz, 1991). Once a treatment is established as empirically supported and is disseminated into clinical practice, treatment integrity continues to play an important role in preventing deviation from and gradual alteration of the treatment manual, referred to as a *therapeutic drift* (Peterson, Homer, & Wonderlich, 1982).

The methodological necessity of treatment integrity has long been recognized (e.g., Marks & Tolsma, 1986; Morris, Turner, & Szykula, 1988). Yet, despite the critical significance of treatment integrity for testing therapeutic efficacy, only a fraction of the psychotherapy outcome studies address this topic. Literature reviews indicate that only 6% to 30% of outcome studies assess and report data on treatment integrity (e.g., Armstrong, Ehrhardt, Cool, & Poling, 1997; Borrelli et al., 2005; Gresham, Gansle, & Noell, 1993; Wiese, 1992). Of those studies that do mention treatment integrity, only 10% to 50% provide quantitative data concerning the degree to which procedures were implemented as designed (e.g., Gresham, Gansle, Noell, Cohen, & Rosenblum, 1993; Gresham et al., 2000). An examination of randomized controlled trials (RCTs) of psychosocial treatments indicated that only about 3.5% of the evaluated RCTs have adequately implemented treatment integrity procedures (Perepletchikova, Treat, & Kazdin, 2007). This may mean that treatment effects from only 3.5% of the examined RCTs can be unambiguously interpreted. Evaluation of barriers to adequately addressing treatment integrity suggests that psychotherapy researchers appreciate its importance but indicate that lack of general knowledge about treatment integrity and specific guidelines hinders adequate attention to treatment integrity (Perepletchikova, Hilt, Chereji, & Kazdin, 2009).

The main goal of this chapter is to provide recommendations on the assessment of treatment integrity. In the chapter, I discuss the importance of treatment integrity assessment, factors that affect assessment procedures, guidelines on assessment strategies, recommendations on evaluating psychometric properties of the assessment instruments, and considerations on data representativeness and accuracy, and I provide an overview of the reporting procedures.

WHY ASSESS TREATMENT INTEGRITY

Assessment of treatment integrity (a) ascertains that inferences drawn about treatment effects are justified, (b) augments therapist training and supervision procedures, (c) prevents therapeutic drift, (d) offers opportunities for isolating active ingredients of change, and (e) may help simplify dissemination procedures (Kazdin, 2003; Miller & Binder, 2002; Moos & Finney, 1983).

Experimental Validity

Assessment of treatment integrity is critical for demonstrating that treatment was delivered as designed. Shadish, Cook, and Campbell (2002) outlined four types of experimental validity—internal, external, construct, and statistical conclusion validity. Establishing which manipulation (treatment or alternative factors) resulted in a change on dependent measures would not be possible without assessment of treatment integrity, and the *internal validity* of the study would be threatened. Indeed, the most cited reason for assessing treatment integrity is to understand ambiguous treatment outcome results or results that were not in the expected direction (Hohmann & Shear, 2002). Assessment of the degree to which a treatment was implemented as intended helps clarify whether such results are due to the failure of the treatment or the failure of the implementation. The failure of the implementation also has to be ruled out when results are in the expected direction, because the breakdown in treatment integrity can indeed enhance the effectiveness of the treatment (Gresham et al., 2000). Deviations can augment procedures and alter the protocol to better suit the treated population. Low treatment integrity does not mean that the treatment is weak, just that it is different from that which was originally intended. When results are in the expected direction but treatment integrity is low, establishing what was actually done by therapists can provide clues for developing a more promising treatment. Thus, data and materials collected as part of a treatment integrity assessment (e.g., sessions tapes, expert ratings, therapist self-reports, clinical notes, written homework assignments, data collection sheets) can be critical for further research.

Lack of treatment integrity assessment can also hinder attempts to replicate the study and evaluate its *external validity*. Generalizability of the findings cannot be established without the exact description of the treatment and how it was delivered. When a treatment is not provided as planned, the *construct validity* of the experiment is also compromised. Imprecision in treatment delivery can cause ambiguity in evaluating what the treatment was and why it produced the effect. When treatment integrity is compromised, the essence of the treatment cannot be separated from the factors that covaried with the treatment. Further, evaluation of the effectiveness of a treatment depends on multiple considerations, including the computational aspects of statistical tests. When treatment is not implemented as intended, *statistical conclusion validity* can be compromised because an unsystematic error is introduced into the data. Such "noise" increases the within-group variability, which reduces the obtained effect size and statistical power and, thus, obscures treatment effect. A treatment might fail to produce significant change on dependent measures because the variability in treatment implementation decreased the likelihood of detecting the effect.

Therapeutic Drift

Assessment of treatment integrity procedures is essential for prevention of the therapeutic drift and can also augment therapist training and supervision methods. Therapeutic drift can result from a multitude of factors. Therapists may not be sufficiently trained in treatment delivery. Further, therapists may adjust their presentation of the prescribed procedures to fit their personality and style of treatment implementation. They might view certain aspects of the protocol as awkward or irrelevant and might alter certain parts. Therefore, failure to adequately train and monitor therapists and assess their performance might threaten the treatment integrity of a protocol. Therapeutic drift is especially common in clinical settings (e.g., Bond, Evans, Salyers, Williams, & Kim, 2000; Tobin, Banker, Weisberg, & Bowers, 2007), and ongoing evaluation of treatment delivery can alert supervisors to its occurrence.

Therapist Training Procedures

Well-trained therapists are less susceptible to deviation from specified treatment protocol (Beidas & Kendall, 2010; Sholomskas et al., 2005). Faithful rendition of the treatment is more likely with direct training procedures that include opportunities for practice and involve procedures such as role-playing, modeling, feedback, rehearsal, and periodic booster sessions (e.g., Kratochwill, Sheridan, Rotto, & Salmon, 1991; Sterling-Turner, Watson, Wildmon, Watkins, & Little, 2001). Still, insufficient opportunities to observe treatment implementation is one of the main problems in therapist training (e.g., Fairburn & Cooper, 2011; Sharpless & Barber, 2009). Video modeling has been shown to increase treatment integrity of implemented techniques (e.g., DiGennaro-Reed, Codding, Catania, & Maguire, 2010; Moore & Fisher, 2007). Over the past decade, e-learning (through electronic media) and Internet-enhanced training have also been gaining interest and recognition as valuable, clinically rich, and easily accessible tools (e.g., Fairburn & Cooper, 2011; Weingardt, Cucciare, Bellotti, & Lai, 2009). Further, training therapists in research and clinical settings to adequate treatment integrity levels can be facilitated by having therapists watch videotapes of sessions by other therapists and rate their performance with treatment integrity measures. Rating adherence and competence of other therapists and comparing these ratings to those made by experts or independent judges may help advance knowledge of treatment components, facilitate learning of required strategies, and improve identification of the adequate and inadequate implementation of treatment procedures. Further, use of self-report measures of treatment integrity by therapists in self-monitoring of treatment integrity levels can greatly enhance training, as well as help therapists continue to adjust their performance after training is completed.

Therapists' self-reports of treatment integrity levels offer immediate access to integrity data. Such access allows ongoing adjustment of treatment delivery and suggestions for improvement via review of self-reports during supervision. Performance feedback on implementation may increase treatment integrity when low levels are detected, may prompt therapists to implement treatment with integrity, and can enhance homogeneity across therapists (Gresham, 1997; K. Jones, Wickstrom, & Friman, 1997). Therapists' self-reports can also be compared with ratings of independent observers or supervisors. Feedback on self-ratings can cue therapists to strategies and procedures that they tend to under- or overrate, overlook, or incorrectly code, as well as further their appreciation of the difference between required and auxiliary procedures and improve their understanding of the competent implementation of treatment components.

Mechanisms of Change

Careful assessment of the implementation of different treatment components can help one identify mechanisms of change. Demonstrating a causal effect between the treatment and the outcome does not establish the way the change occurred. Treatment is a package of components that can be distinguished as essential for change, sufficient ingredients, or facilitative ingredients via dismantling and constructive studies (Kazdin, 2007). Dismantling studies allow for analysis of individual components of a treatment by providing a full intervention package to one group and reduced variation to another group or other groups. Constructive studies are used to evaluate whether adding components to a treatment package enhances the effect of an intervention. For example, in a psychoanalytic treatment, mechanisms research (i.e., dismantling and constructive studies) can help one evaluate whether expressive techniques (e.g., analysis of transference and countertransference) contribute to the therapeutic effect above and beyond the uncovering (e.g., interpretations) facets. However, without an operational definition of each component, meticulous monitoring of implementation, and precise assessment of procedures, such research cannot be done.

Dissemination

Adherence to a protocol is necessary when treatment is defined by all of its representative components, but many of these components may not be essential. Understanding which factors underpin therapeutic effectiveness may simplify the transition of treatments from research laboratories to clinical settings (e.g., Jensen, Weersing, Hoagwood, & Goldman, 2005; Weisz, Weiss, & Donenberg, 1992). Treatments may become more precise and specific once active ingredients of change are known and essential components are separated from sufficient and facilitative ingredients.

FACTORS THAT AFFECT TREATMENT INTEGRITY ASSESSMENT PROCEDURES

Conceptualization of Treatment Integrity

Conceptualization of treatment integrity determines assessment procedures. For example, does assessment encompass adherence, competence, or both? Is treatment differentiation assessed as well? Are proscribed procedures monitored? Is a client's compliance used to determine treatment integrity levels? What treatment components are assessed—those essential for change, required by protocol, and/or auxiliary? The following section elucidates these issues.

Aspects of Treatment Integrity

Treatment integrity consists of three aspects: treatment adherence, therapist competence, and treatment differentiation (e.g., Margison et al., 2000; Waltz, Addis, Koerner, & Jacobson, 1993). *Adherence* refers to the degree to which the therapist utilizes specified procedures and avoids prohibited tasks (e.g., follows the manual verbatim, performs all prescribed tasks and activities). *Competence* refers to the level of skill and judgment shown by a therapist in delivering a treatment (e.g., contingent reinforcement of behavior, provision of prompts and feedback, accurate modeling of techniques). In the context of treatment integrity, competence is conceptualized as the level of skill in performing a specific treatment as opposed to a general therapeutic competence (e.g., empathy, warmth), which is related to common factors. *Differentiation* refers to whether treatments under investigation differ from each other along critical dimensions (e.g., implementing procedures prescribed by the manual for Treatment A and avoiding procedures prescribed for Treatment B and vice versa). Adherence and treatment differentiation are closely related in the sense that a measure of adherence is sufficient to determine whether treatments are distinct (Waltz et al., 1993).

Therapist adherence cannot be substituted for competence. Adherence represents a quantitative aspect of treatment integrity (how frequently a therapist implements prescribed and avoids proscribed procedures), whereas competence is its qualitative aspect (how well prescribed procedures are implemented). Therapists can adhere to a manual and still deliver a treatment incompetently (e.g., appropriate procedures provided in an inappropriate time; application of tasks was not sensitive to the client's needs). If competence is not evaluated, factors that contributed to an obtained effect or lack of effect cannot be identified.

Treatment integrity is sometimes extended to include participant responsiveness (e.g., Dane & Schneider, 1998; Dusenbury, Brannigan, Falco, & Hansen, 2003; H. A. Jones, Clarke, & Power, 2008). However, participant receipt and enactment considerations move treatment integrity beyond implementation aspects to include treatment outcome. Assessing participant compliance with treatment is indeed important and may moderate treatment effect. Yet, treatment integrity may not even be associated with an outcome (Perepletchikova & Kazdin, 2005). If a treatment is not effective, high treatment integrity cannot be expected to lead to better outcomes, regardless of how a client responded to the used strategies or how closely she or he followed the therapist's recommendations. Low treatment integrity, in this case, may actually improve results, as added procedures may better address a client's needs. Further, a client's responsiveness may depend on the multitude of factors not associated with a treatment. Client characteristics can play an important role here, including the client's difficulty (e.g., anger, hostility), cognitive abilities, and developmental level; the problem's severity, duration, and comorbidity; and the client's readiness for change. Treatment integrity answers a question of whether therapy was delivered as intended by a therapist and not whether it was received as intended by a client. The former is the independent variable, whereas the latter is the dependent variable.

Definition of Treatment Integrity

As Sanetti and Kratochwill (2009) pointed out, the field is still a long way from a consensus on a definition of treatment integrity and specification of its aspects. Given the similarities across different conceptual models of treatment integrity, Sanetti and Kratochwill proposed to define treatment integrity as the "extent to which essential intervention components are delivered in a comprehensive and consistent manner by an interventionist trained to deliver the intervention" (p. 448). This conceptualization is much broader and better captures the complexity of the topic. However, although the term *essential component* is frequently used in the treatment integrity literature, such use may lead to some confusion. The question of which ingredients are essential relates to treatment outcome and taps into the mechanisms of change and treatment specificity, rather than implementation. A clear-cut differentiation between essential and nonessential treatment components is not always established. I propose describing the components as "required" instead of "essential." The term *required components* includes components that are regarded as key therapeutic ingredients, consistent with theoretical framework, that differentiate the treatment from other models. Further, the above definition does not include proscribed procedures, the specification of the target, or the framework of delivery. Thus, I propose to extend the definition to incorporate these critical aspects: *Treatment integrity is the extent to which required intervention components are delivered as designed in a competent manner while proscribed procedures are avoided by an interventionist trained to deliver the intervention in a particular setting to a particular population.*

Treatment Specificity

Treatments differ in conceptual approaches, therapeutic components, and operational definition of competent implementation. Thus, requirements for demonstrating adherence and competence and measurement procedures may differ as a function of treatment type. For example, skills-based approaches, such as parenting intervention, may assess adherence in terms of the degree to which prescribed tasks are implemented per each session content (e.g., review last week's practice assignment, discuss time-out technique, show videotaped vignette, role-play techniques; e.g., Breitenstein et al., 2010). Principal-based approaches, such as acceptance and commitment therapy, may be measuring adherence of implemented strategies that are prescribed for all sessions (e.g., identifying thoughts as thoughts and not necessarily as reality, highlighting that thoughts and feelings do not lead to action, facilitating willingness to contact and accept difficult feelings, encouraging commitment to all aspects of life) and avoidance of proscribed strategies (e.g., challenging cognitions, in-session exposure, experiential avoidance change strategies; Plumb & Vilardaga, 2010). Thus, most treatment integrity measures are treatment specific.

Treatment Manual

Assessment of treatment integrity also depends on how the treatment is defined. An operational definition of a treatment provides (a) a clear description of procedures, strategies, and activities that should be implemented and those that should be avoided; (b) specification of the length, duration, and intensity of the services; and (c) definition of the target population. Explicit description of procedures (a) ensures that active ingredients of a treatment are being delivered and proscribed procedures are being avoided; (b) reduces complexity of manipulation checks and amount of inferences required in coding; and (c) increases precision of the assessment measures and data accuracy (e.g., Elkin, Pilkonis, & Sotsky, 1988; Heimberg & Becker, 1984).

Treatment procedures can be detailed in a manual form. Manuals can be developed from conceptual frameworks, pilot studies, and consultations with implementers (Nelsen, 1985). Manuals reduce the variability in treatment implementation (Drozd & Goldfried, 1996; Rounsaville, Chevron, & Weissman, 1984) and enhance treatment integrity (Ehrhardt, Barnett, Lentz, Stollar, & Reifin, 1996; Schinke, Gilchrest, & Snow, 1985). Manuals can (a) discuss the theoretical basis of a treatment, (b) outline its structure, (c) detail required and auxiliary components, (d) specify therapist behaviors (e.g., provide verbatim statements to be made by therapists), (e) describe the sequence of the techniques, (f) give procedures for competent implementation of tasks, and (g) provide procedures for handling deviations (e.g., Dobson & Shaw, 1988; McMahon, 1987; Nelsen, 1985). Nezu and Nezu (2008) suggested developing treatment manuals with treatment integrity implementation and assessment procedures in mind, including detailing adequate and inadequate performance criteria, specifying relevance of therapists' behavior by context, and matching treatment manual and treatment integrity protocol. Further, greater consistency in treatment delivery may arise from allowing some built-in flexibility, in which required therapeutic ingredients are presented in conjunction with procedures that are optional or indicated for just some clients. This built-in flexibility must be reflected in the assessment guidelines and procedures.

Flexibility of an approach may also involve creative presentation of material. Creativity is usually seen as an important aspect of therapist competence; however, when it is used as a key therapeutic component, creativity enters into the domain of treatment adherence. For purposes of assessing adherence, treatment components require operational definition. Yet, meaningfully manualizing creative responding in a moment may be very difficult. For example, training in a humanistic therapy involves providing therapists with an understanding of humanistic philosophy and the theoretical basis of a treatment and facilitating the development of spontaneity, empathy, and genuineness. Creative responding and improvisation in the moment are valued as key ingredients of therapeutic process, whereas specific treatment protocols are viewed as counterproductive (Bohart, O'Hara, & Leitner, 1998). However, such idiosyncratic responding of therapists reduced uniformity in therapists' behavior. Problems with operationalizing treatment are inherent in any psychotherapy research (Frances, Sweeney, & Clarkin, 1985). The task may be challenging because including all potential scenarios of treatment delivery, considering various comorbid diagnoses, and accounting for a client's difficulty is not always possible or feasible. The complexity of the task can at least partially explain the finding that only about 65% of RCTs of psychosocial treatments use specific manuals (Perepletchkova et al., 2007). Yet, lack of a precise operational definition of a treatment introduces random variation into the delivery of a treatment, impedes treatment integrity assessment, reduces statistical power, and compromises the internal and external validity of the study.

ASSESSMENT STRATEGIES

Treatment integrity can be assessed via direct, indirect, and hybrid strategies. In deciding on a strategy, one should consider the strengths and weaknesses of each approach, as detailed next.

Indirect Strategies

Indirect methods of assessment include self-reports, rating scales, interviews, and permanent products of treatment implementation (e.g., homework sheets; Gresham et al., 2000). Self-reports can be obtained directly from therapists and include rating on the degree to which procedures were implemented as intended. Likert scales can be used for such assessment. The Therapy Procedures Checklist (Weersing, Weisz, & Donenberg, 2002), a therapist self-report measure that encompasses psychodynamic, cognitive, behavioral, and family approaches, is notable for its ability to assess treatment differentiation. However, although self-ratings are convenient and easy to obtain, they can be biased and distorted by self-interest. Demand characteristics and a need for social approval can affect the accuracy of the reported adherence and competence.

Clients can be debriefed via interview or questionnaire on what was done by a therapist during treatment sessions. Clients may provide information regarding the manner in which procedures were executed and what was received by subjects (Docherty, 1984; Kazdin, 2003). Subjective recollections may be inaccurate, but responses that vary systematically among experimenters may provide important information about what was implemented. For example, clients may describe specific behaviors of a therapist or report the nature of assignments, monitoring of homework completion, rehearsal of techniques, and clarification of difficult material. Systematic endorsement of a therapist's specific tendencies may provide clues about deviations from the manual and the therapist's competence in treatment delivery.

Research that relies primarily on the indirect, subjective evaluations of treatment integrity is likely to be weak in its ability to measure treatment integrity accurately. Such methods are more likely to be reactive and to be influenced by social desirability and demand characteristics; thus, such methods are less reliable and valid. A potentially more accurate indirect method of treatment integrity assessment includes collection of the permanent products, such as written homework assignments or data collection sheets. Each component of the treatment is referenced to the permanent product corresponding to each treatment step. Evaluation of the presence and absence of the corresponding products is a more reliable indirect method of treatment integrity assessment.

Direct Strategies

Assessments that rely on self-report are subject to various threats to measurement accuracy, as discussed above. Observations conducted by trained staff are considered the gold standard because they can provide a more objective account of the implemented procedures (Hogue, Liddle, & Rowe, 1996; Mowbray, Holter, Teague, & Bybee, 2003). Observations can be done in the treatment setting, by viewing sessions through a one-way mirror or via monitors, or by listening to sessions via review of video/audio records. Attending sessions is more likely when a treatment is provided to a large group of people, such as in a classroom. However, the presence of an observer can alter performance of a therapist and may result in higher adherence to specified procedures during observed sessions as compared to when observations are not conducted (K. Jones et al., 1997; McMahon, 1987). Differential adherence may artificially inflate estimates of treatment integrity and compromise accuracy of integrity data.

To ameliorate reactivity, observers can "spot check" treatment implementations on a variable-time schedule (Peterson et al., 1982). Viewing sessions via monitors or one-way mirror may be a feasible alternative to direct observations in the treatment setting. Such observations are unobtrusive because they can be conducted without therapist awareness, and they may provide more accurate data. Videotaping sessions with subsequent coding by trained observers is a common approach for research protocols. Usually, 20% to 40% of all sessions are observed or videotaped (Schlosser, 2002). Reactivity may be ameliorated when all treatment sessions are videotaped, with subsequent evaluation of a random subset of recordings.

An observational measure, the Therapy Process Observational Coding System for Child Psychotherapy Strategies Scale (TPOCS-S; McLeod & Weisz, 2010), was recently developed to address the limitations of the self-reported Therapy Procedures Checklist. This measure assesses the extent to which treatment procedures from several therapeutic approaches are employed from direct observations of treatment sessions. The ability to examine different therapeutic approaches is a unique strength of this measure, as most treatment integrity assessment instruments are treatment specific. Such a measure can be used to examine implementation of evidence-based approaches in clinical practice. Implementation research is central to understanding the needs and preferences of clinical providers and can inform dissemination efforts. For example, researchers using the TPOCS-S found that usual care therapists utilize multiple approaches and favor nonbehavioral treatments, such as client-centered therapy (McLeod & Islam, 2011).

Hybrid Strategies

Indirect methods of treatment integrity assessment are usually used to supplement direct strategies. Data obtained via direct and indirect measures may be compared to clarify treatment implementation issues (Bergan & Kratochwill, 1990; Gresham, 1989). Only a fraction of sessions is usually utilized for coding of observational data; thus, therapist self-reports collected after each session may offer a more detailed assessment of treatment delivery. Further, therapist self-reports can be used to differentiate between frequently and infrequently used strategies. This information can provide clues to which procedures therapists regard as more effective for further treatment refinement (Carroll et al., 2000).

It should be noted, however, that there is low agreement between direct and indirect methods (Carroll, Nich, & Rounsaville, 1998; Gresham, 1997; Wickstrom, Jones, LaFleur, & Witt, 1998). Some reasons for such disparity include demand characteristics and need for social approval. Inherent limitations of observational ratings may also play a role. Raters are removed from the treatment process and may, therefore, (a) miss subtle strategies or those that are imbedded in reference to previous discussions, (b) misunderstand statements made by therapists, and (c) fail to see the full interaction between client and therapist (e.g., beginning and end of sessions may not always be recorded, and sound and picture quality of the videotapes or TV monitors may preclude accurate representation of a therapist's behaviors; Carroll et al., 2000). Yet, as has been noted, self-reports offer immediate access to the adherence and competence data, and they can be used to adjust treatment delivery.

Reliability of Treatment Integrity Measures

There is no conventional method of establishing reliability of treatment integrity measures. Reliability data have been reported as the percentage of agreement between raters or observers (e.g., Dusenbury, Brannigan, Hansen, Walsh, & Falco, 2005), test–retest reliability (e.g., Resnicow et al., 1998), and intraclass correlations for raters (Carroll et al., 2000). Other methods have been suggested, such as factor analysis to determine internal structure of a measure and internal consistency indices (e.g., coefficient alpha; McGrew, Bond, Dietzen, & Salyers, 1994; Sheridan, Swanger-Gagne, Welch, Kwon, &

Garbacz, 2009). However, coefficient alpha reflects a correlation of variables. As suggested by Gresham (2009), the presence of such a correlation is a dubious assumption, because treatment components cannot be expected to relate to each other. For example, in dialectical behavior therapy, therapeutic strategies assessed for adherence include problem assessment, problem solving, cognitive modification, case management, irreverence, reciprocal communication, exposure-based procedures, and crisis protocols. All of these strategies cannot be expected to correlate. Calculation of interrater reliability, the most common method of establishing measure reliability, is done by dividing the number of agreements by the number of agreements plus the number of disagreements and multiplying by 100%. Agreement can also be calculated by obtaining the kappa coefficient (Cohen, 1960). The kappa coefficient is specifically useful when no raw data are missing, and it may provide better control for chance agreement.

Validation of Treatment Integrity Measures

Validation of measures may be challenging because treatment integrity encompasses constructs—adherence and competence—that are not necessarily related. The validation process may involve examination of how measures behave in relation to one another. Factors (e.g., predictors, causal agents, moderating, mediating variables) that are known to affect constructs under investigation may be used to examine the validity of an instrument. Several factors, including client and treatment characteristics, specificity of a treatment manual, and the levels of therapist training and supervision, are known to be associated with treatment integrity (Perepletchikova & Kazdin, 2005).

Complexity of the treatment, required multiple resources and materials, number of treatment agents, time needed for treatment implementation, and rate of behavioral change are hypothesized to be inversely related to the level of treatment integrity (Gresham, 1989; Gresham et al., 2000; Noell, Gresham, & Gansle, 2002). Construct validity of the treatment adherence measure may be evaluated by examining its association with treatment characteristics. *Construct validity* refers to the relation of a measure to other measures or domains of functioning. Two treatments that differ on the characteristics that negatively affect treatment integrity (e.g., time consuming, requires multiple resources and therapists) may be compared on their effects on adherence levels. Validity may be supported by demonstrating that the characteristics of the treatments are differentially associated with levels of treatment integrity.

Further, evidence on the differential training effects on therapist adherence levels may support validity of a measure. Adherence to protocol is more likely with direct training of therapists (e.g., opportunities for practice and feedback) than with indirect training (e.g., didactic instructions; e.g., Kratochwill et al., 1991; Sterling-Turner et al., 2001). Specificity of a treatment manual may also differentially affect treatment integrity, where higher specificity contributes to greater treatment integrity levels. Manual specificity that differs as a function of treatment may be used to examine construct validity of a treatment integrity measure.

Discriminant validity is suggested if a measure shows little or no correlation with measures with which it is not expected to correlate. Discriminant validity may be supported when the measure of adherence to treatment protocol is associated with the treatment for which the protocol was originally devised (e.g., cognitive-behavioral treatment) and is not associated with the treatment for which conditions are different (e.g., psychodynamic therapy). The same measure of adherence may be employed with both treatments, and significant difference on adherence ratings as a function of therapy type in the expected direction may be indicative of the measure's ability to discriminate between treatments. Further, supervision and monitoring of treatment delivery can help reduce therapeutic drift and may facilitate adherence to the specified treatment protocol. Thus, concurrent validity of a treatment integrity measure may be supported via its association with the levels of provided supervision (i.e., the higher the level of monitoring and feedback, the higher the adherence).

Supervision and ongoing monitoring may also enhance the competence of treatment delivery. Thus, relationship between the measures of the levels of provided supervision with the measure of therapist competence may serve to support the concurrent validity of treatment integrity measures. *Concurrent validity* refers to the association of a measure with performance on another measure at the same point in time. Concurrent validity of the competence measure can also be examined by evaluating the association of therapist competence with the measures of client characteristics, because therapist performance may vary as a function of client difficulty, hostility, high problem severity, duration, and comorbidity (e.g., Detrich, 1999; Foley, O'Malley, Rounsaville, Prusoff, & Weissman, 1987; Waltz et al., 1993).

Criterion validity of a competence measure can be suggested when a measure can distinguish between different therapeutic modalities (e.g., Barber & Crits-Christoph, 1996; Barber, Liese, & Abrams, 2003). *Criterion validity* refers to a correlation of a measure with some other specific or dichotomous criterion. Therapeutic approaches usually have specific requirements for demonstrating competence. For example, cheerleading, self-disclosure, and irreverent communication are commonly used in dialectical behavior therapy but are proscribed for psychoanalytic therapists.

Representativeness of Treatment Integrity Data

Therapists' adherence and competence may vary across subjects, tasks, and time. Representativeness depends upon the number and length of observations and collection of data across treatment phases, therapists, situations, cases, and sessions (Moncher & Prinz, 1991; Peterson et al., 1982). Sampling across these aspects of treatment delivery informs consistency in treatment integrity data (Docherty, 1984).

1. *Across treatment phases.* A treatment usually consists of several phases, such as introduction to therapy and assessment of pathology (Phase 1), skills training (Phase 2), and relapse prevention (Phase 3). Phase 1 may be most conducive to higher treatment integrity ratings, because tasks in this phase are more straightforward. Phase 2, on the other hand, may have lower treatment integrity ratings because more complex tasks, such as the actual training of skills, are administered.

2. *Across therapists.* Therapists may have high variability in their performance due to personality factors, motivation, and previous training and experience (Gresham, 1989; Miller & Binder, 2002; Weissman, Rounsaville, & Chevron, 1982). When data are overrepresentative for some therapists, treatment integrity ratings may be skewed in a particular direction.

3. *Across situations.* At times, therapists may have to deal with unexpected circumstances, such as when a client presents with a crisis. In such situations therapists may have to partially or completely deviate from a treatment protocol in order to address specific concerns. Hence, the integrity of treatment implementation may be lower.

4. *Across sessions.* The material of sessions may vary in complexity and difficulty. Therapists may find it easier to adhere to guidelines when material is more straightforward. When such sessions are overrepresented in the sample, treatment integrity ratings may be higher.

5. *Across cases.* A therapeutic relationship with a difficult (e.g., angry, hostile) client may be less reinforcing for a therapist and may require greater effort. Greater effort in the face of little success may discourage a faithful rendition of the treatment plan. Severe cases may require more direction and coaching and incorporation of additional techniques to address a client's specific concerns. So, treatment integrity may be higher with uncomplicated clients than with more difficult clients.

Further, treatment integrity data may be more informative when they encompass all three aspects involved in their specification: adherence, competence, and treatment differentiation. Adherence measures that include prescribed as well as proscribed procedures can also assess treatment differentiation. Waltz et al. (1993) recommended that adherence measures should include items pertaining to four types of therapist behaviors: (a) those that are unique and essential to the specific treatment (e.g., assigning homework in behavior therapy); (b) those that are essential but not unique to the treatment (e.g., setting treatment goals); (c) those that are compatible with the treatment; that is, not prohibited but neither unique nor essential (e.g., therapeutic self-disclosure); and (d) those that are proscribed (e.g., interpreting resistance or transference in behavior therapy). Competence measures cannot rely on the level of experience and training but should be independently verified by measuring how sensitively the treatment protocol is applied to individual clients. Within this framework, ratings of competence should consider (a) stage of therapy, in terms of information about number of sessions completed and extent of progress; (b) client difficulty, which may impact the level of therapist activity and involvement; and (c) therapist approach to the presenting problem in a manner consistent with the prescribed procedures (Waltz et al., 1993).

Data Accuracy

The accuracy of the rating of treatment integrity depends on the competence of raters, the sophistication of the measures, and the coding procedures. Raters have to be trained in all of the major and minor treatment components and subtle aspects of the treatment (Stein, Sargent, & Rafaels, 2007). Raters who are themselves skilled in the treatment delivery may be most suitable for treatment integrity rating. However, when raters are affiliated with the project, their ratings may be biased. Rater bias occurs when ratings are influenced by the subjectivity of a rater. It can be reduced by (a) using raters not associated with a study; (b) keeping raters unaware of treatment assignment, which is called *blinding;* (c) using multiple raters; and (d) performing consensus ratings and interrater reliability checks (Marcus et al., 2006; Wu, Whiteside, & Neighbors, 2007). Hoyt (2000) offered bias correction procedures to minimize its adverse effect on findings. He proposed four types of rater bias and delineated formulas to correct for attenuation and inflation of observed effect sizes.

Sophistication of the treatment integrity measure can have a significant impact on the accuracy of rating, with less sophisticated measures, such as indirect assessment methods, contributing to higher integrity rates (Miller & Binder, 2002; Robbins & Gutkin, 1994; Wickstrom et al., 1998).

Further, sensitivity and adequacy of the selected measures can affect treatment integrity data. Sensitivity of the measure can be constrained by ceiling or floor effects. Restriction in the range of scores can prevent continued increments in performance and result in a lower treatment integrity rating. A measure may not be comprehensive or specific enough to address constructs of interest. The importance of measurement adequacy was highlighted in the evaluation of the relationship between therapist competence and treatment outcome in the National Institute of Mental Health Treatment of Depression Collaborative Research Program (Shaw et al., 1999). This study showed only weak effects between these variables; however, the competence measure may have failed to tap into important aspects of cognitive-behavioral therapists' performance. The selected scale may have been useful for quality-control monitoring, but it was inadequate as a measure of therapist competence.

Procedures for coding treatment integrity can influence the coding accuracy. Coding of treatment integrity can include evaluation of the occurrence and nonoccurrence of each treatment component and the extent to which each component is performed competently and as specified. Thus, a detailed analysis of each task can increase coding accuracy. Coding videos of sessions in random order can also increase coding accuracy by controlling for observer drift (Kazdin, 1977; O'Leary & Kent, 1973).

Reporting Treatment Integrity

Treatment integrity applies not only to the overall performance of a therapist in treatment delivery but also to the implementation of each treatment component across and within sessions. Reporting of treatment integrity in terms of overall integrity, component integrity, and session integrity is recommended (Gresham, 1997; Schlosser, 2002). *Overall treatment integrity* addresses the degree to which all components were implemented across sessions. *Component integrity* refers to the integrity of implementing each treatment component across sessions. *Session integrity* refers to integrity of all treatment components within one session. Overall treatment integrity and session treatment integrity can be calculated by summing the components that were correctly implemented (across sessions or within one session, respectively) and dividing this number by the total number of components, expressing integrity as a percentage. Component integrity can be calculated by summing the number of sessions during which a component was correctly implemented and dividing this number by the total number of sessions, expressing integrity as a percentage. This approach is regarded as the most relevant because it evaluates the accuracy of treatment implementation (Schlosser, 2002). However, taking into account perspectives of only one observer can weaken this approach; thus, obtaining adequate levels of interrater agreement is also necessary. The current state of the literature on treatment integrity in psychotherapy research indicates that a high integrity level may be demonstrated by 80% to 100% integrity, moderate integrity by a 60% to 80% range, and low integrity by less than 60% integrity (Gansle & McMahon, 1997; Gresham, Gansle, Noell, et al., 1993; Holcombe, Wolery, & Snyder, 1994; Noell et al., 2002).

Calculating all three estimates of treatment integrity is essential, because even though overall treatment integrity may be high, component integrity and/or session integrity may be low. For example, therapist performance may vary as a function of client difficulty (e.g., Foley et al., 1987), and such variability may result in inconsistent treatment delivery within sessions. Although component integrity may be high across sessions, session integrity may be low for a particular session. Failure to measure session integrity may hinder the evaluation of results, especially when treatment failed to produce significant change on dependent measures while overall treatment integrity was high. Treatment components may be more or less critical for successful treatment implementation (e.g., providing a rationale for treatment may be less crucial than contingent delivery of positive reinforcement; Gresham, 1997). Monitoring within-session integrity may supply important information on the degree of competency and consistency in administering each treatment component. Such fine-grained analysis of treatment integrity permits better evaluation of treatment outcome and enhances the credibility and replicability of results. Further, such analysis helps distinguish among treatment components that are essential for change, sufficient, and just facilitative, thus aiding in the identification of the mechanisms of change.

Quantitative adherence and competence data must be presented in a publication on study outcomes, and these data should be informative of the treatment integrity levels. Reporting that utilization of treatment components between treatments was significantly higher for one treatment than for the other does not adequately inform the research consumer about the adherence levels. There may be a statistically significant difference without either treatment having high treatment integrity levels. That is, 50% treatment integrity may be significantly higher than 20% treatment integrity; however, neither represents adequate integrity levels. Further, treatment integrity is sometimes evaluated by asking raters to classify videotapes of therapy sessions by the employed treatment modality (e.g., which tape belongs to cognitive versus interpersonal therapy). This method does not indicate the degree to which therapists were adhering to a manual or were competent in treatment delivery. A tape may be correctly classified because the number of components within a session was higher for one treatment than for the other. However, this classification does not demonstrate that all of the prescribed components were utilized during a session or that proscribed strategies and procedures were avoided.

Only absolute values (not relative to each other) may be informative of treatment integrity levels. To be considered as informative, data may be presented as a percentage (e.g., 85% integrity of treatment delivery), a specific score within a clearly defined range (e.g., the median adherence score on the 5-point Likert scale was 3.8), or a number that can be easily converted into a percentage (e.g., the proportion of strategies consistent with prescribed treatment modality was .82).

CONCLUSION

The question of what represents a satisfactory assurance that treatment was implemented as designed may not have a straightforward answer. Multiple considerations may affect how treatment integrity is addressed, including available funding, study design, setting, level of risk of treatment inaccuracies, and nature of a treatment. Gresham (2009) discussed treatment integrity flexibility, where the required adherence levels depend on the type of the research study, with higher levels necessitated for efficacy studies and less stringent adherence accepted for effectiveness research. This discussion is based on a notion that treatment integrity is related to outcome and that treatments with "drifts" from a protocol can still produce positive effects, while allowing for flexibility under less controlled conditions. However, the main objective of establishing treatment integrity is not to increase the strength of the treatment but to inform the degree to which treatment was implemented as intended. The higher the treatment integrity level, the more closely the implemented treatment approximates the intended treatment. Low treatment integrity levels do not indicate that a treatment is weak but rather that a treatment is different from that originally intended.

A flexible approach to treatment integrity levels can lead to loose operational definition of a treatment and thus increase ambiguity in the interpretation of the findings. Yet, the call for a flexible approach highlights the challenges of consistent treatment delivery in different settings and under different conditions. The flexibility of treatment implementation can be built into the treatment protocol and accounted for in the treatment integrity measures, thus allowing for accurate estimations of integrity levels under variable conditions without compromising the interpretability of the results. Flexibility can be built into the treatment protocol by specifying (a) procedures for handling difficult cases, (b) additional treatment components for addressing comorbid problems, and (c) approaches for working with various populations (e.g., cultural issues, language barriers) and in different settings (e.g., outpatient care, residential facility, inpatient units). Additionally, intervention ingredients are not equally important (e.g., Sanetti & Kratochwill, 2009), and differentiating required components from auxiliary strategies can further augment flexible treatment delivery. These procedures would allow therapists to adapt treatment delivery to the needs of a client and the limitations of a particular setting, while delivering all key elements.

The call for accountability in mental health care necessitates establishing a scientific basis for interventions. Requiring manipulation checks on treatment delivery will improve the quality of research and clinical practice. Although it may be laborious and costly, this adjustment is necessary to advance the psychotherapy field. Redefinition of criteria for clearing the "evidence-based" threshold, standardization and enforcement of treatment integrity procedures, increased funding for research, and provision of incentives for implementing integrity procedures may aid in this quest.

REFERENCES

Armstrong, K. J., Ehrhardt, K. E., Cool, R. T., & Poling, A. (1997). Social validity and treatment integrity data: Reporting in articles published in the *Journal of Developmental and Physical Disabilities*, 1991–1995. *Journal of Developmental and Physical Disabilities*, 9, 359–367. doi:10.1023/A:1024982112859

Barber, J., & Crits-Christoph, P. (1996). Development of a therapist adherence/competence scale for supportive-expressive dynamic psychotherapy: A preliminary report. *Psychotherapy Research*, 6, 81–94. doi:10.1080/10503309612331331608

Barber, J. P., Liese, B., & Abrams, M. J. (2003). Development of the Cognitive Therapy Adherence and Competence Scale. *Psychotherapy Research*, 13, 205–221. doi:10.1093/ptr/kpg019

Beidas, R. S., & Kendall, P. C. (2010). Training therapists in evidence-based practice: A critical review of studies from a systems-contextual perspective. *Clinical Psychology: Science and Practice*, 17, 1–30. doi:10.1111/j.1468-2850.2009.01187.x

Bergan, J. R., & Kratochwill, T. R. (1990). *Behavioral consultation and therapy*. New York, NY: Plenum Press.

Bohart, A. C., O'Hara, M., & Leitner, L. M. (1998). Empirically violated treatments: Disenfranchisement of humanistic and other psychotherapies. *Psychotherapy Research*, 8, 141–157. doi:10.1080/10503309812331332277

Bond, G. R., Evans, L., Salyers, M. P., Williams, J., & Kim, H. W. (2000). Measurement of fidelity in psychiatric rehabilitation. *Mental Health Services Research*, 2, 75–87. doi:10.1023/A:1010153020697

Borrelli, B., Sepinwall, D., Ernst, D., Bellg, A. J., Czajkowski, S., Breger, R., . . . Orwig, D. (2005). A new tool to assess treatment fidelity and evaluation of treatment fidelity across 10 years of health behavior research. *Journal of Consulting and Clinical Psychology, 73*, 852–860. doi:10.1037/0022-006X.73.5.852

Breitenstein, S. M., Fogg, L., Garvey, C., Hill, C., Resnick, B., & Gross, D. (2010). Measuring implementation fidelity in a community-based parenting intervention. *Nursing Research, 59*, 158–165. doi:10.1097/NNR.0b013e3181dbb2e2

Carroll, K. M., Nich, C., & Rounsaville, B. J. (1998). Utility of therapist session checklists to monitor delivery of coping skills treatment for cocaine abusers. *Psychotherapy Research, 8*, 307–320. doi:10.1080/10503309812331332407

Carroll, K. M., Nich, C., Sifry, R. L., Nuro, K. F., Frankforter, T. L., Ball, S. A., . . . Rounsaville, B. J. (2000). A general system for evaluating therapist adherence and competence in psychotherapy research in the addictions. *Drug and Alcohol Dependence, 57*, 225–238. doi:10.1016/S0376-8716(99)00049-6

Cohen, J. (1960). A coefficient of agreement for nominal scales. *Educational and Psychological Measurement, 20*, 37–46. doi:10.1177/001316446002000104

Dane, A. V., & Schneider, B. H. (1998). Program integrity in primary and early secondary prevention: Are implementation effects out of control? *Clinical Psychology Review, 18*, 23–45. doi:10.1016/S0272-7358(97)00043-3

Detrich, R. (1999). Increasing treatment fidelity by matching interventions to contextual variables within the educational setting. *School Psychology Review, 28*, 608–620.

DiGennaro-Reed, F. D., Codding, R., Catania, C. N., & Maguire, H. (2010). Effects of video modeling on treatment integrity of behavioral interventions. *Journal of Applied Behavior Analysis, 43*, 291–295. doi:10.1901/jaba.2010.43-291

Dobson, K. S., & Shaw, B. F. (1988). The use of treatment manuals in cognitive therapy: Experience and issues. *Journal of Consulting and Clinical Psychology, 56*, 673–680. doi:10.1037/0022-006X.56.5.673

Docherty, J. P. (1984). Implications of the technological model of psychotherapy. In J. B. W. Williams & R. L. Spitzer (Eds.), *Psychotherapy research: Where are we and where should we go?* (pp. 139–147). New York, NY: Guilford Press.

Drozd, J. F., & Goldfried, M. R. (1996). A critical evaluation on the state-of-the-art in psychotherapy outcome research. *Psychotherapy: Theory, Research, Practice, Training, 33*, 171–180. doi:10.1037/0033-3204.33.2.171

Dusenbury, L., Brannigan, R., Falco, M., & Hansen, W. B. (2003). A review of research on fidelity of implementation: Implications for drug abuse prevention in school settings. *Health Education Research, 18*, 237–256. doi:10.1093/her/18.2.237

Dusenbury, L., Brannigan, R., Hansen, W. B., Walsh, J., & Falco, M. (2005). Quality of implementation: Developing measures crucial to understanding the diffusion of preventive interventions. *Health Education Research, 20*, 308–313. doi:10.1093/her/cyg134

Ehrhardt, K. E., Barnett, D. W., Lentz, F. E., Jr., Stollar, S. A., & Reifin, L. H. (1996). Innovative methodology in ecological consultation: Use of scripts to promote treatment acceptability and integrity. *School Psychology Quarterly, 11*, 149–168. doi:10.1037/h0088926

Elkin, I., Pilkonis, P. A., & Sotsky, S. M. (1988). Conceptual and methodological issues in comparative studies of psychotherapy and pharmacotherapy, I: Active ingredients and mechanisms of change. *American Journal of Psychiatry, 145*, 909–917.

Fairburn, C. G., & Cooper, Z. (2011). Therapist competence, therapy quality, and therapist training. *Behaviour Research and Therapy, 49*, 373–378. doi:10.1016/j.brat.2011.03.005

Foley, S. H., O'Malley, S., Rounsaville, B. J., Prusoff, B. A., & Weissman, M. M. (1987). The relationship of patient difficulty to therapist performance in interpersonal psychotherapy of depression. *Journal of Affective Disorders, 12*, 207–217. doi:10.1016/0165-0327(87)90029-2

Frances, A., Sweeney, J., & Clarkin, J. (1985). Do psychotherapies have specific effects? *American Journal of Psychotherapy, 39*, 159–174.

Gansle, K. A., & McMahon, C. M. (1997). Component integrity of teacher intervention management behavior using a student self-monitoring treatment: An experimental analysis. *Journal of Behavioral Education, 7*, 405–419. doi:10.1023/A:1022851117439

Gresham, F. M. (1989). Assessment of treatment integrity in school consultation and prereferral interventions. *School Psychology Review, 18*, 37–50.

Gresham, F. M. (1997). Treatment integrity in single-subject research. In R. D. Franklin, D. B. Allison, & B. S. Gorman (Eds.), *Design and analysis of single-case research* (pp. 93–117). Mahwah, NJ: Erlbaum.

Gresham, F. M. (2009). Evolution of the treatment integrity concept: Current status and future directions. *School Psychology Review, 38*, 533–540.

Gresham, F. M., Gansle, K. A., & Noell, G. H. (1993). Treatment integrity in applied behavior analysis with children. *Journal of Applied Behavior Analysis, 26*, 257–263. doi:10.1901/jaba.1993.26-257

Gresham, F. M., Gansle, K. A., Noell, G. H., Cohen, S., & Rosenblum, S. (1993). Treatment integrity of school-based behavioral intervention studies: 1980–1990. *School Psychology Review, 22*, 254–272.

Gresham, F. M., MacMillan, D. L., Beebe-Frankenberger, M. E., & Bocian, K. M. (2000). Treatment integrity in learning disabilities intervention research: Do we really know how treatments are implemented? *Learning Disabilities Research & Practice, 15*, 198–205. doi:10.1207/SLDRP1504_4

Heimberg, R. G., & Becker, R. E. (1984). Comparative outcome research. In M. Hersen, L. Michelson, & A. S. Bellack (Eds.), *Issues in psychotherapy research* (pp. 251–283). New York, NY: Plenum Press.

Hogue, A., Liddle, H. A., & Rowe, C. (1996). Treatment adherence process research in family therapy: A rationale and some practical guidelines. *Psychotherapy: Theory, Research, Practice, Training, 33*, 332–345. doi:10.1037/0033-3204.33.2.332

Hohmann, A. A., & Shear, M. K. (2002). Community-based intervention research: Coping with the "noise" of real life in study design. *American Journal of Psychiatry, 159,* 201–207. doi:10.1176/appi.ajp.159.2.201

Holcombe, A., Wolery, M., & Snyder, E. (1994). Effects of two levels of procedural fidelity with constant time delay on children's learning. *Journal of Behavioral Education, 4,* 49–73. doi:10.1007/BF01560509

Hoyt, W. T. (2000). Rater bias in psychological research: When is it a problem and what can we do about it? *Psychological Methods, 5,* 64–86. doi:10.1037/1082-989X.5.1.64

Jensen, P. S., Weersing, R., Hoagwood, K. E., & Goldman, E. (2005). What is the evidence for evidence-based treatments? A hard look at our soft underbelly. *Mental Health Services Research, 7,* 53–74. doi:10.1007/s11020-005-1965-3

Jones, H. A., Clarke, A. T., & Power, T. J. (2008). Expanding the concept of intervention integrity: A multidimensional model of participant engagement. *In Balance, 23*(1), 4–5.

Jones, K., Wickstrom, K., & Friman, P. (1997). The effects of observational feedback on treatment integrity in school-based behavioral consultation. *School Psychology Quarterly, 12,* 316–326. doi:10.1037/h0088965

Kazdin, A. E. (1977). Artifact, bias, and complexity of assessment: The ABCs of reliability. *Journal of Applied Behavior Analysis, 10,* 141–150. doi:10.1901/jaba.1977.10-141

Kazdin, A. E. (2003). *Research design in clinical psychology* (4th ed.). Boston, MA: Allyn & Bacon.

Kazdin, A. E. (2007). Mediators and mechanisms of change in psychotherapy research. *Annual Review of Clinical Psychology, 3,* 1–27. doi:10.1146/annurev.clinpsy.3.022806.091432

Kratochwill, T. R., Sheridan, S. M., Rotto, P. C., & Salmon, D. (1991). Preparation of school psychologists to serve as consultants for teachers of emotionally disturbed children. *School Psychology Review, 20,* 530–550.

Krumholz, H. M., Radford, M. J., Wang, Y., Chen, J., Heiat, A., & Marciniak, T. A. N. (1998). National use and effectiveness of beta-blockers for the treatment of elderly patients after acute myocardial infarction: National Cooperative Cardiovascular Project. *JAMA: Journal of the American Medical Association, 280,* 623–629. doi:10.1001/jama.280.7.623

Lauritsen, J. (1992, March 30). FDA documents show fraud in AZT trials. *New York Native.* Retrieved from http://www.virusmyth.com/aids/hiv/jlfraud.htm

Marcus, S. M., Gorman, J. M., Tu, X., Gibbons, R. D., Barlow, D. H., Woods, S. W., & Shear, M. K. (2006). Rater bias in a blinded randomized placebo-controlled psychiatry trial. *Statistics in Medicine, 25,* 2762–2770. doi:10.1002/sim.2405

Margison, F. R., McGrath, G., Barkham, M., Clark, J. M., Audit, K., & Connell, J. (2000). Measurement and psychotherapy: Evidence-based practice and practice-based evidence. *British Journal of Psychiatry, 177,* 123–130. doi:10.1192/bjp.177.2.123

Marks, S. E., & Tolsma, R. J. (1986). Empathy research: Some methodological considerations. *Psychotherapy: Theory, Research, Practice, Training, 23*, 4–20. doi:10.1037/h0085591

McGrew, J. H., Bond, G. R., Dietzen, L., & Salyers, M. (1994). Measuring the fidelity of implementation of a mental health program model. *Journal of Consulting and Clinical Psychology, 62*, 670–678. doi:10.1037/0022-006X.62.4.670

McLeod, B. D., & Islam, N. Y. (2011). Using treatment integrity methods to study the implementation process. *Clinical Psychology: Science and Practice, 18*, 36–40. doi:10.1111/j.1468-2850.2010.01232.x

McLeod, B. D., & Weisz, J. R. (2010). The therapy process observational coding system for Child Psychotherapy Strategies Scale. *Journal of Clinical Child and Adolescent Psychology, 39*, 436–443. doi:10.1080/15374411003691750

McMahon, P. M. (1987). Shifts in intervention procedures: A problem in evaluating human service interventions. *Social Work Research & Abstracts, 23*, 13–16. doi:10.1093/swra/23.4.13

Miller, S. J., & Binder, J. L. (2002). The effects of manual-based training on treatment fidelity and outcome: A review of the literature on adult individual psychotherapy. *Psychotherapy: Theory, Research, Practice, Training, 39*, 184–198. doi:10.1037/0033-3204.39.2.184

Moncher, F. J., & Prinz, R. J. (1991). Treatment fidelity in outcome studies. *Clinical Psychology Review, 11*, 247–266. doi:10.1016/0272-7358(91)90103-2

Moore, J. W., & Fisher, W. W. (2007). The effects of videotape modeling on staff acquisition of functional analysis methodology. *Journal of Applied Behavior Analysis, 40*, 197–202. doi:10.1901/jaba.2007.24-06

Moos, R. H., & Finney, J. W. (1983). The expanding scope of alcohol treatment evaluation. *American Psychologist, 38*, 1036–1044. doi:10.1037/0003-066X.38.10.1036

Morris, S. B., Turner, C. W., & Szykula, S. A. (1988). Psychotherapy outcome research: An application of new methods for evaluation research methodology. *Psychotherapy: Theory, Research, Practice, Training, 25*, 18–26. doi:10.1037/h0085319

Mowbray, C. T., Holter, M. C., Teague, G. B., & Bybee, D. (2003). Fidelity criteria: Development, measurement, and validation. *American Journal of Evaluation, 24*, 315–340. doi:10.1177/109821400302400303

Nelsen, J. C. (1985). Verifying the independent variable in single-subject research. *Social Work Research & Abstracts, 21*, 3–8. doi:10.1093/swra/21.2.3

Nezu, A. M., & Nezu, C. M. (2008). *Evidence-based outcome research: A practical guide to conducting randomized controlled trials for psychosocial interventions*. New York, NY: Oxford University Press.

Noell, G. H., Gresham, F. M., & Gansle, K. A. (2002). Does treatment integrity matter? A preliminary investigation of instructional implementation and mathematical performance. *Journal of Behavioral Education, 11*, 51–67. doi:10.1023/A:1014385321849

O'Leary, K. D., & Kent, R. N. (1973). Behavior modification for social action: Research tactics and problems. In L. A. Hamerlynck, P. O. Davidson, & L. E. Acker (Eds.), *Critical issues in research and practice* (pp. 69–96). Champaign, IL: Research Press.

Perepletchikova, F. (2009). *Treatment integrity in treatment outcome research: Adequacy of procedures, associated factors, implications for research and practice, guidelines and recommendations.* Saarbrüken, Germany: Lambert Academic Publishing.

Perepletchikova, F., Hilt, L. M., Chereji, E., & Kazdin, A. E. (2009). Barriers to implementing treatment integrity procedures: Survey of treatment outcome researchers. *Journal of Consulting and Clinical Psychology, 77,* 212–218. doi:10.1037/a0015232

Perepletchikova, F., & Kazdin, A. E. (2005). Treatment integrity and therapeutic change: Issues and research recommendations. *Clinical Psychology: Science and Practice, 12,* 365–383. doi:10.1093/clipsy.bpi045

Perepletchikova, F., Treat, T. A., & Kazdin, A. E. (2007). Treatment integrity in psychotherapy research: Analysis of the studies and examination of the associated factors. *Journal of Consulting and Clinical Psychology, 75,* 829–841. doi:10.1037/0022-006X.75.6.829

Peterson, L., Homer, A. L., & Wonderlich, S. A. (1982). The integrity of independent variables in behavior analysis. *Journal of Applied Behavior Analysis, 15,* 477–492. doi:10.1901/jaba.1982.15-477

Plumb, J. C., & Vilardaga, R. (2010). Assessing treatment integrity in acceptance and commitment therapy: Strategies and suggestions. *International Journal of Behavioral Consultation and Therapy, 6,* 263–295.

Resnicow, K., Davis, M., Smith, M., Lazarus-Yaroch, A., Baranowski, T., Baranowski, J., . . . Wang, D. T. (1998). How best to measure implementation of school health curricula: A comparison of three measures. *Health Education Research, 13,* 239–250. doi:10.1093/her/13.2.239

Robbins, J. R., & Gutkin, T. B. (1994). Consultee and client remedial and preventive outcomes following consultation: Some mixed empirical results and directions for future researchers. *Journal of Educational & Psychological Consultation, 5,* 149–167. doi:10.1207/s1532768xjepc0502_5

Rounsaville, B. J., Chevron, E. S., & Weissman, M. M. (1984). Specification of technique in interpersonal therapy. In J. B. W. Williams & R. L. Spitzer (Eds.), *Psychotherapy research: Where are we and where should we go?* (pp. 160–171). New York, NY: Guilford Press.

Sanetti, L. M. H., & Kratochwill, T. R. (2009). Toward developing a science of treatment integrity: Introduction to the special series. *School Psychology Review, 38,* 445–459.

Schinke, S. P., Gilchrest, L. D., & Snow, W. H. (1985). Skills intervention to prevent cigarette smoking among adolescents. *American Journal of Public Health, 75,* 665–667. doi:10.2105/AJPH.75.6.665

Schlosser, R. W. (2002). On the importance of being earnest about treatment integrity. *Augmentative and Alternative Communication, 18,* 36–44.

Sechrest, L., White, S. O., & Brown, E. D. (Eds.). (1979). *The rehabilitation of criminal offenders: Problems and prospects.* Washington, DC: National Academy of Sciences.

Shadish, W. R., Cook, T. D., & Campbell, D. T. (2002). *Experimental and quasi-experimental designs for generalized causal inference.* New York, NY: Houghton Mifflin.

Sharpless, B. A., & Barber, J. P. (2009). A conceptual and empirical review of the meaning, measurement, development, and teaching of intervention competence in clinical psychology. *Clinical Psychology Review, 29,* 47–56. doi:10.1016/j.cpr.2008.09.008

Shaw, B. F., Elkin, I., Yamaguchi, J., Olmsted, M., Vallis, T. M., Dobson, K. S., . . . Imber, S. D. (1999). Therapist competence ratings in relation to clinical outcome in cognitive therapy of depression. *Journal of Consulting and Clinical Psychology, 67,* 837–846. doi:10.1037/0022-006X.67.6.837

Sheridan, S. M., Swanger-Gagne, M., Welch, G. W., Kwon, K., & Garbacz, S. A. (2009). Fidelity measurement in consultation: Psychometric issues and preliminary examination. *School Psychology Review, 38,* 476–495.

Sholomskas, D. E., Syracuse-Siewert, G., Rounsaville, B. J., Ball, S. A., Nuro, K. F., & Carroll, K. M. (2005). We don't train in vain: A dissemination trial of three strategies of training clinicians in cognitive-behavioral therapy. *Journal of Consulting and Clinical Psychology, 73,* 106–115. doi:10.1037/0022-006X.73.1.106

Stein, K. F., Sargent, J. T., & Rafaels, N. (2007). Intervention research: Establishing fidelity of the independent variable in nursing clinical trials. *Nursing Research, 56,* 54–62. doi:10.1097/00006199-200701000-00007

Sterling-Turner, H. E., Watson, T. S., Wildmon, M., Watkins, C., & Little, E. (2001). Investigating the relationship between training type and treatment integrity. *School Psychology Quarterly, 16,* 56–67. doi:10.1521/scpq.16.1.56.19157

Tobin, D. L., Banker, J. D., Weisberg, L., & Bowers, W. (2007). I know what you did last summer (and it was not CBT): A factor analytic model of international psychotherapeutic practice in the eating disorders. *International Journal of Eating Disorders, 40,* 754–757. doi:10.1002/eat.20426

Vermilyea, B. B., Barlow, D. H., & O'Brien, G. T. (1984). The importance of assessing treatment integrity: An example in the anxiety disorders. *Journal of Behavioral Assessment, 6,* 1–11. doi:10.1007/BF01321456

Waltz, J., Addis, M. E., Koerner, K., & Jacobson, N. S. (1993). Testing the integrity of a psychotherapy protocol: Assessment of adherence and competence. *Journal of Consulting and Clinical Psychology, 61,* 620–630. doi:10.1037/0022-006X.61.4.620

Weersing, V. R., Weisz, J. R., & Donenberg, G. R. (2002). Development of the Therapy Procedures Checklist: A therapist-report measure of technique use in child and adolescent treatment. *Journal of Clinical Child & Adolescent Psychology, 31,* 168–180. doi:10.1207/S15374424JCCP3102_03

Weingardt, K. R., Cucciare, M. A., Bellotti, C., & Lai, W. P. (2009). A randomized trial comparing two models of web-based training in cognitive-behavioral therapy for substance abuse counselors. *Journal of Substance Abuse Treatment, 37,* 219–227. doi:10.1016/j.jsat.2009.01.002

Weissman, M. M., Rounsaville, B. J., & Chevron, E. (1982). Training psychotherapists to participate in psychotherapy outcome studies. *American Journal of Psychiatry, 139,* 1442–1446.

Weisz, J. R., Weiss, B., & Donenberg, G. R. (1992). The lab versus the clinic: Effects of child and adolescent psychotherapy. *American Psychologist, 47,* 1578–1585. doi:10.1037/0003-066X.47.12.1578

Wickstrom, K. F., Jones, K. M., LaFleur, L. H., & Witt, J. C. (1998). An analysis of treatment integrity in school-based behavioral consultation. *School Psychology Quarterly, 13,* 141–154. doi:10.1037/h0088978

Wiese, M. R. R. (1992). A critical review of parent training research. *Psychology in the Schools, 29,* 229–236. doi:10.1002/1520-6807(199207)29:3<229::AID-PITS2310290305>3.0.CO;2-Q

Wu, S. M., Whiteside, U., & Neighbors, C. (2007). Differences in inter-rater reliability and accuracy for a treatment adherence scale. *Cognitive Behaviour Therapy, 36,* 230–239. doi:10.1080/16506070701584367

III

PROMOTING TREATMENT INTEGRITY

7

THE USE OF PERFORMANCE FEEDBACK TO IMPROVE INTERVENTION IMPLEMENTATION IN SCHOOLS

GEORGE H. NOELL AND KRISTIN A. GANSLE

Research examining the use of performance feedback (PFb) to increase intervention implementation by teachers in schools emerged as a sustained line of inquiry with the publication of two studies in 1997 (Noell, Witt, Gilbertson, Ranier, & Freeland, 1997; Witt, Noell, LaFleur, & Mortenson, 1997). These initial studies and the extensions that continue to follow them represent the intersection of an enduring concern in education, child behavior therapy, and behavioral consultation with one of the extensively researched behavior change procedures within psychology. The extent to which teachers, parents, and other treatment agents implement intervention plans as designed following consultation or other planning efforts is an enduring challenge to the effectiveness of many psychological services (Arco & Birnbrauer, 1990; Harchik, Sherman, Sheldon, & Strouse, 1992; Noell & Witt, 1999; Wolery, 1997). Assuring intervention plan implementation remains one of the central challenges facing psychologists working with children and adults

http://dx.doi.org/10.1037/14275-009
Treatment Integrity: A Foundation for Evidence-Based Practice in Applied Psychology, L. M. H. Sanetti and T. R. Kratochwill (Editors)

with developmental disabilities, because in these contexts daily care providers such as parents, teachers, and residential staff are the predominant intervention agents. PFb has a relatively extensive literature base demonstrating that it typically supports behavior change in the desired direction (Alvero, Bucklin, & Austin, 2001; Balcazar, Hopkins, & Suarez, 1985–1986; Casey & McWilliam, 2011). These demonstrations include applications in education and contexts providing services to individuals with developmental disabilities (Arco & Birnbrauer, 1990; Noell et al., 2005).

Viewed in hindsight and from a high level of abstraction, the intersection of PFb and treatment integrity might seem to be an intuitively appealing meeting of a socially significant problem and an extensively researched solution. Although there may be some truth in this observation, the high level of abstraction glosses over complexities at the foundation of whether PFb will be appropriate and effective. Those complexities include recognizing that there are significant challenges in defining PFb and treatment integrity. Additionally, there are role and relationship issues that may emerge specifically within contexts such as behavioral consultation that could suggest that PFb is an inappropriate solution to increasing treatment integrity. The following sections consider selected definitional issues that are central to the intersection of treatment integrity and PFb. Subsequent to those discussions is a summary of the state of the literature examining the application of PFb to increase treatment integrity. The chapter concludes with an examination of key challenges confronting researchers and practitioners.

TREATMENT INTEGRITY VERSUS INTERVENTION PLAN IMPLEMENTATION

Terminology

One of the key challenges in describing the critical facets of treatment integrity and what is known about them is that the term has been used so broadly in the literature that it includes multiple constructs that are related to each other but that are distinct (Noell, 2008; Schulte, Easton, & Parker, 2009). For example, *treatment integrity* has been used extensively to describe the definition and measurement of the independent variable in experimental research (Gresham, Gansle, & Noell, 1993; Peterson, Homer, & Wonderlich, 1982). In this context, it is an issue of the accuracy and reliability of the operation of an experimental apparatus or the behavior of a research staff. It is also worth noting that *integrity*, *fidelity*, *reliability*, *adherence*, and *implementation* have all been used to describe the accuracy of implementation (Dusenbury,

Brannigan, Falco, & Hansen, 2003; Groskreutz, Groskreutz, & Higbee, 2011; Henggeler, Melton, Brondino, Scherer, & Hanley, 1997; Peterson et al., 1982; Sanetti & Fallon, 2011). *Treatment integrity* as it applies to the accuracy of the implementation of the independent variable is a critical issue in the internal validity of experimental research (Johnston & Pennypacker, 1980; Schulte et al., 2009). The literature examining the degree to which researchers provide controls for the implementation of the independent variable in experimental reports in major journals has repeatedly raised the issue that researchers are typically more thorough in documenting the dependent variables than the independent variables (Gresham et al., 1993; Peterson et al., 1982; Schulte et al., 2009).

Conceptual Differences Between Intervention Plan Implementation and Treatment Integrity

In contrast, *treatment integrity* has also been used to describe the implementation of intervention or treatment plans in natural settings by parents, teachers, and students following consultation or training (e.g., Kelleher, Riley-Tillman, & Power, 2008; Wilkinson, 2007). Obviously, assuring in vivo treatment implementation by natural members of those environments is a different problem than assuring integrity of independent variables in experimental reports (Noell, 2008). The literature examining reports of treatment integrity by researchers in premier journals tells us nothing about (a) how implementation should be measured in the natural contexts that matter, (b) the extent to which practitioners successfully obtain implementation in the natural contexts, or (c) how best to assure implementation. Given the competing demands, uncontrolled consequences, and individual differences that exist in natural contexts, this is clearly a different and arguably more socially significant problem than demonstrating that experimental equipment is well calibrated or that research staff are following a detailed procedure. Additionally, the challenge in a natural context is not so much one of assuring the internal validity of an analysis as one of obtaining a level of implementation sufficient to impact children and youth with consultative or intervention services.

Multiple Facets

The emergence of *treatment integrity* as a common label for both implementation of the independent variable in an experiment and implementation of interventions in natural contexts is problematic because it obscures the critical distinctions between them. For example, in much of the literature discussed in this chapter, implementation of an intervention by a teacher, parent, or student was the dependent variable that was influenced by one or more experimental independent variables such as PFb. In the context of child behavior therapy, *treatment integrity* is too imprecise a term because it can describe the implementation of some independent variable designed to influence an outcome, the implementation of a consultation or training process designed to promote behavior change, or the degree to which a planned intervention is implemented by a parent, teacher, student, or peer.

To promote clarity in describing the phenomenon of interest, Noell (2008) recommended adopting three distinct terms in examining treatment implementation in schools and child behavior therapy. First, *treatment integrity* will be reserved for description of the accuracy of the manipulation of an independent variable in an experimental study. *Intervention plan implementation* (IPI) will be used to describe the accuracy of the implementation of an intervention or treatment plan in a natural context. Typically, IPI would describe implementation that is part of practice or is being studied in a way that is hoped to generalize to practice as in studies examining implementation of intervention in the natural context by persons who typically are present in that context (e.g., Auld, Belfiore, & Scheeler, 2010; Rodriguez, Loman, & Horner, 2009). In these cases, IPI is a dependent variable. Finally, *consultation procedural integrity* was recommended for describing the extent to which consultation procedures were implemented as designed (Noell, 2008). This final distinction appears warranted, as typically consultation procedural integrity is a distinct concern in consultation and child behavior therapy practice and research. Having a clear term to differentiate this process from other potential independent variables and the implementation of the intervention appears to have general utility.

Conceptually differentiating IPI from treatment integrity may be necessary to recognizing that IPI is an outcome worthy of study rather than a nuisance factor that needs to be controlled and documented by the experimenter. However, the shift from IPI as a cause controlled by an experimenter to IPI as one possible outcome creates additional challenges. A first and obvious challenge is the operational definition and measurement of IPI. At a conceptual level, assessing IPI is not much different from assessing other behaviors, and it should be amenable to the same self-reports, observations, and rating scales extensively discussed in the literature (Haynes & O'Brien, 2000). However, as one attempts to operationalize an assessment of IPI, complex issues arise (Gresham, 1989). IPI potentially can be assessed on an extremely global scale (e.g., a Likert rating of global implementation) or an extremely molecular level in which hundreds of specific steps are assessed. Neither of these extremes is represented in the literature to an extensive degree due to either low utility (global ratings) or impracticality (documenting hundreds of steps). The predominant strategy has been to measure accuracy of implementation or what has come to be known as *adherence*: to define a modest number of distinct steps (typically in the range of four to 14 steps) and measure completion of those steps (DiGennaro, Martens, & Kleinmann, 2007; Noell et al., 2005). This level of definition has been sufficient to demonstrate both a relationship between IPI and client outcomes and a sensitivity of implementation to experimental manipulation (Noell et al., 2000, 2005). However, the research literature to date has been striking in the degree to which it has failed to consider the differential implementation difficulty of treatment steps, the degree to which steps are serially related, and the degree to which specific treatment steps are pivotal to or determinative of treatment outcome (Noell & Gansle; 2006; Schulte et al., 2009). It is unlikely that each treatment step is equally predictive of outcomes, but there is no practical method for weighting impact for each element of a treatment. Indeed, the importance of specific treatment elements may vary across individuals and time within individuals.

As the professional discussion of treatment integrity has matured, researchers in multiple social science fields have discussed a variety of approaches to describing the multifaceted character of treatment integrity, acknowledging that IPI is not unidimensional and that there are several important planes on which implementation may differ. In their meta-analysis of the effects of integrity on primary and secondary prevention programs, Dane and Schneider (1998) chose five categories in which to classify the treatment integrity described in the studies in their meta-analysis: adherence, exposure, delivery quality exposure, program differentiation, and responsiveness to treatment. All relate either to the quantity or quality of the intervention delivered (Power et al., 2005) and have included such dimensions as the behaviors necessary for the intervention to succeed (Waltz, Addis, Koerner, & Jacobson, 1993); the competence of those delivering the intervention as well as the dosage, adherence, and responsiveness of the participant (Jones, Clarke, & Power, 2008); and IPI seen as content and process variables (Power et al., 2005). Further, given the failure of many researchers to monitor treatment integrity or to do so in only a cursory manner, Power et al. (2005) advocated for a partnership model that would be responsive to community priorities and needs. Instead of the dominant model of procedures for monitoring interventions that are delineated by parties other than those actually implementing the intervention, a partnership model is based on aspects of participatory action research (Reason & Bradbury, 2001). In other words, the control and authority over IPI and monitoring is shared by the research team and the individuals implementing the intervention, thereby programming for the constant analysis and adaptation of interventions to the stakeholders' needs (Power et al., 2005).

Classification System

Schulte et al. (2009) synthesized much of this research into a classification system to guide the study of operational elements of IPI. Based on the previous literature, several different dimensions were selected that can be grouped into three general categories: treatment delivery, treatment receipt, and treatment enactment. The first category, most evident in the literature, and closest conceptually to treatment integrity as measurement of implementation of the independent variable in research, relates to aspects of treatment implementation from the delivery side. Four dimensions of IPI that compose treatment delivery are *adherence*, or the number or proportion of treatment elements delivered; *exposure*, or the "amount" of treatment that is provided by the treatment agent (e.g., number of sessions, how often the treatment was delivered); *quality*, or the extent to which the treatment delivered would be considered mastery practice; and *program differentiation*, or the extent to which the treatment delivered represented elements of the planned intervention and not of some other treatment. The second category of IPI discussed focused on aspects of the receipt of treatment by the treatment target. Three dimensions of IPI that fall into the treatment receipt category include *dose or exposure*, *comprehension* by the target, and *responsiveness* of the target. In other words, how much treatment was received, how much treatment was understood, and the extent to which the target engaged with the treatment or find it relevant, respectively. The third category of dimensions of IPI includes features of treatment enactment, or the extent to which the treatment target used the skills taught. First, was there *mastery* in a controlled setting, and second, was there *use* of the skills in the natural setting?

Measuring Outcomes

Obviously, the discussion of these elements moves description and subsequent measurement of IPI from merely the delivery of a treatment to whether and how it is actually received by the treatment target, and finally, to the outcome: whether the behavior of the treatment target has changed in response to implementation of the intervention. Due to the depth and breadth of these issues, a second critical concern in how IPI is operationalized clearly will be how it is measured. Detailed consideration of the measurement issues surrounding IPI are beyond the scope of this chapter, but it is worth noting that all of the available measurement tools have consequential limitations. Although direct observation is the gold standard, it is susceptible to reactivity, and the resource demands for obtaining an adequate sample can be daunting (Hintze & Matthews, 2004). Permanent product strategies have been used successfully in a number of studies (e.g., Gilbertson, Witt,

Singletary, & VanDerHeyden, 2007; Noell et al., 1997; Resetar, Noell, & Pellegrin, 2006); however, they are limited in the types of treatment behaviors they can capture and are vulnerable to additional sources of measurement error because they are indirect measures of behavior (Haynes & O'Brien, 2000). Self-reports are an intuitively appealing alternative but measure only the respondents' perception of their IPI rather than their actual IPI. Additionally, some research evidence suggests little relationship between teacher-reported IPI and more directly measured IPI with teachers reporting substantially higher levels of implementation than are observed (Noell et al., 2005; Wickstrom, Jones, LaFleur, & Witt, 1998).

In addition to the conceptual and practical issues raised above, choosing to systematically increase IPI raises ethical, professional, and interpersonal issues that can be thorny and have received limited consideration in the literature (Noell, 2008; Noell & Gansle, 2006). Although the raison d'être for consultation and child behavior therapy is to provide beneficial services to a broader range of clients than is possible with direct services alone, the milieu of consultation has typically emphasized a collaborative, coequal approach in which the consultee has the right to refuse recommendations in whole or part (Bergan & Kratochwill, 1990; Erchul et al., 2007; Kelleher et al., 2008). The ethical and professional challenge lies in part in the complexity of adult behavior change. How does one resolve the inconsistency between consultees' stated intent to implement an intervention and their failure to do so? Which provides stronger evidence of consultees' intent, their stated preferences in an interview or their behavioral outcomes in complex environments with many competing demands? In the context of consultation between a parent, educator, and psychologist, who chooses whose behavior to change, and to what extent are those choices freely and knowingly made versus subtly and interpersonally coerced?

Similarly, ethical issues in schools will inevitably emerge between the rights of students and the preferences and professional autonomy of educators (Jacob, Decker, & Hartshorne, 2011). The intent of the preceding was not to create a straw man that consultation is either collaborative or directive. To varying degrees that should be sensitive to the specific situation, it will be both. The purpose in raising the issues described above is to acknowledge that a complex interplay of relationship choices is being made in any context where a psychologist is attempting to change adult behavior to improve life outcomes for a child (increase IPI). Some psychologists may judge PFb to be too intrusive or aversive to be used to support IPI, whereas others may judge it to be perfectly reasonable. It is worth noting that in the limited number of studies examining PFb and IPI, teachers have rated consultants who provide PFb to support IPI favorably (Noell, Duhon, Gatti, & Connell, 2002; Noell et al., 2005).

PERFORMANCE FEEDBACK

Generally, PFb has been defined as information that is provided to an individual or group about the quantity or quality of their behavior that provides information about how well they are doing (Alvero et al., 2001; Prue & Fairbank, 1981; Sulzer-Azaroff & Mayer, 1991). Additionally, it has been argued that PFb provides information that supports performance improvement or increases human capital utilization (Baker, 2010; Smither, London, & Reilly, 2005). Generally, the information would be distinct from or augment the naturally occurring consequences that are already readily available to the individual. For example, observing your missed and made free throws in basketball would not typically be conceptualized as a PFb intervention because observing the outcome is integral to the performance. However, providing the athlete with summary statistics or performance data broken down by context would typically be considered PFb in its most rudimentary from.

Definitions

Although a number of reviews and meta-analyses have all pointed to the efficacy of PFb (Alvero et al., 2001; Balcazar et al., 1985–1986; Casey & McWilliam, 2011; Kluger & DeNisi, 1996), authors have repeatedly identified concerns surrounding definitional issues, functional issues, and occasional paradoxical results. The critical definitional challenges for PFb have to do with the variety of procedures that have been used to deliver feedback, the sources of feedback, and the schedules of delivery. Reaching the conclusion that PFb is effective is distantly parallel to reaching the conclusion that delivering preferred stimuli contingent on the occurrence of a behavior will increase occurrence of that behavior in the future (i.e., will function as a reinforcer). Although that typically may be correct, there are so many variables that potentially can affect this bond (e.g., delivery timing, response effort, ratio, satiation) that one can readily design a context in which the general relationship breaks down.

An early seminal review of PFb research in the workplace found that PFb was most consistently effective when it included goal setting and behavioral consequences, was delivered by a supervisor, included graphic data, and occurred daily or weekly (Balcazar et al., 1985–1986). An updated review generally found similar results with the additional observation that the inclusion of antecedents was also associated with more consistent positive effects (Alvero et al., 2001). Both reviews found instances of mixed results and no positive effect. It is interesting to note that in their meta-analysis of interventions with PFb, Kluger and DeNisi (1996) found an overall positive effect for feedback interventions ($d = 0.41$), but that over a third of feedback interventions resulted in poorer performance. The authors determined that feedback that directs attention away from task learning and performance to metatask processes decreased task performance and that feedback effects were moderated by the nature of the task. They noted that this moderation appears to be complex and remains poorly understood. Further, Kluger and DeNisi examined a broad mixture of studies that included basic laboratory tasks as well as behaviors that are more representative of the workplace. Some of the tasks, participants, and context examined in the Kluger and DeNisi meta-analysis may be so functionally distinct from IPI in the natural context that they would not inform us about the effectiveness of PFb in these contexts. For example, the result of providing PFb to increase reading performance to an undergraduate research participant in a single session experiment may have limited external validity in understanding the impact of PFb on parents implementing a homework management program for their child.

Functional Issues

One of the important challenges in sorting out when PFb works and when it does not is that no broadly accepted conceptual model of the function of PFb has emerged (Alvero et al., 2001; Sulzer-Azaroff & Mayer, 1991; see Exhibit 7.1). It has been argued that PFb can function as positive reinforcement, as negative reinforcement, as a prompt, as a discriminative stimulus, or as instructional feedback, and/or it may elicit rule-governed behavior (Agnew, 1997; Alvero et al., 2001; Noell et al., 2000; Sulzer-Azaroff & Mayer, 1991). For example, a parent might increase IPI to contact praise in the PFb session (positive reinforcement) or to avoid embarrassment about poor implementation (negative reinforcement). Alternatively, the occurrence of the PFb session may serve as a reminder to implement the intervention for a teacher (prompt), or it might signal to the teacher consequences (e.g., supervisory review) that are now in place for IPI beyond the feedback (discriminative stimulus). PFb sessions might provide the opportunity to teach a peer tutor how to implement the procedure correctly (instructional feedback) or may elicit a rule-governed response from the tutor to work

EXHIBIT 7.1
Hypothesized Functional Properties of Performance Feedback

Positive reinforcement
Negative reinforcement
Prompting
Discriminative stimulus
Instructional feedback
Eliciting rule-governed behavior

harder to implement the treatment correctly because that is what he or she committed to do.

Although there have been calls for research focused on the functional properties of PFb, from colleagues adopting both behavioral and cognitive approaches, little progress has been evident in this domain (Alvero et al., 2001; Balcazar et al., 1985–1986; Kluger & DeNisi, 1996). This lack of progress may have more to do with the complexity of the exchange that takes place within PFb than with a lack of interest in sorting out the functions of PFb. In many instances, PFb may have more than one functional property. Further, the functional properties of PFb may not remain stable for individuals over time, and we should expect differences in the functional properties across individuals (Skinner, 1953). For example, initially, PFb may be both embarrassing and instructive such that a teacher increases IPI due to a desire to avoid negative feedback that includes useful information on how to implement the treatment. Subsequently, the same PFb that is now predominantly positive regarding IPI may serve discriminative, positively social reinforcing, and prompting functions. It is also worth recognizing that the function of PFb may be inconsistent across behaviors within individuals. For example, a 360° feedback assessment composed of ratings from supervisors, colleagues, parents, and a teacher regarding a principal's leadership style and management efficacy is a very different sort of assessment than feedback about the implementation of specific steps in a school's positive behavioral support program. It is possible that both PFb procedures could be functional (support behavior change) and useful to the principal, but for very different reasons based on the target behavior, feedback source, and frequency of feedback.

When considering the sheer volume of available studies and the long history of PFb research, it is surprising how much remains unknown about when and why it works. Part of that gap surely is the result of an incomplete consensus regarding the variables that may affect PFb. It may also be the case that PFb is a sufficiently complex social interaction with so many potentially operative elements, that there will remain considerable variability in how and with whom it is effective that only can be sorted out on a case-by-case basis. Those challenges aside for a moment, there are some general findings from previous reviews and meta-analyses of PFb that warrant summary before considering literature examining the application of PFb to IPI specifically.

Across reviews in education and other employment contexts, PFb has been found to be effective in the majority of cases in improving targeted behaviors (Alvero et al., 2001; Balcazar et al., 1985–1986; Casey & McWilliam, 2011). PFb has also been found to be more consistently effective when feedback is delivered by a supervisor, when there are consequences tied to the feedback, and when graphic feedback is provided

(Balcazar et al., 1985–1986; Noell et al., 2002; Sanetti, Luiselli, & Handler, 2007). It is worth noting that graphic feedback frequently is used to present the time course of behavior to participants (e.g., Noell et al., 2002). PFb with goal setting has been found to be more effective than goal setting alone ($d = 0.63$; Neubert, 1998), and goal setting has been reported to make PFb more consistently effective (Alvero et al., 2001; Balcazar et al., 1985–1986). Evidence also suggests that including planned antecedents to support behavior change—to do lists to prompt implementation or implementation prompts from intervention recipients—also improves the consistency of PFb results (Alvero et al., 2001).

Using Performance Feedback to Increase Intervention Plan Implementation

PFb has been provided in schools to support the implementation of instructional programs, behavior management programs, and interventions targeting individual students across a number of studies (Casey & McWilliam, 2011; Codding, Feinberg, Dunn, & Pace, 2005; Rathel, Drasgow, & Christle, 2008). Among published studies examining the use of PFb to increase the implementation of intervention and instructional programs, findings generally have been quite consistent that PFb is effective. PFb as it typically has been implemented in education has consisted of capturing, summarizing, and presenting data to teachers regarding their plan implementation (e.g., Codding et al., 2005; Noell et al., 2005). The focus of these studies typically has been upon whether or not PFb is an effective behavior change strategy for adults specific to implementation behaviors. Generally, one could summarize studies as asking one of two questions. First, is PFb an effective strategy for supporting intervention implementation? Second, does the inclusion of a specific feature of PFb make it more or less effective?

Although the functional properties of PFb have emerged intermittently in the broader literature, rarely have they been the direct focus of investigation, but instead have appeared in the school-based literature serendipitously regarding specific data, on an ad hoc or post hoc basis, and in theoretical discussions (e.g., Noell et al., 2000). Although the functional properties of PFb have not been directly examined, a number of studies were designed in such a way as to reduce the plausibility of instructional feedback as a critical mechanism. In many applications of PFb to support IPI in schools, training was provided such that treatment agents initially exhibited high levels of IPI (e.g., Mortenson & Witt, 1998; Noell et al., 2002). In these instances, there is no ambiguity that the treatment agents had learned the skill of implementing the intervention prior to the implementation of the experimental PFb procedure. In these studies, and the several additional related studies, it seems more plausible that PFb supported behavior through a motivational function (positive or negative reinforcement) or by eliciting some rule-governed behavior.

Initial Studies

The two initial studies that began the line of systematic inquiry into the use of PFb to sustain IPI followed similar structures and generally set the basic design that was used and modified in early studies in this area (Noell et al., 1997; Witt et al., 1997). Both of these studies used single-case multiple baseline designs to examine teachers' implementation of reinforcement-based academic interventions for referred students. Although the same intervention was used for all cases in each study, the specific details of the interventions were developed in consultation with the referring teachers and were tailored to the specific needs of the students involved. In the Witt et al. (1997) study, teachers were provided all of the materials necessary to implement the intervention and were trained in vivo to implement the intervention. The study began with a day of complete intervention implementation prior to baseline, and this was generally the model for subsequent studies. In contrast to the Witt et al. study and the other early studies, the Noell et al. (1997) study provided limited didactic training in a consultation session and did not provide the materials necessary to implement the intervention.

Results were consistent across the two studies (Noell et al., 1997; Witt et al., 1997). In both cases IPI generally was moderate to high in baseline and deteriorated across days. In both cases, implementation improved to high levels with the introduction of PFb on a daily basis. These data provided evidence that implementation of interventions in schools following consultation may deteriorate relatively quickly, and this may occur even following relatively extensive training and the provision of all of the necessary materials (Witt et al., 1997). The studies also demonstrated that PFb was successful in sustaining much higher levels of implementation and that this effect was not dependent on prior training to 100% implementation accuracy prior to receiving PFb. These findings were subsequently replicated and extended in a randomized clinical field trial examining PFb and IPI (Noell et al., 2005). The effect size for the comparison of PFb with the baseline condition was large ($d = 1.3$). Students whose teachers were in the PFb condition also demonstrated greater behavior change than students whose teachers were in the other two groups. An additional comparison group was provided a social influence procedure that emphasized commitment to implement the intervention. PFb was significantly more effective than either weekly meetings without PFb or with commitment emphasis discussions.

Mortenson and Witt (1998) followed the general model of the early studies described above, including the provision of intensive initial training and materials. In contrast to the earlier studies, this study provided PFb on a weekly rather than daily schedule. Although the results were less consistent and strong, this study generally replicated and extended earlier studies demonstrating deteriorating IPI without systematic follow-up and improved implementation with weekly PFb. Pellecchia et al. (2011) demonstrated an alternative approach to increasing the number of teachers for whom a consultant could provide PFb. They provided PFb to special education classroom teaching teams rather than individual general education teachers and found positive results for the targeted teacher behaviors. Although this approach did not increase the number of classes that could be reached, it did demonstrate a method of increasing the number of educators who could be supported under specialized conditions.

Embedding Performance Feedback

Another potential strategy for making PFb around IPI more consistently and widely available is to embed it in the prototypical team-based decision making and intervention routines in schools (Burns, Peters, & Noell, 2008; Duhon, Mesmer, Gregerson, & Witt, 2009). Burns et al. (2008) used a 20-item checklist with problem-solving teams (PSTs) at three schools to provide PFb to those teams. The checklist was derived following the professional literature about PSTs and covered such issues as whether baseline data were collected, whether progress monitoring data were objective, and whether the PST members had designated roles. One checklist was completed by an observer for each case considered by the PST. Following baseline data collection, target behaviors for school staffs were marked by the observer and presented to the PST, which resulted in an increase in the behaviors measured by the checklist. Although there was general improvement by the teams in their adherence to the items on the checklist, important steps such as progress monitoring and assessing intervention effectiveness did not improve. Duhon et al. (2009) delivered verbal and graphed PFb to PSTs regarding treatment elements *not* implemented by the teacher in individual interventions designed by the PST. They demonstrated that weekly PFb delivered in the context of a PST increased teachers' mean IPI to acceptable levels, that it could be maintained with continued PFb in PST meetings, and that removing PFb was associated with swift drops in IPI.

Subsequent studies have examined the importance of the structure and content of the follow-up meetings. Research examining follow-up meetings with and without PFb found that meetings without review of data and PFb were effective for 20% of participating teachers, whereas PFb was successful for 80% of participating teachers (Noell et al., 2000). Research has also examined the importance of the graphic presentation of the time course of IPI as part of the PFb (Noell et al., 2002; Sanetti et al., 2007). In both instances, this line of research was extended to behavior management interventions, and both studies found more positive results with the provision of a time course graph as part of PFb. Two rather different studies have introduced an avoidance contingency into PFb for IPI (DiGennaro, Martens, & McIntyre, 2005; Gilbertson et al., 2007). The Gilbertson et al. (2007) study implemented a response-dependent PFb such that the teacher would receive feedback only when elements of the intervention were omitted as a strategy for thinning PFb. Improved IPI was evident for three of four teachers as PFb was faded through response-dependent PFb and student academic performance improved with implementation of the intervention. In contrast, DiGennaro et al. (2007) combined written PFb with negative reinforcement for teachers in the form of avoiding practicing missed intervention elements. Written PFb with negative reinforcement was found to be effective in sustaining IPI.

Several studies have demonstrated that PFb can be used to change specific teacher behaviors in the classroom. Specifically, PFb has been used to increase behavior-specific praise (Reinke, Lewis-Palmer, & Martin, 2007). It is interesting to note that in this study, PFb was effective even though it was provided only through a graph of past performance without a consultant review of the data. Modeling has been combined with PFb to achieve and maintain a 1:1 or better ratio of praise to behavior correction delivered in three general education classrooms (Pisacreta, Tincani, Connell, & Axelrod, 2011). Reductions of student disruptive behavior and some generalization to classrooms in which training did not occur were also observed. In addition, the use of video has been effective in classrooms to change teacher intervention behavior. Hawkins and Heflin (2011) recorded and edited video of teachers in their classrooms to show behavior-specific praise statements. When PFb was used in tandem with line graphs of the frequency of their behavior-specific praise statements, three high school teachers of students with emotional and behavioral disorders increased their use of such statements. However, only one teacher maintained that behavior once the PFb intervention had ended.

Changing Teacher Behaviors

PFb has been used successfully in combination with other training procedures to change teacher classroom management. Codding and Smyth (2008) demonstrated the impact of providing teachers with feedback about their students' behavior on the teachers' classroom management. Specifically, they found that providing teachers with feedback about the amount of time their students spent in transitions led to changes in teacher classroom management that resulted in decreased transition time and increased student engagement. PFb has also been used successfully to increase preservice teachers' use of differential reinforcement of alternate behavior (Auld et al., 2010), which was associated with increased student hand-raising and decreased talking out in the classroom. In addition, teacher use of evidence-based classroom management strategies in emotional support classes has been improved with the use of PFb (Jeffrey, McCurdy, Ewing, & Polis, 2009).

PFb has been used extensively in clinical and school-related settings with treatment agents other than teachers to improve IPI and management behaviors. PFb combined with positive reinforcement has been demonstrated to increase supervision of staff by clinical directors at a special school (Luiselli, 2008). A number of studies have demonstrated improvements in paraprofessional implementation of routines, interventions, or instructional procedures following PFb from supervisors or research staff (Bolton & Mayer, 2008; Gilligan, Luiselli, & Pace, 2007; Hall, Grundon, Pope, & Romero, 2010; Reedy, Luiselli, & Thibadeau, 2001). Although the effects of PFb on IPI in schools traditionally have been evaluated in the context of interventions designed and implemented for specific behavior or academic problems in classrooms, positive effects of PFb have been demonstrated with a prepackaged interventions as well, and these have been associated with improvements in student behavior (Rodriguez et al., 2009).

Other Clinical and School-Related Settings

Sustaining IPI is the enabling technology that is generally necessary to make much of what is known about effective academic and behavioral intervention for children, youth, and individuals with developmental disabilities effective. Obviously, if we cannot get the intervention implemented, it is not going to be effective. The literature suggests that consulting with teachers, designing an intervention they deem acceptable, providing materials necessary for the intervention, discussing the importance of intervention implementation, and training teachers to implement the intervention are frequently insufficient to support long-term IPI (Codding et al., 2005; DiGennaro et al., 2007; Gilbertson et al., 2007; Noell et al., 2005; Sanetti et al., 2007). PFb has been found to be effective in improving IPI for both academic and behavior interventions, whereas follow-up meetings without data review were inconsistently effective (Noell et al., 2000, 2005). PFb has also been demonstrated to be effective when delivered to teaching teams involving general as well as special educators (Burns et al., 2008; Duhon et al., 2009; Pellecchia et al., 2011). PFb that includes graphic data has been found to be more effective than PFb without graphing (Noell et al., 2002; Sanetti et al., 2007). Avoiding

TABLE 7.1
Findings Related to Procedural Variations Performance Feedback

Issue	Reviews of performance feedback in employment[a]	Studies conducted in school settings
Feedback provider	More effective if delivered by supervisor	Has been effective when delivered by a consultant
Review of data	More effective when graphic feedback is provided	More effective when graphic feedback is provided
Goal setting	More effective	Not studied
Consequences provided	More effective	Has been effective with both praise and escape provided; consequences have not been compared
Antecedents	More effective	Inconsistent evidence on the importance of training
Goal setting	More effective	Not studied

[a]Drawn from Alvero et al. (2001) and Balcazar et al. (1985–1986).

PFb or avoiding practicing parts of an intervention that were missed by the teacher has been demonstrated effective in assuring IPI (DiGennaro et al., 2005; Gilbertson et al., 2007). In addition to improving implementation of specific elements of academic and behavior interventions with teachers, PFb has been demonstrated to be effective for changing teacher behaviors in the classroom that are frequently elements of interventions (Auld et al., 2010; Codding & Smyth, 2008; Hawkins & Heflin, 2011; Jeffrey et al., 2009; Pisacreta et al., 2011; Reinke et al., 2007). Additionally, PFb has been effective with other treatment agents in schools: paraprofessionals, supervisors, staff, and clinical directors (Bolton & Mayer, 2008; Gilligan et al., 2007; Hall et al., 2010; Luiselli, 2008; Reedy et al., 2001), and with custom and prepackaged interventions (Rodriguez et al., 2009). Generally, the findings examining procedural variation in the use of PFb in schools have been consistent with findings in other employment contexts (see Table 7.1).

CHALLENGES FOR RESEARCH AND PRACTICE

Although the progress in what we know has been substantial over the past decade, a number of important challenges remain unresolved or unexamined. One critical challenge confronting the field is how to package this technology for dissemination to new practitioners and the existing workforce. To date, it appears likely that training has followed a mentorship model based on extended contact with more veteran practitioners or has been developed on an ad hoc basis to support research. The key challenge here is that providing PFb in the context of consultation and child behavior therapy is a delicate balance that includes weighing a number of factors. As the first author can attest from training a number of practitioners, it is possible to get it wrong, and those errors can have important consequences.

A second considerable challenge is how consultation that incorporates PFb can be used to support intervention implementation and be adapted to schools to maximize impact. We have plenty of evidence that PFb can work when provided by a consultant in face-to-face meetings. However, there is a broader array of resources available in communities and schools. For example, could PFb regarding IPI be provided by peer teachers or a school counselor? Similarly, would a reciprocal feedback system between parents and teachers work well in a context like conjoint consultation? Is it possible to leverage electronic media allowing consultants to support more teachers, increase the frequency of feedback, or reduce the cost of feedback (see Williams, Noell, Jones, & Gansle, 2012)? As schools and culture continue to evolve, it may become feasible to use electronic social media to communicate about and support intervention implementation across settings and providers in a way that will feel natural to parents and teachers.

A number of fundamental questions remain unanswered regarding how to support IPI. The most practical and effective measurement tools for IPI remain largely unknown. Although there are a few successful ad hoc examples available in the single-case design literature, we have not developed procedures for supporting the minority of teachers who are nonresponders for PFb. In a similar vein, little is known about how best to adapt PFb to fit varied individual teacher needs, schedules, or resources. Similarly, little is known about the factors that moderate IPI (e.g., student, environment, teacher, intervention, referral concern) to identify teachers for whom intensive support is likely to be more necessary and those for whom PFb may not be needed. Finally, we do not know what the predominant functional features of PFb are or how those may evolve over time. Although it appears at the outset that assessing those in practice may not be practical or have a favorable benefit-to-cost ratio, it is possible that research-based insights into this issue could guide new practices that are more effective and efficient.

CONCLUSION

Research over the past 15 years has illuminated some important facts regarding intervention implementation in schools, as can be seen in the preceding review. Research suggests that IPI following consultation is frequently poor and often deteriorates quickly to levels so low that it seems implausible that it would be beneficial. We know that although IPI does not need to be perfect to benefit students and clients, interventions with higher IPI have been found to provide larger, more consistent, and/or quicker benefits than low IPI interventions. Research has repeatedly demonstrated that PFb that includes review of a graphic presentation of implementation data has sustained higher levels of implementation. Additionally, we have evidence that it is possible to sustain implementation with follow-up spaced at weekly intervals once initial implementation has begun. Most important, we now know two important things. First, if consultants do not follow up on implementation in a systematic way, many clients will not receive the planned interventions to a significant degree. Second, we know that, within reasonable parameters, providing PFb to consultees has been found to be effective in supporting intervention implementation across studies, investigators, and sites.

REFERENCES

Agnew, J. L. (1997). The establishing operation in organizational behavior management. *Journal of Organizational Behavior Management, 18,* 7–19. doi:10.1300/J075v18n01_02

Alvero, A. M., Bucklin, B. R., & Austin, J. (2001). An objective review of the effectiveness and essential characteristics of performance feedback in organizational settings (1985–1998). *Journal of Organizational Behavior Management, 21,* 3–29. doi:10.1300/J075v21n01_02

Arco, L., & Birnbrauer, J. S. (1990). Performance feedback and maintenance of staff behavior in residential settings. *Behavioral Residential Treatment, 5,* 207–217. doi:10.1002/bin.2360050307

Auld, R. G., Belfiore, P. J., & Scheeler, M. C. (2010). Increasing pre-service teachers' use of differential reinforcement: Effects of performance feedback on consequences for student behavior. *Journal of Behavioral Education, 19,* 169–183. doi:10.1007/s10864-010-9107-4

Baker, N. (2010). Employee feedback technologies in the human performance system. *Human Resource Development International, 13,* 477–485. doi:10.1080/13678868.2010.501994

Balcazar, F. E., Hopkins, B. L., & Suarez, Y. (1985–1986). A critical, objective review of performance feedback. *Journal of Organizational Behavior Management, 7,* 65–89. doi:10.1300/J075v07n03_05

Bergan, J. R., & Kratochwill, T. R. (1990). *Behavioral consultation and therapy.* New York, NY: Plenum Press.

Bolton, J., & Mayer, M. D. (2008). Promoting the generalization of paraprofessional discrete trial teaching skills. *Focus on Autism and Other Developmental Disabilities, 23,* 103–111. doi:10.1177/1088357608316269

Burns, M. K., Peters, R., & Noell, G. H. (2008). Using performance feedback to enhance implementation fidelity of the problem-solving team process. *Journal of School Psychology, 46*, 537–550. doi:10.1016/j.jsp.2008.04.001

Casey, A. M., & McWilliam, R. A. (2011). The characteristics and effectiveness of feedback interventions applied in early childhood settings. *Topics in Early Childhood Special Education, 31*, 68–77. doi:10.1177/0271121410368141

Codding, R. S., Feinberg, A. B., Dunn, E. K., & Pace, G. M. (2005). Effects of immediate performance feedback on implementation of behavior support plans. *Journal of Applied Behavior Analysis, 38*, 205–219. doi:10.1901/jaba.2005.98-04

Codding, R. S., & Smyth, C. A. (2008). Using performance feedback to decrease classroom transition time and examine collateral effects on academic engagement. *Journal of Educational and Psychological Consultation, 18*, 325–345. doi:10.1080/10474410802463312

Dane, A. V., & Schneider, B. H. (1998). Program integrity in primary and early secondary prevention: Are implementation effects out of control? *Clinical Psychology Review, 18*, 23–45. doi:10.1016/S0272-7358(97)00043-3

DiGennaro, F. D., Martens, B. K., & Kleinmann, A. E. (2007). A comparison of performance feedback procedures on teachers' treatment implementation integrity and students' inappropriate behavior in special education classrooms. *Journal of Applied Behavior Analysis, 40*, 447–461. doi:10.1901/jaba.2007.40-447

DiGennaro, F. D., Martens, B. K., & McIntyre, L. L. (2005). Increasing treatment integrity through negative reinforcement: Effects on teacher and student behavior. *School Psychology Review, 34*, 220–231.

Duhon, G. J., Mesmer, E. M., Gregerson, L., & Witt, J. C. (2009). Effects of public feedback during RTI team meetings on teacher implementation integrity and student academic performance. *Journal of School Psychology, 47*, 19–37. doi:10.1016/j.jsp.2008.09.002

Dusenbury, L., Brannigan, R., Falco, M., & Hansen, W. B. (2003). A review of research on fidelity of implementation: Implications for drug abuse prevention in school settings. *Health Education Research, 18*, 237–256. doi:10.1093/her/18.2.237

Erchul, W. P., DuPaul, G. J., Grissom, P. F., Vile Junod, R. E., Jitendra, A. K., Mannella, M. C. . . . Volpe, R. J. (2007). Relationships among relational communication processes and consultation outcomes for students with attention deficit hyperactivity disorder. *School Psychology Review, 36*, 111–129.

Gilbertson, D., Witt, J. C., Singletary, L. L., & VanDerHeyden, A. (2007). Supporting teacher use of interventions: Effects of response dependent performance feedback on teacher implementation of a math intervention. *Journal of Behavioral Education, 16*, 311–326. doi:10.1007/s10864-007-9043-0

Gilligan, K. T., Luiselli, J. K., & Pace, G. M. (2007). Training paraprofessional staff to implement discrete trial instruction: Evaluation of a practical performance feedback intervention. *Behavior Therapist, 30*, 63–66.

Gresham, F. M. (1989). Assessment of treatment integrity in school consultation and prereferral intervention. *School Psychology Review, 18,* 37–50.

Gresham, F. M., Gansle, K. A., & Noell, G. H. (1993). Treatment integrity in applied behavior analysis with children. *Journal of Applied Behavior Analysis, 26,* 257–263. doi:10.1901/jaba.1993.26-257

Groskreutz, N. C., Groskreutz, M. P., & Higbee, T. S. (2011). Effects of varied levels of treatment integrity on appropriate toy manipulation in children with autism. *Research in Autism Spectrum Disorders, 5,* 1358–1369. doi:10.1016/j.rasd.2011.01.018

Hall, L. J., Grundon, G. S., Pope, C., & Romero, A. B. (2010). Training paraprofessionals to use behavioral strategies when educating learners with autism spectrum disorders across environments. *Behavioral Interventions, 25,* 37–51. doi:10.1002/bin.294

Harchik, A. E., Sherman, J. A., Sheldon, J. B., & Strouse, M. C. (1992). Ongoing consultation as a method of improving performance of staff members in a group home. *Journal of Applied Behavior Analysis, 25,* 599–610. doi:10.1901/jaba.1992.25-599

Hawkins, S. M., & Heflin, L. J. (2011). Increasing secondary teachers' behavior-specific praise using a video self-modeling and visual performance feedback intervention. *Journal of Positive Behavior Interventions, 13,* 97–108. doi:10.1177/1098300709358110

Haynes, S. N., & O'Brien, W. (2000). *Principles and practice of behavioral assessment.* Dordrecht, the Netherlands: Kluwer Academic. doi:10.1007/978-0-306-47469-9

Henggeler, S. W., Melton, G. B., Brondino, M. J., Scherer, D. G., & Hanley, J. H. (1997). Multisystemic therapy with violent and chronic juvenile offenders and their families: The role of treatment fidelity in successful dissemination. *Journal of Consulting and Clinical Psychology, 65,* 821–833. doi:10.1037/0022-006X.65.5.821

Hintze, J. M., & Matthews, W. J. (2004). The generalizability of systematic direct observations across time and setting: A preliminary investigation of the psychometrics of behavioral observation. *School Psychology Review, 33,* 258–270.

Jacob, S., Decker, D. M., & Hartshorne, T. S. (2011). *Ethics and law for school psychologists* (6th ed.). Hoboken, NJ: Wiley.

Jeffrey, J. L., McCurdy, B. L., Ewing, S., & Polis, D. (2009). Classwide PBIS for students with EBD: Initial evaluation of an integrity tool. *Education & Treatment of Children, 32,* 537–550. doi:10.1353/etc.0.0069

Johnston, J. M., & Pennypacker, H. S. (1980). *Strategies and tactics of human behavioral research.* Hillsdale, NJ: Erlbaum.

Jones, H. A., Clarke, A. T., & Power, T. J. (2008). Expanding the concept of intervention integrity: A multidimensional model of participant engagement. *InBalance, 23*(1), 4–5. doi:10.1037/e597762009-004

Kelleher, C., Riley-Tillman, T. C., & Power, T. J. (2008). An initial comparison of collaborative and expert-driven consultation on treatment integrity. *Journal of Educational and Psychological Consultation, 18*, 294–324. doi:10.1080/10474410802491040

Kluger, A. N., & DeNisi, A. (1996). The effects of feedback interventions on performance: A historical review, a meta-analysis, and a preliminary feedback intervention theory. *Psychological Bulletin, 119*, 254–284. doi:10.1037/0033-2909.119.2.254

Luiselli, J. K. (2008). Effects of a performance management intervention on frequency of behavioral supervision at a specialized school for students with developmental disabilities. *Journal of Developmental and Physical Disabilities, 20*, 53–61. doi:10.1007/s10882-007-9079-z

Mortenson, B. P., & Witt, J. C. (1998). The use of weekly performance feedback to increase teacher implementation of a prereferral academic intervention. *School Psychology Review, 27*, 613–627.

Neubert, M. J. (1998). The value of feedback and goal setting over goal setting alone and potential moderators of this effect: A meta-analysis. *Human Performance, 11*, 321–335. doi:10.1207/s15327043hup1104_2

Noell, G. H. (2008). Appraising and praising systematic work to support systems change: Where we might be and where we might go. *School Psychology Review, 37*, 333–336.

Noell, G. H., Duhon, G. J., Gatti, S. L., & Connell, J. E. (2002). Consultation, follow-up, and implementation of behavior management interventions in general education. *School Psychology Review, 31*, 217–234.

Noell, G. H., & Gansle, K. A. (2006). Assuring the form has substance: Treatment plan implementation as the foundation of assessing response to intervention. *Assessment for Effective Intervention, 32*, 32–39. doi:10.1177/15345084060320010501

Noell, G. H., & Witt, J. C. (1999). When does consultation lead to intervention implementation? Critical issues for research and practice. *Journal of Special Education, 33*, 29–35. doi:10.1177/002246699903300103

Noell, G. H., Witt, J. C., Gilbertson, D. N., Ranier, D. D., & Freeland, J. T. (1997). Increasing teacher intervention implementation in general education settings through consultation and performance feedback. *School Psychology Quarterly, 12*, 77–88. doi:10.1037/h0088949

Noell, G. H., Witt, J. C., LaFleur, L. H., Mortenson, B. P., Ranier, D. D., & LeVelle, J. (2000). Increasing intervention implementation in general education following consultation: A comparison of two follow-up strategies. *Journal of Applied Behavior Analysis, 33*, 271–284. doi:10.1901/jaba.2000.33-271

Noell, G. H., Witt, J. C., Slider, N. J., Connell, J. E., Gatti, S. L., & Williams, K. L. . . . Duhon, G. J. (2005). Treatment implementation following behavioral consultation in schools: A comparison of three follow-up strategies. *School Psychology Review, 34*, 87-106.

Pellecchia, M., Connell, J. E., Eisenhart, D., Kane, M., Schoener, C., Turkel, K., . . . Mandell, D. S. (2011). We're all in this together now: Group performance feedback to increase classroom team data collection. *Journal of School Psychology, 49*, 411–431. doi:10.1016/j.jsp.2011.04.003

Peterson, L., Homer, A. L., & Wonderlich, S. A. (1982). The integrity of independent variables in behavior analysis. *Journal of Applied Behavior Analysis, 15*, 477–492. doi:10.1901/jaba.1982.15-477

Pisacreta, J., Tincani, M., Connell, J. E., & Axelrod, S. (2011). Increasing teachers' use of a 1:1 praise-to-behavior correction ratio to decrease student disruption in general education classrooms. *Behavioral Interventions, 26*, 243–260. doi:10.1002/bin.341

Power, T. J., Blom-Hoffman, J., Clarke, A. T., Riley-Tillman, T. C., Kelleher, C., & Manz, P. H. (2005). Reconceptualizing intervention integrity: A partnership-based framework for linking research with practice. *Psychology in the Schools, 42*, 495–507. doi:10.1002/pits.20087

Prue, D. M., & Fairbank, J. A. (1981). Performance feedback in organizational behavior management: A review. *Journal of Organizational Behavior Management, 3*, 1–16. doi:10.1300/J075v03n01_01

Rathel, J. M, Drasgow, E., & Christle, C. C. (2008). Effects of supervisor performance feedback on increasing preservice teachers' positive communication behaviors with students with emotional and behavioral disorders. *Journal of Emotional and Behavioral Disorders, 16*, 67–77. doi:10.1177/1063426607312537

Reason, P., & Bradbury, H. (Eds.). (2001). *Handbook of action research: Participative inquiry and practice*. London, England: Sage.

Reedy, P., Luiselli, J. K., & Thibadeau, S. (2001). Improving staff performance in a residential child-care setting using computer-assisted feedback. *Child & Family Behavior Therapy, 23*, 43–51. doi:10.1300/J019v23n01_04

Reinke, W. M., Lewis-Palmer, T., & Martin, E. (2007). The effect of visual performance feedback on teacher use of behavior-specific praise. *Behavior Modification, 31*, 247–263. doi:10.1177/0145445506288967

Resetar, J. L., Noell, G. H., & Pellegrin, A. L. (2006). Teaching parents to use research-supported systematic strategies to tutor their children in reading. *School Psychology Quarterly, 21*, 241–261. doi:10.1521/scpq.2006.21.3.241

Rodriguez, B. J., Loman, S. L., & Horner, R. H. (2009). A preliminary analysis of the effects of coaching feedback on teacher implementation fidelity of First Step to Success. *Behavior Analysis in Practice, 2*(2), 11–21.

Sanetti, L. M. H., & Fallon, L. M. (2011). Treatment integrity assessment: How estimates of adherence, quality, and exposure influence interpretation of implementation. *Journal of Educational and Psychological Consultation, 21*, 209–232. doi:10.1080/10474412.2011.595163

Sanetti, L. M. H., Luiselli, J. K., & Handler, M. W. (2007). Effects of verbal and graphic performance feedback on behavior support plan implementation in a public elementary school. *Behavior Modification, 31,* 454–465. doi:10.1177/0145445506297583

Schulte, A. C., Easton, J. E., & Parker, J. (2009). Advances in treatment integrity research: Multidisciplinary perspectives on the conceptualization, measurement, and enhancement of treatment integrity. *School Psychology Review, 38,* 460–475.

Skinner, B. F. (1953). *Science and human behavior.* New York, NY: Macmillan.

Smither, J. W., London, M., & Reilly, R. R. (2005). Does performance improve following multisource feedback? A theoretical model, meta-analysis, and review of empirical findings. *Personnel Psychology, 58,* 33–66. doi:10.1111/j.1744-6570.2005.514_1.x

Sulzer-Azaroff, B., & Mayer, G. R. (1991). *Behavior analysis for lasting change.* Fort Worth, TX: Holt, Rinehart, and Winston.

Waltz, J., Addis, M. E., Koerner, K., & Jacobson, N. S. (1993). Testing the integrity of a psychotherapy protocol: Assessment of adherence and competence. *Journal of Consulting and Clinical Psychology, 61,* 620–630. doi:10.1037/0022-006X.61.4.620

Wickstrom, K. F., Jones, K. M., LaFleur, L. H., & Witt, J. C. (1998). An analysis of treatment integrity in school-based behavioral consultation. *School Psychology Quarterly, 13,* 141–154. doi:10.1037/h0088978

Wilkinson, L. A. (2007). Assessing treatment integrity in behavioral consultation. *International Journal of Behavioral Consultation and Therapy, 3,* 420–432.

Williams, K. L., Noell, G. H., Jones, B. A., & Gansle, K. A. (2012). Modifying students' classroom behaviors using an electronic daily behavior report card. *Child & Family Behavior Therapy, 34,* 269–289. doi:10.1080/07317107.2012.732844

Witt, J. C., Noell, G. H., LaFleur, L. H., & Mortenson, B. P. (1997). Teacher use of interventions in general education settings: Measurement and analysis of the independent variable. *Journal of Applied Behavior Analysis, 30,* 693–696. doi:10.1901/jaba.1997.30-693

Wolery, M. (1997). Encounters with general early education: Lessons being learned. *Journal of Behavioral Education, 7,* 91–98. doi:10.1023/A:1022897605627

8

PRODUCING HIGH LEVELS OF TREATMENT INTEGRITY IN PRACTICE: A FOCUS ON PREPARING PRACTITIONERS

DEAN L. FIXSEN, KAREN A. BLASE, ALLISON J. METZ, AND SANDRA F. NAOOM

Treatment integrity is essential to the delivery of effective human services (Century, Rudnick, & Freeman, 2010; Schoenwald, 2011). In this chapter, we use the definition proposed by Sanetti and Kratochwill (2009): "Treatment integrity is the extent to which essential intervention components are delivered in a comprehensive and consistent manner by an interventionist trained to deliver the intervention" (p. 448). In pharmacology (and other atom-based sciences), the evidence base is built into the composition of a pill or serum that can be mass produced in laboratories and provided to those who can benefit. The intervention (e.g., the chemical composition of the pill or serum) is the same no matter who delivers it. In human services

Preparation of this article was supported, in part, by funds from the U.S. Department of Education Office of Special Education Programs (H326K070003) and from the Frank Porter Graham Child Development Institute. The views expressed are those of the authors and should not be attributed to the funding sources. We would like to thank our National Implementation Research Network colleagues who provide continual inspiration and delight: Leah Bartley, Michelle Duda, Barbara Sims, and Melissa Van Dyke.

http://dx.doi.org/10.1037/14275-010
Treatment Integrity: A Foundation for Evidence-Based Practice in Applied Psychology, L. M. H. Sanetti and T. R. Kratochwill (Editors)

(and other interaction-based sciences), the evidence base is "built into" what practitioners do as they provide services to those who can benefit (Fixsen, Blase, Duda, Naoom, & Van Dyke, 2010). In interaction-based sciences, there are human beings on each side of the interaction, each influencing the other. The intervention is not the same no matter who provides it; rather, the intervention should be expected to vary within practitioners over time as well as across practitioners. In human services, once an intervention is established, treatment integrity is not a characteristic of practitioners (McGrew, Bond, Dietzen, & Salyers, 1994). Treatment integrity needs to be continually assessed in practice to assure the intervention is still present and potent (Bauman, Stein, & Ireys, 1991; Schoenwald, 2011). Thus, intervention delivery is more complicated in interaction-based sciences than in atom-based sciences. This complexity is not a reason to give up on treatment integrity, however, but a reason to develop sophisticated methods and measures that account for the complexity of human beings interacting with one another.

TREATMENT INTEGRITY AND HUMAN SERVICES

Human services have been slow to develop measures of treatment integrity and to require high levels of treatment integrity in practice (Dane & Schneider, 1998; Durlak & DuPre, 2008; Paine, Bellamy, & Wilcox, 1984). This is a serious omission. Low levels of treatment integrity are associated with unnecessary human suffering and loss of life. Despite major investments in developing evidence-based interventions, national reviews of human services in the United States reveal that many publicly funded human services are deemed ineffective and sometimes harmful (Kohn, Corrigan, & Donaldson, 2000; U.S. Department of Health and Human Services, 1999). For example, medical error is the third leading cause of death in the United States (Starfield, 2000), and literacy outcomes for 9-year-old students have remained at a consistently and unacceptably low level for over 40 years (Grigg, Daane, Jin, & Campbell, 2003). Lack of treatment integrity is also costly. Multiple scholars have concluded that the benefits of effective use of known interventions far outweigh the potential benefits of any new interventions that might be invented (Clancy, 2006; Durlak & DuPre, 2008; Woolf & Johnson, 2005). Kessler and Glasgow (2011) recommended a moratorium on funding the development of any new evidence-based interventions until we learn to use the ones we have effectively.

Our purpose in this chapter is to briefly review how to produce adequate treatment integrity in practice with the end result in mind: improved outcomes of human services to benefit individuals and society. In this chapter, we have organized content around the concepts in the Active Implementation

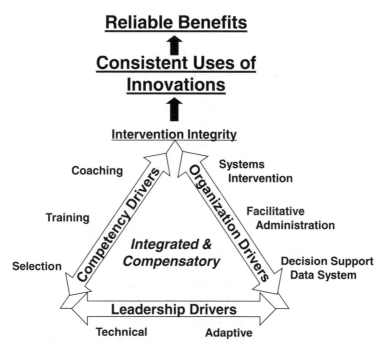

Reliable Benefits

Consistent Uses of Innovations

Intervention Integrity

Coaching

Systems Intervention

Training

Facilitative Administration

Competency Drivers

Organization Drivers

Integrated & Compensatory

Selection

Decision Support Data System

Leadership Drivers

Technical   Adaptive

Figure 8.1. Active Implementation Framework for systematically producing high levels of treatment integrity and reliable outcomes for individuals. The components arrayed around the triangle are implementation drivers.

Framework (see Figure 8.1; Fixsen, Naoom, Blase, Friedman, & Wallace, 2005). We discuss (a) essential intervention components, (b) the implementation drivers associated with preparing practitioners to deliver the intervention, and (c) how to assure the delivery of essential implementation drivers in a comprehensive and consistent manner.

ESSENTIAL INTERVENTION COMPONENTS

In the rush for rigor to establish evidence-based interventions, "interventions" themselves have not been given the same scholarly attention as "evidence." This is unfortunate because it is interventions, not the requirements for methodological rigor, that practitioners use to produce desired outcomes in human services. When an intervention is evaluated and found to be "evidence based," what exactly is the intervention that needs to be taught and learned and used in practice?

Fixsen, Blase, Metz, and Van Dyke (2013) outlined criteria for describing interventions: (a) descriptions of underlying philosophy, values, and principles; (b) descriptions of essential components that define the intervention;

(c) operational definitions of each essential component; and (d) assessments of treatment integrity in practice that are highly correlated with desired outcomes. These criteria describe the essential components of an intervention, and those components guide the assessment of the presence and strength of the intervention. Put simply, if we don't know what "it" is, it is difficult to detect the presence of "it" in practice.

Reviews of outcome studies across a wide range of human services have been reported by Dane and Schneider (1998); Durlak and DuPre (2008); McIntyre, Gresham, DiGennaro, and Reed (2007); and Naleppa and Cagle (2010). Overall, these reviews of over 1,200 outcome studies report that less than 20% of researchers measured the independent variable and only a fraction of those used the measure of the independent variable in analyses of the outcome data. Consequently, in the majority of outcome studies, very little is known about the essential components of the evaluated intervention or how to assess those components in practice.

Mental health managers are cautioned that assertions by intervention developers and researchers about the essential components of interventions are no substitute for data linking those putative essential components to outcomes. Jensen, Weersing, Hoagwood, and Goldman (2005) examined intervention research studies and concluded:

> When positive effects were found, few studies systematically explored whether the presumed active therapeutic ingredients actually accounted for the degree of change, nor did they often address plausible alternative explanations, such as nonspecific therapeutic factors of positive expectancies, therapeutic alliance, or attention. (p. 53)

Without adequate descriptions of interventions, presumptive active ingredients cannot be ruled in and alternative explanations cannot be ruled out. Thus, mental health managers must find ways to define interventions so they can be taught, used in practice, and assessed for integrity.

IMPLEMENTATION DRIVERS ASSOCIATED WITH PREPARING PRACTITIONERS

If evidence-based interventions are to produce their intended benefits, they must be used fully and effectively in practice. It is well documented that implementation is the missing link in the science-to-service chain (Fixsen et al., 2005; Glasgow, Klesges, Dzewaltowski, Bull, & Estabrooks, 2004; Greenhalgh, Robert, MacFarlane, Bate, & Kyriakidou, 2004). Fortunately, the science and best practices of implementation are now better established, and the knowledge base is growing rapidly. Methods to reliably produce high treatment integrity when interventions are used in typical human services settings are becoming better known.

Figure 8.1 depicts the Active Implementation Framework, derived from a thorough review of the implementation evaluation literature (Fixsen et al., 2005) and from a series of reviews of implementation in practice (Blase, Fixsen, Naoom, & Wallace, 2005). The *implementation drivers* arrayed around the triangle are in support of practitioners' consistent use of the chosen evidence-based interventions or other effective innovations. Intervention and implementation activities related to the competency, organizational, and leadership drivers come together at the top of the triangle, with intervention integrity (i.e., treatment integrity) as a major outcome. Treatment integrity is not only an outcome, however. It is also a major contributor to the reliable production of benefits for children, families, and individuals. Like so many factors in implementation science, treatment integrity is a dependent variable at one level (i.e., the outcome of implementation drivers) and an independent variable at the next level (i.e., influences client outcomes).

All implementation drivers illustrated in Figure 8.1 are meant to improve the skills of practitioners and other staff and thus produce greater benefits to children, families, and individuals. Although all organizational and leadership drivers are equally important and contribute to practitioner performance, the current chapter focuses on competency drivers (staff selection, training, and coaching), which most directly facilitate consistent practitioner treatment integrity.

Staff Selection and Treatment Integrity

If the evidence base needs to be built into what practitioners do, then practitioners should have a lot to say about the effective use of evidence-based interventions. Evidence-based interventions are not for everyone. For example, a psychologist with a strong psychodynamic orientation might be a poor choice for using an evidence-based behavior-analytic intervention. In that case, there might be a poor fit between the philosophy, values, and current practices of the practitioner and the requirements of the evidence-based intervention. Readiness to effectively use evidence-based interventions is an important issue (Aarons, 2004) that affects eventual outcomes for those being treated (Feifer et al., 2004).

The advantage of the active implementation drivers is that human services managers do not need to simply wait for readiness. Readiness can be created and other "soft" qualifications can be assessed during a staff selection interview. Staff selection is often lamented (Mancini et al., 2009) but rarely studied in human services. In business and manufacturing, staff selection is seen as critical to success and is the subject of considerable attention (Macan,

2009). For example, McDaniel, Whetzel, Schmidt, and Maurer (1994) conducted a meta-analysis of research on selection. The authors found that structured interviews that included inquiries about education and background, exchanges of information related to the work to be done, and role-play/behavior vignettes (job samples) were effective interview techniques that related to later work outcomes for employees.

In human services, structured selection interviews are used in national implementation of evidence-based interventions such as the teaching-family model (Blase, Fixsen, & Phillips, 1984; Wolf, Kirigin, Fixsen, Blase, & Braukmann, 1995) and multisystemic therapy (Reiter-Lavery, 2004). Maloney et al. (1983) analyzed the relationship between selection factors and later job performance for applicants for practitioner positions in teaching-family model programs. They found that compared with applicants who were not hired, applicants who were hired scored significantly higher on responses to behavioral vignettes, receptivity to training, and overall interview performance. On the basis of an evaluation of their later performance on the job (after 3–4 months), practitioners who were hired were divided into two groups: above or below the median performance for the group. The better performers were found to have differed significantly on their responses to the behavioral vignettes during the interview (but not on the other interview components). The better performers also had higher grade point averages (the other background measures were not significant). Follow-up data indicated the practitioners who scored higher in the interview also stayed significantly longer on the job. These methods and findings are consistent with the outcomes of the meta-analysis by McDaniel et al. (1994).

In our current work in a variety of human services organizations, the best practices for staff selection are often rated as "not in place." The same organizations describe the difficulties they face with practitioners who already are employed and who are only mildly (if at all) interested in making use of evidence-based interventions. Implementation of evidence-based interventions with adequate levels of treatment integrity begins with staff selection and mutually informed consent to engage in practices consistent with the intervention. With existing staff groups, an interview process can be used to select practitioners who will be the first to be prepared to use an evidence-based intervention. According to Prochaska, Prochaska, and Levesque (2001), about 20% of the current staff might be ready for change, 60% might be willing to think about it and prepare for change, and 20% may not be ready for change anytime soon. A manager who insists on change when practitioners are not prepared for it will annoy the practitioners and frustrate those who are trying to support the use of an evidence-based intervention in the provider agency. Time and resources may be better spent on those who were engaged in a selection process and consent to changing their practices.

Training and Treatment Integrity

Perhaps the most consistent finding in implementation science is that training by itself is insufficient for producing high levels of treatment integrity by practitioners and good outcomes for children, families, individuals, and society (Fixsen et al., 2010). Training by itself may result in about 5% to 15% of the practitioners using an evidence-based intervention (Joyce & Showers, 2002), with only a fraction of them using the intervention with high treatment integrity (Vernez, Karam, Mariano, & DeMartini, 2006). Nevertheless, training is an important implementation driver.

When best practices are used for training, information about history, theory, philosophy, and rationales for intervention components and practices is conveyed in lecture and discussion formats geared to impart knowledge and facilitate understanding. Skills and abilities related to carrying out the intervention components and practices are demonstrated (live or on tape), then followed by behavior rehearsal to practice the skills and receive feedback (Blase et al., 1984; Joyce & Showers, 2002; Kealey, Peterson, Gaul, & Dinh, 2000).

Training is common in human services organizations but often does not include best practices related to behavior rehearsal to criterion or pre- and postassessments of knowledge and skills (Joyce & Showers, 2002). Effective training is a critical support for the use of evidence-based interventions. Over the course of a decade, there is steady turnover among frontline practitioners, providing many opportunities to improve the effectiveness and efficiency of staff selection and staff training. Effective training that is focused on the essential components of an intervention is a key step toward the full and effective implementation of an evidence-based intervention.

Coaching and Treatment Integrity

Selection and training are preparation for the real learning that occurs on the job with the support of a competent coach. Three findings are clear from the literature on coaching (Fixsen et al., 2005). First, newly learned behavior is crude compared with the skillful performance of a master practitioner. Second, newly learned skills are fragile and likely will not be sustained in the face of reactions from consumers and colleagues. Third, newly learned skills are incomplete and need to be expanded in practice. It is the job of a coach to help practitioners develop, sustain, and expand their skills to benefit those they serve. After decades of research on training teachers, Joyce and Showers (2002) began to think of training and coaching as one continuous set of operations designed to produce actual changes in the classroom behavior of teachers. One without the other is insufficient.

Spouse (2001) noted that formal knowledge and skills that were part of training ("episteme") needs to be supplemented with craft knowledge ("phronesis") so practitioners can learn to see the relevance of what they have learned to the situations at hand. Coaching needs to be work based, opportunistic, readily available, and reflective (e.g., debriefing discussions). Spouse described four main roles of a coach: (a) supervision, (b) teaching while engaged in practice activities, (c) assessment and feedback, and (d) provision of emotional support. In keeping with this advice, a survey of staff in public mental health facilities by Kavanagh et al. (2003) found that the extent to which coaches taught new skills, strengthened confidence, offered safety in sessions, and spent time on discipline-specific skills accounted for 62% of the variance in perceived impact on practice. There also is evidence that coaching done well contributes substantially to eventual outcomes (Hattie, 2009; Schoenwald, Sheidow, & Letourneau, 2004).

For practitioners to routinely make full and effective uses of an intervention, coaching begins immediately after training. Ideally, the coach was a part of the practitioner selection interview and part of the behavior rehearsals during training (see Figure 8.1; the implementation drivers are "integrated" by people who perform multiple roles). As part of the coaching supports for practitioners, coaches directly observe practitioners in action, review records, and interview those associated with the practitioner to see how the practitioner is doing in his or her work with children, families, and others. In essence, the coach is doing minitreatment integrity assessments frequently, and the practitioner becomes accustomed to being observed and acclimated to receiving positive, constructive, and helpful feedback to improve outcomes for children, families, and individuals.

Coaching plays a key role in developing the competence of practitioners who have been selected and trained to use an evidence-based intervention or other effective innovation. Selection interviews and training are episodic and are conducted within fairly narrow boundaries (a 90-minute interview; a 4-day workshop). On the other hand, coaching supports for practitioners start immediately after training and never end. Coaching in the form of observation, advice, and continued skill development related to making practical use of evidence-based programs is more frequent and intensive right after training. As practitioners master all aspects of the evidence-based intervention, coaching may become more reflective and occur less frequently. It also means that coaching is a difficult set of skills to teach and to maintain at a high level. Given that coaches interact with and support a pool of practitioners, a good coach can do a lot of good and a poor coach can do a lot of harm (Hattie, 2009; Schoenwald et al., 2004). Thus, coaching is an important key to high treatment integrity by practitioners and to achieving desired outcomes for children, families, individuals, and society.

Performance Assessment and Treatment Integrity

Treatment integrity assessments are not a standard part of human services (Crosse et al., 2011; Durlak & DuPre, 2008). This is a costly omission in terms of human suffering and wasted resources. The relative absence of treatment integrity assessments in research on evidence-based interventions contributes to the current state of the field. McGrew et al. (1994) noted that the development of treatment integrity measures is hampered by three factors: (a) most interventions are not well defined conceptually, making it difficult to identify essential intervention components; (b) when essential intervention components have been identified, they are not operationally defined with agreed-upon criteria for use in practice; and (c) only a few interventions have been around long enough to study planned and unplanned variations of their uses in typical human services settings. A recent summary of the field by Durlak and DuPre (2008) indicates little has changed since McGrew et al. made their observations. From an implementation point of view, any intervention (evidence based or otherwise) is incomplete without a good measure of treatment integrity to detect the presence and strength of the intervention in practice.

For managers of human services organizations, treatment integrity is not just of academic importance. Treatment integrity data can be used to inform competency drivers (i.e., selection, training, and coaching) and improve the skill levels of practitioners and other staff, thus facilitating greater benefits to children, families, and individuals. As noted by Naoom, Van Dyke, Fixsen, Blase, and Villagomez (2012):

> Staff performance assessments are designed to assess the use of the skills that are required for full and effective use of the evidence-based approach. In well-integrated evidence-based programs, staff performance criteria [are] known and understood by the staff through coaching that takes into account the performance assessment criteria. Performance assessment criteria are also communicated and bolstered through the training of critical skills and through an implementation-informed selection process that takes into account and communicates the performance criteria. (p. 454)

Thus, treatment integrity data inform selection criteria and the efficient allocation of training and coaching supports.

Treatment integrity data also help managers and others discriminate implementation problems from intervention problems and help guide problem solving to improve outcomes. As shown in Table 8.1, Blase et al. (1984) described how information about treatment integrity and outcomes can be linked to possible solutions to continually improve intended outcomes. The desired combination is high-integrity use of an intervention that produces

TABLE 8.1

Combining Data on Treatment Integrity Assessments and Outcomes Helps
to Identify the Actions Needed to Improve Benefits to Society

Outcome	High treatment integrity	Low treatment integrity
Good	Celebrate!	Reexamine the intervention; modify the treatment integrity assessment.
Poor	Modify the intervention.	Start over.

good outcomes. When high treatment integrity is consistently linked with good outcomes, it is time to celebrate and continue to use the intervention strategies and implementation support strategies with confidence. The next best quadrant in Table 8.1 is where high treatment integrity is achieved but outcomes are poor. This clearly points to an intervention that is being implemented as intended but is ineffective in practice. In this case, it is clear that the intervention needs to be changed or discarded. The quadrants in Table 8.1 in the low treatment integrity column have corrective actions that are less clear. Low treatment integrity in combination with good outcomes points to a poorly described intervention, a poor measure of treatment integrity, or both. In any of these cases, it is not clear what is producing the good outcomes and may indicate a need for evaluation of potentially related issues or circumstances to better understand what mechanisms are at work. Low treatment integrity associated with poor outcomes leaves users in a quandary. It may be a good time to start again to develop or find an effective intervention and develop effective implementation supports.

Thus, human services managers, coaches, and practitioners need to have information about treatment integrity as well as outcomes. Without data on treatment integrity, outcomes are difficult to interpret, required actions are not clear, and services will likely remain inconsistent, ineffective, and sometimes harmful (Kohn et al., 2000).

Other Implementation Drivers and Treatment Integrity

Leadership and organizational implementation drivers are integrated with competency drivers discussed above. For example, human service organization leaders and facilitative administrators support the staff selection, training, and coaching described above (see Figure 8.1). These active implementation drivers help to routinely produce the practitioner behavior required to deliver the intervention as intended. Treatment integrity assessment, as a measure of the presence and strength of the evidence-based intervention in practice, can be used to inform (a) coaching for practitioner improvement, (b) leadership about current practices, and (c) how an organization evolves to produce improved outcomes. By taking into account client outcomes and treatment integrity data, practitioners, managers, and leaders can work together to provide data-based answers to important implementation questions (e.g., Are we doing what we intend? Is it producing desired outcomes?). Such data-based decision making will facilitate their ability to achieve greatly improved outcomes for children, families, and individuals.

ENSURING CONSISTENT DELIVERY OF ESSENTIAL INTERVENTION COMPONENTS

Who does the work of implementation (see Figure 8.1) to support practitioners' effective use of interventions? Systematic implementation of evidence-based interventions in practice can be supported by implementation teams that function within an organization (e.g., county mental health system, school district in an education system, a hospital in the medical system; Fixsen et al., 2005; Greenhalgh et al., 2004; Higgins, Weiner, & Young, 2012). Implementation teams are made up of individuals who have special expertise related to the intervention, as well as expertise related to implementation and improvement strategies. They are accountable for actively supporting and guiding the implementation of interventions, from exploration to full, effective, and sustained use of evidence-based interventions. An implementation team's focus is on (a) creating readiness, (b) installing and sustaining the implementation drivers, (c) monitoring treatment integrity, and (d) assessing achievement of intended outcomes. Implementation teams typically are internal to an agency or community (Whitley, Gingerich, Lutz, & Mueser, 2009), although some of the active implementation drivers may be provided by others (Schoenwald, Brown, & Henggeler, 2000). Implementation capacity that is built within the community or agency can create a structure that is more easily sustained (team functions are more sustainable than those provided by individuals; Higgins et al., 2012; Patras & Klest, in press).

In a human services organization with multiple practitioners and multiple evidence-based interventions in place, the assessment function requires considerable preparation and organization on the part of implementation team members. The constructive uses of treatment integrity data are many. Constructive uses of treatment integrity information depend upon implementation team members who understand how to secure, process, and analyze the data and make targeted changes to improve practitioners' uses of the intervention and the outcomes for those being served. Unfortunately, there are few implementation teams currently available in human services systems to do this work. Thus, creating implementation capacity in human services systems is a priority if society hopes to realize the promise of evidence-based interventions.

CONCLUSION

Attending to treatment integrity is important and, in human services systems, it is the product of implementation done well. Practitioners do the work of delivering an evidence-based intervention to the intended beneficiaries of the service, while organization managers attempt to support practitioners so they can work more effectively and efficiently. Currently, implementation of evidence-based interventions and other innovations is left to overworked practitioners and managers to "just do it," and, somehow, about 10% to 15% of them get it done eventually (e.g., Aladjem & Borman, 2006; Dane & Schneider, 1998; Joyce & Showers, 2002). However, 10% to 15% use of evidence-based interventions after 17 years (Balas & Boren, 2000) is not sufficient to produce benefits to society. The implementation framework presented highlights three categories of drivers that facilitate high levels of treatment integrity: leadership, organization, and competency drivers.

Although an integration of all of these drivers is essential to high levels of treatment integrity, the discussion above focused on how practitioner selection, training, and coaching can increase levels of treatment integrity. If managers interview candidates with particular skill sets and behavioral repertoires in mind, provide high-quality training, and support ongoing implementation through coaches, it is more likely that those being served will experience better outcomes. Treatment integrity data can be used to inform managers of the intervention skills necessary for implementers, training objectives, and foci of coaching. These data can help managers use scarce resources more efficiently to improve outcomes (e.g., Fixsen et al., 2010; Greenhalgh et al., 2004; Hall & Hord, 1987).

Assessments of treatment integrity are uncommon in research studies, however. This is a major barrier for those interested in using evidence-based interventions. If human services systems and organizations are going to help practitioners make use of evidence-based interventions with integrity, there needs to be evidence of and confidence in the link between assessments of treatment integrity and outcomes. Without data-based knowledge of the essential components of an intervention, what is it that program managers should insist upon "no matter what" in the hectic world of human services programs? The academic debates about "adapt to adopt" have little meaning for managers. They want to know the essential practices that must be in place to produce the outcomes promised by evidence-based interventions.

The near absence of treatment integrity measures established by researchers and developers of evidence-based interventions is a major barrier to achieving socially important outcomes for evidence-based interventions in practice (Perepletchikova, Treat, & Kazdin, 2007). The lack of operationalization of interventions by developers makes the task of creating treatment integrity measures difficult, leaving it to others to guess at the essential components, operationalize interventions, and develop reliable indicators of treatment integrity.

Such implementation work can be effectively done by implementation teams; however, these teams are not common in human services. With implementation teams providing purposeful supports for practitioners and organizations, the likelihood of successful use of evidence-based interventions is increased, and the time required to reach sustained use is decreased (Fixsen, Blase, Timbers, & Wolf, 2001). Directors and managers of human services organizations need to incorporate the active implementation drivers (see Figure 8.1) and create implementation teams. Given the central role of treatment integrity in practice and the cost–benefits of producing better outcomes for those being served, it is worth investing in producing treatment integrity reliably.

REFERENCES

Aarons, G. A. (2004). Mental health provider attitudes toward adoption of evidence-based practice: The Evidence-Based Practice Attitude Scale (EBPAS). *Mental Health Services Research, 6*, 61–74. doi:10.1023/B:MHSR.0000024351.12294.65

Aladjem, D. K., & Borman, K. M. (Eds.). (2006). *Examining comprehensive school reform*. Washington, DC: Urban Institute Press.

Balas, E. A., & Boren, S. A. (2000). Managing clinical knowledge for health care improvement. In J. H. van Bemmel & A. T. McCray (Eds.), *Yearbook of medical informatics 2000: Patient-centered systems* (pp. 65–70). Stuttgart, Germany: Schattauer Verlagsgesellschaft.

Bauman, L. J., Stein, R. E. K., & Ireys, H. T. (1991). Reinventing fidelity: The transfer of social technology among settings. *American Journal of Community Psychology, 19*, 619–639. doi:10.1007/BF00937995

Blase, K. A., Fixsen, D. L., Naoom, S. F., & Wallace, F. (2005). *Operationalizing implementation: Strategies and methods*. Tampa: University of South Florida, Louis de la Parte Florida Mental Health Institute.

Blase, K. A., Fixsen, D. L., & Phillips, E. L. (1984). Residential treatment for troubled children: Developing service delivery systems. In S. C. Paine, G. T. Bellamy, & B. L. Wilcox (Eds.), *Human services that work: From innovation to standard practice* (pp. 149–165). Baltimore, MD: Brookes.

Century, J., Rudnick, M., & Freeman, C. (2010). A framework for measuring fidelity of implementation: A foundation for shared language and accumulation of knowledge. *American Journal of Evaluation, 31,* 199–218. doi:10.1177/1098214010366173

Clancy, C. (2006). The $1.6 trillion question: If we're spending so much on healthcare, why so little improvement in quality? *Medscape General Medicine, 8,* 58. Retrieved from http://www.ncbi.nlm.nih.gov/pmc/articles/PMC1785188/

Crosse, S., Williams, B., Hagen, C. A., Ristow, L., DiGaetano, R., Broene, P., . . . Derzon, J. H. (2011). *Prevalence and implementation fidelity of research-based prevention programs in public schools: Final report.* Washington, DC: U.S. Department of Education.

Dane, A. V., & Schneider, B. H. (1998). Program integrity in primary and early secondary prevention: Are implementation effects out of control? *Clinical Psychology Review, 18,* 23–45. doi:10.1016/S0272-7358(97)00043-3

Durlak, J. A., & DuPre, E. P. (2008). Implementation matters: A review of research on the influence of implementation on program outcomes and the factors affecting implementation. *American Journal of Community Psychology, 41,* 327–350. doi:10.1007/s10464-008-9165-0

Feifer, C., Fifield, J., Ornstein, S., Karson, A. S., Bates, D. W., Jones, K. R., & Vargas, P. A. (2004). From research to daily clinical practice: What are the challenges in "translation"? *Joint Commission Journal on Quality Improvement, 30,* 235–245.

Fixsen, D., Blase, K., Metz, A., & Van Dyke, M. (2013). Statewide implementation of evidence-based programs. *Exceptional Children, 79,* 213–230.

Fixsen, D. L., Blase, K. A., Duda, M. A., Naoom, S. F., & Van Dyke, M. (2010). Implementation of evidence-based treatments for children and adolescents: Research findings and their implications for the future. In J. R. Weisz & A. E. Kazdin (Eds.), *Evidence-based psychotherapies for children and adolescents* (2nd ed., pp. 435–450). New York, NY: Guilford Press.

Fixsen, D. L., Blase, K. A., Timbers, G. D., & Wolf, M. M. (2001). In search of program implementation: 792 replications of the teaching-family model. In G. A. Bernfeld, D. P. Farrington, & A. W. Leschied (Eds.), *Offender rehabilitation in practice: Implementing and evaluating effective programs* (pp. 149–166). London, England: Wiley.

Fixsen, D. L., Naoom, S. F., Blase, K. A., Friedman, R. M., & Wallace, F. (2005). *Implementation research: A synthesis of the literature.* Tampa: University of South Florida, Louis de la Parte Florida Mental Health Institute, National Implementation Research Network.

Glasgow, R. E., Klesges, L. M., Dzewaltowski, D. A., Bull, S. S., & Estabrooks, P. (2004). The future of health behavior change research: What is needed to improve translation of research into health promotion practice? *Annals of Behavioral Medicine, 27,* 3–12. doi:10.1207/s15324796abm2701_2

Greenhalgh, T., Robert, G., MacFarlane, F., Bate, P., & Kyriakidou, O. (2004). Diffusion of innovations in service organizations: Systematic review and recommendations. *Milbank Quarterly, 82*, 581–629. doi:10.1111/j.0887-378X.2004.00325.x

Grigg, W. S., Daane, M. C., Jin, Y., & Campbell, J. R. (2003). *The nation's report card: Reading 2002*. Washington, DC: U.S. Department of Education, Institute of Education Sciences.

Hall, G. E., & Hord, S. M. (1987). *Change in schools: Facilitating the process*. Albany: State University of New York.

Hattie, J. A. C. (2009). *Visible learning: A synthesis of over 800 meta-analyses relating to achievement*. London, England: Routledge.

Higgins, M. C., Weiner, J., & Young, L. (2012). Implementation teams: A new lever for organizational change. *Journal of Organizational Behavior, 33*, 366–388. doi:10.1002/job.1773

Jensen, P. S., Weersing, R., Hoagwood, K. E., & Goldman, E. (2005). What is the evidence for evidence-based treatments? A hard look at our soft underbelly. *Mental Health Services Research, 7*, 53–74. doi:10.1007/s11020-005-1965-3

Joyce, B. R., & Showers, B. (2002). *Student achievement through staff development* (3rd ed.). Alexandria, VA: Association for Supervision and Curriculum Development.

Kavanagh, D. J., Spence, S. H., Strong, J., Wilson, J., Sturk, H., & Crow, N. (2003). Supervision practices in allied mental health: Relationships of supervision characteristics to perceived impact and job satisfaction. *Mental Health Services Research, 5*, 187–195. doi:10.1023/A:1026223517172

Kealey, K. A., Peterson, A. V., Jr., Gaul, M. A., & Dinh, K. T. (2000). Teacher training as a behavior change process: Principles and results from a longitudinal study. *Health Education & Behavior, 27*, 64–81. doi:10.1177/109019810002700107

Kessler, R., & Glasgow, R. E. (2011). A proposal to speed translation of healthcare research into practice: Dramatic change is needed. *American Journal of Preventive Medicine, 40*, 637–644. doi:10.1016/j.amepre.2011.02.023

Kohn, L. T., Corrigan, J. M., & Donaldson, M. S. (Eds.). (2000). *To err is human: Building a safer health system*. Washington, DC: National Academies Press.

Macan, T. (2009). The employment interview: A review of current studies and directions for future research. *Human Resource Management Review, 19*, 203–218. doi:10.1016/j.hrmr.2009.03.006

Maloney, D. M., Warfel, D. J., Blase, K. A., Timbers, G. D., Fixsen, D. L., & Phillips, E. L. (1983). A method for validating employment interviews for residential child care workers. *Residential Group Care & Treatment, 1*, 37–50. doi:10.1300/J297v01n04_06

Mancini, A. D., Moser, L. L., Whitley, R., McHugo, G. J., Bond, G. R., Finnerty, M. T., & Burns, B. J. (2009). Assertive community treatment: Facilitators and barriers to implementation in routine mental health settings. *Psychiatric Services,* *60*, 189–195. doi:10.1176/appi.ps.60.2.189

McDaniel, M. A., Whetzel, D. L., Schmidt, F. L., & Maurer, S. D. (1994). The validity of employment interviews: A comprehensive review and meta-analysis. *Journal of Applied Psychology, 79*, 599–616. doi:10.1037/0021-9010.79.4.599

McGrew, J. H., Bond, G. R., Dietzen, L., & Salyers, M. (1994). Measuring the fidelity of implementation of a mental health program model. *Journal of Consulting and Clinical Psychology, 62*, 670–678. doi:10.1037/0022-006X.62.4.670

McIntyre, L. L., Gresham, F. M., DiGennaro, F. D., & Reed, D. D. (2007). Treatment integrity of school-based interventions with children in the *Journal of Applied Behavior Analysis* 1991–2005. *Journal of Applied Behavior Analysis, 40*, 659–672. doi:10.1901/jaba.2007.659-672

Naleppa, M. J., & Cagle, J. G. (2010). Treatment fidelity in social work intervention research: A review of published studies. *Research on Social Work Practice, 20*, 674–681. doi:10.1177/1049731509352088

Naoom, S. F., Van Dyke, M., Fixsen, D. L., Blase, K. A., & Villagomez, A. N. (2012). Developing implementation capacity of organizations and systems to support effective uses of family literacy programs. In B. H. Wasik (Ed.), *Handbook of family literacy* (2nd ed., pp. 447–464). New York, NY: Routledge.

Paine, S. C., Bellamy, G. T., & Wilcox, B. L. (Eds.). (1984). *Human services that work: From innovation to standard practice.* Baltimore, MD: Brookes.

Patras, J., & Klest, S. (in press). Group size and therapists' workplace ratings: Three is the magic number. *Journal of Social Work.*

Perepletchikova, F., Treat, T. A., & Kazdin, A. E. (2007). Treatment integrity in psychotherapy research: Analysis of the studies and examination of the associated factors. *Journal of Consulting and Clinical Psychology, 75*, 829–841. doi:10.1037/0022-006X.75.6.829

Prochaska, J. M., Prochaska, J. O., & Levesque, D. A. (2001). A transtheoretical approach to changing organizations. *Administration and Policy in Mental Health and Mental Health Services Research, 28*, 247–261. doi:10.1023/A:1011155212811

Reiter-Lavery, L. (2004, January). *Finding great MST therapists: New and improved hiring guidelines.* Paper presented at the Third International MST Conference, Charleston, SC.

Sanetti, L. M. H., & Kratochwill, T. R. (2009). Toward developing a science of treatment integrity: Introduction to the special series. *School Psychology Review, 38*, 445–459.

Schoenwald, S. K. (2011). It's a bird, it's a plane, it's . . . fidelity measurement in the real world. *Clinical Psychology: Science and Practice, 18*, 142–147. doi:10.1111/j.1468-2850.2011.01245.x

Schoenwald, S. K., Brown, T. L., & Henggeler, S. W. (2000). Inside multisystemic therapy: Therapist, supervisory, and program practices. *Journal of Emotional and Behavioral Disorders, 8*, 113–127. doi:10.1177/106342660000800207

Schoenwald, S. K., Sheidow, A. J., & Letourneau, E. J. (2004). Toward effective quality assurance in evidence-based practice: Links between expert consultation, therapist fidelity, and child outcomes. *Journal of Clinical Child and Adolescent Psychology, 33*, 94–104. doi:10.1207/S15374424JCCP3301_10

Spouse, J. (2001). Bridging theory and practice in the supervisory relationship: A sociocultural perspective. *Journal of Advanced Nursing, 33*, 512–522. doi:10.1046/j.1365-2648.2001.01683.x

Starfield, B. (2000). Is US health really the best in the world? *Journal of the American Medical Association, 284*, 483–485. doi:10.1001/jama.284.4.483

U.S. Department of Health and Human Services. (1999). *Mental health: A report of the Surgeon General.* Rockville, MD: Author.

Vernez, G., Karam, R., Mariano, L. T., & DeMartini, C. (2006). *Evaluating comprehensive school reform models at scale: Focus on implementation.* Santa Monica, CA: RAND.

Whitley, R., Gingerich, S., Lutz, W. J., & Mueser, K. T. (2009). Implementing the illness management and recovery program in community mental health settings: Facilitators and barriers. *Psychiatric Services, 60*, 202–209. doi:10.1176/appi.ps.60.2.202

Wolf, M. M., Kirigin, K. A., Fixsen, D. L., Blase, K. A., & Braukmann, C. J. (1995). The teaching-family model: A case study in data-based program development and refinement (and dragon wrestling). *Journal of Organizational Behavior Management, 15*, 11–68. doi:10.1300/J075v15n01_04

Woolf, S. H., & Johnson, R. E. (2005). The break-even point: When medical advances are less important than improving the fidelity with which they are delivered. *Annals of Family Medicine, 3*, 545–552. doi:10.1370/afm.406

9

BEHAVIOR ANALYTIC TECHNIQUES TO PROMOTE TREATMENT INTEGRITY

FLORENCE D. DiGENNARO REED, JASON M. HIRST,
AND VERONICA J. HOWARD

Numerous professional task forces (e.g., American Psychological Association, Evidence-Based Practices Special Interest Group of the Association for Behavior Analysis International, Council for Exceptional Children), nationally regarded organizations (e.g., Association for Science in Autism Treatment, National Autism Center), and government agencies (e.g., National Research Council, New York State Department of Health) have synthesized large bodies of research and applied criteria to develop standards of evidence-based intervention practices (e.g., American Psychological Association Presidential Task Force on Evidence-Based Practice, 2006; Lord & McGee, 2001; National Autism Center, 2009). Others seek to promote evidence-based practice in their mission and disseminate valuable information to aid psychologists and interventionists (e.g., American Psychological Association Task Force on Evidence-Based Practice with Children and Adolescents, National Guideline Clearinghouse, Promising

http://dx.doi.org/10.1037/14275-011
Treatment Integrity: A Foundation for Evidence-Based Practice in Applied Psychology, L. M. H. Sanetti and T. R. Kratochwill (Editors)

Practices Network, Center on Instruction). In many ways, these reviews have simplified the clinical decision making of psychologists, consultants, behavior analysts, and other professionals who must decide among an array of appropriate and potentially effective treatment options for any given referral issue. Fortunately, many (though not all) clinical care, behavioral, and educational concerns have emerging or well-established research to guide intervention efforts. Compared with the educational and care opportunities offered only decades ago, the potential for high-quality service delivery is greatly improved given these resources.

The availability of these resources, even combined with an increased focus on accountability and use of "scientifically based research" in clinical practice and educational settings (e.g., Individuals with Disabilities Education Improvement Act of 2004; No Child Left Behind Act of 2001), does not imply that interventionists will implement the evidence-based intervention practices with adequate treatment integrity (i.e., consistently and accurately) over time (Jahr, 1998; Parsons, Reid, & Green, 1993; Reid & Green, 1990). Interventionists need support in initiating and maintaining the behavior changes associated with implementing these intervention practices with adequate treatment integrity. Behavior analytic techniques have a long history of effectively supporting behavior change, and several such techniques (e.g., direct training, feedback) can produce dramatic changes in treatment integrity (e.g., Salmento & Bambara, 2000; Schepis & Reid, 1994; van Vonderen, de Swart, & Didden, 2010). A number of other behavior analytic techniques are available to guide professional interactions between psychologists and interventionists with the goal of promoting high levels of treatment integrity. The purpose of this chapter is to (a) describe behavior analysis and how it may serve as a framework to conceptualize treatment integrity promotion; (b) summarize behavior analytic techniques to improve or maintain treatment integrity; and (c) describe social validity, a central tenet in behavior analysis, within the intervention delivery process.

ABC MODEL OF TREATMENT INTEGRITY PROMOTION

Behavior analysis is the scientific (i.e., experimental) study of behavior. Its focus is on identifying causes of behavior in the environment and outside of the individual (Skinner, 1953). An advantage of adopting this philosophical approach is the notion that we can influence interventionist behavior by arranging the environment in strategic, carefully planned ways. Treatment integrity (interventionist behavior) is impacted by the events that precede (i.e., antecedents) and follow (i.e., consequences) plan implementation (i.e., the ABC model; see Table 9.1). The collective body

TABLE 9.1
Antecedent–Behavior–Consequence (ABC Model)

Antecedent	Behavior	Consequence
Psychologist provides behavioral skills training (i.e., modeling, coaching, and feedback) until the interventionist meets a competency criterion during role play.	Interventionist implements the treatment plan with high treatment integrity.	Client problem behavior decreases; psychologist publicly recognizes and acknowledges interventionist's high treatment integrity in a team meeting.

of behavior analytic research provides valuable information with respect to the antecedents and consequences that may promote treatment integrity. As a result, the remainder of the chapter is organized consistent with the ABC model. That is, we will first describe antecedent-based techniques to prevent treatment integrity failures and then summarize consequence-based techniques to improve low treatment integrity (and/or maintain high treatment integrity).

We recognize that varied conceptualizations of treatment integrity exist, and the techniques we describe are likely to apply regardless of the particular conceptualization adopted. It is important to note, however, that although the techniques discussed below have been effective across a wide range of behaviors, there is not yet experimental research supporting the effectiveness of these techniques related to treatment integrity. This chapter assumes readers have consulted Chapters 7 and 8 of this book. It is outside the scope of this chapter to summarize ways to measure and report treatment integrity; readers are encouraged to read Chapters 4, 5, and 6 for discussions of this relevant issue.

BEHAVIOR ANALYTIC PROMOTION TECHNIQUES

Antecedent- and consequence-based techniques can be used in isolation or as part of a training package. Incorporating some combination of training techniques produces the most robust change in treatment integrity (van Oorsouw, Embregts, Bosman, & Jahoda, 2009). A wide variety of antecedents may precede high treatment integrity in the natural environment (e.g., psychologist or supervisor enters the room, a timer beeps reminding the interventionist to perform a particular behavior). As a result, we will focus on the provision of high-quality training in our summary of antecedent-based techniques. Various consequence-based techniques are offered in this chapter as options to improve treatment integrity, including natural and contrived reinforcement, performance feedback, and directed rehearsal.

Antecedent-Based Techniques

Interventionists will not likely have the requisite knowledge and skills necessary to ensure high treatment integrity of all intervention procedures they are asked to implement across their career. As a result, a period of initial training will be necessary to provide interventionists with the skills needed to effectively carry out an intervention plan recommended for a particular client. Meta-analytic research documents improved training effectiveness when more than one training method is adopted (van Oorsouw et al., 2009), which supports the common practice of using training packages and multiple training methods to teach interventionists how to implement a plan (Roscoe & Fisher, 2008; Sarokoff & Sturmey, 2004; Sepler & Myers, 1978). Summaries of effective, empirically supported training techniques are offered elsewhere (e.g., DiGennaro Reed, Hirst, & Howard, 2013; Reid & Green, 1990) and include behavioral skills training (e.g., modeling skills interventionists are expected to perform, providing real-time support or coaching and immediate feedback) among others. We refer readers to these resources for specific details about the training techniques themselves.

The goal of training is to ensure lasting and sustainable interventionist behavior change (i.e., treatment plan implementation) across environments. Unfortunately, high-quality training that requires interventionists to emit high treatment integrity to an established training criterion is insufficient to ensure treatment integrity outside the training environment (e.g., DiGennaro, Martens, & Kleinmann, 2007; DiGennaro, Martens, & McIntyre, 2005; Noell et al., 2000). We conceptualize treatment integrity promotion as a *generalization* issue from the training to the naturalistic environment (Scheeler, 2008). Psychologists (i.e., trainers) must design initial training to ensure that interventionists can implement plans with high treatment integrity across time in the complex and varied treatment environment. Stated simply, psychologists should program for generalization within their training techniques. Stokes and Baer (1977) offered nine generalization strategies, several of which are useful in the current context and are summarized in Table 9.2.

Use Common Stimuli

A practical technique that may promote long-term treatment integrity is to identify and make available physical stimuli (e.g., written protocol, video model of treatment procedures) present in both the training and natural

TABLE 9.2
Antecedent-Based Techniques

Technique	Description	Example
Program common stimuli	During training, identify and use physical stimuli that will be present in the natural environment.	Teacher is trained to use a checklist and specific materials to prompt appropriate plan implementation during an academic intervention carried out with a student.
Train sufficient exemplars	Provide many exemplars that are both representative of the actual environment in which the intervention will take place and that reflect the range of conditions and situations that may be present during implementation.	A parent asked to implement a behavior management plan practices various scenarios during rehearsal with multiple people playing the role of the child. Training also includes practice with actual child in various contexts and activities.
Mediate generalization	Train skills that are widely applicable and are likely to be used across many contexts.	Staff hired at a specialized school for children with disabilities are trained to minimize reinforcement for any problem behaviors encountered and to keep a log of their own behaviors during treatment implementation: two skills that can apply across their caseload.

environment. Interventionists may be taught to use these stimuli during training to aid plan implementation, and then refer back to them once training is complete. A wide variety of physical stimuli may be available depending on the intervention plan being implemented. For example, a common practice is to develop a written protocol or task analysis of the intervention procedures and provide interventionists with this written document. Although ineffective as the *only* training technique in generating skillful performance (e.g., DiGennaro Reed, Codding, Catania, & Maguire, 2010; Fixsen, Naoom, Blase, Friedman, & Wallace, 2005; Sterling-Turner, Watson, & Moore, 2002), the presence of a particular stimulus may effectively serve as a prompt for correct plan implementation if made available across both environments as part of a training package.

Creating a video to model correct performance may also serve as a common stimulus in both the training and natural environments. Video modeling has gained empirical support as an effective training tactic (e.g., C. N. Catania, Almeida, Liu-Constant, & DiGennaro Reed, 2009; Lavie & Sturmey,

2002; Moore & Fisher, 2007) and may also be used to promote generalization. In video modeling, treatment procedures that interventionists are expected to implement are modeled and recorded. After initial training is complete, the video model could be saved in a digital file format that allows convenient playback on accessible devices, such as tablet computers (e.g., iPad, iPod) or smart phones. When used in this way, video models could be quickly watched by interventionists before an intervention session to facilitate high treatment integrity. For guidance on using video modeling technology, readers are encouraged to consult Collier-Meek, Fallon, Johnson, Sanetti, and Del Campo (2012), who outlined procedures for creating, editing, and implementing video models.

When adopted in the ways offered above, programming common stimuli is used as a prompt to primarily address skill deficits. Limited experimental research is available to guide psychologists on the best way to use this generalization strategy, but it could be adapted in creative ways based on the procedures that interventionists are asked to implement as well as each unique treatment environment. Some physical stimuli may be inappropriate given these particular features (e.g., use of vulnerable populations during training; prompts that impede treatment integrity or cannot always be present during treatment, such as supervisor reminders), whereas others quickly appear as appropriate options (e.g., video model, electronic prompting devices such as timers or tactile prompts, use of the natural context for training). For example, electronic prompting devices, such as the MotivAider, can be programmed to vibrate at set intervals. When worn on the belt or tucked in a pocket, these devices may prompt interventionists to engage in a particular behavior at a set time with little disruption to the natural environment. Stimuli such as these can be widely applicable across environments and treatment settings.

Train Sufficient Exemplars

An important consideration during initial interventionist training is to provide exemplars that are good (i.e., representative of the intervention environment) and varied (i.e., reflect the range of situations one will encounter within a complex environment). Training sufficient and diverse exemplars prepares the interventionist to emit high treatment integrity despite evolving intervention conditions. For example, during behavioral rehearsal, the interventionist is asked to implement the intervention in an analogue role-play situation with the psychologist (i.e., trainer) who behaves like the client receiving the intervention. To promote generalization, a variety of realistic role-play scenarios could be presented to the interventionist so that he or she must practice implementing the intervention procedures in the face of a changing environment, much like the real-world intervention environment. Training that makes use of modeling (i.e., the interventionist is asked to imitate a skill performed correctly by the trainer) has been shown to be effective when used with other training techniques (Nigro-Bruzzi & Sturmey, 2010; Sarokoff & Sturmey, 2004) and is most effective when multiple examples of high-quality models are provided (Ducharme & Feldman, 1992; Moore & Fisher, 2007), which provides support for this generalization tactic. For example, a video modeling procedure could incorporate multiple situations and different contexts with models displaying high treatment integrity. An interventionist observing varied models and contexts is provided with more information about how to implement the intervention during changing conditions.

Mediate Generalization

Interventionists may be trained to mediate generalization through the use of self-recording or self-monitoring techniques. This strategy provides in vivo, real-time treatment integrity information to interventionists that allows them to modify their behavior during actual plan implementation. Although certainly a benefit, monitoring and recording one's behavior may be challenging while simultaneously teaching and implementing an intervention plan. Moreover, early research documented that interventionists do not accurately monitor their own behavior during plan implementation (Wickstrom, Jones, LaFleur, & Witt, 1998). More recent research, however, supports the effective use of self-recording by interventionists. Sanetti and Kratochwill (2009) not only demonstrated improvements in treatment integrity when teachers were asked to complete self-recording assessments daily but also showed that teachers were able to accurately record their own behavior amidst plan implementation within the classroom environment.

Another strategy that psychologists might consider to help interventionists mediate generalization is to train skills that are applicable and transferable across intervention plans or referral concerns. For example, interventionists who are effectively taught to minimize reinforcement for problem behavior and instead provide contingent reinforcement for socially appropriate behavior can apply these principles and skills across a wide variety of behavioral issues in the treatment environment. Interventionists may more easily generalize these concepts across intervention plans to produce higher levels of treatment integrity. The success of this tactic, however, is a function of the procedures used to teach interventionists these skills (Scheeler, 2008) and promote generalization. One strategy the organizational behavior management literature suggests that may effectively mediate generalization is to teach employees (in this case, interventionists) to develop and follow verbal rules applicable across environments (Sigurdsson & Austin, 2006). Although research on this application is limited, this generalization strategy could be adopted for a large number of instructional and behavior management techniques. For example, an interventionist who was taught to implement a planned ignoring procedure for a student who screamed loudly in class to gain her attention might develop the rule to "implement planned ignoring when any child engages in mild disruptive behavior for attention-seeking purposes."

Consequence-Based Techniques

A variety of consequence-based techniques have been effectively used as a follow-up approach to improve poor treatment integrity or maintain adequate or high treatment integrity. Reinforcement may be used to address performance deficits, whereas feedback may be adopted for both skill and performance deficits. These and other techniques are summarized below; however, readers should consult Chapter 7 of this book for additional information about performance feedback. Table 9.3 summarizes the techniques described next.

Behavioral Traps

One way to maintain treatment integrity is through behavioral trapping. A *behavioral trap* refers to a behavior that comes into contact with natural reinforcement through contrived methods but is maintained over time via natural reinforcement (Baer & Wolf, 1970). Improvements in client behavior may serve as a natural reinforcer for maintaining high treatment integrity of an intervention. For example, decreases in a difficult client's anxiety symptoms may be a natural reinforcer for a psychologist to maintain high treatment integrity of an exposure and response prevention protocol. However, research suggests that changes in client behavior may not always function as a reinforcer. For example, DiGennaro et al. (2007) showed that reductions of student problem behavior in the classroom were not sufficient to maintain teachers' high treatment integrity of behavior change interventions. We recommend that psychologists arrange reinforcement opportunities and avoid making assumptions that improvements in client behavior function as reinforcers. It may be possible to arrange naturally occurring environmental conditions to mediate the behavior of interventionists. For example, DeWein and Miller (2008) attempted to improve the degree to which preschool staff implemented a behavioral procedure aimed to increase the engagement of a child with developmental delays through the use of a daily written report (i.e., an arranged reinforcement opportunity). The written reports were made available to the student's mother at the end of the day to provide an arranged opportunity for feedback to the teaching staff. Results indicate that teaching staff implemented the engagement procedure more frequently during conditions when the written report was present, and they received parental praise

TABLE 9.3
Consequence-Based Techniques

Technique	Description	Example
Behavioral traps	Behavior is artificially brought into contact with natural contingencies that will help maintain the behavior.	A supervisor initially provides artificial reinforcement to a therapist for correctly implementing a behavior support plan. The supervisor eventually arranges for parents or caregivers of clients to provide positive feedback on the progress of the client as a more natural source of reinforcement.
Schedules of reinforcement	Reinforcers are delivered according to a predetermined schedule based on the passage of time or a number of responses.	Supervisors of therapists in a residential service setting arrange for immediate and frequent reinforcement of appropriate implementation behaviors during initial training. Over time, feedback and reinforcement are thinned to a variable schedule in order to program for maintenance and increase resistance to extinction.
Positive reinforcement	A pleasant condition or event is provided following some behavior that results in an increased probability of that behavior occurring in the future.	Teachers observed to appropriately implement a treatment plan in the classroom are entered into a lottery, the winner of which receives a monetary prize or an extra privilege.
Negative reinforcement	An unpleasant condition or event is avoided or removed following some behavior that results in an increased probability of that behavior occurring in the future.	When direct-service therapists are observed to make an error in implementation, a supervisor calls a meeting to discuss missed steps and practice them. If the therapists maintain high or perfect implementation, they may avoid the meeting and the associated loss of time.
Performance feedback	Feedback is information that enables an individual to make changes to his or her future behavior; feedback compares performance with a standard or benchmark and provides information on how to improve.	During a home observation of a parent implementing a treatment procedure, the psychologist provides a description of steps performed correctly. The psychologist also models the appropriate implementation of steps missed.
Directed rehearsal	An error correction procedure in which an interventionist repeatedly practices missed intervention steps	Staff members committing errors in plan implementation for residential clients are asked to practice the steps missed or implemented incorrectly until they demonstrate the correct implementation five times consecutively.

and feedback (i.e., reinforcement), than in the reversal condition when the report was absent. The authors also simulated postresearch effects by fading researcher support and demonstrated that teaching staff continued to use written report under naturalistic conditions and, consequently, continued to implement the engagement procedure with high treatment integrity. The authors speculated that it was possible to bring the teaching staff into contact with natural reinforcers (i.e., parental praise and feedback) through the use of an arranged reinforcement opportunity (i.e., home–school communication via daily written report).

Schedules of Reinforcement

We may better understand interventionist treatment integrity by understanding how schedules of reinforcement influence behavior. First explored by Ferster and Skinner (1957), a *schedule of reinforcement* refers to the relationship between a person's behavior and the subsequent delivery of consequences. In short, a schedule of reinforcement can be conceptualized as the rule describing which behaviors will be followed by contingent reinforcement. Schedules of reinforcement produce predictable effects on the frequency of behavior, the time that passes between each occurrence of behavior, and the resistance of behavior to change (Mace, Pratt, Zangrillo, & Steege, 2011). They play a particularly salient role in the acquisition and maintenance of behavior—two factors directly related to interventionist treatment integrity (Lentz & Daly, 1996). Psychologists might improve their effectiveness in promoting treatment integrity through an awareness of the influence of reinforcement schedules on interventionist behavior (i.e., implementing treatment procedures). To grant a better understanding of the role of reinforcement schedules on behavior, the most basic schedules of reinforcement are summarized next.

Extinction is a schedule of reinforcement in which planned consequences (both positive and negative reinforcers) are withheld (Mace et al., 2011). Often, interventionists are expected to demonstrate adequate levels of treatment integrity as part of their typical responsibilities; thus, no specific consequences (e.g., positive reinforcement) are planned to increase treatment integrity. In these cases, treatment integrity could be said to be "on extinction." Numerous studies, however, have shown that under these typical conditions (i.e., extinction), treatment integrity levels tend to be inadequate, even if interventionists implemented procedures adequately during initial training. For example, Mortenson and Witt (1998) and Noell et al. (2000) showed that teacher treatment integrity decreased to low levels in a posttraining condition absent of planned consequences. Despite exhibiting high treatment integrity during typical conditions when the consultant was available for immediate support (a planned consequence), teachers' performance dramatically reduced within several intervention sessions during a baseline condition that included extinction (i.e., no planned consequence of immediate support from a consultant). Interestingly, when extinction is *gradually* introduced (i.e., slowly decrease how much reinforcement is delivered), rather than suddenly introduced (i.e., stop reinforcement altogether), treatment integrity remains high (DiGennaro et al., 2005; Gilbertson, Witt, Singletary, & VanDerHeyden, 2007). This procedure is known as *fading* and may be used successfully as a way to reduce the amount of support provided to interventionists while maintaining high treatment integrity. For example, feedback may be provided to an interventionist after each intervention episode immediately. Over time and as treatment integrity remains high, feedback may be faded to delivery after every other episode to once a week and even less (DiGennaro et al., 2007, 2005).

Ratio schedules refer to those schedules where reinforcement is delivered following a specified number of responses. In *fixed-ratio* (FR) schedules, the number of responses required to earn reinforcement is set (or fixed), and reinforcement is delivered following the same number of responses. For example, a special education teacher might praise her new paraprofessional after every three lessons delivered to a special education student. In this case, the special education teacher delivers the reinforcer (praise) after an FR of every third lesson delivered. FR schedules produce a pattern of responding referred to as a "break-and-run" pattern epitomized by a high rate of responding until reinforcement is delivered, then a pause following reinforcement. Behavior reinforced on this schedule is less likely to maintain over time for three reasons. First, this schedule of reinforcement results in frequent reinforcement delivery, which could result in *satiation* (or programmed reinforcers being less effective due to overuse). Next, less frequent reinforcement could produce *ratio strain*, which refers to pausing that takes place due to an increase in the effort required or how difficult it is to obtain reinforcement. During ratio strain, the person simply stops behaving in the desired manner. Finally, because of the predictability of reinforcement, behaviors reinforced on FR schedules will more quickly decrease in frequency when reinforcement is no longer available (i.e., during extinction). This schedule of reinforcement, however, is incredibly effective when teaching skills initially. When training interventionists to use new skills, a psychologist would be well served to use an FR schedule (such as FR 1, when reinforcement is delivered after every behavior instance or session) to reinforce target skills often and predictably before fading to another schedule of reinforcement.

Variable-ratio (VR) schedules of reinforcement are similar to FR schedules in that the delivery of reinforcement is based on the number of responses.

However, unlike FR schedules, the number of responses necessary to earn reinforcement varies, but reinforcement is delivered following some average number of responses. For example, the treatment supervisor in a group home might provide praise to direct care workers after they complete an average of five correct social skills interactions. Sometimes the supervisor would provide praise after two correct social skills interactions, sometimes after eight correct social skills interactions, but the praise would be delivered on average after every five social skills interactions. Behavior reinforced on a VR schedule of reinforcement is more resistant to extinction (i.e., the person continues to behave in the same manner) than behavior reinforced on FR schedules. This schedule of reinforcement produces a consistent pattern of responding at relatively high rates. This schedule of reinforcement would be effective to use if the aim is to maintain relatively high rates of a behavior (e.g., if the aim was to increase the number of praise statements [i.e., rate] made to clients during interactions).

Interval schedules of reinforcement include delivery of reinforcement for the first response following a prespecified period. *Fixed-interval* (FI) schedules of reinforcement occur when the amount of time is identical from opportunity to opportunity, and *variable-interval* (VI) schedules of reinforcement occur when the amount of time varies with each new reinforcement opportunity, but averages a fixed amount of time. For example, a supervisor who is able to remotely monitor treatment being delivered in the clinical setting might schedule observations to monitor the integrity of his or her direct care workers. If this supervisor monitored the intervention on a consistent daily, weekly, or monthly schedule (e.g., every Tuesday at 1 p.m.), and deliver praise or feedback about obtaining high treatment integrity at a consistent time, the direct care workers would be on an FI schedule of reinforcement. If the supervisor were less consistent in his or her observations, or specifically programmed observations to occur more randomly to avoid reactivity (e.g., Reed, Fienup, Luiselli, & Pace, 2010), the direct care workers' behavior would be on a VI schedule of reinforcement. FI schedules of reinforcement produce a pattern of responding known as scalloping, though there is some question as to whether this pattern of responding occurs in humans (Hyten & Madden, 1993). Following the delivery of reinforcement during FI schedules, the individual will respond at low rates (at or near zero), but the rate of responding occurs more frequently as the end of the interval approaches, ultimately resulting in irregular patterns of behavior. This schedule of reinforcement also produces behavior that is highly susceptible to extinction (i.e., frequency of behavior decreases as soon as reinforcement is no longer provided). VI schedules of reinforcement produce patterns of responding that are relatively low rate, yet consistent, and are highly resistant to extinction.

Positive Reinforcement

Positive reinforcement takes place when an individual engages in a behavior that produces a consequence he or she desires (e.g., approval, items of value), resulting in an increase in the future probability of the same behavior (A. C. Catania, 2007). Delivering the consequence contingent on behavior strengthens the behavior it follows; thus, positive reinforcement is used to increase the likelihood of the behavior occurring again. Evidence of the effectiveness of a variety of positive reinforcers to increase interventionist performance is available in the literature including monetary rewards (e.g., Luiselli et al., 2009; Pommer & Streedback, 1974), privileges (e.g., a letter of commendation, parking space, free lunch, an extra work break; Green, Reid, Perkins, & Gardner, 1991), vacation days or schedule changes (e.g., Iwata, Bailey, Brown, Foshee, & Alpern, 1976; Reid, Schuh-Wear, & Brannon, 1978), and other tangible items (e.g., coupons, meals; Reid & Whitman, 1983). A common reinforcer used in interventions to improve treatment integrity is performance feedback in the form of praise for treatment components performed correctly (performance feedback is summarized below and elsewhere in this book). Psychologists should carefully consider the schedule of reinforcement they wish to use and make every effort to identify items that actually function as reinforcers (i.e., serve to increase treatment integrity).

Negative Reinforcement

Negative reinforcement takes place when an individual engages in behavior that terminates or prevents an unpleasant event, resulting in an increase in the future probability of the same behavior (A. C. Catania, 2007). Similarly to positive reinforcement, negative reinforcement involves strengthening behavior, but the increase is due to the removal of an event rather than the addition of one. Negatively reinforced behaviors are those that can be referred to as *escape* or *avoidance* behaviors. A common classroom example includes students who engage in disruptive behavior to escape or avoid a difficult academic task. If the disruptive behavior results in the student escaping the aversive task (perhaps due to being sent to the office), the student is more likely to behave similarly when faced with aversive tasks in the future. Negative reinforcement can also be used to achieve desired intervention implementation results. For example, DiGennaro et al. (2007, 2005) used a negative reinforcement contingency to improve the treatment integrity of teachers implementing an intervention to reduce the occurrence of disruptive behaviors in the classroom. First, teachers were provided with intervention training consisting of modeling, coaching, and feedback. Then teachers implemented the interventions independently. When teachers demonstrated low treatment integrity, a meeting was held during which the consultant and teacher reviewed and practiced missed intervention steps. The authors posited that time is a valuable resource for teachers and avoiding the loss of time to attend meetings with the consultant might serve to motivate teachers to improve their performance. Teachers were thus able to avoid the meeting by implementing the intervention correctly. When teachers were made to attend the meetings, the consultant incorporated performance feedback and directed rehearsal (described below). The package of feedback, directed rehearsal, and negative reinforcement showed consistent positive effects in that all teachers achieved high levels of treatment integrity.

The addition of a negative reinforcement contingency to other procedures was also shown to be effective by Noell et al. (2000). The goal of the study was to improve the implementation of a peer tutoring intervention by general education teachers. The researchers primarily used performance feedback to achieve this goal. However, one teacher did not respond to the feedback alone. When reminded about a meeting with the student's parents and the school principal at the end of the intervention, her performance improved. This finding suggests that making accountability more salient may serve as an unpleasant consequence that could be avoided by improving performance.

We do not recommend that aversive control methods take precedence over positive reinforcement or feedback procedures. Whenever possible, antecedent training procedures and positive consequences should be used first. However, in instances where those procedures are not effective, negative reinforcement procedures may be an alternative. The literature has provided examples of relatively tame consequences, such as avoiding the loss of time, which may prove to be more socially acceptable and palatable than reprimands or monetary penalties, which are forms of punishment.

Performance Feedback

Feedback has been studied extensively as an effective method for improving performance in a variety of settings including, but not limited to, food service (Johnson & Masotti, 1990), health care (DeVries, Burnette, & Redmon, 1991), industry (Komaki, Barwick, & Scott, 1978), and education (Auld, Belfiore, & Scheeler, 2010). Most definitions describe *feedback* as information provided to an individual about performance (e.g., Wilder, Austin, & Casella, 2009), the purpose of which is to enable an interventionist to make adjustments to his or her performance. The function of feedback—or the process by which feedback changes behavior—may vary. Some researchers have proposed that feedback serves as an antecedent for the next occasion where a certain task is attempted (Daniels, 1994). That is, the feedback interventionists receive following their last performance provides instructions for how to change their performance the next time they implement an intervention. Others have proposed that feedback serves as a behavioral consequence for the performance it follows (Komaki et al., 1978; Sulzer-Azaroff & Mayer, 1991). Finally, feedback has been described as a contingency-specifying stimulus (Agnew, 1997; Agnew & Redmon, 1993). That is, the feedback provides an individual with a rule that, if followed, will result in a positive consequence. The varying content or format of feedback suggests that it can have several functions. For this reason, it has been suggested that feedback not be used as a technical term but rather as a sort of professional slang (Peterson, 1982). In the absence of research indicating which function feedback serves, we have opted to describe it as a consequence-based strategy.

Although the function of performance feedback remains uncertain, there is a substantial body of evidence supporting its effectiveness in improving performance in a variety of settings. In cases in which performance refers to the treatment integrity with which interventionists implement procedures or protocols, feedback may serve as an effective intervention. Particularly when used in conjunction with other behavioral techniques, performance feedback has been shown to have reliable and consistent effects (Alvero, Bucklin, & Austin, 2001; Balcazar, Hopkins, & Suarez, 1985–1986). For example, Noell et al. (2000) demonstrated that performance feedback was more effective than standard weekly follow-up meetings in improving the implementation of a peer tutoring procedure. The experimenter met with the teacher each morning to review the teacher's performance on the previous day. During these meetings, performance feedback was delivered in the form of simple graphs depicting both the students' performance and the teacher's performance. In addition to sharing the graphs, the experimenter provided information on which steps were completed or missed and provided specific recommendations on how to improve performance. The frequency of the meetings was thinned over time as teacher performance improved. The results of the study showed that the feedback was effective in improving the teaching performance of three out of four teachers. Auld et al. (2010) used performance feedback to improve the implementation of a classroom-based differential reinforcement procedure by preservice teachers. Following an initial training program, the teachers were observed in the classroom and attended weekly meetings with the researchers. During the meetings, the researchers shared performance data—data indicating which steps were completed or missed—with the teacher. Additionally, the components of the intervention were reviewed, and specific recommendations were made for how to respond to incidents that arise in the classroom. The training and feedback package produced significant increases in teacher performance and concurrently an improvement in student behavior in the classroom.

Daniels and Daniels (2006) suggested that simply providing information does not constitute feedback; instead, feedback should serve two purposes. First, the information should compare current performance to some benchmark; second, feedback should contain information on how to improve performance in the future. Meta-analytic research has supported that feedback used in isolation is not likely to be as effective as in combination with antecedents to behavior such as staff training procedures, task analyses/checklists, written objectives, or prompts from supervisors or managers; or consequences for behavior such as incentives or other forms of reinforcement (Alvero et al., 2001).

Directed Rehearsal

Directed rehearsal, sometimes referred to as *positive practice*, is an error correction procedure where an individual is made to repeatedly practice a specific skill following an error in performing that skill (Ward, Johnson, & Konukman, 1998). A distinction has been made between directed rehearsal and positive practice such that positive practice is considered to be a punishment procedure used to reduce the occurrence of inappropriate behaviors and directed rehearsal is used to describe procedures used to increase the occurrence of desired behaviors (Lenz, Singh, & Hewett, 1991).

Two related studies by Ward and colleagues (Ward, Smith, & Makasci, 1997; Ward et al., 1998) demonstrated the effectiveness of directed rehearsal in improving the teaching performance of preservice physical education teachers. When participants made an error in the teaching procedure, they were asked to attend a follow-up meeting with the researchers where they had to perform the missed steps 10 times consecutively before being allowed to leave for the day. This procedure effectively improved performance. Moreover, teachers only required the rehearsal contingency on nine occasions in the former study (Ward et al., 1997) and on five occasions in the latter (Ward et al., 1998). More recent research suggests that the criterion of 10 consecutive correct rehearsals may not be necessary. Two studies (e.g., DiGennaro et al., 2007, 2005) asked teachers to practice missed steps three times and showed similar positive results.

In these cases, directed rehearsal was made contingent on participants making an error in the teaching procedure. The authors suggested that the effectiveness of the rehearsal procedure may have been derived from the negative reinforcement contingency represented by avoiding practice (Ward et al., 1998) or avoiding the loss of time associated with the rehearsal meetings (DiGennaro et al., 2007).

Technique Selection

It is important to iterate the value of assessing the reasons interventionists emit low treatment integrity. In the simplest sense, poor treatment integrity may be a function of a skill deficit (i.e., *can't do* problem; lacks skills or does not know how to implement the intervention) or a performance deficit (i.e., *won't do* problem; has skills but does not use them). Particular behavior analytic techniques are appropriate given the type of deficit identified. Antecedent techniques are generally appropriate for skill deficits, and consequence-based techniques are generally appropriate for performance deficits, but these helpful rules are not universal.

Researchers commonly use a combination of the above-described antecedents and consequences to quickly impact interventionist behavior (Roscoe & Fisher, 2008; Sarokoff & Sturmey, 2004, 2008; Sepler & Myers, 1978). Unfortunately, a comparison of the effectiveness of these techniques in isolation using component analysis has not been conducted, which makes it challenging to provide guidance about the best way to select among these options. We endorse reliance on high-quality training (e.g., modeling, rehearsal, coaching) and positive follow-up techniques (e.g., performance feedback, positive reinforcement) to facilitate high levels of treatment integrity. In the absence of any empirical data to further guide decision making, we also recommend assessing the perceptions of individuals affected by the interventions to better understand the social validity of the techniques being adopted and the outcomes obtained.

TREATMENT ACCEPTABILITY ASSESSMENT

Social validity refers to the extent to which the procedures, goals, and effects of intervention are significant, appropriate, and important to consumers including students, caregivers, interventionists, and others (e.g., immediate and extended community members; Wolf, 1978). Treatment acceptability is one aspect of social validity assessing "whether treatment is appropriate for the problem, whether treatment is fair, reasonable, and intrusive, and whether treatment meets with conventional notions about what treatment should be" (Kazdin, 1980, p. 259). Although considerations of social validity may play a key role in effective consultation, Carter (2007) posited that treatment acceptability assessment is an important component of ensuring an individual's right to effective treatment. Measuring the acceptability of intervention procedures used with clients has been adopted in empirical research (e.g., Martens, Witt, Elliott, & Darveaux, 1985) and primarily focuses on interventions designed to reduce behavior problems of children (Jones, Eyberg, Adams, &

Boggs, 1998). More recently, however, researchers have explored the acceptability of the consultation process as well as techniques used by psychologists to improve or maintain treatment integrity (e.g., McDougal, Clonan, & Martens, 2000; Ward et al., 1997, 1998; Weinkauf, Zeug, Anderson, & Ala'i-Rosales, 2011; Yetter, 2010). Findings are mixed with respect to the relationship between treatment integrity and interventionist acceptability ratings of the interventions implemented with clients (Watson & Skinner, 2004). We were unable to locate any research evaluating the relationship between treatment integrity and interventionist acceptability ratings of the consultation or training and support process. In the absence of research, we encourage psychologists to ask interventionists to rate the acceptability of intervention training and support procedures. Questionnaires consisting of 6-point (e.g., DiGennaro et al., 2007, 2005; DiGennaro Reed et al., 2010) and 3-point Likert-type scales (Ward et al., 1998) have been successfully used; however, the psychometric properties of these scales are unknown, indicating the need for validation research. In addition to treatment acceptability assessment, psychologists should include assessment of other aspects of social validity such as the social importance and significance of treatment goals and outcomes. We encourage psychologists to involve multiple stakeholders in social validity assessment such as students, caregivers, and teachers.

CONCLUSION

In this chapter, we have detailed a behavior analytic approach to treatment integrity promotion and included a summary of antecedent- and consequence-based techniques to support interventionist implementation efforts. We recommend adopting high-quality training techniques and positive follow-up techniques to promote treatment integrity. However, negative reinforcement (when used with directed rehearsal) has been shown to be an effective and acceptable intervention to improve treatment integrity. Identifying reasons for low treatment integrity (i.e., skill or performance deficit) will guide the efforts of psychologists and inform appropriate follow-up techniques. Equally important is assessment of the acceptability of interventions used with clients, as well as those implemented with interventionists to improve or maintain treatment integrity.

REFERENCES

Agnew, J. L. (1997). The establishing operation in organizational behavior management. *Journal of Organizational Behavior Management, 18,* 7–19. doi:10.1300/J075v18n01_02

Agnew, J. L., & Redmon, W. K. (1993). Contingency specifying stimuli: The role of "rules" in organizational behavior management. *Journal of Organizational Behavior Management, 12*, 67–76. doi:10.1300/J075v12n02_04

Alvero, A. M., Bucklin, B. R., & Austin, J. (2001). An objective review of the effectiveness and essential characteristics of performance feedback in organizational settings (1985–1998). *Journal of Organizational Behavior Management, 21*, 3–29. doi:10.1300/J075v21n01_02

American Psychological Association Presidential Task Force on Evidence-Based Practice. (2006). Evidence-based practice in psychology. *American Psychologist, 61*, 271–285. doi:10.1037/0003-066X.61.4.271

Auld, R. G., Belfiore, P. J., & Scheeler, M. C. (2010). Increasing pre-service teachers' use of differential reinforcement: Effects of performance feedback on consequences for student behavior. *Journal of Behavioral Education, 19*, 169–183. doi:10.1007/s10864-010-9107-4

Baer, D. M., & Wolf, M. M. (1970). The entry into natural communities of reinforcement. In R. Ulrich, T. Stachnik, & J. Mabry (Eds.), *Control of human behavior: Vol. 2. From cure to prevention* (pp. 319–324). Glenview, IL: Scott, Foresman.

Balcazar, F. E., Hopkins, B. L., & Suarez, Y. (1985–1986). A critical, objective review of performance feedback. *Journal of Organizational Behavior Management, 7*, 65–89. doi:10.1300/J075v07n03_05

Carter, S. L. (2007). Review of recent treatment acceptability research. *Education and Training in Developmental Disabilities, 42*, 301–316.

Catania, A. C. (2007). *Learning: Interim (4th) edition*. Cornwall-on-Hudson, NY: Sloan.

Catania, C. N., Almeida, D., Liu-Constant, B., & DiGennaro Reed, F. D. (2009). Video modeling to train staff to implement discrete-trial instruction. *Journal of Applied Behavior Analysis, 42*, 387–392. doi:10.1901/jaba.2009.42-387

Collier-Meek, M. A., Fallon, L. M., Johnson, A. H., Sanetti, L. M. H., & Del Campo, M. A. (2012). Constructing self-modeling videos: Procedures and technology. *Psychology in the Schools, 49*, 3–14. doi:10.1002/pits.20614

Daniels, A. C. (1994). *Bringing out the best in people*. New York, NY: McGraw-Hill.

Daniels, A. C., & Daniels, J. E. (2006). *Performance management: Changing behavior that drives organizational effectiveness*. Atlanta, GA: Performance Management.

DeVries, J. E., Burnette, M., & Redmon, W. K. (1991). AIDS prevention: Improving nurses' compliance with glove wearing through performance feedback. *Journal of Applied Behavior Analysis, 24*, 705–711. doi:10.1901/jaba.1991.24-705

DeWein, M., & Miller, L. K. (2008). The effect of a teacher report on the sustainability of an intervention to facilitate engagement by a child with developmental delays. *Education & Treatment of Children, 31*, 333–349. doi:10.1353/etc.0.0002

DiGennaro, F. D., Martens, B. K., & Kleinmann, A. E. (2007). A comparison of performance feedback procedures on teachers' implementation integrity and students' inappropriate behavior in special education classrooms. *Journal of Applied Behavior Analysis, 40*, 447–461. doi:10.1901/jaba.2007.40-447

DiGennaro, F. D., Martens, B. K., & McIntyre, L. L. (2005). Increasing treatment integrity through negative reinforcement: Effects on teacher and student behavior. *School Psychology Review, 34,* 220–231.

DiGennaro Reed, F. D., Codding, R., Catania, C. N., & Maguire, H. (2010). Effects of video modeling on treatment integrity of behavioral interventions. *Journal of Applied Behavior Analysis, 43,* 291–295. doi:10.1901/jaba.2010.43-291

DiGennaro Reed, F. D., Hirst, J. M., & Howard, V. J. (2013). Empirically supported staff selection, training, and management strategies. In D. D. Reed, F. D. DiGennaro Reed, & J. K. Luiselli (Eds.), *Handbook of crisis intervention for individuals with developmental disabilities* (pp. 71–85). New York, NY: Springer. doi:10.1007/978-1-4614-6531-7_5

Ducharme, J. M., & Feldman, M. A. (1992). Comparison of staff training strategies to promote generalized teaching skills. *Journal of Applied Behavior Analysis, 25,* 165–179. doi:10.1901/jaba.1992.25-165

Ferster, C. B., & Skinner, B. F. (1957). *Schedules of reinforcement.* New York, NY: Appleton-Century-Crofts. doi:10.1037/10627-000

Fixsen, D. L., Naoom, S. F., Blase, K. A., Friedman, R. M., & Wallace, F. (2005). *Implementation research: A synthesis of the literature.* Tampa: University of South Florida, Louis de la Parte Florida Mental Health Institute, National Implementation Research Network.

Gilbertson, D., Witt, J. C., Singletary, L. L., & VanDerHeyden, A. (2007). Supporting teacher use of interventions: Effects of response dependent performance feedback on teacher implementation of a math intervention. Journal of Behavioral Education, *16,* 311-326. doi:10.1007/s10864-007-9043-0

Green, C. W., Reid, D. H., Perkins, L. I., & Gardner, S. M. (1991). Increasing habilitative services for persons with profound handicaps: An application of structural analysis to staff management. *Journal of Applied Behavior Analysis, 24,* 459–471. doi:10.1901/jaba.1991.24-459

Hyten, C., & Madden, G. J. (1993). The scallop in human fixed-interval research: A review of problems with data description. *Psychological Record, 43,* 471–500.

Individuals with Disabilities Education Improvement Act of 2004, H.R. 1350, 108th Cong. (2004).

Iwata, B. A., Bailey, J. S., Brown, K. M., Foshee, T. J., & Alpern, M. A. (1976). A performance-based lottery to improve residential care and training by institutional staff. *Journal of Applied Behavior Analysis, 9,* 417–431. doi:10.1901/jaba.1976.9-417

Jahr, E. (1998). Current issues in staff training. *Research in Developmental Disabilities, 19,* 73–87. doi:10.1016/S0891-4222(97)00030-9

Johnson, C. M., & Masotti, R. M. (1990). Suggestive selling by waitstaff in family-style restaurants: An experiment and multisetting observations. *Journal of Organizational Behavior Management, 11,* 35–54. doi:10.1300/J075v11n01_04

Jones, M. L., Eyberg, S. M., Adams, C. D., & Boggs, S. R. (1998). Treatment acceptability of behavioral interventions for children: An assessment by mothers of children with disruptive behavior disorders. *Child & Family Behavior Therapy*, 20, 15–26. doi:10.1300/J019v20n04_02

Kazdin, A. E. (1980). Acceptability of alternative treatments for deviant child behavior. *Journal of Applied Behavior Analysis*, 13, 259–273. doi:10.1901/jaba.1980.13-259

Komaki, J., Barwick, K. D., & Scott, L. R. (1978). A behavioral approach to occupational safety: Pinpointing and reinforcing sale performance in a food manufacturing plant. *Journal of Applied Psychology*, 63, 434–445. doi:10.1037/0021-9010.63.4.434

Lavie, T., & Sturmey, P. (2002). Training staff to conduct a paired-stimulus preference assessment. *Journal of Applied Behavior Analysis*, 35, 209–211. doi:10.1901/jaba.2002.35-209

Lentz, F. E., Jr., & Daly, E. J., III. (1996). Is the behavior of academic change agents controlled metaphysically? An analysis of the behavior of those who change behavior. *School Psychology Quarterly*, 11, 337–352. doi:10.1037/h0088939

Lenz, M., Singh, N. N., & Hewett, A. M. (1991). Overcorrection as an academic remediation procedure: A review and reappraisal. *Behavior Modification*, 15, 64–73. doi:10.1177/01454455910151004

Lord, C., & McGee, J. P. (Eds.). (2001). *Educating children with autism*. Washington, DC: National Academy Press.

Luiselli, J. K., DiGennaro Reed, F. D., Christian, W. P., Markowski, A., Rue, H. C., St. Amand, C., & Ryan, C. J. (2009). Effects of an informational brochure, lottery-based financial incentive, and public posting on absenteeism of direct-care human services employees. *Behavior Modification*, 33, 175–181. doi:10.1177/0145445508320624

Mace, F. C., Pratt, J. L., Zangrillo, A. N., & Steege, M. W. (2011). Schedules of reinforcement. In W. W. Fisher, C. C. Piazza, & H. S. Roane (Eds.), *Handbook of applied behavior analysis* (pp. 55–75). New York, NY: Guilford Press.

Martens, B. K., Witt, J. C., Elliott, S. N., & Darveaux, D. X. (1985). Teacher judgments concerning the acceptability of school-based interventions. *Professional Psychology: Research and Practice*, 16, 191–198. doi:10.1037/0735-7028.16.2.191

McDougal, J. L., Clonan, S. M., & Martens, B. K. (2000). Using organizational change procedures to promote the acceptability of prereferral intervention services: The school-based intervention team project. *School Psychology Quarterly*, 15, 149–171. doi:10.1037/h0088783

Moore, J. W., & Fisher, W. W. (2007). The effects of videotape modeling on staff acquisition of functional analysis methodology. *Journal of Applied Behavior Analysis*, 40, 197–202. doi:10.1901/jaba.2007.24-06

Mortenson, B. P., & Witt, J. C. (1998). The use of weekly performance feedback to increase teacher implementation of a prereferral academic intervention. *School Psychology Review*, 27, 613–627.

National Autism Center. (2009). *National standards report*. Randolph, MA: Author.

Nigro-Bruzzi, D., & Sturmey, P. (2010). The effects of behavioral skills training on mand training by staff and unprompted vocal mands by children. *Journal of Applied Behavior Analysis, 43*, 757–761. doi:10.1901/jaba.2010.43-757

No Child Left Behind Act of 2001, H.R. 1, 107th Cong. (2001).

Noell, G. H., Witt, J. C., LaFleur, L. H., Mortenson, B. P., Ranier, D. D., & LeVelle, J. (2000). Increasing intervention implementation in general education following consultation: A comparison of two follow-up strategies. *Journal of Applied Behavior Analysis, 33*, 271–284. doi:10.1901/jaba.2000.33-271

Parsons, M. B., Reid, D. H., & Green, C. W. (1993). Preparing direct service staff to teach people with severe disabilities: A comprehensive evaluation of an effective and acceptable training program. *Behavioral Residential Treatment, 8*, 163–185. doi:10.1002/bin.2360080302

Peterson, N. (1982). Feedback is not a new principle of behavior. *Behavior Analyst, 5*, 101–102. Retrieved from http://www.ncbi.nlm.nih.gov/pmc/articles/PMC2742013/

Pommer, D. A., & Streedback, D. (1974). Motivating staff performance in an operant learning program for children. *Journal of Applied Behavior Analysis, 7*, 217–221. doi:10.1901/jaba.1974.7-217

Reed, D. D., Fienup, D. M., Luiselli, J. K., & Pace, G. M. (2010). Performance improvement in behavioral health care: Collateral effects of planned treatment integrity observations as an applied example of schedule-induced responding. *Behavior Modification, 34*, 367–385. doi:10.1177/0145445510383524

Reid, D. H., & Green, C. W. (1990). Staff training. In J. L. Matson (Ed.), *Handbook of behavior modification with the mentally retarded* (2nd ed., pp. 71–90). New York, NY: Plenum Press.

Reid, D. H., Schuh-Wear, C. L., & Brannon, M. E. (1978). Use of a group contingency to decrease staff absenteeism in a state institution. *Behavior Modification, 2*, 251–266. doi:10.1177/014544557822006

Reid, D. H., & Whitman, T. L. (1983). Behavioral staff management in institutions. A critical review of effectiveness and acceptability. *Analysis and Intervention in Developmental Disabilities, 3*, 131–149. doi:10.1016/0270-4684(83)90011-3

Roscoe, E. M., & Fisher, W. W. (2008). Evaluation of an efficient method for training staff to implement stimulus preference assessments. *Journal of Applied Behavior Analysis, 41*, 249–254. doi:10.1901/jaba.2008.41-249

Salmento, M., & Bambara, L. M. (2000). Teaching staff members to provide choice opportunities for adults with multiple disabilities. *Journal of Positive Behavior Interventions, 2*, 12–21. doi:10.1177/109830070000200103

Sanetti, L. M. H., & Kratochwill, T. R. (2009). Treatment integrity assessment in the schools: An evaluation of the Treatment Integrity Planning Protocol. *School Psychology Quarterly, 24*, 24–35. doi:10.1037/a0015431

Sarokoff, R. A., & Sturmey, P. (2004). The effects of behavioral skills training of stall implementation of discrete-trial teaching. *Journal of Applied Behavior Analysis, 37*, 535–538. doi:10.1901/jaba.2004.37-535

Sarokoff, R. A., & Sturmey, P. (2008). The effects of instructions, rehearsal, modeling, and feedback on acquisition and generalization of staff use of discrete trial teaching and student correct responses. *Research in Autism Spectrum Disorders*, *2*, 125–136. doi:10.1016/j.rasd.2007.04.002

Scheeler, M. C. (2008). Generalizing effective teaching skills: The missing link in teacher preparation. *Journal of Behavioral Education*, *17*, 145–159. doi:10.1007/s10864-007-9051-0

Schepis, M. M., & Reid, D. H. (1994). Training direct service staff in congregate settings to interact with people with severe disabilities: A quick, effective, and acceptable program. *Behavioral Interventions*, *9*, 13–26. doi:10.1002/bin.2360090103

Sepler, H. J., & Myers, S. L. (1978). The effectiveness of verbal instruction on teaching behavior-modification skills to nonprofessionals. *Journal of Applied Behavior Analysis*, *11*, 198. doi:10.1901/jaba.1978.11-198

Sigurdsson, S. O., & Austin, J. (2006). Institutionalization and response maintenance in organizational behavior management. *Journal of Organizational Behavior Management*, *26*, 41–77. doi:10.1300/J075v26n04_03

Skinner, B. F. (1953). *Science and human behavior.* New York, NY: Macmillan.

Sterling-Turner, H. E., Watson, T. S., & Moore, J. W. (2002). The effects of direct training and treatment integrity on treatment outcomes in school consultation. *School Psychology Quarterly*, *17*, 47–77. doi:10.1521/scpq.17.1.47.19906

Stokes, T. F., & Baer, D. M. (1977). An implicit technology of generalization. *Journal of Applied Behavior Analysis*, *10*, 349–367. doi:10.1901/jaba.1977.10-349

Sulzer-Azaroff, B., & Mayer, G. R. (1991). *Behavior analysis for lasting change.* Fort Worth, TX: Holt, Rinehart, and Winston.

van Oorsouw, W. M. W. J., Embregts, P. J. C. M., Bosman, A. M. T., & Jahoda, A. (2009). Training staff serving clients with intellectual disabilities: A meta-analysis of aspects determining effectiveness. *Research in Developmental Disabilities*, *30*, 503–511. doi:10.1016/j.ridd.2008.07.011

van Vonderen, A., de Swart, C., & Didden, R. (2010). Effectiveness of instruction and video feedback on staff's use of prompts and children's adaptive responses during one-to-one training in children with severe to profound intellectual disability. *Research in Developmental Disabilities*, *31*, 829–838. doi:10.1016/j.ridd.2010.02.008

Ward, P., Johnson, M., & Konukman, F. (1998). Directed rehearsal and preservice teachers' performance of instructional behaviors. *Journal of Behavioral Education*, *8*, 369–380. doi:10.1023/A:1022827415544

Ward, P., Smith, S., & Makasci, K. (1997). Teacher training: Effects of directed rehearsal on the teaching skills of physical education majors. *Journal of Behavioral Education*, *7*, 505–517. doi:10.1023/A:1022863520165

Watson, T. S., & Skinner, C. H. (Eds.). (2004). *Encyclopedia of school psychology.* New York, NY: Kluwer Academic/Plenum. doi:10.1007/978-0-387-22556-2

Weinkauf, S. M., Zeug, N. M., Anderson, C. T., & Ala'i-Rosales, S. (2011). Evaluating the effectiveness of a comprehensive staff training package for behavioral interventions for children with autism. *Research in Autism Spectrum Disorders, 5*, 864–871. doi:10.1016/j.rasd.2010.10.001

Wickstrom, K. F., Jones, K. M., LaFleur, L. H., & Witt, J. C. (1998). An analysis of treatment integrity in school-based behavioral consultation. *School Psychology Quarterly, 13*, 141–154. doi:10.1037/h0088978

Wilder, D. A., Austin, J., & Casella, S. (2009). Applying behavior analysis in organizations: Organizational behavior management. *Psychological Services, 6*, 202–211. doi:10.1037/a0015393

Wolf, M. M. (1978). Social validity: The case for subjective measurement or how applied behavior analysis is finding its heart. *Journal of Applied Behavior Analysis, 11*, 203–214. doi:10.1901/jaba.1978.11-203

Yetter, G. (2010). Assessing the acceptability of problem-solving procedures by school teams: Preliminary development of the Pre-Referral Intervention Team Inventory. *Journal of Educational & Psychological Consultation, 20*, 139–168.

IV

APPLYING TREATMENT INTEGRITY ASSESSMENT AND PROMOTION METHODS

10

LEGAL AND ETHICAL ISSUES RELATED TO TREATMENT INTEGRITY IN PSYCHOLOGY AND EDUCATION

JULIA E. McGIVERN AND MARTHA J. WALTER

Ethical dilemmas in psychology and education often arise because advances in knowledge, practices, and technology outpace the refinement of ethical codes (e.g., Barnett, Behnke, Rosenthal, & Koocher, 2007; Jacob, Decker, & Hartshorne, 2011). As examples, consider revisions to the most influential psychological ethics code, the American Psychological Association's (APA's) "Ethical Principles of Psychologists and Code of Conduct" (hereafter the APA Ethics Code), necessitated by psychologists' widespread use of electronic storage and transfer of information and of test scoring and interpretation services (APA, 2002, 2010, Standards 4.01 and 4.02). As suggested in these examples, ethical standards are often reactive; they are bound to the time frame in which they are written. Ethical standards are also intentionally broad and are not intended to answer all the specific questions that arise in the course of professional life (e.g., APA, 2002, 2010; Barnett et al., 2007). Similarly,

http://dx.doi.org/10.1037/14275-002
Treatment Integrity: A Foundation for Evidence-Based Practice in Applied Psychology, L. M. H. Sanetti and T. R. Kratochwill (Editors)

laws may be subject to multiple interpretations that must be clarified in court, especially as contexts change (e.g., Zirkel, 2011b).

The context of psychological and educational practice today—including an emphasis on evidence-based interventions and practice, accountability, and multitiered service delivery—has led to increased and warranted attention to the construct of treatment integrity (e.g., Sanetti & Fallon, 2011; Sanetti & Kratochwill, 2009; Schulte, Easton, & Parker, 2009). Although the APA Ethics Code and other ethics codes in psychology and education (e.g., the National Association of School Psychologists [NASP], 2010, Principles for Professional Ethics) do not specifically mention treatment integrity, some ethical standards can be interpreted to reflect aspects of treatment integrity. Exhibit 10.1 presents a summary of the APA Ethical Principles and Standards most closely linked to the construct.

Similarly, the most sweeping federal education statutes and regulations (e.g., the No Child Left Behind Act of 2001 [NCLB] and the Individuals with Disabilities Education Improvement Act [IDEA], 2004) do not directly address the issue of treatment integrity, leaving professionals[1] to determine the course of ethical and legal behavior with insufficient guidance (e.g., Zirkel & Rose, 2009). However, many state statutes are specifically requiring measurement of treatment integrity of classroom interventions as a condition of evaluation for specific learning disabilities (Zirkel & Thomas, 2010).

The purposes of this chapter are to (a) identify the most critical ethical and legal issues relevant to treatment integrity, (b) present information about the guidance provided by current ethical codes and laws, and (c) provide recommendations to guide professionals until research answers important questions that remain about treatment integrity. In our review of the treatment integrity literature in psychology and education, we identified seven questions that need to be answered before professionals have adequate direction regarding the ethical issues related to treatment integrity and before a standard of practice can be established that acquires the force of law. These questions, which are addressed in the following sections, are

1. What is treatment integrity?
2. Should professionals measure treatment integrity?
3. What legal–ethical challenges do professionals face in measuring treatment integrity?
4. What degree of treatment integrity must be attained to determine that treatment has been implemented? In other words, how much treatment integrity is enough?
5. Is it ethical and/or legal to provide an intervention when it will not be implemented with treatment integrity?

---

[1]We are using the term *professionals* to refer to researchers and practitioners.

EXHIBIT 10.1
American Psychological Association Ethical Principles and Standards Most Closely Related to Treatment Integrity

Principle C: Integrity: Psychologists seek to promote accuracy, honesty, and truthfulness. . . .

Principle D: Justice: Psychologists recognize that fairness and justice entitle all persons to access to and benefit from the contributions of psychology and to equal quality in the . . . services being conducted by psychologists . . . .

Principle E: Respect for People's Rights and Dignity: Psychologists respect the dignity and worth of all people. . . .

Standard 2.01: Boundaries of Competence
(e) In those emerging areas in which generally recognized standards for preparatory training do not yet exist, psychologists . . . take reasonable steps to ensure the competence of their work and to protect . . . others from harm.

Standard 2.04: Bases for Scientific and Professional Judgments
Psychologists' work is based upon established scientific and professional knowledge of the discipline.

Standard 3.10: Informed Consent
(a) When psychologists conduct research or provide assessment, therapy, counseling, or consulting services . . . they obtain the informed consent of the individual or individuals . . . .

Ethical Standard 6.01: Documentation of Professional and Scientific Work and Maintenance of Records
Psychologists create, and . . . maintain, disseminate, store, retain, and dispose of records and data relating to their professional and scientific work in order to (1) facilitate provision of services . . . (2) allow for replication of research. . . .

Ethical Standard 9.01: Bases for Assessments
(a) Psychologists base the opinions contained in their recommendations, reports, and diagnostic or evaluative statements . . . on information and techniques sufficient to substantiate their findings.

Ethical Standard 9.02: Use of Assessments
(a) Psychologists administer, adapt, score, interpret, or use assessment techniques, interviews, tests, or instruments in a manner and for purposes that are appropriate . . . .
(b) Psychologists use assessment instruments whose validity and reliability have been established . . . .

Ethical Standard 9.03: Informed Consent in Assessments
(a) Psychologists obtain informed consent for assessments, evaluations, or diagnostic services . . . .

Ethical Standard 9.05: Test Construction
Psychologists who develop . . . assessment techniques use appropriate psychometric procedures and current scientific or professional knowledge for test design, standardization, validation . . . .

Ethical Standard 10.01: Informed Consent to Therapy
(a) When obtaining informed consent to therapy . . . psychologists inform clients/ patients . . . about the nature and anticipated course of therapy . . . .

Note. From "Ethical Principles of Psychologists and Code of Conduct," by American Psychological Association, 2002, *American Psychologist, 57,* pp. 1060–1073. Copyright 2002 by American Psychological Association.

6. What are the legal–ethical implications of promoting treatment integrity?
7. How should professionals proceed while awaiting answers to critical questions about treatment integrity?

Relevant ethical principles, federal and state statutes and regulations, and case law will be referenced as we examine these questions.

WHAT IS TREATMENT INTEGRITY?

Treatment integrity has traditionally been defined as the degree to which an intervention is implemented as designed (e.g., Gresham, 1989). Other terms that have been used synonymously with treatment integrity include *treatment fidelity, intervention fidelity,* and *implementation fidelity* (Gansle & Noell, 2007; Moncher & Prinz, 1991; Schulte et al., 2009).

Recent conceptualizations of treatment integrity identify it as a multi-dimensional construct that includes not only issues of treatment delivery (Gresham, 2009; Moncher & Prinz, 1991; Perepletchikova, Treat, & Kazdin, 2007) but also dimensions such as treatment receipt (the extent to which the participant understands and is engaged in the treatment) and treatment enactment (the extent to which the participant uses skills acquired through treatment in natural environments; Schulte et al., 2009). Some authors have argued for expansion of the construct of treatment integrity to include factors common to most treatments, such as the therapeutic alliance (McLeod & Islam, 2011; McLeod, Southam-Gerow, & Weisz, 2009).

Increased recognition of the importance of treatment integrity is reflected in training and research arenas. For example, the Assessment of Competency Benchmarks Work Group, authorized by the APA Board of Educational Affairs, included "Implements interventions with fidelity to empirical models and flexibility to adapt where appropriate" (Fouad et al., 2009, p. S19) among competencies to be mastered by psychology trainees. In the research domain, increased emphasis on treatment integrity is evident in the Institute of Education Sciences' (2012) requirement that research proposals contain a description of how intervention implementation with treatment integrity will be facilitated.

Thus, in spite of questions about the dimensions of treatment integrity, consensus is building around the importance of the construct; the most basic and universal element of treatment integrity, adherence to interventions as designed; and the critical role of treatment integrity in intervention implementation (e.g., Durlak & DuPre, 2008; Gresham, 2009; Perepletchikova et al., 2007; Sanetti & Kratochwill, 2009). As researchers within psychology and education further define treatment integrity with respect to the unique aspects of their fields, increased understanding of treatment integrity will allow providers to identify the dimensions of treatment integrity most relevant to their work.

SHOULD PROFESSIONALS MEASURE TREATMENT INTEGRITY?

The goal of measuring treatment integrity is to help determine whether a treatment contributed to observed outcomes; without treatment integrity data, an intervention cannot be said to be responsible for changes in behavior (e.g., Gresham, 1989; Moncher & Prinz, 1991; Perepletchikova et al., 2007). Without evidence of treatment integrity, both internal and external validity are compromised, and professionals cannot assume that the treatment is responsible for changes in behavior (internal validity) or that treatment can be generalized to other settings (external validity; e.g., Gresham, 1989; Moncher & Prinz, 1991; Sanetti & Kratochwill, 2005). Multiple interpretations of outcomes may be possible without good knowledge about treatment implementation (e.g., Gresham, 2009). For example, it is possible that poor outcomes might be attributed incorrectly to an effective treatment because the treatment was not implemented or was implemented poorly. Conversely, positive outcomes could be attributed to an ineffective treatment when the treatment was significantly adapted during implementation and undocumented factors have positively influenced outcomes. Use of treatment integrity data can assist in determining whether to adapt and improve the treatment (when it is well implemented but ineffective) or to increase the treatment integrity (when the intervention is poorly implemented; Wood, Umbreit, Liaupsin, & Gresham, 2007).

Reviews of treatment studies across numerous fields of psychology and education have found that reporting information about treatment integrity is the exception rather than the norm (Gresham, MacMillan, Beebe-Frankenberger, & Bocian, 2000; Perepletchikova et al., 2007; Sanetti, Dobey, & Gritter, 2012; Sanetti, Gritter, & Dobey, 2011). In addition, although school-based practitioners report believing that treatment integrity is important to measure, very few of them assess treatment integrity in practice (Cochrane & Laux, 2008).

Contextual Influences Related to Treatment Integrity Assessment

In considering whether and how to assess treatment integrity, professionals must be aware of the contextual influences in the field today. Research has demonstrated that, overall, interventions implemented with higher treatment integrity are associated with better outcomes than interventions implemented with lower treatment integrity (e.g., Durlak & DuPre, 2008; Gresham, 2009). But low levels of treatment integrity do not necessarily negatively affect all participants, and some interventions may be less negatively affected by low treatment integrity than others (e.g., Noell, 2008). The specific contexts relevant to interventions can influence the importance of treatment integrity.

Evidence-Based Treatments and Practice

One of the major forces in psychology and education in recent years is the focus on evidence-based treatments (EBTs) and evidence-based practice (EBP; e.g., APA Presidential Task Force on Evidence-Based Practice, 2006; APA Task Force on Evidence-Based Practice With Children and Adolescents, 2008; Chambless & Hollon, 1998; Kratochwill & Stoiber, 2002). Although there has been debate about the pros and cons of EBTs (see, e.g., Weisz, Jensen-Doss, & Hawley, 2006), increasingly, psychological associations (e.g., APA, NASP) and public agencies (e.g., U.S. Department of Education) have called for rigorous research to identify EBTs, increased training in implementation of EBTs, and dissemination of EBTs to consumers (e.g., APA Task Force on Evidence-Based Practice With Children and Adolescents, 2008; Coalition for Evidence-Based Policy, 2003). Implicit in the advancement of EBTs is the assumption that interventions will be implemented as planned; indeed, Greenwood (2009) stated, "Treatment integrity is the key to wide-scale application of EBPs and to reaching a discipline of greater effectiveness" (p. 548).

Response-to-Intervention

Multitiered service delivery systems, such as response-to-intervention (RTI) models, are advocated in education today (e.g., Burns, Deno, & Jimerson, 2007; National Association of State Directors of Special Education [NASDSE], 2005) to address the varied needs of today's youth. In these models, interventions are provided in tiers of increasingly intensive service as need is demonstrated by students (NASDSE, 2005). Treatment integrity is a critical element of implementation of RTI models (e.g., Gresham, 2009; Sanetti & Kratochwill, 2009). As Gresham (2009) noted, "One cannot legitimately claim to practice response to intervention in the absence of determining the extent to which the 'I' (intervention) was implemented" (p. 538).

Consultation Services

Many interventions are implemented by consultees who are supported by consultants. This indirect or mediated service delivery model raises additional questions about treatment integrity. In psychological and educational consultation, a distinction is made between consultation procedural integrity and treatment plan implementation (Gansle & Noell, 2007). To capture both aspects of consultation, Sheridan, Swanger-Gagné, Welch, Kwon, and Garbacz (2009) called consultation a "two-tiered" intervention (p. 478). Although the degree to which consultation procedural integrity is related to treatment plan implementation and treatment outcomes has yet to be determined, mediated service delivery adds a layer to the assessment of treatment integrity (Gresham, 2009; Sheridan et al., 2009). As researchers (e.g., Gresham, 2009; Sanetti & Kratochwill, 2009; Sheridan et al., 2009) have suggested, an absence of knowledge about treatment plan implementation in consultation, as with direct services, results in lack of knowledge about internal validity: Can outcomes be attributed to interventions taught to consultees if we do not know whether the interventions were actually implemented?

Ethical Issues and Guidance

The APA (2002) Ethics Code provides some guidance about the importance of determining whether treatments are implemented as planned. First, in Principle C, Integrity, the Ethics Code identifies the aspirational goal of promoting "accuracy, honesty, and truthfulness" (p. 1062) in the practice of psychology. To claim that an intervention has been implemented, professionals must measure treatment integrity.

Also, Ethical Standard 2.04 of the APA (2002) Ethics Code calls for psychologists to be guided by the "scientific and professional knowledge of the discipline" (p. 1064). A growing body of literature about treatment integrity argues that this construct is firmly established in the knowledge base in psychology and education and that the most universal and critical element of treatment integrity is adherence to the discrete steps of an intervention. Consequently, ethical practice today includes, at the very least, assessment of adherence to intervention components.

Legal Issues and Guidance

NCLB (2001) has positioned the science of education research squarely at the center of its thrust; NCLB references the term *scientifically based research* more than 100 times (Zucker, 2004). Similarly, IDEA (2004) and the 2006 IDEA regulations used the term *scientifically based research* or a variant 41 times in the IDEA legislative and regulatory provisions and an additional 141 times in the commentary (Zirkel & Rose, 2009). IDEA accepts the definition of *scientifically based research* detailed in NCLB, which states, "The term 'scientifically based research'—(A) means research that involves the application of rigorous, systematic, and objective procedures to obtain reliable and valid knowledge relevant to education activities and programs . . . ." (§ 7801(37)). The focus of

NCLB and IDEA on scientifically based research suggests a heightened valuing of the scientific process. These federal laws require that providers select interventions grounded in scientific research, which today includes measurement of treatment integrity. By extension, to meet the standards in NCLB and IDEA, researchers carrying out and reporting about research studies must ensure that interventions have been delivered as planned and must report data about treatment integrity for consumers' use. Many state laws and some court decisions (to be discussed in later sections) provide further guidance about mandates to implement interventions with treatment integrity.

WHAT LEGAL–ETHICAL CHALLENGES DO PROFESSIONALS FACE IN MEASURING TREATMENT INTEGRITY?

Given experts' consensus about the importance of treatment integrity, it is imperative that professionals have access to high-quality tools for measuring treatment integrity. Treatment integrity assessment, however, is challenging and raises many methodological issues.

Measurement Issues

One of the critical issues that arise in measurement of treatment integrity concerns the measurement strategies used. There are numerous ways to measure treatment integrity, including both direct and indirect means. Lane, Bocian, MacMillan, and Gresham (2004) discussed five methods of assessing treatment integrity: (a) direct observation, (b) feedback from consultants, (c) self-reporting and behavioral interview techniques, (d) review of permanent products, and (e) manualization of interventions. There are ethical implications involved in the decisions regarding which types of assessment to use. Some methods, such as direct observation, may be more accurate, but are very time and resource intensive (Sheridan et al., 2009; Smith, Daunic, & Taylor, 2007). Other methods, such as teacher self-monitoring and self-reporting, may be less accurate but more cost-effective. Researchers suggest measuring treatment integrity first using direct means (e.g., direct observation) and supplementing these data through indirect assessment methods (e.g., review of permanent products; Gresham et al., 2000). Given that the five methods outlined by Lane et al. are not mutually exclusive, multiple methods can be implemented concurrently (Smith et al., 2007). However, as Gansle and Noell (2007) noted, "Any given treatment can be task analyzed to the point that measuring implementation of all its steps is more costly than implementing the intervention itself" (p. 247). Budgetary constraints likely will require professionals to consider a cost–benefit analysis in the assessment of treatment integrity. Several additional issues, discussed below, arise in measurement of treatment integrity.

Ethical Issues and Guidance

Although treatment integrity is not addressed specifically in the APA (2002, 2010) Ethics Code, the code does provide significant guidance regarding assessment in general that can be applied to the assessment of treatment integrity specifically. The code reviews the appropriate use of assessments, the need to obtain informed consent for assessment, and considerations in test construction. Other relevant issues, including boundaries of competence, delegation of work to others, confidentiality, and maintenance of records, are also addressed in the APA Ethics Code.

Treatment Integrity Instruments

The APA (2002) Ethics Code (Standard 9.02) stipulates that professionals should use assessment instruments with established validity and reliability levels. Therefore, professionals measuring treatment integrity are ethically bound to use instruments that are reliable and valid for the purpose of assessing treatment integrity. Current scientific and professional knowledge suggests that multiple forms of validity are important to consider in the assessment of treatment integrity, including (a) internal validity, (b) external validity, (c) construct validity, and (d) statistical conclusion validity (Sanetti & Kratochwill, 2005; for further discussions of these, see Chapters 5 and 6, this volume). Considerations of validity are essential in treatment integrity assessment given the potential ramifications of using instruments without adequate psychometric properties. Such instruments may not accurately measure levels of treatment integrity, thus failing to provide professionals with the information needed to understand treatment outcomes and depriving practitioners of valuable information needed to make decisions regarding next steps in their clients' treatment plans.

Psychologists who develop tests, such as treatment integrity assessments, are ethically obligated to do so using "appropriate psychometric procedures" and "current scientific or professional knowledge" in the design and validation of the instrument (APA, 2002, Standard 9.05, p. 1072). Although some advances are being made (e.g., McKenna, Rosenfield, & Gravois's, 2009, Level of Implementation Interview Scale for use in measuring treatment integrity in instructional consultation), additional research is needed in the area of treatment integrity assessment (Sanetti & Kratochwill, 2009). Currently, the majority of existing instruments are specific to particular interventions, thus decreasing their utility across different types of interventions (Schoenwald, Henggeler, Brondino, & Rowland, 2000). Experts suggest that research is needed to develop treatment integrity instruments that are both efficient and feasible for practitioners to implement in applied settings (Sanetti & Kratochwill, 2009).

Competence/Training and Professional Role Issues. A crucial issue to address is *who* will be assessing the treatment integrity of interventions being implemented. Part of this decision will be determined by the type of assessment (e.g., direct observation, self-report) being conducted. Several ethical considerations emerge in this decision-making process.

First, it is critical that the individuals conducting the treatment integrity assessment are trained to do so. Psychologists are ethically bound only to provide services that fall within their scope of competence (APA, 2002, Standard 2.01). If they are not competent to conduct treatment integrity assessments, they are ethically obligated to seek training, consultation, and/ or experience prior to conducting the assessments. Similarly, professionals should ensure that any individuals to whom they delegate treatment integrity assessment (e.g., teachers, other personnel) are trained and qualified to carry out the assessment (APA, 2002, Standards 2.05 and 9.07). This process can be particularly challenging when the individuals conducting the treatment integrity assessment do not value the promotion of treatment integrity and/or feel that it conflicts with their professional roles. In addition to being qualified to conduct assessments, it is critical that individuals who assess treatment integrity are knowledgeable about the interventions so that their judgments about intervention implementation are accurate.

Consent and Confidentiality. Ethical guidelines require professionals to obtain informed consent from appropriate individuals (e.g., the client or a minor client's legal guardians) prior to conducting assessment (APA, 2002, Standard 9.03) and therapy (APA, 2002, Standard 10.01). An exception to the assessment standard exists if "testing is conducted as a routine educational, institutional, or organizational activity" (APA, 2002, Standard 9.03, p. 1071). Given that development of treatment integrity instruments is in its infancy, it is likely that assessment of treatment integrity has not yet become a "routine" activity in many institutions. Therefore, professionals will need to decide if they are ethically obligated to obtain consent from individuals prior to assessing the treatment integrity of interventions they are implementing. If it is determined that consent is required, professionals will need to ensure that a full explanation of the nature and purpose of the assessment, including use of the assessment data, involvement of other personnel at the institution, and limits of confidentiality, is provided (APA, 2002, Standards 4.02 and 9.03).

Psychologists have "a primary obligation" to maintain confidentiality of information provided by persons or organizations with whom they have a professional relationship (APA, 2002, Standards 4.01 and 4.02, p. 1066). In the context of treatment integrity assessment, this may mean not sharing assessment results with any individuals who do not have a legitimate need to know the information. Any necessary release of information to other individuals (e.g., an employee's supervisor or a school principal) must be discussed when consent is obtained from the individual whose intervention delivery is being assessed (APA, 2002, Standard 3.11). If an individual's intervention implementation is going to be audio- or video-recorded for assessment purposes, permission should be obtained ahead of time (APA, 2002, Standard 4.03).

Storage of Data. Ethical guidelines require secure storage of records related to professionals' work (APA, 2002, Standards 6.01 and 6.02). Because treatment integrity assessment data will likely be linked to a particular individual or group of individuals, it is important for the data to be stored in a secure location with access only by individuals with a legitimate need to view the information. If the data will be stored in a database to which others have access, the data should be de-identified (APA, 2002, Standard 6.02).

Legal Issues and Guidance

Federal legislation indicates that states "must permit the use of a process based on the child's response to scientific, research-based intervention" in specific learning disability identification (IDEA, 2004; C.F.R. § 300.307(a)(2)). Many states now require the use of RTI procedures in specific learning disability identification, and some states (e.g., Wisconsin) specify that the scientific, research-based interventions provided to struggling students must be delivered with "adequate fidelity" (Wisconsin Administrative Code, 2012, PI § 11.36(6)). To document that they provided interventions with adequate fidelity, practitioners need a method of assessing treatment integrity. This legislative guidance highlights the importance of identifying methods of treatment integrity assessment that have sufficient psychometric properties and are feasible to implement in applied settings.

HOW MUCH TREATMENT INTEGRITY IS ENOUGH?

One of the biggest challenges in psychology and education today is determining to what extent interventions must be implemented as designed to achieve targeted outcomes and what degree of adaptation is permissible or even encouraged (e.g., Durlak & DuPre, 2008; Gansle & Noell, 2007; Randall & Biggs, 2008). Fixsen, Naoom, Blase, Friedman, and Wallace (2005) defined *implementation* as "a specified set of activities designed to put into practice an activity or program of known dimensions" (p. 5). As Gresham (2009) noted, "The problem our field faces in this regard is that we do not know what level of integrity is necessary with what treatments to produce beneficial outcomes. We also do not know how far we might 'drift' away from a treatment protocol and still have positive effects" (p. 537). Experts agree that intervention adaptation will occur. Durlak and DuPre's 2008 review of the intervention implementation literature identified over 500 studies that included self-report or observer evaluation of implementation factors and levels. These authors found that few studies attained greater than 80% treatment integrity and that positive results were often obtained with treatment integrity of 60%.

Is All Adaptation Bad?

Intervention agents may deviate from an intervention protocol in two ways. First, an agent may implement unplanned deviations from the protocol ("therapist drift"; Peterson, Homer, & Wonderlich, 1982, p. 480). Unplanned deviations present a particular problem because they may be more difficult to identify and measure, especially if it is the intervention agent who is measuring treatment integrity. Second, an agent may intentionally alter an intervention protocol, which can occur for multiple reasons, such as desire to adapt an intervention for a particular population (e.g., Huey & Polo, 2008; Kumpfer, Pinyuchon, Teixeira de Melo, & Whiteside, 2008).

Researchers have found that some intentional adaptations of interventions are desirable (e.g., Barber et al., 2006; Durlak & DuPre, 2008; Kendall, Gosch, Furr, & Sood, 2008). In fact, the APA (2006) defined EBP as "the integration of the best available research with clinical expertise in the context of patient characteristics, culture, and preferences" (p. 273). The challenge for the professional is to determine how much or what kind of adaptation facilitates improved interventions—or how much treatment integrity is too little. The answer may depend on the kind of adaptation. Some researchers have stressed the importance of understanding the theoretical underpinnings of intervention components (e.g., Durlak & DuPre, 2008; Schulte et al., 2009). Fixsen et al. (2005) noted that "understanding and adhering to the principles of intervention underlying each core component may allow for flexibility in form (e.g., processes and strategies) without sacrificing the function associated with the component" (p. 25). However, researchers have yet to identify the essential core components—or active ingredients—of most interventions (e.g., Durlak & DuPre, 2008; Noell, 2008; Noell & Gansle, 2006).

Even in the absence of evidence-based core components, some researchers are studying ways to increase the appropriateness of interventions with specific populations by relying on knowledge about populations and about theoretical underpinnings of interventions. As Durlak and DuPre (2008) noted, providers who are familiar with their communities may be able to make programs more effective in specific settings. And researchers are studying ways in which to make interventions more powerful with specific cultural populations (e.g., Barrera, Castro, Strycker, & Toobert, 2013; Kumpfer et al., 2008). Barrera et al. (2013) identified a series of questions that need to be answered to help intervention developers and therapists understand how to accomplish this, including "Under what conditions are cultural adaptations justified? How might such adaptations be achieved? What intervention activities should be added or modified in the development of cultural adaptations? Are culturally adapted interventions effective?" (p. 196).

Durlak and DuPre (2008) argued that the fidelity–adaptation debate is inappropriately framed dichotomously; intervention agents do not just implement an intervention with treatment integrity or not. Treatment integrity is a matter of degree, and we cannot determine the most advantageous blend of adherence and adaptation without carefully measuring what is implemented with treatment integrity and what is adapted. However, Durlak and DuPre suggested that there may be a threshold beyond which further treatment integrity contributes little to desired outcomes, particularly if research has identified the core treatment components and these are delivered with treatment integrity.

Ethical Issues and Guidance

There are no specific ethical standards that answer the question of how much treatment integrity is enough. However, Ethical Standard 2.04 (APA, 2002) makes clear that it is the responsibility of psychologists to be sure their work "is based upon established scientific and professional knowledge of the discipline" (APA, 2002, p. 1064). The body of treatment integrity knowledge in psychology and education does provide some direction regarding adaptations to treatments. Planned adaptations, such as those that adapt treatments to clients' contexts and preferences (APA, 2006), may be supportable. However, the state of knowledge today also suggests that professionals must measure treatment integrity to determine whether an intervention has influenced outcomes—especially when adaptations have occurred (e.g., Huey & Polo, 2008). In acting with integrity (APA Principle C), psychologists are honest about interventions delivered and guard against unplanned deviations from intervention protocols.

Legal Issues and Guidance

To date, the literature base in psychology and education indicates that legal issues regarding the degree of treatment integrity required in intervention implementation have arisen primarily in the education domain. The following discussion addresses issues that have been the focus of recent statutes, regulations, and case law in education.

Response-to-Intervention and Specific Learning Disabilities

Relevant to treatment integrity, IDEA (2004) and its 2006 regulations provide direction to states and local education agencies regarding identification of specific learning disabilities (SLD) by requiring states to permit and by permitting local education agencies (LEAs) to use "a process that determines if the child responds to scientific, research-based intervention as part of the evaluation procedures" (C.F.R. § 300.307(a)(2)). Treatment integrity is a core characteristic of models that incorporate the examination of students' response to scientifically based interventions (Gresham, 2009; Duhon, Mesmer, Gregerson, & Witt, 2009). However, federal laws do not, at this time, specify what degree of treatment integrity is required.

In response to the reauthorization of IDEA in 2004, states have revised their criteria for identification of students with SLD to be consistent with federal law. As of 2011, fifteen states had passed laws requiring use of an RTI model for determining SLD eligibility for at least some subject areas and/or grades (Zirkel, 2011b). Zirkel and Thomas (2010) conducted an analysis of state laws and guidelines regarding RTI implementation. These authors found that of the 45 states in which SLD eligibility laws had changed to be consistent with IDEA, 15 (plus Wisconsin, which has since approved its administrative rule governing identification of SLD) explicitly require treatment integrity measures in their laws and/or guidelines. Other states implicitly require or recommend treatment integrity measures, and only a few states did not address treatment integrity.

As school systems become legally mandated to consider treatment integrity in implementation of RTI models and in identification of SLD, practitioners will be required to measure treatment integrity. How they do this and what criteria they invoke for treatment integrity remain to be determined as states implement new laws and regulations.

Implementation of the Individualized Education Program

Another education issue related to treatment integrity concerns the implementation of the individualized education program (IEP) for students with disabilities. The IEP is intended to guide the provision of a free, appropriate, public education (FAPE) for students with disabilities (IDEA, 2004). The question of whether an intervention delivered with a low level of treatment integrity satisfies the school's obligation to implement the IEP has been raised in the educational and legal professional literature and in the courts. This question is framed in the literature as an issue of procedural due process (e.g., Duhon et al., 2009; Gansle & Noell, 2007), which prohibits states from taking away a liberty or property right (e.g., education) without implementing an appropriate procedure in which an individual is told what the state is proposing and is provided an opportunity to be heard (14th Amendment to the U.S. Constitution).

Some legal scholars (e.g., Huefner, 2008; Romberg, 2011) have argued that lack of IEP implementation violates an individual's due process rights, and that IDEA (2004) requires a higher standard of treatment integrity of IEP implementation than was determined by the U.S. Supreme Court in *Board of Education of Hendrick Hudson Central School District v. Rowley* (1982) to achieve delivery of FAPE. In *Rowley*, the court determined that its role was to provide "a basic floor of opportunity" and to ascertain whether the student's IEP was "reasonably calculated to enable the child to receive educational benefits" (p. 207).

Romberg (2011) argued that under IDEA (2004) a school district has three distinct procedural obligations regarding the IEP. First, it must collaborate with the child's family in developing the IEP; second, its decision-making process must be individualized to the child; and third, "after the district has arrived at this collaborative, individualized set of decisions documented in the IEP, the resulting document is, in effect, a contract" (p. 451). Huefner (2008) stated that "failure to meet and implement the . . . IEP requirements is no harmless error. These requirements are the substantive heart of FAPE" (p. 378).

Several U.S. circuit courts have ruled on issues of IEP implementation since the Supreme Court's 1982 *Rowley* decision. In *Van Duyn v. Baker School District 5J* (2007), the Ninth Circuit Court established a standard for assessing lack of implementation of IEPs. The Ninth Circuit Court determined that only a "*material* failure to implement an IEP violates the IDEA" (p. 822). A "material failure occurs when there is more than a minor discrepancy between the services provided to a disabled child and those required by the IEP" (p. 815). In *Houston Independent School District v. Bobby R.* (2000), the Fifth Circuit Court determined that

> to prevail on a claim under the IDEA, a party challenging the implementation of an IEP must show more than a *de minimis* failure to implement all elements of that IEP, and, instead, must demonstrate that the school board or other authorities failed to implement substantial or significant provisions of the IEP. (p. 349)

The court acknowledged that there had been implementation failures in the IEP, but determined that the most significant portions of the IEP had been implemented and, thus, the student had received educational benefit. In the Eighth Circuit Court's decision in *Neosho R-V School District v. Clark*

(2003), IDEA was determined to have been violated if there is evidence that the school actually failed to implement an essential element of the IEP that was necessary for the child to receive an educational benefit. The court ruled that because the child's behavior was not adequately addressed, the child was unable to obtain benefit from his educational program.

In 2010, the Ninth Circuit Court again ruled in a case regarding FAPE and IEP implementation, *J. L. v. Mercer Island School District*. After a series of appeals, the Ninth Circuit Court determined the student had been provided FAPE by the standard set in *Rowley* (1982) and rejected arguments that Congress, in revisions to IDEA since *Rowley*, had established a higher benchmark for provision of FAPE.

The cases and decisions described above raise questions about the level of IEP implementation necessary to determine whether FAPE has been provided. What specifically, for example, is a "material failure" (*Van Duyn*, 2007, p. 815)? Whether courts or Congress in the future adopt a broader interpretation of FAPE, one that includes a greater focus on IEP implementation and thus treatment integrity, remains to be seen.

Behavior Intervention Plans

A related issue has arisen regarding the implementation of behavior intervention plans (BIPs) in schools (Etscheidt, 2006; Zirkel, 2011a). Zirkel (2011a) completed a review of hearing officer decisions and published court decisions regarding BIPs between 1998 and 2010. Of the 149 cases regarding BIPs, only 19 related to implementation of the IEP; the majority of cases related to access to appropriate education and appropriateness of the IEP. In general, decisions in BIP cases were divided evenly in favor of parents and districts. However, in cases related to implementation of the BIP, cases were "relatively infrequent but heavily favored school districts" (p. 200). Zirkel (2011a) hypothesized that this disparity is related to the lack of clear guidelines regarding BIPs and the fact that courts have generally used a standard of "equitable rather than 100% compliance as the standard" (p. 205).

IS IT ETHICAL AND/OR LEGAL TO PROVIDE AN INTERVENTION WHEN IT WILL NOT BE IMPLEMENTED WITH TREATMENT INTEGRITY?

There are times when practitioners might predict that intervention enablers or core treatment components or doses of an intervention will not be delivered. Should that intervention be implemented? As suggested earlier, treatment integrity is viewed today as a multidimensional construct (e.g., Sanetti & Kratochwill, 2009; Schulte et al., 2009). Schulte et al. (2009) identified multiple dimensions, including treatment delivery, treatment receipt, and treatment enactment. Critical to comprehensive analysis of treatment integrity is consideration of all three components.

Ethical Issues and Guidance

The APA (2002) Ethics Code preamble states that "it has as its goals the welfare and protection of the individuals and groups with whom psychologists work" (p. 1062). Logically, this code would extend to maximizing the likelihood that treatments enacted are actually received by the client.

The dimension of *treatment delivery* (Schulte et al., 2009) includes factors such as therapist adherence (core treatment elements delivered), exposure (number of sessions and their length), and quality (competence and skill of the therapist). There are times when core components and recommended doses of treatments are not delivered or are delivered by persons other than those intended to deliver the interventions. For example, treatments designed for implementation in community settings are often adapted to school settings (e.g., Merrell, 2008). These adaptations frequently involve decreasing the number of sessions or dose. If an adolescent misses 50% of a drug treatment program, has that program been delivered to that adolescent?

Schulte et al.'s (2009) *treatment receipt* and *treatment enactment* dimensions relate to the treatment participant and are also critical dimensions of treatment integrity to be addressed. The degree to which participants are present at intervention sessions, understand the content delivered, and engage with the treatment are elements of treatment receipt. For example, if a depression intervention is provided when a client is severely depressed (possibly influencing engagement), has that intervention been provided with treatment integrity?

Schulte et al. (2009) considered treatment enactment to comprise participant ability to use new skills during treatment and participant generalization of skills to new settings. For example, if a participant in a group intervention for anxiety cannot generate a coping thought to use in an anxiety-provoking situation, has that intervention been provided with treatment integrity? Another issue to consider regarding treatment receipt and enactment is that intervention participants might be differentially affected by breakdowns in treatment integrity (Gansle & Noell, 2007). This issue relates to justice and equality (APA, 2002, Principle D: Justice).

APA Principle D: Justice (see Exhibit 10.1), suggests that psychologists strive to ensure that all persons benefit from services and that psychologists ensure "equal quality" (APA, 2002, p. 1062) in the services delivered. Basically, this is an issue of fairness. As Kratochwill and Stoiber (2002) noted in a discussion of cultural diversity, we cannot assume the "universality of intervention effectiveness" (p. 365). Ethically, professionals must assess the wide range of factors that influence intervention implementation (e.g., Burns, Jacob, & Wagner, 2008; Durlak & DuPre, 2008; Schulte et al., 2009), including factors that influence client receipt and engagement, to maximize the likelihood that interventions have been delivered as planned.

Legal Issues and Guidance

Legal issues regarding the treatment integrity of intervention delivery arise in education and psychology in relation to RTI, as discussed earlier. But legal issues also arise regarding treatment receipt and enactment. In the 1970s, preceding and foreshadowing the Education of All Handicapped Children Act (1975) and IDEA (2004), the *Pennsylvania Association for Retarded Children (PARC) v. Commonwealth of Pennsylvania* (1972) and *Mills v. Board of Education of District of Columbia* (1972) decisions affirmed the rights of students with mental retardation (*PARC*) and students with behavioral, emotional, and learning impairments (*Mills*) to public education. *Mills* required that the public education be "free and suitable" regardless of the level of the student's impairment (p. 878). These and other cases brought forth in that era laid the groundwork for the IEP provisions in IDEA. The *individualized* nature of the IEP implies that students' needs and capabilities are considered in the development of the IEP. And students' needs must be met via implementation of core treatment elements identified in the IEP. In *Sumter County School District Number 17 v. Joseph Heffernan* (2011), in the Fourth Circuit Court of Appeals, parents prevailed in their argument that the IEP was not implemented when behavior therapy provided to the student was provided by untrained personnel who did not understand the appropriate use of core behavioral strategies and techniques.

WHAT ARE THE LEGAL–ETHICAL IMPLICATIONS OF PROMOTING TREATMENT INTEGRITY?

How far should practitioners go to promote treatment integrity? Ethical issues arise particularly around issues of methods of promotion of treatment integrity and a right to self-determination. Field, Martin, Miller, Ward, and Wehmeyer (1998) defined *self-determination* as "a combination of skills, knowledge, and beliefs that enable a person to engage in goal-directed, self-regulated, autonomous behavior" (p. 2).

Many researchers have identified strategies for increasing treatment adherence (Fixsen et al., 2005; Randall & Biggs, 2008). Yet inherent in the notion of client behavior change is the ethical issue of choosing behavior change for others (e.g., Noell & Gansle, 2009). Monahan et al. (2005) noted that "treating people with mental disorders without their consent has always been the defining human rights issue in mental health law" (p. 37). At what point does encouragement of client treatment adherence become coercion that interferes with self-determination? The same question can be asked about treatment agents. If an intervention is delivered with low treatment integrity—for example, a therapist does not like a particular behavioral intervention recommended by a supervisor and therefore does not fully implement it—how does the supervisor weigh lack of treatment acceptability (Kazdin, 1980) versus potential client benefits?

How far should mental health and criminal justice systems go in encouraging client adherence to treatment? Some methods for encouraging client adherence to treatment, such as motivational interviewing (Miller & Rollnick, 2002), are intended to increase the client's interest in change while respecting the client's autonomy; other interventions, such as leveraging, are more coercive. In the mental health system (Monahan et al., 2005), leveraging is being used to increase client adherence. As Jaeger and Rossler (2010) noted, "Interventions aimed at enhancing psychiatric patients' outpatient treatment adherence frequently include informal coercion such as inducements and threats of negative sanctions" (p. 48). Although providers are likely to judge that the mental health interventions are critical for clients' positive outcomes, such inducements (e.g., lenient treatment by the courts and subsidized housing) may conflict with individuals' right to self-determination (e.g., Field et al., 1998).

Ethical Issues and Guidance

The APA (2002) Ethics Code's first principle, Beneficence and Nonmalfeasance, states that psychologists strive to benefit those with whom they work and to do no harm. Principle E, Respect for People's Rights and Dignity, exhorts psychologists to respect the rights of individuals to self-determination, but also to consider "special safeguards" that persons who may not be capable of "autonomous decision making" may require (p. 1063). These principles suggest that psychologists must carefully weigh the benefit that clients will obtain from treatment against the rights of persons to determine their own course of action, especially with persons with reduced decision-making capabilities. However, psychologists must be cautious in making such determinations. APA Ethical Standard 3.10 requires psychologists to obtain informed consent to treatment. When working with people who are not capable of providing informed consent, psychologists "consider such persons' preferences and best interests" (p. 1065).

Legal Issues and Guidance

Promoting client treatment adherence through coercive means such as leveraging is common with individuals with significant mental health disorders (Jaeger & Rossler, 2010; Redlich, Steadman, Robbins, & Swanson, 2006). Monahan et al. (2005) found that up to 59% of individuals with mental illness receiving active outpatient treatment in a large, multisite study had experienced at least one type of community treatment mandate.

Increased understanding of the psychological and legal ramifications of leveraging is necessary to inform the debate about the desirability and effectiveness of these practices. Redlich et al. (2006) found no association between criminal justice leveraging and treatment compliance in the arena of mental health, suggesting that additional research is needed to determine what, if any, benefits are accrued to clients through these practices.

HOW SHOULD PROFESSIONALS PROCEED WHILE AWAITING ANSWERS TO CRITICAL QUESTIONS ABOUT TREATMENT INTEGRITY?

In spite of questions that remain to be answered regarding how researchers and practitioners can engage in ethical and legal practice in the area of treatment integrity, general recommendations do emerge from the literature. We offer the following recommendations to guide professionals until critical questions regarding the construct of treatment integrity are answered:

- Develop an understanding, and help others develop understanding, of treatment integrity and its relationship to internal and external validity (e.g., Gresham, 1989).
- When identifying interventions, determine whether they can be implemented with treatment integrity. Are required resources (e.g., persons, materials) and prerequisites (e.g., training) available (e.g., Fixsen et al., 2005)?
- Understand the theoretical underpinnings of interventions and focus on implementing core features with treatment integrity (e.g., Durlak & DuPre, 2008).
- Carefully consider adaptations to interventions; document the use of adaptations intended to enhance interventions in a specific context (e.g., Barrera et al., 2013).
- Identify methods of treatment integrity measurement that are cost-effective yet provide critical information about internal and external validity and are appropriate for the questions being asked (e.g., Sanetti & Kratochwill, 2005).

- Use the data generated to improve interventions or provide feedback to others (e.g., Wood et al., 2007).
- Generate practice-based evidence (Kratochwill et al., 2012) to extend the knowledge base about interventions; disseminate findings to others through publications, conferences, and professional meetings.

CONCLUSION

As research provides answers to questions about treatment integrity, and as ethical codes, statutes, regulations, and case law propel the fields of education and psychology toward more effective practices, the body of knowledge about treatment integrity will grow. In the meantime, professionals can examine the contexts of their work to identify practices related to treatment integrity that increase the likelihood that conclusions reached about intervention outcomes are valid and that facilitate the development and use of effective interventions.

REFERENCES

American Psychological Association. (2002). Ethical principles of psychologists and code of conduct. *American Psychologist, 57*, 1060–1073. doi:10.1037/0003-066X.57.12.1060

American Psychological Association. (2010). 2010 amendments to the 2002 "Ethical Principles of Psychologists and Code of Conduct." *American Psychologist, 65*, 493. doi:10.1037/a0020168

American Psychological Association Presidential Task Force on Evidence-Based Practice. (2006). Evidence-based practice in psychology. *American Psychologist, 61*, 271–285. doi:10.1037/0003-066X.61.4.271

American Psychological Association Task Force on Evidence-Based Practice With Children and Adolescents. (2008). *Disseminating evidence-based practice for children and adolescents: A systems approach to enhancing care*. Washington, DC: American Psychological Association. doi:10.1037/e582412010-001

Barber, J. P., Gallop, R., Crits-Christoph, P., Frank, A., Thase, M. E., Weiss, R. D., & Gibbons, M. B. C. (2006). The role of therapist adherence, therapist competence, and alliance in predicting outcome of individual drug counseling: Results from the National Institute Drug Abuse Collaborative Cocaine Treatment Study. *Psychotherapy Research, 16*, 229–240. doi:10.1080/10503300500288951

Barnett, J. E., Behnke, S. H., Rosenthal, S. L., & Koocher, G. P. (2007). In case of ethical dilemma, break glass: Commentary on ethical decision making in practice. *Professional Psychology: Research and Practice, 38*, 7–12. doi:10.1037/0735-7028.38.1.7

Barrera, M., Jr., Castro, F. G., Strycker, L. A., & Toobert, D. J. (2013). Cultural adaptations of behavioral health interventions: A progress report. *Journal of Consulting and Clinical Psychology, 81*, 196–205. doi:10.1037/a0027085

Board of Education of Hendrick Hudson Central School District v. Rowley, 458 U.S. 176 (1982).

Burns, M. K., Deno, S. L., & Jimerson, S. R. (2007). Toward a unified response-to-intervention model. In S. R. Jimerson, M. K. Burns, & A. M. VanDerHeyden (Eds.), *Handbook of response to intervention: The science and practice of assessment and intervention* (pp. 428–440). New York, NY: Springer. doi:10.1007/978-0-387-49053-3_32

Burns, M. K., Jacob, S., & Wagner, A. R. (2008). Ethical and legal issues associated with using response-to-intervention to assess learning disabilities. *Journal of School Psychology, 46*, 263–279. doi:10.1016/j.jsp.2007.06.001

Chambless, D. L., & Hollon, S. D. (1998). Defining empirically supported therapies. *Journal of Consulting and Clinical Psychology, 66*, 7–18. doi:10.1037/0022-006X.66.1.7

Coalition for Evidence-Based Policy. (2003). *Identifying and implementing educational practices supported by rigorous evidence: A user friendly guide*. Washington, DC: U.S. Department of Education.

Cochrane, W. S., & Laux, J. M. (2008). A survey investigating school psychologists' measurement of treatment integrity in school-based interventions and their beliefs about its importance. *Psychology in the Schools, 45*, 499–507. doi:10.1002/pits.20319

Duhon, G. J., Mesmer, E. M., Gregerson, L., & Witt, J. C. (2009). Effects of public feedback during RTI team meetings on teacher implementation integrity and student academic performance. *Journal of School Psychology, 47*, 19–37. doi:10.1016/j.jsp.2008.09.002

Durlak, J. A., & DuPre, E. P. (2008). Implementation matters: A review of research on the influence of implementation on program outcomes and the factors affecting implementation. *American Journal of Community Psychology, 41*, 327–350. doi:10.1007/s10464-008-9165-0

Education of All Handicapped Children Act, Pub. L. No. 94-142 (1975).

Etscheidt, S. (2006). Behavioral intervention plans: Pedagogical and legal analysis of issues. *Behavioral Disorders, 31*, 223–243.

Field, S., Martin, J., Miller, R., Ward, M., & Wehmeyer, M. (1998). *A practical guide for teaching self-determination*. Reston, VA: Council for Exceptional Children.

Fixsen, D. S., Naoom, S. F., Blase, K. A., Friedman, R. M., & Wallace, F. (2005). *Implementation research: A synthesis of the literature*. Tampa: University of South Florida, Louis de la Parte Florida Mental Health Institute, National Implementation Research Network.

Fouad, N. A., Grus, C. L., Hatcher, R. L., Kaslow, N. J., Hutchings, P. S., Madson, M. B., . . . Crossman, R. E. (2009). Competency benchmarks: A model for understanding and measuring competence in professional psychology across training levels. *Training and Education in Professional Psychology, 3*, S5–S26. doi:10.1037/a0015832

Gansle, K. A., & Noell, G. H. (2007). The fundamental role of intervention implementation in assessing response to intervention. In S. R. Jimerson, M. K. Burns, & A. M. VanDerHeyden (Eds.), *Handbook of response to intervention: The science and practice of assessment and intervention* (pp. 244–251). New York, NY: Springer. doi:10.1007/978-0-387-49053-3_18

Greenwood, C. R. (2009). Treatment integrity: Revisiting some big ideas. *School Psychology Review, 38*, 547–553.

Gresham, F. M. (1989). Assessment of treatment integrity in school consultation and prereferral intervention. *School Psychology Review, 18*, 37–50.

Gresham, F. M. (2009). Evolution of the treatment integrity concept: Current status and future directions. *School Psychology Review, 38*, 533–540.

Gresham, F. M., MacMillan, D. L., Beebe-Frankenberger, M. E., & Bocian, K. M. (2000). Treatment integrity in learning disabilities intervention research: Do we really know how treatments are implemented? *Learning Disabilities Research & Practice, 15*, 198–205. doi:10.1207/SLDRP1504_4

Houston Independent School District v. Bobby R., 200 F.3d 341 (5th Cir. 2000).

Huefner, D. S. (2008). Updating the FAPE standard under IDEA. *Journal of Law & Education, 37*, 367–379.

Huey, S. J., Jr., & Polo, A. J. (2008). Evidence-based psychosocial treatments for ethnic minority youth. *Journal of Clinical Child & Adolescent Psychology, 37*, 262–301. doi:10.1080/15374410701820174

Individuals with Disabilities Education Improvement Act of 2004, Pub. L. No. 108-446 (2004).

Institute of Education Sciences. (2012). *Requests for applications: Special education research grants: CFDA Number 84-324A*. Washington, DC: U.S. Department of Education.

Jacob, S., Decker, D. M., & Hartshorne, T. S. (2011). *Ethics and law for school psychologists* (6th ed.). Hoboken, NJ: Wiley.

Jaeger, M., & Rossler, W. (2010). Enhancement of outpatient treatment adherence: Patients' perceptions of coercion, fairness and effectiveness. *Psychiatry Research, 180*, 48–53. doi:10.1016/j.psychres.2009.09.011

J. L. v. Mercer Island School District, 592 F.3d 938 (9th Cir. 2010).

Kazdin, A. E. (1980). Acceptability of alternative treatments for deviant child behavior. *Journal of Applied Behavior Analysis, 13*, 259–273. doi:10.1901/jaba.1980.13-259

Kendall, P. C., Gosch, E., Furr, J. M., & Sood, E. (2008). Flexibility within fidelity. *Journal of the American Academy of Child & Adolescent Psychiatry, 47*, 987–993. doi:10.1097/CHI.0b013e31817eed2f

Kratochwill, T. R., Hoagwood, K. E., Kazak, A. E., Weisz, J. R., Hood, K., Vargas, L. A., & Banez, G. A. (2012). Practice-based evidence for children and adolescents: Advancing the research agenda in schools. *School Psychology Review, 41*, 215–235.

Kratochwill, T. R., & Stoiber, K. C. (2002). Evidence-based interventions in school psychology: Conceptual foundations of the *Procedural and Coding Manual* of Division 16 and the Society for the Study of School Psychology Task Force. *School Psychology Quarterly, 17*, 341–389. doi:10.1521/scpq.17.4.341.20872

Kumpfer, K. L., Pinyuchon, M., Teixeira de Melo, A., & Whiteside, H. O. (2008). Cultural adaptation process for international dissemination of the Strengthening Families Program. *Evaluation & the Health Professions, 31*, 226–239. doi:10.1177/0163278708315926

Lane, K. L., Bocian, K. M., MacMillan, D. L., & Gresham, F. M. (2004). Treatment integrity: An essential—but often forgotten—component of school-based interventions. *Preventing School Failure, 48*, 36–43. doi:10.3200/PSFL.48.3.36-43

McKenna, S. A., Rosenfield, S., & Gravois, T. A. (2009). Measuring the behavioral indicators of instructional consultation: A preliminary validity study. *School Psychology Review, 38*, 496–509.

McLeod, B. D., & Islam, N. Y. (2011). Using treatment integrity methods to study the implementation process. *Clinical Psychology: Science and Practice, 18*, 36–40. doi:10.1111/j.1468-2850.2010.01232.x

McLeod, B. D., Southam-Gerow, M. A., & Weisz, J. R. (2009). Conceptual and methodological issues in treatment integrity measurement. *School Psychology Review, 38*, 541–546.

Merrell, K. W. (2008). *Helping students overcome depression and anxiety: A practical guide* (2nd ed.). New York, NY: Guilford Press.

Miller, W. R., & Rollnick, S. (2002). *Motivational interviewing: Preparing people for change* (2nd ed.). New York, NY: Guilford Press.

Mills v. Board of Education of District of Columbia, 348 F. Supp. 866 (D. D.C. 1972).

Monahan, J., Redlich, A. D., Swanson, J., Robbins, P. C., Appelbaum, P. S., Petrila, J., . . . McNiel, D. E. (2005). Use of leverage to improve adherence to psychiatric treatment in the community. *Psychiatric Services, 56*, 37–44. doi:10.1176/appi.ps.56.1.37

Moncher, F. J., & Prinz, R. J. (1991). Treatment fidelity in outcome studies. *Clinical Psychology Review, 11*, 247–266. doi:10.1016/0272-7358(91)90103-2

National Association of School Psychologists. (2010). *Principles for professional ethics*. Bethesda, MD: Author. Retrieved from http://www.nasponline.org/standards/2010standards/1_%20Ethical%20Principles.pdf

National Association of State Directors of Special Education. (2005). *Response to intervention: Policy considerations and implementation*. Alexandria, VA: Author.

Neosho R-V School District v. Clark, 315 F.3d 1022, n.3 (8th Cir. 2003).

No Child Left Behind Act of 2001, Pub. L. No. 107-110 (2001).

Noell, G. H. (2008). Research examining the relationships among consultation process, treatment integrity, and outcomes. In W. P. Erchul & S. M. Sheridan (Eds.), *Handbook of research in school consultation* (pp. 323–342). New York, NY: Erlbaum.

Noell, G. H., & Gansle, K. A. (2006). Assuring the form has substance: Treatment plan implementation as the foundation of assessing response to intervention. *Assessment for Effective Intervention, 32*, 32–39. doi:10.1177/15345084060320 010501

Noell, G. H., & Gansle, K. A. (2009). Moving from good ideas in educational systems change to sustainable program implementation: Coming to terms with some of the realities. *Psychology in the Schools, 46*, 79–89. doi:10.1002/pits.20355

Pennsylvania Association for Retarded Children (PARC) v. Commonwealth of Pennsylvania, 343 F. Supp. 279 (E.D. Pa. 1972).

Perepletchikova, F., Treat, T. A., & Kazdin, A. E. (2007). Treatment integrity in psychotherapy research: Analysis of the studies and examination of the associated factors. *Journal of Consulting and Clinical Psychology, 75*, 829–841. doi:10.1037/0022-006X.75.6.829

Peterson, L., Homer, A. L., & Wonderlich, S. A. (1982). The integrity of independent variables in behavior analysis. *Journal of Applied Behavior Analysis, 15*, 477–492. doi:10.1901/jaba.1982.15-477

Randall, C. J., & Biggs, B. K. (2008). Enhancing therapeutic gains: Examination of fidelity to the model for the intensive mental health program. *Journal of Child and Family Studies, 17*, 191–205. doi:10.1007/s10826-007-9159-9

Redlich, A. D., Steadman, H. J., Robbins, P. C., & Swanson, J. W. (2006). Use of the criminal justice system to leverage mental health treatment: Effects on treatment adherence and satisfaction. *Journal of the American Academy of Psychiatry and the Law, 34*, 292–299.

Romberg, J. (2011). The means justify the ends: Structural due process in special education law. *Harvard Journal on Legislation, 48*, 415–466. Retrieved from http://www.harvardjol.com/wp-content/uploads/2011/07/Romberg_Article.pdf

Sanetti, L. H., & Kratochwill, T. R. (2005). Treatment integrity assessment within a problem-solving model. In R. Brown-Chidsey (Ed.), *Assessment for intervention: A problem-solving approach* (pp. 304–325). New York, NY: Guilford Press.

Sanetti, L. M. H., Dobey, L. M., & Gritter, K. L. (2012). Treatment integrity of interventions with children in the *Journal of Positive Behavior Interventions* from 1999 to 2009. *Journal of Positive Behavior Interventions, 14*, 29–46. doi:10.1177/1098300711405853

Sanetti, L. M. H., & Fallon, L. M. (2011). Treatment integrity assessment: How estimates of adherence, quality, and exposure influence interpretation of implementation. *Journal of Educational and Psychological Consultation, 21*, 209–232. doi:10.1080/10474412.2011.595163

Sanetti, L. M. H., Gritter, K. L., & Dobey, L. M. (2011). Treatment integrity of interventions with children in the school psychology literature from 1995 to 2008. *School Psychology Review, 40*, 72–84.

Sanetti, L. M. H., & Kratochwill, T. R. (2009). Toward developing a science of treatment integrity: Introduction to the special series. *School Psychology Review, 38,* 445–459.

Schoenwald, S. K., Henggeler, S. W., Brondino, M. J., & Rowland, M. D. (2000). Multisystemic therapy: Monitoring treatment fidelity. *Family Process, 39,* 83–103. doi:10.1111/j.1545-5300.2000.39109.x

Schulte, A. C., Easton, J. E., & Parker, J. (2009). Advances in treatment integrity research: Multidisciplinary perspectives on the conceptualization, measurement, and enhancement of treatment integrity. *School Psychology Review, 38,* 460–475.

Sheridan, S. M., Swanger-Gagné, M., Welch, G. W., Kwon, K., & Garbacz, S. A. (2009). Fidelity measurement in consultation: Psychometric issues and preliminary examination. *School Psychology Review, 38,* 476–495.

Smith, S. W., Daunic, A. P., & Taylor, G. G. (2007). Treatment fidelity in applied educational research: Expanding the adoption and application of measures to ensure evidence-based practice. *Education & Treatment of Children, 30,* 121–134. doi:10.1353/etc.2007.0033

Sumter County School District Number 17 v. Joseph Heffernan, 642 F.3d 478 (4th Cir. 2011).

Van Duyn v. Baker School District 5J, 502 F.3d 811 (9th Cir. 2007).

Weisz, J. R., Jensen-Doss, A., & Hawley, K. M. (2006). Evidence-based youth psychotherapies versus usual clinical care: A meta-analysis of direct comparisons. *American Psychologist, 61,* 671–689. doi:10.1037/0003-066X.61.7.671

Wisconsin Administrative Code, PI § 11.36(6) (2012).

Wood, B. K., Umbreit, J., Liaupsin, C. J., & Gresham, F. M. (2007). A treatment integrity analysis of function-based intervention. *Education & Treatment of Children, 30,* 105–120. doi:10.1353/etc.2007.0035

Zirkel, P. A. (2011a). Case law for functional behavior assessments and behavior intervention plans: An empirical analysis. *Seattle University Law Review, 35,* 175–212.

Zirkel, P. A. (2011b). What does the law say? *Teaching Exceptional Children, 43,* 65–67.

Zirkel, P. A., & Rose, T. (2009). Scientifically based research and peer-reviewed research under the IDEA. *Journal of Special Education Leadership, 22,* 36–50.

Zirkel, P. A., & Thomas, L. B. (2010). State laws and guidelines for implementing RTI. *Teaching Exceptional Children, 43,* 60–73.

Zucker, S. (2004). *Scientifically based research: NCLB and assessment* (Policy report). San Antonio, TX: Harcourt Assessment.

11

TREATMENT INTEGRITY IN CONJOINT BEHAVIORAL CONSULTATION: ACTIVE INGREDIENTS AND POTENTIAL PATHWAYS OF INFLUENCE

SUSAN M. SHERIDAN, KRISTIN M. RISPOLI,
AND SHANNON R. HOLMES

The statistical precision by which intervention outcomes are evaluated has increased in recent years in an effort to improve their viability in addressing emotional, social, behavioral, and academic issues. Despite these advances, *treatment integrity*, a vital aspect in evaluating the merit of a given intervention, remains largely overlooked. Definitions of treatment integrity include the accuracy and consistency with which an intervention is implemented (Wolery, 2011) and whether the intervention is delivered as intended (Knoche, Sheridan, Edwards, & Osborn, 2010). For our purposes, we share the perspective of Dane and Schneider (1998), who defined treatment integrity as the extent to which treatment agents deliver an intervention as intended with sufficient precision, reliability, and distinction.

Preparation of this chapter was supported in part by a grant (R324A100115) awarded to the first author by the Institute of Education Sciences. The opinions expressed here belong to the authors and are not to be viewed as representing those of the funding agency.

http://dx.doi.org/10.1037/14275-012
Treatment Integrity: A Foundation for Evidence-Based Practice in Applied Psychology, L. M. H. Sanetti and T. R. Kratochwill (Editors)

School-based interventions are often implemented by natural treatment agents (e.g., teachers) through indirect service delivery (e.g., consultation). Behavioral or problem-solving consultation is a service delivery model whereby a consultant with expertise in data-based problem solving and intervention development works with a consultee (e.g., teacher, parent) to identify and analyze specific targets for intervention and develop, implement, and evaluate strategies to address identified concerns (Sheridan & Kratochwill, 1992). Unique to consultation is its indirect nature, whereby treatments are implemented by individuals who are part of children's natural environments (e.g., teachers, parents) and not trained behavioral therapists in a "pull-out" (e.g., small group therapy, individual therapy) fashion. Contextual factors inherent in consultation-based intervention implementation in schools (e.g., lack of specialized intervention training, environmental disruptions, resistance from students) pose threats to treatment integrity that, if undetected, may lead to erroneous conclusions regarding intervention effectiveness (Elliott, Witt, Kratochwill, & Stoiber, 2002). In this chapter, we introduce conjoint behavioral consultation (CBC) as a coordinated, cross-system approach to consultation; identify and describe active ingredients of CBC (including those representing both collaborative problem solving and behavioral intervention plan implementation); explore the various dimensions of treatment integrity for CBC research; articulate integrity variables in need of investigation; and offer specific research directions.

CBC (Sheridan & Kratochwill, 2008) is a variant of behavioral consultation involving a similar structured problem-solving procedure and implementation of behavioral interventions by parents and teachers in a coordinated and collaborative (i.e., conjoint) fashion. CBC is predicated on ecological–behavioral theory (Bronfenbrenner, 1977) and a belief that positive connections between individuals from the primary ecological systems in a child's life maximize developmental progress. CBC seeks to improve child concerns that disrupt learning, enhance the capacity of families and schools to foster child functioning, and bolster family–school relationships. To this end, embedded throughout CBC is the development of collaborative partnerships between families and schools to facilitate joint problem-solving interactions that maximize change in child behaviors across the home and school contexts. It aims to develop a sense of shared responsibility between parents and teachers, such that current and future needs are addressed through a cooperative problem-solving process (Sheridan, Eagle, Cowan, & Mickelson, 2001). Within this larger aim is the goal to increase communication between parents and teachers by fostering open and equal participation in the consultative process. Likewise, CBC focuses on improving relationships between parents and teachers such that all parties establish a sense of respect for the expertise and contribution of the other in addressing the child's needs. With a focus on systems, CBC promotes the examination of needs as present across settings, leading to more accurate problem conceptualization and the development of comprehensive plans to address them (Sheridan & Colton, 1994).

Structurally, CBC is implemented through a series of four stages that guide the consultative process, with three of four completed via a structured interview. In the *problem (needs) identification* stage and the concomitant Conjoint Needs Identification Interview, the consultant guides the parent and teacher in discussing the child's strengths and areas of need. With the support of the consultant, the parent and teacher identify a common priority and operationally define the target skill or behavior that becomes the focus of consultation. A goal is then developed, along with a plan to collect baseline data on the priority behavior. In the *problem (needs) analysis* stage (and Conjoint Needs Analysis Interview), data that have been collected are discussed, and team members examine possible contributing factors (e.g., setting events, antecedents, consequences, environmental conditions) that may be influencing behavior. Team members together develop a plan for home and school that includes the use of evidence-based strategies, and plan for ongoing data collection to assess behavior change. In the *treatment implementation* stage, the plan is implemented with agreed-upon strategies and procedures. Finally, in the *plan evaluation* stage (and Plan Evaluation Interview), the team discusses successes and difficulties encountered while implementing the plan across environments. Together members determine features of the plan that may need to be altered and whether continuation of the plan and future meetings are warranted. Methods for maintaining ongoing communication among team members are introduced and encouraged by the consultant (Sheridan & Kratochwill, 2008). Although structured and designed in a specific sequence, the practice of CBC often mandates flexibility and recurring movement between stages (Sheridan et al., 2001).

DUAL COMPONENTS, OBJECTIVES, AND ACTIVE INGREDIENTS OF CBC

Within behavioral consultation, two parallel components function together to influence a child's behaviors: (a) the structured problem-solving procedures invoked by consultants to guide the team in plan development and evaluation (i.e., collaborative problem solving) and (b) the intervention that is implemented by treatment agents in the child's environment (i.e., behavioral intervention plan). An important caveat within the context of assessing CBC treatment integrity as compared with other forms of behavioral consultation is that each aspect of the problem-solving and plan implementation process must be implemented collaboratively in a manner that considers the inputs and perspectives of both home and school. This approach reflects the emphasis in CBC on joint ownership, mutual decision making, and coordination and continuity in an effort to maximize the impact of the intervention.

To examine the integrity with which the CBC intervention (including collaborative problem-solving and behavioral intervention plans; see Table 11.1) is implemented, it is necessary to identify the unique criteria that define it as an intervention. By extension, observation of these criteria is necessary to determine that the CBC intervention is in place. These criteria are thought to be the active ingredients of CBC, reflecting the fundamental elements that operate to produce positive effects in accordance with the objectives of the CBC intervention. Thus, they are conceptualized as necessary to define CBC implementation. If not present, conclusions regarding the efficacy of CBC will not be possible, nor will a determination that changes observed in students, parents, or teachers are attributable to CBC. It should be noted that the active ingredients reported here are presumed to be related to important consultation outcomes; they have not been tested empirically and require systematic investigation to determine their functional role in producing desired effects.

Table 11.1 outlines the active ingredients of CBC organized according to common objectives of the model within the collaborative problem-solving and behavioral intervention plan components. Strategies used by consultants are also discussed to illustrate behavioral indicators that allow for the evaluation of the integrity of the model's active ingredients.

Component 1: Collaborative Problem Solving

Foster, Develop, and Maintain a Working Partnership

The first objective of CBC is to foster, develop, and maintain a working partnership between parents and teachers. There are several active ingredients of the CBC process organized under this objective. Specifically, a working partnership between parents and teachers is achieved through (a) active participation and cooperation among participants, (b) sensitivity and responsiveness to participants, and (c) reinforcement of participants' skills and competencies. The presence of these active ingredients is indicated by a host of consultant strategies such as providing supportive, affirming, and validating statements to participants. The use of positive feedback by the consultant fosters a sense of competence in parents and teachers by reinforcing parents' and teachers' expertise regarding the child's needs and their contributions to the consultation process. Other strategies may include the consultant's efforts to understand and consider the culture of the family and school, remain sensitive to the potential influence of cultural background in shaping the relationship between

TABLE 11.1
Active Ingredients of Dual Components of Conjoint Behavioral Consultation

Objective	Active ingredients	Strategies
Component 1: Collaborative problem solving		
Foster, develop, and maintain a working partnership	Encourage active participation and cooperation/collaboration among participants Demonstrate sensitivity and responsiveness to participants Reinforce participants' skills and competencies	Provide supportive, affirming, and validating statements (e.g., use active listening, empathetic statements) Work to understand and consider the influence of family and school culture (e.g., tailor treatment content to teachers' and parents' values, beliefs, and practicing styles)
Communicate effectively	Establish effective communication channels; engage in multidirectional communication Share information with the team that is pertinent to the child's development and that facilitates the consultation process	Use clear and inclusive language Use nonverbal and verbal communication to establish a friendly and supportive atmosphere Provide feedback and relevant developmental information Establish method by which families and schools continue communication following consultation (e.g., home–school notes, e-mail, phone calls)
Determine and maintain roles and responsibilities	Establish joint responsibility among participants Make joint decisions throughout the consultation process	Emphasize the contribution of all participants by discussing and defining roles at the outset of consultation Ensure roles are maintained throughout the relationship Encourage parents and teachers to provide their insight throughout the process

(continues)

TABLE 11.1

Active Ingredients of Dual Components of Conjoint Behavioral Consultation   (Continued)

Objective	Active ingredients	Strategies
Determine current level of performance through data-based means	Discuss strengths and needs of the child Select and define a target behavior based on family and teacher priorities Establish and agree upon data collection procedures Ensure that data are collected, shared, and reviewed Identify/confirm the function of the behavior through use of baseline or related data Agree on a goal for behavior change	Use expertise in child development to aid team in determining developmental appropriateness of behavioral priorities Build on parents' and teachers' expertise, perspectives, and relevant experiences to determine child's competencies and deficits Guide parents and teachers to operationally define the target behavior in observable and measurable terms Check in with parents and teachers about data collection through phone calls and/or classroom visits Aid in determining the function of the behavior by emphasizing the antecedents and consequences of the behavior Encourage parents and teachers to set goals that are challenging yet attainable for the child
Develop and implement plan	Develop an intervention plan with specific procedures regarding implementation (who, when, where, how) Support implementation of intervention plan across settings	Work to integrate evidence-based practices into plans Invite parents and teachers to express opinions regarding plan viability across home and school Complete classroom observations, home visits, and data collection Provide feedback on plan implementation; support to improve implementation (e.g., modeling, role play)
Evaluate efficacy of plan through data-based means	Determine if the goal for behavior change was met across settings	Facilitate sharing of data collected, anecdotal observations, and feedback

Evaluate the effectiveness of the plan at producing change in the target behavior

Determine the need to continue, change, or remove the plan

Use data-based decision-making procedures to guide team in evaluation of plan

Component 2: Behavioral intervention plans

Verify that research evidence exists supporting use of the intervention at addressing the target behavior for students at a similar developmental level

Ensure intervention includes a motivational component to build new skills

Determine match between the function of the behavior and intervention selection

Provide support and/or training of consultees' implementation of coordinated strategies across home and school

Consider treatment modifications as necessary to facilitate goal attainment

Observe the child in his or her natural setting to clarify function of behavior and link intervention components to functional assessment

Brainstorm and cocreate appropriate reinforcers to support the child's use of desired behavior and/or discourage engagement in negative behavior

Establish communication mechanisms between home and school to promote regular family–teacher contact regarding child's behavioral progress

Maintain contact through phone calls, school observations, and home visits throughout implementation

Provide training regarding intervention implementation, including role plays or modeling, review of collected data, and provision of feedback and suggestions

Acknowledge and work to overcome barriers related to contextual or environmental issues that may interfere with implementation families and schools, and tailor treatment content to the values and beliefs of participants (Webster-Stratton, Reinke, Herman, & Newcomber, 2011). Additionally, consultants define the roles of each participant and discuss their importance early in the process as a strategy to ensure that all participants view themselves as active contributors in CBC. The important contribution each participant will make with his or her expertise is emphasized.

Communicate Effectively

The second objective of CBC is to foster effective communication between home and school. This objective is obtained through active ingredients, including (a) establishing effective communication channels and demonstration of multidirectional communication and (b) sharing information that is pertinent to the child's development and facilitative of the consultation process. A strategy used by consultants that reflects these active ingredients includes the use of clear and inclusive language. That is, consultants who avoid the use of technical jargon and instead use terms that can be easily understood by parents and teachers are practicing in a manner consistent with this criterion. Moreover, consultants may use nonverbal and verbal communication as a strategy to establish a friendly and supportive atmosphere that invites participation by all parties involved. Consultants also foster collaboration between families and schools by providing feedback and relevant factual (e.g., developmental) information when appropriate. Consultants practicing CBC with high treatment integrity also aim to establish a partnership between families and schools that will continue following termination of CBC, and as such establish means for families and schools to continue communication following CBC completion.

Determine and Maintain Roles and Responsibilities

The third CBC objective involves determining and maintaining roles in the problem-solving partnership. The active ingredients subsumed under this objective require that (a) the responsibility for problem solving is shared among participants and (b) decisions are made jointly throughout the consultation process. Strategies used by consultants that are indicative of these active ingredients include defining roles early in the process; ensuring roles are maintained throughout the relationship; and encouraging both families and school personnel to provide insight regarding efforts to change the behavior, the outcome of such efforts, and the need for ongoing support. Consultants practicing with high treatment integrity ensure that participants are engaged throughout the process in ways that uniquely and collaboratively support change (i.e., they contribute to target behavior identification, data collection, and behavioral plan implementation consistent with their roles).

Determine Current Level of Performance Through Data-Based Means

The fourth CBC objective is to determine the current level of student performance through data-based means. The active ingredients characterizing this objective require that (a) the strengths and needs of the child are discussed; (b) a target behavior based on family and teacher priorities is selected and defined; (c) data collection procedures are established and agreed upon; (d) data are collected, shared, and reviewed; (e) the function of the behavior is determined; and (f) a goal for behavior change is agreed upon. Strategically, CBC consultants use their expertise in child development to aid the team in determining the developmental appropriateness of behavioral priorities, simultaneously building on parents' and teachers' expertise, perspectives, and relevant experiences to determine the child's competencies and areas of need. After a behavioral priority has been determined, consultants guide parents and teachers to operationally define the target behavior in observable and measurable terms, and support data collection by checking in with parents and teachers through phone calls and/or classroom visits. Using the data collected by parents and teachers, consultants support the team in determining the function of the behavior by emphasizing the antecedents and consequences of behavior, and encourage parents and teachers to set goals that are challenging yet attainable for the child.

Develop and Implement the Plan

The fifth objective of CBC concerns the specification of a treatment plan to be implemented by parents and teachers. There are several criteria associated with this objective that collectively depict active ingredients. Specifically, it is necessary that (a) an intervention plan with specific procedures regarding implementation (i.e., who, when, where, how) is developed and (b) implementation of the intervention plan across settings is supported by the consultant and evident via the actions of teachers and parents. Strategies employed by consultants include conducting classroom observations and home visits and assisting with data collection. Consultants can ensure that the agreed-upon strategies will be feasible across home and school by inviting parents and teachers to express their opinion regarding the viability of the intervention plan.

Evaluate the Efficacy of the Plan Through Data-Based Means

The sixth CBC objective involves evaluating the efficacy of the plan through data-based means. Active ingredients essential to the attainment of this objective include the evaluation and determination of (a) the effectiveness of the plan at producing change in the target behavior; (b) whether the goal for behavior change was met across settings; and (c) the need to continue, change, or remove the plan. Strategies used by consultants that reflect these active ingredients include facilitating discussion of aspects of the plan that were successful and those that were not in an effort to identify strengths of the plan as well as elements that may require modification.

Component 2: Behavioral Intervention Plans

The second component of the CBC intervention concerns the behavioral intervention plan implemented by parents and teachers in natural home and school settings. In addition to considering the integrity of the collaborative problem-solving process, the degree to which the behavioral plans are put into place in the home and school may predict the degree of behavioral change that can be expected. Thus, active ingredients of behavioral plans must be identified and measured in consultation research and practice. Although the specifics of each intervention plan vary according to the child's unique strengths and needs, certain active ingredients can be identified that are necessary for all intervention plans implemented by parents and teachers (see Table 11.1). Specifically, within the CBC context, it is important that there be (a) research evidence for the intervention to address the target behavior for students at a similar developmental level; (b) a motivational or skill-building component targeting desired behaviors; (c) a match between the function of the behavior and intervention selection; (d) consultant support and/or training of consultees' implementation of coordinated strategies across home and school; and (e) treatment modifications as necessary to facilitate goal attainment.

Strategies used by consultants in developing a behavioral intervention plan include observing the child in his or her natural setting to clarify the function of behavior and linking intervention components to the outcome of this assessment (Swanger-Gagné, Garbacz, & Sheridan, 2009), brainstorming and cocreating appropriate reinforcers to support the child's use of desired behavior and/or discourage his or her engagement in negative behavior, and establishing communication mechanisms between home and school to promote regular contact between the family and teacher regarding the child's behavioral progress. Additional strategies include ongoing contact through phone calls, school observations, and home visits throughout the implementation phase (Sheridan et al., 2001). During observations and home visits, consultants may review collected data and provide feedback and suggestions, provide training regarding intervention implementation through the use of role plays or modeling, and augment existing strengths and resources of families and school personnel through affirmations and validations (Sheridan, Clarke, Knoche, & Edwards, 2006).

It is noteworthy that treatment plans implemented across home and school do not necessarily need to be identical, but they should be based on the same behavioral principles and complement one another. In some cases, distinctive behavioral plans may be implemented in one setting only. Nevertheless, elements of treatment plan implementation across settings are always essential features of CBC, evidenced by programs such as home–school notes or communication systems, to ensure shared responsibility and partnership.

DIMENSIONS OF TREATMENT INTEGRITY FOR CBC RESEARCH

Within the treatment integrity construct are inbuilt dimensions critical for adequately determining the degree of implementation. These dimensions include adherence, quality, participant responsiveness, dosage, and program differentiation, and are typically assessed through participant and expert reports and ratings, interviews, direct observations, and permanent products (Dane & Schneider, 1998; Dusenbury, Brannigan, Falco, & Hansen, 2003; Sheridan, Swanger-Gagné, Welch, Kwon, & Garbacz, 2009). Evaluation of these implementation dimensions is a necessary consideration when determining a given intervention's effect on student outcomes (Derzon, Sale, Springer, & Brounstein, 2005; Webster-Stratton et al., 2011).

Adherence, also referred to as compliance or faithful replication (Durlak & DuPre, 2008), is concerned with whether key intervention components are implemented as originally proposed (Dane & Schneider, 1998; O'Donnell, 2008). In contrast, *quality* is the degree to which implementers deliver the intervention components effectively using given strategies, processes, or methods (Cordray & Pion, 2006; O'Donnell, 2008). *Participant responsiveness* is described as participants' level of engagement and interest in program activities (Dane & Schneider, 1998; O'Donnell, 2008). *Dosage* refers to the total amount of the intervention to which individuals are exposed (Durlak & DuPre, 2008; Sheridan et al., 2009). Finally, *program differentiation* considers whether the program's key elements distinguish the treatment from comparison conditions during efficacy studies (O'Donnell, 2008; Sheridan et al., 2009). This dimension is typically restricted to comparisons across treatment and control groups in randomized clinical trials, and thus will receive little further attention here.

A multimethod, multisource framework for assessing the key dimensions of treatment integrity across the dual components of CBC research is presented in Table 11.2. Treatment integrity (adherence, quality, participant responsiveness, and dosage) of both the collaborative problem-solving process

TABLE 11.2
Measurement of Fidelity Dimensions Across the Dual Components
of Conjoint Behavioral Consultation

Measure	Adherence	Quality	Participant response	Dosage
Component 1: Collaborative problem solving				
Observations/coding of parent–teacher meetings	X	X		
Parent Engagement in Consultation Scale			X	
Teacher Engagement in Consultation Scale			X	
Parent Participation in Problem Solving			X	
Teacher Participation in Problem Solving			X	
Contact logs (parent and teacher)				X
Consultant contact logs				X
Component 2: Behavioral intervention				
Self-report	X			X
Direct observations	X	X	X	X
Permanent products	X			
Classroom Environmental Scan Checklist			X	

Note. All measures are available by request from Susan M. Sheridan.

and the behavioral strategies implemented at home and school are included to fully capture the scope of aspects comprising the CBC intervention.

Component 1: Treatment Integrity of Collaborative Problem Solving

Adherence of collaborative problem solving is the dimension of treatment integrity assessed most commonly in CBC practice and research (e.g., Sheridan et al., 2006, 2009, 2012; Swanger-Gagné et al., 2009). It is often measured by determining the percentage of components implemented by treatment agents (Sheridan et al., 2009). As such, CBC adherence is often defined as the percentage of interview objectives met (i.e., verbalizations reflecting problem-solving objectives) as they pertain to home and school. This approach provides an initial determination of whether the CBC consultant adheres to the model as specified, and is often achieved via observation of consultant verbalizations during the CBC interview sequence. Previous research (e.g., Sheridan et al., 2001, 2006) has used simple checklists corresponding to the stated objectives of the CBC interviews (Sheridan & Kratochwill, 2008) to indicate adherence to the model as procedurally operationalized through a series of conjoint problem-solving meetings. For example, each CBC interview can be described as composed of a number of statements or objectives. Adherence can be measured by self-report or observation (via recordings, transcripts, or interview protocols) of whether the objectives were met through the verbal exchanges in each meeting. An alternative approach lies in the specification of overall model criteria (i.e., active ingredients). Techniques associated with assessing adherence to the model are achieved in a global manner (vs. a system assessing discrete interview objectives) with a coding system that tracks the attainment of CBC active ingredients (see Table 11.1).

Most previous CBC research studies that have included assessments of treatment integrity have focused on adherence only. To date, researchers have not explored issues of quality of CBC implementation. Quality, assessed through observer and implementer reports and ratings of use of recommended techniques (Hansen, Graham, Wolkenstein, & Rohrbach, 1991), extends the information gleaned from adherence in several ways. Rather than assess merely whether a CBC criterion (e.g., active ingredient) is met in a dichotomous (yes/no) fashion, as is the case with adherence ratings, quality assessments evaluate the extent to which relevant information is obtained in a manner that is useful to data-based problem solving, and whether information is obtained in a manner that supports the parent–teacher relationship. To generate such ratings, Likert scales can be developed wherein each anchor on a scale is defined to quantify and operationalize quality with numerical scoring criteria. Sample items from a rating scale that incorporates both adherence to and quality with which objectives are met in the Conjoint Needs Identification Interview (i.e., the structured interview that guides the problem identification stage) are in Appendix 11.1.

Participant responsiveness is another important dimension of treatment integrity to be assessed in CBC. It has typically been assessed through examinations of implementers' understanding of and receptiveness to key intervention components (Hansen, 1996; Sheridan et al., 2009). Other methods for assessing responsiveness of the parent and teacher consultees to the collaborative problem-solving process are available. For example, coding systems can be used to assess parent and teacher engagement in CBC based on verbalizations made on the audio recordings or transcripts from CBC meetings. Such coding systems evaluate active participation, engagement, or collaboration as demonstrated by consultees. Scales assessing these and related constructs have been developed for research (Sheridan, 2005) and are available to evaluate responsiveness from multiple sources and utilizing multiple methods. For example, the Engagement in Consultation Scale (Parent and Teacher forms; Sheridan, 2005) has been used in research to measure the degree to which parents and teachers demonstrate engagement during each of the formal CBC meetings as manifested through behaviors such as sharing information, participating in decision making, communicating effectively, making supportive statements, responding to others in the CBC meetings, and following through on actions to facilitate positive child outcomes. The scale can be completed by consultants in practice or independent observers in research. Similarly, the Participation in Problem Solving Scale (Parent and Teacher forms; Sheridan, 2004) is also available to provide data on the degree to which parents and teachers participate actively in problem solving.

Finally, dosage of CBC represents a treatment integrity dimension that has rarely been considered in CBC practice or research. It can be measured by the number, length, frequency, and/or intensity of consultation sessions (Dane & Schneider, 1998), examined through contact logs and meeting checklists (Dusenbury et al., 2003). In most applications, CBC is considered an intensive intervention comprising participant meetings, on-site supports, data-based monitoring functions, and evaluation practices. Variations in strength (e.g., time, effort) of CBC are likely, and may influence its efficacy at producing desired changes in child behaviors and parent–teacher relationships. Amount of support (dosage) provided by consultants can be documented by recording tangible actions, such as hours of meeting time, minutes spent in the classroom or conducting home visits, number of e-mail messages or phone calls to consultees, and time preparing behavioral interventions or assessing and documenting their effects on child performance. To date, no research has determined the optimal amount of support (and associated time and effort) needed to produce desired effects. Thus, as measures of dosage become available, researchers may pursue questions that can guide optimal levels of practice and link expended efforts to expected outcomes.

Component 2: Treatment Integrity of Behavioral Plan Implementation

The second component of CBC involves implementation of behavioral interventions by parents and teachers in their respective home and school settings. The same treatment integrity dimensions of adherence, quality, participant responsiveness, and dosage are relevant. In the consultation literature, studies that have addressed treatment integrity of behavioral intervention implementation have tended to focus on adherence to plan steps by consultees (e.g., Sheridan et al., 2009). Multiple methods have been used, yielding basic information about the plan components delivered to students via CBC. For example, self-report measures typically require delineation of the steps comprising an intervention (i.e., treatment integrity criteria) on a checklist, on which consultees record completion of treatment steps. Self-report adherence assessments yield an estimate of consultees' compliance with intervention implementation, often computed as a percentage of steps completed. They typically require few resources for data collection and provide a simple and sometimes instructive approach (Sanetti & Kratochwill, 2008). The accuracy of self-report adherence data as reflecting intervention treatment integrity has been debated, with some researchers (Lane, 2007; Wickstrom, Jones, LaFleur, & Witt, 1998) suggesting that they overestimate implementation and others (Sheridan et al., 2009) reporting close concordance between self-reports and other objective methods (i.e., permanent products, direct observations).

Permanent products have also been used to provide tangible evidence of adherence to treatment plans. Examples of permanent products used for this purpose are intervention records (with intervention components clearly identified), charts, and tokens. When structured to specify treatment plan criteria, permanent products may yield a record of adherence quantified as the percentage of intervention steps completed. They offer a relatively simple measurement procedure by providing a natural source of data in many circumstances (as in the use of intervention tools such as home–school notes and reward charts) with little reactivity from parents and teachers (Sanetti & Kratochwill, 2008). However, some intervention components may not yield a permanent product, and certain steps may be impossible to capture via this method (Sheridan et al., 2009).

Direct observation as a method to assess adherence involves a trained and reliable individual, ideally independent from the consultation and intervention team, assessing direct, objective implementation of treatment plan components in naturalistic settings. Despite their apparent objectivity, direct observations of treatment plan implementation are less common than other assessment methods, perhaps due to their resource-intensive nature. Specifically, additional individuals (e.g., independent observers) are often necessary to conduct direct observations, and depending on the complexity of the intervention, numerous observations may be required to capture all intervention components in practice. Observations may also produce reactivity among teachers and parents implementing the intervention.

Quality of treatment implementation is measured less often in consultation and CBC research, although it represents an important dimension to capture unique aspects of interventions being implemented. The quality of implementation by experts or independent judges can be rated through direct observations of implementation by treatment agents (live or via recordings; e.g., Jones, Wickstrom, & Friman, 1997; Mills & Ragan, 2000) or by self-report scales completed by individuals delivering or receiving the intervention (e.g., Weiner, Sheridan, & Jenson, 1998). Likert scales can be constructed to capture the quality with which treatment agents deliver an intervention, requiring careful specification of the criteria constituting qualitative ratings and mastery training by raters. Given that treatment plans delivered in consultation-based contexts are individualized and implemented with unique child- and setting-specific considerations, the feasibility of this approach in most practice settings is limited.

Participant responsiveness, or the degree to which children serving as clients in CBC respond to the behavioral interventions, is a relevant dimension variable worthy of consideration. Behaviors such as attending to and engaging in the plan elements (e.g., collecting stickers on a chart, moving tokens into a jar, receiving earned rewards) provide documentation of student "buy in" or responsiveness to the intervention. These can be collected via direct observation of permanent products. Global ratings of classrooms using a measure such as the Classroom Environment Scan Checklist (Sheridan, 2011) can also be assessed to determine the degree to which teachers respond to CBC by invoking effective behavioral or instructional strategies as a function of CBC structure and support.

Measurement of dosage of behavioral intervention implementation is important to evaluate the level of effort expended by consultees to influence child behavior. Indices such as the amount of time spent by teachers and parents delivering interventions, monitoring child behavior, and providing documentation can all be considered aspects of treatment plan dosage. Measurement is possible through self-monitoring on intervention records or through the use of electronic methods such as time stamps denoting start and stop points, simple time-keeping devices, and other portable tools.

TREATMENT INTEGRITY VARIABLES IN CBC RESEARCH

The conceptualization of treatment integrity in consultation has focused primarily on its utility in practice, with much less attention to its role as a critical variable in consultation research. Whereas the importance of promoting and ensuring accurate implementation of intervention plans in practice is clear, an understanding of its function in affecting treatment outcomes is essential to advance the construct empirically.

The goals of CBC include improving behavioral outcomes for children for whom there are specific concerns, enhancing skills and practices among parents and teachers to promote children's functioning, and strengthening parent–teacher relationships. To date, the processes by which these goals are achieved in a collective and integrated fashion, and the role of treatment integrity, have not been researched. By definition, CBC is composed of problem-solving practices led by a consultant to produce desired changes in a client indirectly. As an indirect model, it is implied that CBC operates through mechanisms other than consultants' behaviors to produce the desired outcomes on children's behaviors. Investigating the process by which

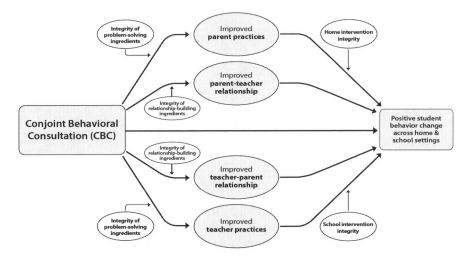

Figure 11.1. Theoretical model specifying independent, dependent, mediating, and moderating variables in conjoint behavioral consultation.

CBC serves to produce desired changes in student performance requires the specification of experimental variables in CBC research. Figure 11.1 is presented as a theoretical model specifying these variables, including treatment integrity, and their hypothesized relationships within the CBC intervention. Next, we define the research variables requiring specification to advance an empirical understanding of the efficacy of CBC and the role of treatment integrity.

Independent and Dependent Variables

The aims of intervention research are generally concerned with determining a treatment's effects on outcomes of interest. In consultation research, a common research question takes the form of "Does intervention *x* (in this case, CBC) produce outcome y (the ultimate goal being changes in student performance)?" This classic research question calls for a design that considers CBC as an independent variable and student performance indicators (e.g., behavioral, academic, social-emotional, health outcomes) as dependent variables. Many CBC studies have followed this tradition (e.g., Galloway & Sheridan, 1994; Lasecki, Olympia, Clark, Jenson, & Heathfield, 2008; Sheridan et al., 2001; Wilkinson, 2005) and reported very favorable results.

Other potential dependent variables including parent and teacher practices and the parent–teacher relationship are also relevant in CBC research. That is, CBC is expected to produce indirect effects on clients and direct effects on parent and teacher practices and the parent–teacher relationship. For example, given the educational aspects associated with consultation-based interventions, changes in teachers' knowledge and skills, including the use of evidence-based interventions in the classroom, are desirable outcomes and reflect direct effects of CBC. Improvements in home–school communication, parents' effective use of praise, contingent reinforcement, and precision commands are similar examples of important outcomes (i.e., dependent variables) associated with participation in CBC.

Mediating and Moderating Variables

Specification of CBC as an independent variable and measurement of parent and teacher practices and child performance as dependent variables provide an initial understanding of their relevance; however, the pathways by which these variables operate or cooperate causally has not been clarified. Exploration of pathways of influence allows one to identify mechanisms or mediators and how they work to effect change. Some proposed pathways or possible explanations for the impact of CBC on desired outcomes are specified in Figure 11.1.

Recently, researchers have found that the parent–teacher relationship partially mediates the effects of CBC on the social and adaptive behaviors of students with externalizing concerns (Sheridan et al., 2012); however, the specific role of parent and teacher practices has not been investigated. It is possible that CBC directly influences parent and/or teacher practices, which leads to desired child outcomes (e.g., behavioral change). Treatment integrity of the problem-solving process (i.e., a consultant's use of certain active ingredients that focus on problem solving, such as selecting and defining a target behavior based on family and teacher priorities, or supporting implementation of intervention plan across settings) may moderate parent and teacher skills and practices. That is, teachers' and parents' use of efficacious practices may depend on CBC consultants' adherence to or quality of the use of these and other active ingredients addressing the problem-solving sequence. In like fashion, the treatment integrity with which parents and teachers implement behavioral strategies may moderate observed changes in student behavior across the home and school settings.

Similarly, a consultant's use of active ingredients that promote a partnership between parents and teachers, such as making joint decisions throughout the consultation process and reinforcing participants' skills and competencies, may moderate the development of a positive parent–teacher relationship. In other words, the development of a positive parent–teacher relationship may be possible only under conditions when consultants practice certain active ingredients to create a partnership (e.g., shared decision making and mutual goal setting) with treatment integrity. In this case, it is possible to explore whether the goal of strengthening parent–teacher relationships is achieved under conditions wherein consultants adhere to the relationship-building ingredients of CBC, and do so with quality. To date, little to no research has explored these direct and indirect effects of CBC. Given their presumed importance, such investigation is necessary.

RESEARCH DIRECTIONS

As a first step in CBC treatment integrity research, it is necessary to explore the psychometric properties of measures used to assess the various features or dimensions of treatment integrity. There is some preliminary evidence of convergence across treatment integrity assessment methods (Sheridan et al., 2009); however, basic indicators of reliability, sensitivity, and generalizability have not been researched. Only through the availability of reliable and valid measures will researchers be equipped to explore the unique dimensions of treatment integrity, their relationship to desired outcomes, and their role as mediating and moderating variables.

Careful specification and effective measurement of treatment integrity (including treatment integrity of the dual components of the collaborative problem-solving process and behavioral strategies used by consultees) will advance intervention science in significant ways. Such careful attention will allow researchers to explore many facets of intervention design and implementation and ultimately result in the proliferation of effective interventions. To date, the active ingredients of CBC have not been empirically derived. By systematically analyzing the presumed active ingredients of CBC, researchers could determine with precision its critical and operative features. A related issue involves an empirical determination of whether each ingredient is required, optimal, or sufficient to treatment utility (defined in terms of its tactical role in producing desired treatment effects). This level of scrutiny has not been examined in CBC research and warrants careful attention.

Seemingly opposite to the dissection of an intervention for its active ingredients is a line of research aimed at determining threshold and saturation levels of an intervention. A global assessment of threshold levels can elucidate the intervention strength required for CBC to "take hold" (the level at which significant treatment effects can be expected), or the level required to produce optimal performance. Similarly, a global assessment can determine saturation, or the point at which effects of CBC may have reached and surpassed their peak effects and suggest the need for modifications focused on maintenance. To achieve this nuanced understanding of

CBC dosage and its relationship to or effects on outcomes, the measurement of the treatment integrity of its critical implementation elements is necessary. Likewise, it is possible that interactions with certain child variables (e.g., target behavior, severity, disability status), parent–teacher variables (e.g., skill, knowledge, background), or relationship variables (e.g., history of joint problem solving, quality of relationship, communication) may influence both threshold and saturation, yielding yet another important line of research.

Methods for determining "treatment as usual" and treatment integrity indicators that differentiate active treatment and nontreatment conditions are necessary for randomized clinical trials. Aspects of the intervention on which programs may be differentiated include interactions between parents and teachers and strategies used to support child development or manage behavior. Procedurally, this focus allows for the assessment of control or counterfactual conditions in experimental intervention research to determine empirically the uniqueness of the CBC intervention and its relative effects on outcomes of interest.

Despite a great deal of attention in the practice literature, little field-based research attention has attempted to identify factors that contribute to treatment integrity across both the collaborative problem-solving process and behavioral intervention implementation. This line of inquiry is critical as researchers move forward in designing, developing, implementing, and evaluating CBC-based educational interventions. Further investigation of factors that contribute to treatment integrity of both aspects of CBC will advance our ability to determine necessary or sufficient consultation intervention elements and how integrity of these components contributes to salient outcomes.

Finally, it is necessary to begin empirically examining the theory proposed in Figure 11.1 by testing relationships and determining the mechanisms by which CBC operates, and the role of variations of treatment integrity. Specifically, it is possible that the treatment integrity with which the active ingredients are practiced serves as a moderator of parent and teacher practices. It is also possible that the success of promoting parent–teacher partnerships via CBC is a function of the strategies consultants use to build those relationships (e.g., inclusive questioning, joining statements, perspective taking, modeling). By testing treatment integrity as a moderator or independent variable in its own right, researchers may begin to explore whether parents' and teachers' practices and relationships are influenced by the integrity with which consultants utilize the active ingredients of CBC. As such, treatment integrity research serves a primary role in moving us closer to an understanding of the mechanisms by which CBC effects change and the conditions under which such effects are maximized.

Sample Items for Measuring Adherence and Quality of Active Ingredients

Objective	Active ingredient	0 (not present or not effective)	1 (present and moderately effective)	2 (present and highly effective)
Meeting participants collaboratively selected and defined a target behavior	Decided upon a specific priority behavior to target after understanding the general needs	• Participants did not identify a target behavior or • The target behavior was selected without being informed by a discussion of the needs	• The target behavior was informed by the needs discussed and either • Decided on by one participant (e.g., parent, teacher, facilitator) or • Decided on by the facilitator and either the parent or the teacher but not both	• The target behavior was informed by the needs discussed and • Decided on by at least the parent and the teacher
	Defined the target behavior objectively	• Participants did not define the target behavior objectively and measurably (e.g., unobservable or subjective terms were used)	• The target behavior was defined objectively and measurably (i.e., observable terms were used and subjective terms were clarified) and • Either the teacher or the parent but not both contributed to, acknowledged, or agreed with the definition of the target behavior	• The target behavior was defined objectively and measurably (i.e., observable terms were used and subjective terms were clarified) and • Both the teacher and the parent contributed to, acknowledged, or agreed with the definition of the target behavior
	Selected and clarified a priority setting in which to address the target behavior	• Participants did not identify a target setting that included a specific time and place	• A specific time and/or location was indicated and • Either the teacher or the parent but not both contributed to, acknowledged, or agreed with the time and location	• A specific time and/or location was indicated and • Both the teacher and the parent contributed to, acknowledged, or agreed with the time and location

REFERENCES

Bronfenbrenner, U. (1977). Toward an experimental psychology of human development. *American Psychologist, 32,* 513–531. doi:10.1037/0003-066X.32.7.513

Cordray, D. S., & Pion, G. M. (2006). Treatment strength and integrity: Models and methods. In R. R. Bootzin & P. E. McKnight (Eds.), *Strengthening research methodology: Psychological measurement and evaluation* (pp. 103–124). Washington, DC: American Psychological Association. doi:10.1037/11384-006

Dane, A. V., & Schneider, B. H. (1998). Program integrity in primary and early secondary prevention: Are implementation effects out of control? *Clinical Psychology Review, 18,* 23–45. doi:10.1016/S0272-7358(97)00043-3

Derzon, J. H., Sale, E., Springer, J. F., & Brounstein, P. (2005). Estimating intervention effectiveness: Synthetic projection of field evaluation results. *Journal of Primary Prevention, 26,* 321–343. doi:10.1007/s10935-005-5391-5

Durlak, J. A., & DuPre, E. P. (2008). Implementation matters: A review of research on the influence of implementation on program outcomes and the factors affecting implementation. *American Journal of Community Psychology, 41,* 327–350. doi:10.1007/s10464-008-9165-0

Dusenbury, L., Brannigan, R., Falco, M., & Hansen, W. B. (2003). A review of research on fidelity of implementation: Implications for drug abuse prevention in school settings. *Health Education Research, 18,* 237–256. doi:10.1093/her/18.2.237

Elliott, S. N., Witt, J. C., Kratochwill, T. R., & Stoiber, K. C. (2002). Selecting and evaluating classroom interventions. In M. R. Shinn, H. M. Walker, & G. Stoner (Eds.), *Interventions for academic and behavior problems II: Preventive and remedial approaches* (pp. 243–294). Bethesda, MD: National Association of School Psychologists.

Galloway, J., & Sheridan, S. M. (1994). Implementing scientific practices through case studies: Examples using home–school interventions and consultation. *Journal of School Psychology, 32,* 385–413. doi:10.1016/0022-4405(94)90035-3

Hansen, W. B. (1996). Pilot test results comparing the All Stars program with seventh grade D.A.R.E.: Program integrity and mediating variable analysis. *Substance Use & Misuse, 31,* 1359–1377. doi:10.3109/10826089609063981

Hansen, W. B., Graham, J. W., Wolkenstein, B. H., & Rohrbach, L. A. (1991). Program integrity as a moderator of prevention program effectiveness: Results for fifth-grade students in the adolescent alcohol prevention trial. *Journal of Studies on Alcohol, 52,* 568–579.

Jones, K. M., Wickstrom, K. F., & Friman, P. C. (1997). The effects of observational feedback on treatment integrity in school-based behavioral consultation. *School Psychology Quarterly, 12,* 316–326. doi:10.1037/h0088965

Knoche, L. L., Sheridan, S. M., Edwards, C. P., & Osborn, A. Q. (2010). Implementation of a relationship-based school readiness intervention: A multidimensional approach to fidelity measurement for early childhood. *Early Childhood Research Quarterly, 25,* 299–313. doi:10.1016/j.ecresq.2009.05.003

Lane, K. L. (2007). Identifying and supporting students at risk for emotional and behavioral disorders within multi-level models: Data driven approaches to conducting secondary interventions with an academic emphasis. *Education & Treatment of Children, 30,* 135–164.

Lasecki, K., Olympia, D., Clark, E., Jenson, W., & Heathfield, L. (2008). Using behavioral interventions to assist children with type 1 diabetes manage blood glucose levels. *School Psychology Quarterly, 23,* 389–406. doi:10.1037/1045-3830.23.3.389

Mills, S. C., & Ragan, T. J. (2000). A tool for analyzing implementation fidelity of an integrated learning system. *Educational Technology Research and Development, 48,* 21–41. doi:10.1007/BF02300498

O'Donnell, C. L. (2008). Defining, conceptualizing, and measuring fidelity of implementation and its relationship to outcomes in K–12 curriculum intervention research. *Review of Educational Research, 78,* 33–84. doi:10.3102/0034654307313793

Sanetti, L. M. H., & Kratochwill, T. R. (2008). Treatment integrity in behavioral consultation: Measurement, promotion, and outcomes. *International Journal of Behavioral Consultation and Therapy, 4,* 95–114.

Sheridan, S. M. (2004). *Parent Participation in Problem Solving (PPPS).* Unpublished scale, University of Nebraska–Lincoln.

Sheridan, S. M. (2005). *Parent Engagement in Consultation Scale (PECS).* Unpublished scale, University of Nebraska–Lincoln.

Sheridan, S. M. (2011). *Classroom Environment Scan Checklist (CESC).* Unpublished scale, University of Nebraska–Lincoln.

Sheridan, S. M., Bovaird, J. A., Glover, T. A., Garbacz, S. A., Witte, A., & Kwon, K. (2012). A randomized trial examining the effects of conjoint behavioral consultation and the mediating role of the parent–teacher relationship. *School Psychology Review, 41,* 23–46.

Sheridan, S. M., Clarke, B. L., Knoche, L. L., & Edwards, C. P. (2006). The effects of conjoint behavioral consultation in early childhood settings. *Early Education and Development, 17,* 593–617. doi:10.1207/s15566935eed1704_5

Sheridan, S. M., & Colton, D. L. (1994). Conjoint behavioral consultation: A review and case study. *Journal of Educational & Psychological Consultation, 5,* 211–228. doi:10.1207/s1532768xjepc0503_2

Sheridan, S. M., Eagle, J. W., Cowan, R. J., & Mickelson, W. (2001). The effects of conjoint behavioral consultation: Results of a 4-year investigation. *Journal of School Psychology, 39,* 361–385. doi:10.1016/S0022-4405(01)00079-6

Sheridan, S. M., & Kratochwill, T. R. (1992). Behavioral parent–teacher consultation: Conceptual and research considerations. *Journal of School Psychology, 30,* 117–139. doi:10.1016/0022-4405(92)90025-Z

Sheridan, S. M., & Kratochwill, T. R. (2008). *Conjoint behavioral consultation: Promoting family–school connections and interventions* (2nd ed.). New York, NY: Springer.

Sheridan, S. M., Swanger-Gagné, M., Welch, G. W., Kwon, K., & Garbacz, S. A. (2009). Fidelity measurement in consultation: Psychometric issues and preliminary examination. *School Psychology Review, 38,* 476–495.

Swanger-Gagné, M. S., Garbacz, S. A., & Sheridan, S. M. (2009). Intervention implementation integrity within conjoint behavioral consultation: Strategies for working with families. *School Mental Health, 1,* 131–142. doi:10.1007/s12310-009-9012-y

Webster-Stratton, C., Reinke, W. M., Herman, K. C., & Newcomber, L. L. (2011). The Incredible Years teacher classroom management training: The methods and principles that support fidelity of training delivery. *School Psychology Review, 40,* 509–529.

Weiner, R. K., Sheridan, S. M., & Jenson, W. R. (1998). The effects of conjoint behavioral consultation and a structured homework program on math completion and accuracy in junior high students. *School Psychology Quarterly, 13,* 281–309. doi:10.1037/h0088986

Wickstrom, K. F., Jones, K. M., LaFleur, L. H., & Witt, J. C. (1998). An analysis of treatment integrity in school-based behavioral consultation. *School Psychology Quarterly, 13,* 141–154. doi:10.1037/h0088978

Wilkinson, L. A. (2005). An evaluation of conjoint behavioral consultation as a model for supporting students with emotional and behavioral difficulties in mainstream classrooms. *Emotional and Behavioural Difficulties, 10,* 119–136. doi:10.1177/1363275205054163

Wolery, M. (2011). Intervention research: The importance of fidelity measurement. *Topics in Early Childhood Special Education, 31,* 155–157. doi:10.1177/0271121411408621

12

TREATMENT INTEGRITY IN URBAN, COMMUNITY-BASED PREVENTION PROGRAMS

COURTNEY N. BAKER, STEPHEN S. LEFF, KATHERINE BEVANS,
AND THOMAS J. POWER

A substantial number of children experience behavioral, emotional, and social problems that result in considerable personal and societal costs (Foster & Jones, 2005; Merikangas et al., 2010). Recent estimates suggest that only 20% to 50% of children in the United States who need psychosocial treatment receive it, and much of this treatment is incomplete or of low quality (Leaf et al., 1996; Merikangas et al., 2010). These problems are more pervasive in low-income, chronically disadvantaged communities (Brooks-Gunn, Rouse, & McLanahan, 2007), where the challenges associated with accessing high-quality interventions are compounded by poverty, institutionalized

This work was supported by grants to Stephen S. Leff from the Centers for Disease Control and Prevention (cooperative agreement 5U49CE001093) and the National Institutes of Health (R21RR026311) and to Thomas J. Power from the Health Resources and Services Administration, Maternal and Child Health Bureau (R40MC08964), and the Department of Education, Office of Special Education Programs (325D060008). We wish to thank Janis Kupersmidt for allowing us to include the Building Bridges Project as our preschool-based program example.

http://dx.doi.org/10.1037/14275-013
Treatment Integrity: A Foundation for Evidence-Based Practice in Applied Psychology, L. M. H. Sanetti and T. R. Kratochwill (Editors)

discrimination, and a shortage of providers and programs. Socioeconomically disadvantaged individuals are less likely to seek and receive high-quality services and have worse health and educational outcomes (McGinnis, Williams-Russo, & Knickman, 2002; Smedley, Stith, & Nelson, 2003; U.S. Department of Health and Human Services, 2001).

It is well known that many prevention efforts are associated with strong and lasting positive outcomes (Olds et al., 1998; Smokowski, Mann, Reynolds, & Fraser, 2004; Webster-Stratton, Reid, & Hammond, 2001). In addition, prevention saves considerable costs when compared with reactive or tertiary care. For example, recent estimates suggest that the Nurse Family Partnership, a prevention program for first-time, low-income mothers that delivers education and support in the mother's home, is associated with state and local fiscal benefits of $15,273 per family, outweighing the $8,000 to $10,000 cost (Bartik, 2009). Thus, community-based prevention programs have the potential to minimize sociodemographic disparities in health and education outcomes in a cost-effective manner.

Though research supports the potential of prevention programs to promote positive outcomes among children, the benefits of many programs have been modest (La Greca, Silverman, & Lochman, 2009). The modest effects are partially attributable to the challenges associated with translating evidence-based programs into community settings (Glasgow, Lichtenstein, & Marcus, 2003; Miller & Shinn, 2005). Treatment integrity, a multidimensional construct that characterizes how much treatment is provided, how well it is provided, and how well it is received (Dane & Schneider, 1998; Power et al., 2005; Sanetti & Kratochwill, 2009), has been clearly linked to intervention outcomes (Durlak & DuPre, 2008) but is particularly difficult to optimize in community-based settings (Hulleman & Cordray, 2009).

The conceptualization of treatment integrity depends on whether an intervention is offered directly or indirectly to children or youth (hereafter referred to as children). In community settings, practitioners often provide direct interventions by engaging children in individual (e.g., counseling, academic tutoring) or group interventions (e.g., social skill groups, leadership promotion groups). Other interventions are provided indirectly by training and consulting with parents, teachers, counselors, and coaches who thereafter intervene directly with children. With indirect intervention, the process of understanding treatment integrity is more complex because it involves assessing (a) how practitioners (consultants) deliver the intervention to direct agents (consultees), (b) how it is received by the consultees, (c) how the consultees deliver the intervention directly to children, and finally (d) how the intervention is received by children. The direct and indirect pathways of community-based intervention delivery are depicted in Figure 12.1.

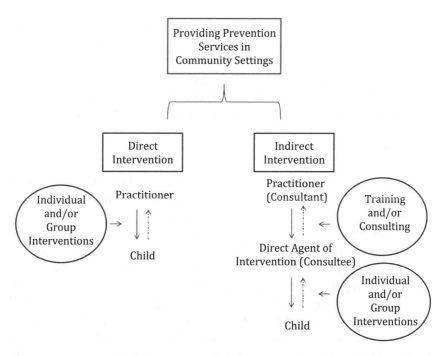

Figure 12.1. Direct and indirect pathways of intervention delivery in community-based prevention programs (solid arrows) including feedback loops (dotted arrows).

In this chapter, we describe common barriers to treatment integrity when prevention services targeting behavioral, emotional, and social problems are provided in community settings, specifically focusing on those programs that are implemented in underserved communities. We then offer recommendations for promoting the treatment integrity of programs offered in these contexts. Last, we provide examples of how treatment integrity has been monitored and promoted in the context of prevention services across a variety of community settings.

CHALLENGES ASSOCIATED WITH PROVIDING HIGH-QUALITY PREVENTION SERVICES IN URBAN, LOW-INCOME, ETHNICALLY DIVERSE COMMUNITY CONTEXTS

Multiple factors impede the high-quality implementation of prevention services at one or more levels of the program engagement and delivery process shown in Figure 12.1. These challenges may disproportionally affect the quality of interventions delivered in underserved urban, low-income, and often ethnic minority communities, thus contributing to disparities in health and academic performance (Adler & Newman, 2002; Smedley et al., 2003). Given the clear importance of these issues, attention has increasingly been focused on identifying and addressing the challenges associated with providing high-quality community-based prevention services (O'Connell, Boat, & Warner, 2009), including barriers to access, insufficient program dose, low-quality intervention implementation, and inadequate consideration of contextual factors.

Service Access

Many challenges prevent children from accessing community-based prevention services. If children and families are unable or unwilling to access services, then even the most efficacious prevention programs cannot be successful. Prevention services and service providers are scarce in many urban, low-income communities (Galea & Vlahov, 2005). Research also suggests that logistical factors, including lack of time, scheduling conflicts, transportation difficulties, unavailability of child care, and competing family commitments, reduce participation in prevention programs (Garvey, Julion, Fogg, Kratovil, & Gross, 2006). Many of these logistical challenges disproportionately affect socioeconomically disadvantaged families, and marshaling the resources to participate in prevention programming is likely even more difficult for families experiencing economic hardship.

Even when prevention programs actively address these logistical factors by providing resources to reduce the burden of program participation, enrollment can be strikingly low (Garvey et al., 2006; Spoth & Redmond, 2000). For example, Baker, Arnold, and Meagher (2011) reported that only 48% of interested parents enrolled in a behavioral parent training prevention program for low-income preschoolers, even though barriers were addressed by holding sessions at community sites and by providing child care and meals. In this study, enrollment was associated with higher socioeconomic status, dual-parent households, and ethnic majority status. Although low-income parents report that they find parent training programs interesting and potentially helpful (Gross, Julion, & Fogg, 2001), resources clearly play a critical role in their ability to enroll in these types of prevention programs. Barriers to service access for disadvantaged families are likely deeper and more pervasive than previously assumed, and additional factors must be considered, such as issues related to family and community capacity and parents' concerns that programs may not be relevant, useful, or delivered in a culturally appropriate manner.

Program Dose

Even when families are able to access services, they may be exposed to lower-than-intended doses of the intervention because program content is abbreviated or because participants drop out of the program prior to its completion (Dane & Schneider, 1998). Many common prevention programs require training and materials that may be too expensive for community sites to purchase. In cases in which materials are purchased and staff trained, the scarcity of resources such as space and high rates of staff turnover in socio-economically disadvantaged communities pose additional barriers to the implementation of prevention services at their intended doses. In addition, prevention programs often include 10 or more sessions (e.g., Committee for Children, 2002; Leff et al., 2010), and even the briefest programs require mul-tiple visits (Shaw, Dishion, Supplee, Gardner, & Arnds, 2006). Consultees in particular may be unable or unwilling to implement such lengthy programs in their entirety; as a result, the children enrolled in preventive interventions may be exposed to inadequate doses (e.g., Baker, Kupersmidt, Voegler-Lee, Arnold, & Willoughby, 2010).

Children and families may also receive an incomplete dose if they dis-continue participation in programs, and research has demonstrated that indi-viduals who drop out are less likely to receive the full benefit of treatments (Prinz & Miller, 1994). All families, regardless of socioeconomic status, report that time-related demands are barriers to involvement in prevention programs (Spoth, Redmond, Hockaday, & Shin, 1996). In addition, there is growing evidence that socioeconomically disadvantaged parents experience greater difficulty than their higher income peers (a) paying for health-related programming and associated transportation and child care necessary to take advantage of health-related programs, (b) understanding program content and feeling confident in their communication with those who implement the intervention, and (c) having access to flexible work schedules that allow them to participate (Gage, 2010). By default, those families that enroll in prevention programs are not seeking services to resolve a particular problem. Unsurprisingly, families that experience the target of the prevention program as a problem are more likely to stay involved (Baker et al., 2011; Garvey et al., 2006; Reid, Webster-Stratton, & Baydar, 2004). Thus, the fit and relevance of the program are critical to consider in maximizing retention in prevention contexts.

Implementation Quality

Poor implementation quality, or how well the intervention is being both delivered and received, can impact the quality of community-based preven-tion programs (Power et al., 2005; Sanetti & Kratochwill, 2009). Unlike dose, which is defined as *how much* of the program is delivered, implementation quality refers to *how well* the program is delivered (Dane & Schneider, 1998). Socioeconomic factors have been associated with implementation quality, including both the quality of intervention implementation and participants' response to the intervention (Gullan, Feinberg, Freedman, Jawad, & Leff, 2009). Implementation quality includes content integrity (e.g., implementing the content specified by the manual), as well as process integrity (e.g., the quality of the relationships between, and the level of engagement of, the practitioners, consultees, and children). If community-based providers lack an understanding of evidence-based programs, they may omit active ingredients of an intervention, thus compromising the program's content integrity. This challenge is further compounded for indirect interventions. Practitioners working in community-based settings may train consultees to implement the intervention in the context of a one-time workshop, but they are often not adequately resourced to provide ongoing feedback, consultation, and technical support to their consultees (Fixsen, Naoom, Blase, Friedman, & Wallace, 2005).

Though less well studied (Durlak & DuPre, 2008), process integrity has also been linked to outcomes (e.g., Nix, Bierman, McMahon, & The Conduct Problems Prevention Research Group, 2009). In direct intervention routes, prevention programs may be implemented by practitioners from outside the community and/or at sites that are not situated within one's community, potentially leading to cultural mismatches and difficulties building therapeutic relationships. When considering indirect intervention routes, the relatively high rates of turnover and low qualifications among staff at some community sites reduce the quality and continuity of service delivery (Kushman, 1992). As a result, children who receive services in these contexts may have fewer opportunities to establish therapeutic relationships with program staff, and consultees may have trouble keeping children and families engaged in prevention programs. Both therapeutic alliance and treatment engagement are critical components of the process integrity of any intervention, and low levels of either likely dampen program benefits (Karver, Handelsman, Fields, & Bickman, 2006).

Consideration of Context

If those implementing prevention programs in community settings fail to adequately consider contextual factors, then these programs are unlikely to be successful (Baker et al., 2010; Fixsen et al., 2005; Nastasi et al., 2000). A prime example of such a factor is culture; if prevention programs are not culturally relevant and/or those who implement the interventions are not culturally competent, then the program will be inappropriate for the community's needs at best and offensive at worst. Staff who deliver services in socioeconomically and ethnically diverse communities must understand the ways in which cultural and linguistic differences influence how children view and interact with their environment, learn, and behave (Sheridan, 2000). In the context of program implementation, these practitioners must be *culturally competent,* which is defined as the extent to which a counselor has developed the awareness, knowledge, and skills necessary to work with children and families from diverse backgrounds (Sue et al., 1982). In addition, treatment integrity is maximized if the intervention itself is culturally competent, such that the intervention goals and procedures are developed or adapted with sensitivity to children's culture and the realities of their daily lives (Bridge, Massie, & Mills, 2008). When the practices and procedures of an intervention are considered reasonable, appropriate, fair, and respectful of participants' social and cultural values, then that program is considered acceptable (Carter, 2007; Elliott, Witt, Galvin, & Peterson, 1984). Children's responsiveness to and engagement in prevention programs depends, in part, on the degree to which the intervention goals and activities are meaningful to them (Bellg et al., 2004). For example, a violence prevention program targeting urban, low-income youth should be conducted with sensitivity to urban children's increased risk for exposure to violence in their communities (Leff et al., 2010). Awareness of the importance of culturally competent practitioners/consultants and consultees and culturally relevant programs is fairly recent (American Psychological Association, 2003), and the field continues to struggle with effectively training practitioners, evaluating the impact of cultural competency training, and linking culturally competent interventions to better outcomes (e.g., Betancourt & Green, 2010).

Treatment integrity can also be influenced by systemic factors. For example, implementation of the Building Bridges multicomponent preventive intervention was strongly related to systemic factors, including preschool teachers' perceptions about their jobs, workplaces, and center directors (Baker et al., 2010). In that study, teachers who were one standard deviation above the mean in their perception that their workplace was supportive and collaborative completed approximately 23% more activities than teachers who were one standard deviation below the mean, a difference that amounted to approximately 57 additional activities over the course of this particular program. Notably, considerable variance in teacher implementation was accounted for by preschool center. Durlak and DuPre (2008) similarly reported that level of implementation differed widely between practitioners and sites. Together, these findings suggest that the relevance, acceptability, and feasibility of programs given specific community contexts are critical to consider in order to maximize treatment integrity.

RECOMMENDATIONS FOR PROMOTING
TREATMENT INTEGRITY

Factors that have a negative impact on treatment integrity can reduce the effectiveness of evidence-based programs for children and families. The next section provides suggestions for promoting treatment integrity, with specific recommendations for research and practice included in Table 12.1.

Attend to and Monitor Treatment Integrity

Given the impact of treatment integrity, program content (e.g., practitioner delivered a section of the manual) and process (e.g., practitioner was warm and encouraging during the session) should be monitored to ensure high-quality intervention implementation (Durlak & DuPre, 2008). Unfortunately, treatment integrity has been adequately evaluated in less than 4% of randomized controlled trials of psychosocial interventions recently published in top journals (Perepletchikova, Treat, & Kazdin, 2007). Further, the prevalence of treatment integrity monitoring in research studies likely overestimates the frequency with which it is evaluated in real-world settings, because staff in community agencies may lack both the resources required to adequately monitor treatment integrity and a full understanding of why treatment integrity monitoring is a critical component of evidence-based practice. Despite these challenges, community agencies are increasingly pressured by funding agencies and legislative bodies to select, implement, and monitor the treatment integrity of evidence-based programs.

The monitoring of treatment integrity varies widely, and typical methods include self-report checklists, record reviews, and live observations (for a review of methods used to assess implementation, see Durlak & DuPre, 2008, Table 1). The accuracy of checklists can be undermined by self-reporting and recall biases because they are typically completed by program facilitators, often long after the sessions are completed. Record reviews provide more accurate information but rarely include implementation quality data of any depth. Live observation in community settings has consequences related to the intrusiveness of the procedures and the reactive effects of being observed. Technology can be assistive in the monitoring of treatment integrity, including using checklists accessed via the Internet or a cell phone and making video recordings of sessions for later coding. Technology is not foolproof, however, and its failure can result in permanent loss of data. When considering indirect service models, the issue is even more complex; specifically, the treatment integrity by which the consultee interacts with the child is separate but dependent on the treatment integrity by which the consultee has been trained and/or is supervised by the practitioner/consultant. Though the

TABLE 12.1

Recommendations for Promoting Treatment Integrity

Type of treatment integrity	Overall recommendation	Specific recommendations for research and practice
All types	Attend to and monitor treatment integrity	• Encourage the monitoring and reporting of treatment integrity across research and practice settings. • Standardize and streamline treatment integrity monitoring methods to increase ease of use. • Ensure that monitoring methods assess content and process aspects of treatment integrity. • Embrace a model of "flexibility within fidelity," which in part suggests that treatment manuals should encourage a flexible implementation with room for therapist creativity and consideration of patient characteristics (Kendall & Beidas, 2007). • Ensure that monitoring methods address the training pathway between practitioners/consultants and consultees. • Improve community agencies' capacity to implement evidence-based programs, including collecting and evaluating data related to treatment integrity.
Service access	Provide services in flexible locations	• Implement community-based prevention programs at hubs of activity, potentially including recreation centers and churches. • Develop outreach and home delivery models (e.g., a group of families that were interested in parent training but were unable to attend groups held at community sites benefited from home-delivered services; Nix, Pinderhughes, Bierman, Maples, & The Conduct Problems Prevention Research Group, 2005). • Utilize technology to deliver prevention programming in minimally intrusive and maximally convenient ways, such as Internet-based, self-administered interventions. • Integrate brief prevention programming into other services children already receive (e.g., primary care settings).
Service access	Address deep barriers to participation	• Conduct research to better understand parents' possible concerns about enrolling in community-based prevention programs (e.g., that they may not be relevant, useful, or delivered in a culturally appropriate manner).

(continues)

TABLE 12.1
Recommendations for Promoting Treatment Integrity *(Continued)*

Type of treatment integrity	Overall recommendation	Specific recommendations for research and practice
		• Foster interdisciplinary efforts with public health and public policy to develop a better understanding of the intersection between program implementation in community settings and the development of family and community capacity.
Program dose	Streamline programs and develop recommendations for minimum dosage	• Actively engage families after they miss, and/or support consultees after they fail to implement, even one session.
		• Conduct research to better understand why families drop out and/or consultees stop implementing programs.
		• Develop and implement retention strategies applicable to both families and consultees, such as Nock and Kazdin's (2005) brief intervention for parents in behavioral parent training programs, which focused on addressing barriers and increasing motivation for treatment.
		• Conduct treatment outcome research to determine adequate dosage of programs with the goal of providing benchmarks for practitioners (Sanders, 1999).
		• Identify the active ingredients of current evidence-based interventions toward the goal of creating more streamlined, shorter, or modular programs (Collins, Murphy, Nair, & Strecher, 2005).
Program dose	Reconsider the role of prevention	• Market prevention programming effectively to attract families that could benefit.
		• Ensure that the prevention programming provided in a given community setting is relevant to the children or families that would benefit.
		• Actively address issues of relevance and fit early in a prevention program by discussing the rationale of the program with participants.
		• Reconceptualize program dose in the context of these factors such that families have the option of opting out of nonrelevant program components or picking and choosing aspects of a program that are most helpful to them.

Implementation quality	Improve the therapeutic alliance and level of treatment engagement	• Train practitioners/consultants to be culturally competent and actively foster the process aspects of treatment integrity. • Utilize indirect intervention to tap into and bolster the strengths of the community. • Provide education and training to community-based consultees around treatment integrity in the context of evidence-based treatments. • Embrace a model of consulting and on-site mentoring that is associated with improved treatment integrity in school and mental health settings, including technology-assisted consultation (Noell, Duhon, Gatti, & Connell, 2002).
Implementation quality	Utilize culturally competent and socially valid prevention programs	• Select culturally appropriate and relevant interventions when possible. • Continue conducting research focused on the process of developing culturally sensitive interventions. • Implement nonadapted interventions using the model of "fidelity within flexibility," which allows clinicians to meet the needs of the child and family by incorporating relevant examples and other content while maintaining the active components of the intervention (Kendall & Beidas, 2007).
Consideration of context	Address system-level factors	• Conduct research to better understand system-level factors and their influences on program implementation. • Actively engage and partner with individuals at the administrative level of community sites to foster their buy-in and support. • Develop companion interventions that actively address system-level issues. • Incorporate system-level interventions into a more holistic approach to prevention programming.
All types	Embrace a partnership model	• Embrace a partnership model when implementing prevention programs in community settings. • Utilize collaborative approaches like community-based participatory research (CBPR) when conducting research on community-based prevention programming. • Investigate the role of partnership-based approaches (e.g., CBPR) or other techniques that facilitate site staff buy-in that may improve the acceptability of and outcomes associated with evidence-based programs implemented in community settings.

interaction between the consultee and child can be monitored by the methods elaborated above, the interaction between the consultee and the practitioner/ consultant typically falls into the domains of training, consultation, and supervision and is rarely monitored for treatment integrity.

Provide Services in Flexible Locations

Though there has been considerable effort to develop effective and accessible prevention programs for children and families, interventions provided in traditional mental health settings are associated with considerable barriers to access (McGinnis et al., 2002). Integrating services into alternative community settings, including home-based and self-administered interventions, may provide greater access to services.

Address Deep Barriers to Participation

Even when programs actively address surface-level or logistical barriers (e.g., child care, transportation), rates of enrollment remain low (e.g., Baker et al., 2011). Disparities in service utilization are partial contributors to the gap in educational and health outcomes (McGinnis et al., 2002; Smedley et al., 2003). Additional factors, such as families' potential concerns about the program and/or program implementers and the social networks of families, must be considered in promoting access to services for disadvantaged families (Eiraldi, Mazzuca, Clarke, & Power, 2006).

Streamline Programs and Develop Recommendations for Minimum Dosage

Perfect implementation is unrealistic, with dosage rarely exceeding 80% and positive outcomes frequently associated with programs even when implementation levels are as low as 60% (Durlak & DuPre, 2008). Though doses specified in treatment manuals are consistently higher than 60%, these recommendations may be based on theory rather than on treatment outcome data. In addition, doses of prevention programs across both direct and indirect intervention routes have been demonstrated to decrease precipitously over time and especially after the first session, suggesting that far fewer children and families benefit from the content covered in later sessions (Baker et al., 2011, 2010). Current versions of many evidence-based interventions may be too onerous to be as useful as they could be, and it is well documented that concerns about the program, which frequently relate to the amount of time it will take to implement, are strongly related to poorer treatment integrity (Baker et al., 2010; Elliott et al., 1984).

Reconsider the Role of Prevention

When families decide to commit to a prevention program, they are likely deciding against equally attractive alternative uses of their time. Because prevention programs by nature do not address preexisting problems, the issue of ensuring that prevention programs are relevant and useful to families is even more critical in keeping them involved (Baker et al., 2011; Garvey et al., 2006; Reid et al., 2004). For this reason, it is important to consider whether a prevention program will be meaningful and timely for families and related to their future goals, or whether some other program would be more appropriate.

Improve the Therapeutic Alliance and Level of Treatment Engagement

Building a trusting relationship and becoming engaged in a program are both critical aspects of treatment integrity and effectiveness (Nix et al., 2009; Shaw et al., 2006). In the context of community-based prevention work, direct intervention often features practitioners from outside the community, who may experience difficulty maintaining high levels of process integrity due to not sharing the same racial, ethnic, socioeconomic, or linguistic background as community members. Indirect routes of intervention are more likely to feature community members as the implementers of programs. These approaches can facilitate community member input into program development, build the capacity of community agencies, pave the way for sustainable programming, and enhance buy-in from the children and families engaged in the program. However, the same issues of trust and engagement apply to the relationship between the consultee, as a member of the community, and the practitioner/consultant, as an outsider. In addition, recent research suggests that community members as program implementers in clinical research contexts may encounter extremely stressful work conditions that lead them to engage in numerous misbehaviors, including making mistakes, engaging in ethical misconduct to enroll and retain families, and reporting false information to the researcher or practitioner/consultant in an effort to meet expectations (True, Alexander, & Richman, 2011). In these situations, community members recruited for indirect implementation efforts may face the difficult task of balancing the immediate needs of the individuals within their community and engaging in evidence-based practice, sometimes in the context of research, where the benefits to families may seem quite distant.

Utilize Culturally Competent and Socially Valid Prevention Programs

The importance of making cultural adaptations to psychosocial interventions for children has been long known (Forehand & Kotchick, 1996), but making these adaptations remains a challenge in the field. Effective preventive interventions in community settings must balance fidelity of implementation and adaptation of the program to meet the needs of the community (Castro, Barrera, & Martinez, 2004). Recently, researchers have focused on developing culturally sensitive interventions (for a review, see Jackson, 2009), which blend empirically supported interventions with the cultural context of the children and families that are intended to benefit from the program.

Address System-Level Factors

Though many prevention programs are focused on the individual or group level, factors at the system level still greatly impact treatment integrity (Baker et al., 2010). Such factors might include the administration or leaders at a community site, the interpersonal dynamics of a team, or the environmental characteristics of a community venue. Though they are understudied, inadequate consideration of these contextual factors likely negatively affect treatment integrity.

Embrace a Partnership Model

Those using traditional approaches have encountered considerable difficulties in translating evidence-based interventions into community settings (Glasgow et al., 2003; Miller & Shinn, 2005). Community-based participatory research (CBPR), on the other hand, is a collaborative approach that equitably involves academic and community partners in all phases of the research process while continuously recognizing the strengths of each partner (Nastasi et al., 2000). Given the nature of CBPR, it lends itself well to initiatives focused on community-based programming in urban, ethnic minority, and socioeconomically disadvantaged communities. Specifically, CBPR is a methodology for blending empirical research findings with critical community stakeholder feedback, which has the potential to result in interventions that are more likely to be effective because they are culturally appropriate and feasible to implement with relatively high levels of treatment integrity (Kelleher, Riley-Tillman, & Power, 2008).

STRATEGIES FOR ASSESSING AND PROMOTING TREATMENT INTEGRITY: FOUR SETTINGS FOR COMMUNITY-BASED PROGRAMMING

In this section, we discuss four settings of community-based programming, including after-school sites, preschool-based programs, primary health care practices, and home settings. We discuss the ways in which those who implemented the prevention programs across these urban, low-income community contexts addressed the challenges of monitoring and promoting treatment integrity associated with providing prevention services. In each example, we will focus on discussing strategies for monitoring treatment integrity, which can be used to provide feedback to those responsible for developing (e.g., researchers, program developers) and implementing programs (e.g., practitioners/consultants, consultees).

After-School Sites

A number of researchers have begun examining after-school as a setting for prevention programming, as this setting provides structured activities during high-risk nonacademic time and allows access to parents and community resources (Durlak & Weissberg, 2007). In the context of a broad range of after-school settings, our team of researchers and community leaders used a CBPR approach to develop the PARTNERS youth violence prevention program (Leff et al., 2010). PARTNERS is a 10-session social problem-solving and leadership promotion group intervention designed specifically for urban youth 10 to 14 years of age, which occurs in combination with a series of parent and community workshops. Treatment integrity of the PARTNERS program is assessed in vivo by external observers using two rating scales. The first allows observers to rate content integrity (e.g., "Facilitators discussed leadership") and process integrity (e.g., "Facilitators encouraged all youth to participate") on a scale ranging from 0 (*not implemented at all*) to 2 (*fully implemented*). The second allows observers to evaluate process integrity in more detail by rating process items (e.g., "Student interest and enthusiasm in the session," "Facilitators encouraging students to participate and setting up successful session context," and "Enthusiasm of facilitators") on a scale including values of 1 (*extremely poor*), 5 (*at average/expected level*), and 10 (*truly outstanding*). The structure of this global process integrity rating scale has been developed to maximize variability in ratings and limit the possibility of ceiling effects (for a more detailed description, see Gullan et al., 2009). Preliminary results suggest that high levels of content and process integrity can be achieved. Ongoing research is being conducted to develop and validate additional implementation quality measures that more directly address important process variables like therapeutic alliance, group dynamics, treatment engagement, cultural competence, and social validity.

Preschool-Based Programs

Preschool-based approaches to prevention programming, especially early childhood consultation, have garnered recent attention as effective ways to promote the preacademic and socioemotional skills necessary for young children to succeed in school (Brennan, Bradley, Allen, & Perry, 2008). The Building Bridges Project, a classroom-based preventive intervention for low-income preschoolers, features the program developers as well as practitioners/consultants who trained preschool teachers to implement the program via workshops. In the context of a broader research study, approximately half of the preschool teachers in the intervention condition were randomly assigned to a "workshops plus" condition and also received weekly on-site mentoring. The consultants were (a) specialists in either early childhood education or children's mental health, (b) extensively trained in the Building Bridges program, and (c) closely supervised by a licensed clinical psychologist to ensure treatment integrity in the consultant–consultee interaction. Their consultation with preschool teachers included reviewing the skills taught in the workshops, providing teachers with individualized feedback based upon baseline assessments, setting goals, and reviewing goals informally each week and formally three times per intervention year. All preschool teachers were required to implement 10 preacademic and socioemotional intervention activities per week over the course of the program. Consultants regularly observed teachers implementing Building Bridges activities at which time they completed an observation form that documented whether the teacher completed the goals of the activity, followed the script for the activity with fidelity, and engaged his or her students in the activity (see Kupersmidt et al., 2012, for more information). Preschool teachers also filled out a checklist following each activity that they completed, which provided similar content and process integrity information (see Baker et al., 2010). In this example of indirect intervention implementation, both the consultant–consultee and the consultee–child interactions were monitored for content and process integrity.

Primary Care

Primary care provides an opportune venue for promoting physical and mental health (Coleman, Austin, Brach, & Wagner, 2009). Partnering to Achieve School Success (PASS) is an indicated prevention program for children with attention and behavior problems in the context of urban primary care practices. The program consists of multiple components, including brief parent training, consultation with teachers, collaborative management with primary care providers to address medical issues, and crisis intervention when needed. PASS services are provided by a mental health clinician and a community partner, a resident of the community who is knowledgeable about the health and school systems. Treatment integrity monitoring has focused on content integrity, including which components have been provided and the dosage of each component (Power, Lavin, Mautone, & Blum, 2010). For example, in a pilot study, 78% of families in PASS received school consultation, and families received 2.5 school consultation sessions, on average. In addition, treatment integrity checklists have been developed for clinicians to conduct a self-assessment and for external observers to provide an evaluation of process integrity. The checklists obtain information about how well each of the components of PASS (e.g., "Monitors status of the family–school relationship," "Affirms parents for engagement in treatment," and "Monitors barriers to treatment and problem solves as indicated") has been implemented on a scale ranging from 0 (*not implemented at all*) to 2 (*fully implemented*). The checklist also indicates whether the community partner participated with the clinician and family in providing each component. Last, parent adherence is assessed via the collection of between-session "homework" assignments given to parents. Future research will investigate quality of implementation by analyzing audio- and videotapes of sessions, as well as parent adherence via the use of structured homework assignments.

Home Visitation

An alternative venue for the delivery of services to children and their families is the home, and home visitation programs have been used to deliver a wide range of prevention and health promotion services focused on children's physical health, mental health, development, and successful transition to school (Sweet & Appelbaum, 2004). Assessing treatment integrity in the context of a home visit can be especially challenging. Researchers have developed checklists to be used by home visitors and observers to assess the duration of each session, the content addressed during the home visit, and how much of the session was child focused versus parent focused (Raikes et al., 2006). Observations can be conducted by a staff member who accompanies the home visitor or via audio recording with parent permission. Typically there is much less emphasis on monitoring the quality of the visit. In contrast to most work in this area, Roggman, Boyce, Cook, and Jump (2001) developed methods for obtaining information from caregivers about the quality of the services provided as well as the quality of the relationship between home visitor and caregiver. Future research should focus on parent adherence to strategies addressed during home visitation, including conducting observations of the home context and parent–child interactions and evaluating permanent products.

CONCLUSION

Implementing evidence-based prevention programs with high levels of treatment integrity in underserved community settings has been challenging (Glasgow et al., 2003; Hulleman & Cordray, 2009; Miller & Shinn, 2005).

Children and families from urban, low-income, often ethnic minority communities disproportionately encounter barriers to accessing services, insufficient program dose, low-quality intervention implementation, and services that fail to take into account important contextual factors. As a result, programs may be less effective, and positive outcomes are less likely, contributing to disparities in health and education (Adler & Newman, 2002; Smedley et al., 2003). Addressing the unique challenges of monitoring and promoting treatment integrity in community settings is critical, and this chapter includes a variety of recommendations for researchers and practitioners to consider in this effort.

REFERENCES

Adler, N. E., & Newman, K. (2002). Socioeconomic disparities in health: Pathways and policies. *Health Affairs, 21*, 60–76. doi:10.1377/hlthaff.21.2.60

American Psychological Association. (2003). Guidelines on multicultural education, training, research, practice, and organizational change for psychologists. *American Psychologist, 58*, 377–402. doi:10.1037/0003-066X.58.5.377

Baker, C. N., Arnold, D. H., & Meagher, S. (2011). Enrollment and attendance in a parent training prevention program for conduct problems. *Prevention Science, 12*, 126–138. doi:10.1007/s11121-010-0187-0

Baker, C. N., Kupersmidt, J. B., Voegler-Lee, M. E., Arnold, D. H., & Willoughby, M. T. (2010). Predicting teacher participation in a classroom-based, integrated preventive intervention for preschoolers. *Early Childhood Research Quarterly, 25*, 270–283. doi:10.1016/j.ecresq.2009.09.005

Bartik, T. J. (2009). *Estimated state and local fiscal effects of the Nurse Family Partnership program* (Upjohn Institute Staff Working Paper No. 09-152). doi:10.2139/ssrn.1447868

Bellg, A. J., Borrelli, B., Resnick, B., Hecht, J., Minicucci, D. S., Ory, M., . . . Czajkowski, S. (2004). Enhancing treatment fidelity in health behavior change studies: Best practices and recommendations from the NIH Behavior Change Consortium. *Health Psychology, 23*, 443–451. doi:10.1037/0278-6133.23.5.443

Betancourt, J. R., & Green, A. R. (2010). Commentary: Linking cultural competence training to improved health outcomes: Perspectives from the field. *Academic Medicine, 85*, 583–585. doi:10.1097/ACM.0b013e3181d2b2f3

Brennan, E. M., Bradley, J. R., Allen, M. D., & Perry, D. F. (2008). The evidence base for mental health consultation in early childhood settings: Research synthesis addressing staff and program outcomes. *Early Education and Development, 19*, 982–1022. doi:10.1080/10409280801975834

Bridge, T. J., Massie, E. G., & Mills, C. S. (2008). Prioritizing cultural competence in the implementation of an evidence-based practice model. *Children and Youth Services Review, 30*, 1111–1118. doi:10.1016/j.childyouth.2008.02.005

Brooks-Gunn, J., Rouse, C. E., & McLanahan, S. (2007). Racial and ethnic gaps in school readiness. In R. C. Pianta, M. J. Cox, & K. L. Snow (Eds.), *School readiness and the transition to kindergarten in the era of accountability* (pp. 283–306). Baltimore, MD: Brookes.

Carter, S. L. (2007). Review of recent treatment acceptability research. *Education and Training in Developmental Disabilities, 42,* 301–316.

Castro, F. G., Barrera, M., Jr., & Martinez, C. R., Jr. (2004). The cultural adaption of prevention interventions: Resolving tensions between fidelity and fit. *Prevention Science, 5,* 41–45. doi:10.1023/B:PREV.0000013980.12412.cd

Coleman, K., Austin, B. T., Brach, C., & Wagner, E. H. (2009). Evidence on the chronic care model in the new millennium. *Health Affairs, 28,* 75–85. doi:10.1377/hlthaff.28.1.75

Collins, L. M., Murphy, S. A., Nair, V. N., & Strecher, V. J. (2005). A strategy for optimizing and evaluating behavioral interventions. *Annals of Behavioral Medicine, 30,* 65–73. doi:10.1207/s15324796abm3001_8

Committee for Children. (2002). *Second Step: A violence prevention curriculum, Grades Pre/K* (3rd ed.). Seattle, WA: Author.

Dane, A. V., & Schneider, B. H. (1998). Program integrity in primary and early secondary intervention: Are implementation effects out of control? *Clinical Psychology Review, 18,* 23–45. doi:10.1016/S0272-7358(97)00043-3

Durlak, J. A., & DuPre, E. P. (2008). Implementation matters: A review of research on the influence of implementation on program outcomes and the factors affecting implementation. *American Journal of Community Psychology, 41,* 327–350. doi:10.1007/s10464-008-9165-0

Durlak, J. A., & Weissberg, R. P. (2007). *The impact of after-school programs that promote personal and social skills.* Chicago, IL: Collaborative for Academic, Social, and Emotional Learning.

Eiraldi, R. B., Mazzuca, L. B., Clarke, A. T., & Power, T. J. (2006). Service utilization among ethnic minority children with ADHD: A model of help-seeking behavior. *Administration and Policy in Mental Health and Mental Health Services Research, 33,* 607–622. doi:10.1007/s10488-006-0063-1

Elliott, S. N., Witt, J. C., Galvin, G. A., & Peterson, R. (1984). Acceptability of positive and reductive behavioral interventions: Factors that influence teachers' decisions. *Journal of School Psychology, 22,* 353–360. doi:10.1016/0022-4405(84)90022-0

Fixsen, D. L., Naoom, S. F., Blase, K. A., Friedman, R. M., & Wallace, F. (2005). *Implementation research: A synthesis of the literature.* Tampa: University of South Florida, Louis de la Parte Florida Mental Health Institute, National Implementation Research Network.

Forehand, R., & Kotchick, B. A. (1996). Cultural diversity: A wake-up call for parent training. *Behavior Therapy, 27,* 187–206. doi:10.1016/S0005-7894(96)80014-1

Foster, E. M., & Jones, D. E. (2005). The high costs of aggression: Public expenditures resulting from conduct disorder. *American Journal of Public Health, 95,* 1767–1772. doi:10.2105/AJPH.2004.061424

Gage, E. (2010). Examining the most relevant conceptualization of the socio-economic status construct for cancer research. *Cancer Nursing, 33*, E1–E9. doi:10.1097/NCC.0b013e3181c29583

Galea, S., & Vlahov, D. (2005). Urban health: Evidence, challenges, and directions. *Annual Review of Public Health, 26*, 341–365. doi:10.1146/annurev.publhealth.26.021304.144708

Garvey, C., Julion, W., Fogg, L., Kratovil, A., & Gross, D. (2006). Measuring participation in a prevention trial with parents of young children. *Research in Nursing & Health, 29*, 212–222. doi:10.1002/nur.20127

Glasgow, R. E., Lichtenstein, E., & Marcus, A. C. (2003). Why don't we see more translation of health promotion research to practice? Rethinking the efficacy-to-effectiveness transition. *American Journal of Public Health, 93*, 1261–1267. doi:10.2105/AJPH.93.8.1261

Gross, D., Julion, W., & Fogg, L. (2001). What motivates participation and dropout among low-income urban families of color in a prevention intervention? *Family Relations, 50*, 246–254. doi:10.1111/j.1741-3729.2001.00246.x

Gullan, R. L., Feinberg, B. E., Freedman, M. A., Jawad, A., & Leff, S. S. (2009). Using participatory action research to design an intervention integrity system in the urban schools. *School Mental Health, 1*, 118–130. doi:10.1007/s12310-009-9006-9

Hulleman, C. S., & Cordray, D. S. (2009). Moving from the lab to the field: The role of fidelity and achieved relative intervention strength. *Journal of Research on Educational Effectiveness, 2*, 88–110. doi:10.1080/19345740802539325

Jackson, K. F. (2009). Building cultural competence: A systematic evaluation of the effectiveness of culturally sensitive interventions with ethnic minority youth. *Children and Youth Services Review, 31*, 1192–1198. doi:10.1016/j.childyouth.2009.08.001

Karver, M. S., Handelsman, J. B., Fields, S., & Bickman, L. (2006). Meta-analysis of therapeutic relationship variables in youth and family therapy: The evidence for different relationship variables in the child and adolescent treatment outcome literature. *Clinical Psychology Review, 26*, 50–65. doi:10.1016/j.cpr.2005.09.001

Kelleher, C., Riley-Tillman, T. C., & Power, T. J. (2008). An initial comparison of collaborative and expert-driven consultation on treatment integrity. *Journal of Educational and Psychological Consultation, 18*, 294–324. doi:10.1080/10474410802491040

Kendall, P. C., & Beidas, R. S. (2007). Smoothing the trail for dissemination of evidence-based practices for youth: Flexibility within fidelity. *Professional Psychology: Research and Practice, 38*, 13–20. doi:10.1037/0735-7028.38.1.13

Kupersmidt, J. B., Voegler-Lee, M. E., Arnold, D. H., Willoughby, M., Field, S., Bryant, D., & Peisner-Feinberg, E. (2012). *Professional development and curriculum enhancements for behavioral and academic kindergarten readiness: The Building Bridges program*. Unpublished manuscript.

Kushman, J. W. (1992). The organizational dynamics of teacher workplace commitment: A study of urban elementary and middle schools. *Educational Administration Quarterly, 28,* 5–42. doi:10.1177/0013161X92028001002

La Greca, A. M., Silverman, W. K., & Lochman, J. E. (2009). Moving beyond efficacy and effectiveness in child and adolescent intervention research. *Journal of Consulting and Clinical Psychology, 77,* 373–382. doi:10.1037/a0015954

Leaf, P. J., Alegria, M., Cohen, P., Goodman, S. H., Horwitz, S. M., Hoven, C. W., . . . Regier, D. A. (1996). Mental health service use in the community and schools: Results from the four-community MECA study. *Journal of the American Academy of Child & Adolescent Psychiatry, 35,* 889–897. doi:10.1097/00004583-199607000-00014

Leff, S. S., Thomas, D. E., Vaughn, N. A., Thomas, N. A., MacEvoy, J. P., Freedman, M. A., . . . Fein, J. A. (2010). Using community-based participatory research to develop the PARTNERS youth violence prevention program. *Progress in Community Health Partnerships: Research Education and Action, 4,* 207–216. doi:10.1353/cpr.2010.0005

McGinnis, J. M., Williams-Russo, P., & Knickman, J. R. (2002). The case for more active policy attention to health promotion. *Health Affairs, 21,* 78–93. doi:10.1377/hlthaff.21.2.78

Merikangas, K. R., He, J.-P., Brody, D., Fisher, P. W., Bourdon, K., & Koretz, D. S. (2010). Prevalence and treatment of mental disorders among US children in the 2001–2004 NHANES. *Pediatrics, 125,* 75–81. doi:10.1542/peds.2008-2598

Miller, R. L., & Shinn, M. (2005). Learning from communities: Overcoming difficulties in dissemination of prevention and promotion efforts. *American Journal of Community Psychology, 35,* 169–183. doi:10.1007/s10464-005-3395-1

Nastasi, B. K., Varjas, K., Schensul, S. L., Silva, K. T., Schensul, J. J., & Ratnayake, P. (2000). The participatory intervention model: A framework for conceptualizing and promoting intervention acceptability. *School Psychology Quarterly, 15,* 207–232. doi:10.1037/h0088785

Nix, R. L., Bierman, K. L., McMahon, R. J., & The Conduct Problems Prevention Research Group. (2009). How attendance and quality of participation affect treatment response to parent management training. *Journal of Consulting and Clinical Psychology, 77,* 429–438. doi:10.1037/a0015028

Nix, R. L., Pinderhughes, E. E., Beirman, K. L., Maples, J. J., & The Conduct Problems Prevention Research Group. (2005). Decoupling the relation between risk factors for conduct problems and the receipt of intervention services: Participation across multiple components of a prevention program. *American Journal of Community Psychology, 36,* 307–325. doi:10.1007/s10464-005-8628-9

Nock, M. K., & Kazdin, A. E. (2005). Randomized controlled trial of a brief intervention for increasing participation in parent management training. *Journal of Consulting and Clinical Psychology, 73,* 872–879. doi:10.1037/0022-006X.73.5.872

Noell, G. H., Duhon, G. J., Gatti, S. L., & Connell, J. E. (2002). Consultation, follow-up, and implementation of behavior management interventions in general education. *School Psychology Review, 31*, 217–234.

O'Connell, M. E., Boat, T., & Warner, K. E. (Eds.). (2009). *Preventing mental, emotional, and behavioral disorders among young people: Progress and possibilities.* Washington, DC: National Academies Press.

Olds, D. L., Henderson, C. R., Jr., Cole, R., Eckenrode, J., Kitzman, H., Luckey, D., . . . Powers, J. (1998). Long-term effects of nurse home visitation on children's criminal and antisocial behavior: 15-year follow-up of a randomized controlled trial. *Journal of the American Medical Association, 280*, 1238–1244. doi:10.1001/jama.280.14.1238

Perepletchikova, F., Treat, T. A., & Kazdin, A. E. (2007). Treatment integrity in psychotherapy research: Analysis of the studies and examination of the associated factors. *Journal of Consulting and Clinical Psychology, 75*, 829–841. doi:10.1037/0022-006X.75.6.829

Power, T. J., Blom-Hoffman, J., Clarke, A. T., Riley-Tillman, T. C., Kelleher, C., & Manz, P. H. (2005). Reconceptualizing intervention integrity: A partnership-based framework for linking research with practice. *Psychology in the Schools, 42*, 495–507. doi:10.1002/pits.20087

Power, T. J., Lavin, H. J., Mautone, J. A., & Blum, N. J. (2010). Partnering to Achieve School Success: A collaborative care model of early intervention for attention and behavior problems in urban contexts. In B. Doll, W. Pfohl, & J. Yoon (Eds.), *Handbook of youth prevention science* (pp. 375–392). New York, NY: Routledge.

Prinz, R. J., & Miller, G. E. (1994). Family-based treatment for childhood antisocial behavior: Experimental influences on dropout and engagement. *Journal of Consulting and Clinical Psychology, 62*, 645–650. doi:10.1037/0022-006X.62.3.645

Raikes, H., Green, B. L., Atwater, J., Kisler, E., Constantine, J., & Chazan-Cohen, R. (2006). Involvement in Early Head Start home visiting services: Demographic predictions and relations to child and parent outcomes. *Early Childhood Research Quarterly, 21*, 2–24. doi:10.1016/j.ecresq.2006.01.006

Reid, M. J., Webster-Stratton, C., & Baydar, N. (2004). Halting the development of conduct problems in Head Start children: The effects of parent training. *Journal of Clinical Child and Adolescent Psychology, 33*, 279–291. doi:10.1207/s15374424jccp3302_10

Roggman, L. A., Boyce, L. K., Cook, G. A., & Jump, V. K. (2001). Inside home visits: A collaborative look at process and quality. *Early Childhood Research Quarterly, 16*, 53–71. doi:10.1016/S0885-2006(01)00085-0

Sanders, M. R. (1999). Triple P-Positive Parenting Program: Towards an empirically validated multilevel parenting and family support strategy for the prevention of behavior and emotional problems in children. *Clinical Child and Family Psychology Review, 2*, 71–90. doi:10.1023/A:1021843613840

Sanetti, L. M. H., & Kratochwill, T. R. (2009). Toward developing a science of treatment integrity: Introduction to the special series. *School Psychology Review, 38,* 445–459.

Shaw, D. S., Dishion, T. J., Supplee, L., Gardner, F., & Arnds, K. (2006). Randomized trial of a family-centered approach to the prevention of early conduct problems: 2-year effects of the Family Check-Up in early childhood. *Journal of Consulting and Clinical Psychology, 74,* 1–9. doi:10.1037/0022-006X.74.1.1

Sheridan, S. M. (2000). Considerations of multiculturalism and diversity in behavioral consultation with parents and teachers. *School Psychology Review, 29,* 344–453.

Smedley, B. D., Stith, A. Y., Nelson, A. R. (Eds.). (2003). *Unequal treatment: Confronting racial and ethnic disparities in health care.* Washington, DC: National Academies Press.

Smokowski, P. R., Mann, E. A., Reynolds, A. J., & Fraser, M. W. (2004). Childhood risk and protective factors and late adolescent adjustment in inner city minority youth. *Children and Youth Services Review, 26,* 63–91. doi:10.1016/j.childyouth.2003.11.003

Spoth, R., & Redmond, C. (2000). Research on family engagement in preventive interventions: Toward improved use of scientific findings in primary prevention practice. *Journal of Primary Prevention, 21,* 267–284. doi:10.1023/A:1007039421026

Spoth, R., Redmond, C., Hockaday, C., & Shin, C. Y. (1996). Barriers to participation in family skills preventive interventions and their evaluations: A replication and extension. *Family Relations, 45,* 247–254. doi:10.2307/585496

Sue, D. W., Bernier, J. E., Durran, A., Feinberg, L., Pedersen, P., Smith, E. J., & Vasquez-Nuttall, E. (1982). Position paper: Cross-cultural counseling competencies. *Counseling Psychologist, 10,* 45–52. doi:10.1177/0011000082102008

Sweet, M. A., & Appelbaum, M. I. (2004). Is home visiting an effective strategy? A meta-analytic review of home visiting programs for families with young children. *Child Development, 75,* 1435–1456. doi:10.1111/j.1467-8624.2004.00750.x

True, G., Alexander, L. B., & Richman, K. A. (2011). Misbehaviors of front-line research personnel and the integrity of community-based research. *Journal of Empirical Research on Human Research Ethics, 6,* 3–12. doi:10.1525/jer.2011.6.2.3

U.S. Department of Health and Human Services. (2001). *Mental health: Culture, race and ethnicity: A supplement to mental health: A report of the Surgeon General.* Rockville, MD: Substance Abuse and Mental Health Services Administration.

Webster-Stratton, C., Reid, M. J., & Hammond, M. (2001). Preventing conduct problems, promoting social competence: A parent and teacher partnership in Head Start. *Journal of Clinical Child Psychology, 30,* 283–302. doi:10.1207/S15374424JCCP3003_2

INDEX

303

Training. *See also* Practitioner
    preparation
  in behavior analytic techniques,
    205–206
  best practices for, 191
  exemplars for, 208–209
  for health services providers, 17,
    27–29
  and implementation, 44–45
  of interventionists, 22–23
  legal and ethical issues with, 238
  in performance feedback, 171–172
  procedures for, 134–135
  recommendations for, 27–28
  stimuli for, 206–207
  techniques for, 219
Transparent Reporting of Evaluations
    with Nonrandomized Designs
    (TREND), 28
Transtheoretical model (TTM), 64–68
Traps, behavioral, 210–212
Trauma-focused group therapy (TFGT),
    60
Treat, T. A., 20–21
Treatment effect norms, 125–126
Treatment fidelity. *See also* Treatment
    integrity
  and dissemination, 27
  in health services research, 19–21
  in medical settings, 16
  monitoring, 18, 19, 23, 24, 39, 47
  of prevention interventions, 37
Treatment integrity. *See also specific
    headings*
  conceptualization of, 136–138, 205,
    232
  definitions of, 17, 131, 185, 255
  evolution of, 5–6
  in health services research, 16–21
  overall, 147, 148
Treatment manuals, 138–140
Treatment phase, 145
Treatment receipt
  conceptualization of, 114
  defined, 17
  in health services research, 22, 23
  legal and ethical issues with, 245
TREND (Transparent Reporting of
    Evaluations with Nonrandomized
    Designs), 28

TTM (transtheoretical model), 64–68
Type I error, 18
Type II error, 18

Urban contexts, 281–285
User characteristics, educational
    innovations and, 101–102

Validity
  of assessment measures, 143–144
  concurrent, 144
  construct, 115–116, 133, 143
  content, 122
  criterion, 144
  and dependent variable, 116
  discriminant, 144
  in experimental research, 115–116,
    133
  external, 115, 121, 133
  and independent variable, 116
  of inferences, 114–117
  internal, 115, 133
  social, 219–220
  statistical conclusion, 116, 133
Van Duyn v. Baker School District 5J,
    243
Van Dyke, M., 187–188, 193
Variability, 116
Variable-interval (VI) schedules, 214
Variable-ratio (VR) schedules,
    213–214
Variables
  in CBC research, 270–273
  in data analysis, 117–118
  dependent, 110, 111, 116, 271–272
  in educational innovations,
    100–105
  independent, 111–112, 116, 120–
    121, 162–163, 271–272
  with practitioner, 117–118
Video recordings
  for adherence assessment, 148–149
  as direct assessment strategy, 141
  for modeling performance,
    207–208
  for therapist training, 134
Villagomez, A. N., 193
VI (variable-interval) schedules, 214
Visitation, home, 295

ABOUT THE EDITORS

Lisa M. Hagermoser Sanetti, PhD, is an associate professor at the University of Connecticut, a research scientist with the Center for Behavioral Education and Research, and a licensed psychologist in Connecticut. Dr. Sanetti's research interests involve implementation science, treatment integrity assessment and promotion, and evidence-based practice in schools. In 2012, she received the Lightner Witmer Award from the American Psychological Association for her early career scholarship related to treatment integrity.

Thomas R. Kratochwill, PhD, is Sears Roebuck Foundation-Bascom Professor at the University of Wisconsin–Madison, director of the School Psychology Program, and a licensed psychologist in Wisconsin. Dr. Kratochwill is the author of more than 200 journal articles and book chapters. He has written or edited more than 30 books and has made over 300 professional presentations. His research interests include problem-solving consultation, transportability of evidence-based interventions to practice, children's anxiety disorders, and single-case research design and data analysis.